LEGISLATIVE PETITIONS
of the
Town and County
of
Alexandria, Virginia
1778-1861

Wesley E. Pippenger

HERITAGE BOOKS
2008

HERITAGE BOOKS
AN IMPRINT OF HERITAGE BOOKS, INC.

Books, CDs, and more—Worldwide

For our listing of thousands of titles see our website at
www.HeritageBooks.com

Published 2008 by
HERITAGE BOOKS, INC.
Publishing Division
100 Railroad Ave. #104
Westminster, Maryland 21157

Copyright © 1995 Wesley E. Pippenger

All rights reserved. No part of this book may be reproduced or transmitted in any form or by any means, electronic or mechanical, including photocopying, recording or by any information storage and retrieval system without written permission from the author, except for the inclusion of brief quotations in a review.

International Standard Book Numbers
Paperbound: 978-1-58549-379-1
Clothbound: 978-0-7884-7742-3

DEDICATED

TO

DR. JAMES D. MUNSON

WITH ADMIRATION AND GRATITUDE

LEGISLATIVE PETITIONS
of the
Town and County of Alexandria, Virginia
1778-1861

egislative petitions, a practice which was carried over from British law, were used as a means to seek remedy for grievance for a number of types of actions ranging from divorce to taxation. In studying the petitions which have survived for Alexandria, one wonders if some persons who were routinely represented therein had much else to do in life. The lists of petitioners may prove invaluable in determining neighbors, comrades or kin. Because an issue may be more irksome to one social or religious group than another, some petitions show a higher involvement by these groups than otherwise might be found.

At Archives and Records Division of The Library of Virginia in Richmond, a number of archival boxes contain original legislative petitions which were either associated with or initiated by the inhabitants of the town or county of Alexandria. For the town of Alexandria, five smaller boxes are identified "A" through "E," and one oversized container is labeled "5A." Petitions for Alexandria County are maintained in a single archival box. Though not widely available to researchers, most of these petitions were abstracted by Hamilton J. Eckenrode and published as "Calendar of Legislative Petitions, Arranged by Counties; Accomac to Bedford," in <u>Fifth Annual Report of the Library Board of the Virginia State Library, 1907-1908</u>, at pages 61-87. Presentation in the "Eckenrode" record is sequenced by the unique identifying number which was assigned each document by the Library.

This work contains abstracts of 205 legislative petitions (excluding duplicates), which contain signatures of more than 6,000 different petitioners. Each record is headed by the parties initiating the petition. This is followed by the date the petition was received by the General Assembly in Richmond, Virginia, the unique identifying number assigned by the Library (when available), and abstracts and transcriptions of text found in the original document. When available, the status of the petition is given, e.g. *Rejected, Referred, [Found] Reasonable, Bill Drawn*, etc., and the archival box in which the original is found is noted. This compiler has used the Eckenrode abstracts as a foundation for the present work, inserted the petitions found which were not previously included therein, and made notations regarding further documentation or outcome of the petitions.

The original signatures contained in most legislative petitions can be very useful for historical or genealogical research. Unfortunately, not all signatures are legible. Signatures found illegible to the compiler are indicated by an asterisk "*", and questionable letters are underscored "_". One outstanding

Legislative Petitions of the Town and County of Alexandria, Virginia

value in seeing multiple signatures in a list is to, perhaps long at last, witness primary evidence that multiple instances of the same name shows different individuals.

Along with most entries, a list of petitioners has been devised by the compiler from the original signatures. In a few cases, names of petitioners were obviously transcribed and no original signatures were present. For this record, the names are presented in the sequence in which they are found on each page. Please note, however, that the original sequence of a petition's pages is not always known. Oftentimes pages were dispersed geographically, then assembled with glue (or later pins) in an order which may or may not be significant. Because of the age of these documents and the frequent advanced state of deterioration, it is difficult to determine the original configuration of the petition materials.

Sometimes numbering in excess of 600 per cause, each signature is unique in some way. A number of them are virtually illegible to those outside of the person's immediate family; some are in French, others in German. It is interesting to watch how the spelling of a name evolves, and realize that a person may spell his own name differently over time. A signature can indicate a decline in health or condition. In compiling the lists of names, the margin for error can be quite high in interpreting each signature, ranging from the elementary to the cryptic or elaborate. In an effort to reduce this, comparisons were made of outside court records.

Often the handwriting of the original petition is abominable, or the condition of the paper and ink deplorable. Two 20th century readers may thus have differing conclusions on certain words, names or dates. As a consequence, these abstracts are not offered as the "ultimate, definitive" texts. They are, however, especially with the footnotes and index of both names and subjects, an eminently useful way to finding whether they cover one's research subject at all. Generous amounts of verbatim and summarized petition texts then confirm it. Specialists may want still further to examine the originals in Richmond, or microfilm copies, but can know that whatever the effort to do so will be certain of success.

I am indebted to Dr. James D. Munson of Arlington, Virginia, for his outstanding craft and ability in interpreting history. He has greatly assisted and encouraged me in completing this project.

Wesley E. Pippenger
Arlington, Virginia

Legislative Petitions of the Town and County of Alexandria, Virginia

ABSTRACTS

Trustees of Alexandria.
1778, 20 NOV. A456. Petitioners, under the law of 1748[1] for erection of town at Hunting Creek Warehouse, built in 1775 a warehouse on Phil. Alexander's land which became property of town. They have lately rented parcels of this land to Thomas Fleming, and parcels at Point West to Thomas Moxley, Richard Conway, Robert Mease and Robt. Adam for period of 63 years, with final reversion to town.[2] They have built a warehouse on south side of Oronoka Street at expense of £700. Notwithstanding these leases and buildings, Oronoka Street is 66 feet wide, and the county and town wharf gives a clear space of 18,000 square feet. There is a certain piece of sunken ground adjoining land bought by town for establishment of town at Hunting Creek, and belonging to Philip Alexander, but purchased from him by Major Lawrence Washington, Nathaniel Chapman, Wm. Ramsay and Messrs. Carlyle & Dalton for 200 pistoles. John Carlyle and Wm. Ramsay, being only surviving partners of this purchase, sold this sunken land with intention of giving money obtained therefrom to town, and petitioners ask that this sale and other proceedings be confirmed. Signed by Wm. Ramsay, Robert Adam, John Muir, Thomas Fleming and Richd. Conway. *Bill Drawn.* Box A.

Inhabitants.
1778, 20 NOV. A457. The lots left by Jno. Alexander in fee simple require an annual rent, upon condition that a brick, stone or wooden-framed house 20 ft. sq. be put up within two years, in default of which it will revert to Jno. Alexander and his heirs.[3] On account of contest with Great Britain, it has been impracticable to comply with conditions of improvement of said lots. And by the descent of the lots to the infant

---

[1] William Waller Hening, The Statutes at Large; Being a Collection of All the Laws of Virginia (Richmond: Franklin Press, 1820 et seq.), Vol. 6, p. 214, October 1748, "An act for erecting a town at Hunting Creek warehouse, in the county of Fairfax." Hereafter cited as Hening.
[2] Hening, Vol. 8, Chapter LII, pp. 613-15, February 1772, "An act to encourage the further settlement of the town of Alexandria, in the county of Fairfax." Page 615, And whereas it is represented, by the said trustees, that the wharf at Point West, in the said town, originally built by the public, was afterwards rebuilt by them, at a considerable expence, and that the same is now in a ruinous condition, occasioned chiefly by ships, and other vessels heaving down by the mooring at the said wharf; and the said trustees have petitioned that such a wharfage may be imposed upon such vessels as will enable them to repair and extend the same...
[3] Hening, Vol. 8, Chapter X, pp. 49-51, "An act for encouraging the settlement of the towns of Alexandria and Falmouth, and for other purposes therein mentioned." Because it was felt that placing a time restriction for building on vacant lots was injurious to the development of Alexandria, an act was passed in October 1764, which repealed all previous acts limiting the time within which purchasers of lots should improve the same, but should be at liberty to build thereon when they should think fit.

Legislative Petitions of the Town and County of Alexandria, Virginia

heir of Jno. Alexander, deceased, it is impossible for the petitioners to come to any agreement or compromise with heir.[4] They therefore pray that the Assembly will prolong the time for improving the lots and that the said lots and streets may be made town lands. Signed by John Finley, Edward Ramsay, Wm. Hartshorne, John Butcher, Wm. Hartshorne for John Saunders, Wm. McKnight, Adam Lynn, Peter Wise, John Fitzgerald, Wm. Herbert, William Munday, Pattr. Murray and James Parsons.[5] *Reasonable.* 3 NOV 1779. Box A.

Inhabitants of the Town of Alexandria.

1778, 2 DEC. A458. Incorporation of the town,[6] with the necessary regulations for governing it and an election of town officers to be held annually. Also that the town boundaries be extended.[7] That from the present number and daily increase of the Inhabitants and great improvements made and continuing to be made in the said Town, many necessary regulations for the well ordering and governing the same are wanting; and that they conceive that many very great advantages would arise to them from an incorporation of the Town; they therefore humbly pray that the same may be made an incorporate Town, to be Governed by one Mayor, one Recorder, four Aldermen and six common Councilmen, elective annually by the Inhabitants of the Town; and that the bounds thereof may be extended and Begin at the Mill dam to be made at the head of the Race, now cutting to the Mill of Robert Adam, Esqr. on four mile Creek, thence down the said Creek, the several courses thereof to the River Potomac, thence down the River to the mouth of Great Hunting Creek thence up the same the several Courses thereof to the place where the Colchester Road crosses the said Creek, and from thence by a straight line to the place of begining... And that such person who shall be elected first Mayor for the Town, shall, within one week after his Election, before the Eldest Magistrate then in the County of Fairfax, take an oath, or if conscienciously scrupulous of swearing an oath, make solemn affirmation for the due execution of his

---

[4] Hening, Vol. 10, 1779-1781, Chapter XXXI, pp. 192-93, "An act to confirm certain sales and leases made by the trustees of the town of Alexandria, and to enlarge the said town."

[5] Petitioners had a vested interest by having purchased entire or partial lots from John Alexander: On 19 DEC 1774, John Finley, copartner and joint merchant with Windsor Brown, purchased Lot 106 at the southeast corner of Duke and St. Asaph streets [Fairfax Co. Deeds, Bk. M, pp. 78-82]; Edward Mitchell Ramsay, joiner, purchased Lot 99 [Bk. M, pp. 93-96]; William Hartshorne, merchant, purchased a parcel comprising part of Lots 90 and 99 at Royal and Wolfe streets [Bk. M, pp. 112-115]; John Saunders, joiner, purchased Lot 98 [Bk. M, pp. 96-100]; William McKnight, cabinet maker, purchased Lot 110 [Bk. M, pp. 109-112]; Peter Wise purchased Lot 118 [Bk. M, pp. 86-89]; William Munday, joiner, purchased Lot 102 [Bk. M, pp. 82-86]; Patrick Murray purchased Lot 112 [Bk. M, pp. 121-124]; James Parsons purchased Lot 108 [Bk. M, pp. 115-118]; and on 20 DEC 1774, Andrew Stewart and William Herbert, joint merchants and partners, and John Fitzgerald and Valentine Peers, merchants, obtained Lots 94 and 95 [Bk. M, pp. 127-131];

[6] Hening, Vol. 10, 1779-1781, Chapter XXV, pp. 172-76, "An act for incorporating the town of Alexandria in the county of Fairfax, and the town of Winchester in the county of Frederick."

[7] Hening, Vol. 10, 1779-1781, Chapter XXXI, pp. 192-93, "An act to confirm certain sales and leases made by the trustees of the town of Alexandria, and to enlarge the said town."

office... that no person shall exercise the office of Mayor within the said Town for more than one year within any two years, but that after the intervention of one year he may again be eligible to that office... that the Mayor, Recorder and Aldermen of the said Town for the time being, shall be justices of the peace, and be impowered to act, within the said Town, as fully and amply as any justice or justices of the peace... have power and authority to hear and inquire into all and all manner of Treasons, Murders, manslaughters and all manner of Felonies and other crimes and offences capital and criminal whatsoever arising within the said Town... that the Town Constable, for the time being, be impowered to serve, levy and return all process issuing from the said Court... that the Mayor, Recorder, Aldermen and Common Councilmen of the said Town shall when elected, and their successors shall and may forever hereafter hold and keep within the said Town, two Market days in every week of the Year, the one on Wednesday and the other upon Saturday in such place or places as is shall or may be appointed for that purpose by the Commonalty or their successors from time to time and may forever hereafter nominate and from time to time appoint the Clerk of the Market who shall have assize of bread, wine, beer, wood and other things... appoint a Town Constable, Clerk of the Court and all and other officer and officers that may and shall hereafter be necessary within the Corporation for carrying into execution the Lawful ordinance, orders and regulations of the Mayor and Commonalty within the same...

Signed by: Samuel Simmons (p. order), James Collins, Thomas Reed, Michl. Gretter, Philip Jackson, Richd. M. Gerrard, Dennis Ramsay, Robert Muir, George Row?, Robt. Hay, John Frisby, Jno. Clements, John Shaw, Henry Rozier (p. order), *, Jas. Muir, John Harper, Senr., Shubael Pratt, John Harper, Lawrence Hooff, James Steuart, Ralph Longden, John Gretter, Robert Anderson, Tobias Zimmerman, Timothy Zimmerman, Thomas West, Thomas Moxley, Joel Cooper, Wilm. Ward, Robert Lyles, Michael Barnett (p. order), Saml. Kelly, Henry Stroman, Oliver Price, J. Meyler, Ch. Langmarch, Peter Wise, Peter Dow, Colin McIver, James McDonald, George Nash, Jno. Oliphant, Thomas Rose, Thos. Kirkpatrick, Gerrard T. Conn, Jno. Winterbery, John Lott (p. order), Wm. Bushby, Wm. McKnight, William Munday, Cys. Copper, Lewis Weston, Thos. Fletcher, William Hunter, Richard Sanford, Washer Blunt, Charles Jones, Jos. Watson, John Mills, Isaac Gostling, Edwd. Sanford, Val: Peers, Edwd. Owens, Wm. Duvall, Charles Alexander, Geo. Duncan, Roger Chew, John Longden, Richd. Conway, John Lomax, Charles Bryan, James Chapman, Robert Adam, George Gilpin, James Parsons, Richard Arell, Robert McCrea, William Hartshorne, R. Hooe, George Swan, Thomas Fleming, D. Arell, James Hendricks, James Adam, Ed. Ramsey, Guy Evans, John Bowling, Thomas Wilkinson, Adam Lynn, Wm. Rumney, Wm. Herbert, Robert Allison, Robert Mease, J. Allison, Michael Thorn, James Lawrason, Wm. Paton, John Butcher, Jacob Cox, Neal Mooney, M. Tandy, Jos. Caverly and John Korn. *Reasonable.* Oversize. Box 5A.

Merchants & Adventurers to Sea, at Alexandria.

1779, 25 OCT. A459. Fairfax County, Oct. 19, 1779. Establishment of a naval office in town[8] for the safety of inhabitants and foreigners. Petition and several depositions. *Reasonable.* Box A.

Petition signed by: William McFarland, Richard Arell, Jacob Cox, *, Washer Blunt, Benja. Chapin, John Muir, Thos. Kirkpatrick, George Ross, Meyler E. Lungermann, John Carlyle, Wm. Ramsay, John Mills, Michael Thorn, James Lawrason, Honorable Alexander Lory, Robert Harper, Wm. Tandy, Wm. Paton, James Steuart, Allison & Ramsay, Saml. Arell, Edwd. Owens, Wm. Hunter, Wm. Herbert, R.A. Contee, James Adam, Richd. Conway, Robert Adam, Joseph Harper, Hooe & Harrison, Josiah Watson, Wm. Hartshorne, McCrea & Mease, Fitzgerald & Peers, John Harper, and Dow & McIver. *Reasonable.* Oversize. Box 5A.

The deposition of Capt. John Sandford taken before me one of the Magistrates for the County aforesaid & in the Commonwealth of Virginia. The Deponent being sworn deposeth and saith that he has sailed from the Town of Alexandria to sea these eight years past in the course of which time the vessels to which he belonged & commanded have frequently been detain'd by calling at the Naval Office so as to loose a fair wind that would have carried them to sea immediately, & that thereby they have been obliged to wait till a shift of wind which has taken up many days; that the case has been the same oftentimes on their return from sea with a fair wind that would have brought them quite to Alexandria, they have by being obliged to stop to enter, been detained so as to loose their wind and taken up several days afterwards in getting to the aforesaid Town against head winds-- That in the Winter Fall & Spring the winds frequently blow so violently upon the Virginia shore as to oblige vessels to anchor on the Maryland side, that then they have about 12 to 15 miles to go in their Boats to the Virginia office & that during the continuance of the Wind no row Boat can return on board the vessels on the Maryland shore. That he on his return from Cape Francois last December 12 Mo. came too in the schooner Sidney opposite the Virginia office to enter, that the Wind came on so violently as to part both his cables, that he was obliged & with difficulty it was he got the vessel under way, that he stood back & forward in the River during a whole night, and next morning run his vessel ashore in Smith's Creek on the Maryland side & there lay till he could lower Anchors-- that he had almost his whole cargo to unlade on the beach before he could get his vessel off again, that one of his Anchors he found again & that thereafter he totally left. That the office lyes extremely open to the Enemy and that he has known them to be as high up the River in any times and has frequently heard of their taking vessels thereabout, and further saith not. Sworn before: Robert Adam.

---

[8] Hening, Vol. 10, 1779-1781, Chapter XLV, p. 208, "An act concerning the naval office of the district of South Potowmack."

Legislative Petitions of the Town and County of Alexandria, Virginia

Deposition of Captain Lawrence Sandford, October 19, 1779, Fairfax County. The deponent being sworn, deposeth and saith that he has sailed from the Town of Alexandria to Sea these Fifteen years past...

Deposition of Captain Benjamin Earle, October 19, 1779, Fairfax County. The deponent being Sworn deposeth and saith, that he has sailed out of the port of Alexandria for some time past, during which time he has always met with delay at the South Potomack Naval Office, sometimes loosing a fair wind...

Deposition of Captain Robert Conway, October 19, 1779, ...that he has sailed from the Town of Alexandria for several years past, in the course of which time he has been detain'd at the South Potomack Naval Office, that in his opinion the Harbour at said office is extremely dangerous...

Subjects of the State & Adventurers in Trade.
1780, 27 MAY. A460. Taxes laid upon merchants are unjust and tend to give Maryland, Carolina and Pennsylvania an advantage. Merchants are taxed 2½ percent upon actual worth of their goods, while lands are taxed 2 percent and valued very much below worth. Also land is taxed but one a year, while the trader is taxed 2½ percent every time he turns his money over. Besides if trade must be taxed heavily, inland traders should be taxed more than importers. Large dealers should not be sacrificed for retailers. Signed by Hooe & Harrison,[9] Richard Conway and John Harper. *Referred to Ways & Means.* Box A.

John Carlyle (1720-1780).
1780, 3 JUN. A461. Removal of Hunting Creek inspection to another place. Petitioner is manager of estate of Mrs. Sybil West, which will descend, upon her death,[10] to George William Carlyle, his son. Hunting Creek tobacco warehouses are surrounded by other houses and are, therefore, in great danger in case of fire, and besides petitioner can use the lots to better advantage... That the inconveniences of inspection might be redressed by moving the inspection either to the lands of Baldwin Dade above the Town or John Alexander below the Town, to both which places there were public roads and proper landings... Not signed. Box A.

Another paper by memorialist Sibyl West, of Fairfax County, most humbly sheweth That the warehouses on Great Hunting Creek for Inspection of Tobacco have for many years before the Erection of Alexandria, been fixed on land belonging to her husband, the late Hugh

---

[9] Records of the firm of Richard Harrison and Robert T. Hooe, general merchandise, 1789-1796, are included in the manuscript collection of the Alexandria Library, Lloyd House.
[10] Fairfax County Wills, Bk. E, 1784-1791, pp. 235-36, will of Sybil West, relict of Hugh West, Senior, of the County of Fairfax, makes no mention of any Ramsay member as a legatee, but names Col. Dennis Ramsay of Alexandria, my kinsman, as an executor along with Robert McCrea, Josiah Watson and William Triplett. Dated 16 SEP 1786, proved 18 JUN 1787.

Legislative Petitions of the Town and County of Alexandria, Virginia

West; and when the said Town was established, its Trustees appropriated a particular Lott of ground within its limits to the use and express Purpose of an Inspection of Tobacco. That accordingly, the Husband of your memorialist erected Buildings on said Lott; and after his decease in 1754[11] your memorialist, his widow, did, from time to time as necessity required, increase Buildings for the Reception of Tobacco... Box A.

Inhabitants of the Town of Alexandria.
1782, 27 MAY. A462. Establishment of ferries from the town to Hawkin's, Addison's or Rozier's on the Maryland side of the Potomac River, to be under immediate direction of mayor and common council. The mayor and council be empowered to collect from all sea vessels using the town wharf, the customary wharfage, to be applied to the use and benefit of the town. And that the mayor and common council be empowered to extend Water Street [now Lee Street] through the town from north to south, and to open and lay off Union Street from north to south.[12] People for some time past, by right of number of inhabitants, have been entitled to representation in House of Delegates and pray that they may send to Assembly a Burgess, the voting to be by ballot in same manner as they vote for their town council.

Signed by: Oliver Price, Robert Lyle, Wm. Paton, Jacob Cox, John Harper, John Saunders, Lewis Weston, Washer Blunt, Robert McCrea, Robert Allison, Wm. Duvall, Lawrence Hooff, Philip Webster, Geo. Duncan, Saml. Arell, John Hendricks, Peter Wise, Wm. Hartshorne, Josiah Watson, Wm. Hepburn, James Parsons, Joseph Robinson, Benjamin Shreve, John Butcher, Aaron Hewes, Edward Ramsay, James Lawrason, Wm. Ramsay, R. Hooe, Robert Adam, Richd. Conway, James Adam, John Lomax, Jesse Taylor, Josiah P. Adams, Wm. Lyles, Jr., Henry Lyles, Robert Harper, James Hendricks, [M. Bryan?], W. McKnight, Charles Bryan, Robert Muir, Adam Lynn, Wm. Hunter, Ch. Simms, Jos. Caverly, John Sanford, Thos. Wilkinson, Michael Thorn, Andw. Wales, Wm. Bird, and John Finley. *Bill drawn.* Box A.

Bryan Fairfax (d. 1802).
1783, 5 DEC. A463. Retention of the Northern Neck as the property of Robert, Lord Fairfax and Denny Martin,[13] it having been a purchase

---

[11] Fairfax County Wills, Bk. B, 1752-1767, p. 74, will of Hugh West, dated 9 FEB 1754, proved 21 NOV 1754, executor Nathaniel Chapman.

[12] Hening, Vol. 11, 1782-1784, Chapter XXIV, pp. 44-5, "An act to empower the mayor, recorder, aldermen and common council of the town of alexandria to lay a wharfage tax, and to extend water and Union-streets."

[13] [Kenton Kilmer and Donald Sweig, The Fairfax Family in Fairfax County (Fairfax: Fairfax County Office of Comprehensive Planning, 1975), p. 35]. Robert Fairfax, Seventh Baron of Cameron, was Denny Martin's uncle. Robert was unable to claim his Virginia inheritance in 1782, as acts passed by the Virginia Assembly in 1779 and 1782 prohibited British subjects from holding Virginia lands, and specifically exempted them from holding lands in the Northern Neck. As a result of the action, in 1792, Robert was awarded funds pursuant to an act of Parliament for the relief of American loyalists.

made by their ancestors. They have enjoyed the lands since 1680,[14] and their possession has been confirmed by acts of 1736, 1748,[15] and 1777. Land was acquired by real purchase and not by royal favor. *To lie on table.* Petition not found.

Richard Sanford & Richard Webster, Tobacco Inspectors at Alexandria Warehouse.
1784, 5 JUN. A464. Grant of a salary equal to that of the Dumfries and Quantico Inspectors. Signed by Richd. Sanford, and Richd. Webster. *Reported.* Box A.

Shubael Pratt (d. 1785).[16]
1784, 12 JUN. A465. Pay for fifteen months' service in Alexandria Hospital, for which petitioner never received satisfaction. *Reasonable.* Box A.

Mayor, Aldermen and Commonalty.
1784, 2 DEC. A466. At a meeting of the mayor, recorded, alderman and common councilmen of the town of Alexandria, May 14, 1784. Measures are needed for a general improvement of Alexandria streets.[17] Consequently petitioners ask that an act be passed vesting Robert Adam, Richard Conway, George Gilpin, John Saunders and Neill Mooney with power to take a general level of the streets and to direct manner of digging them down and raising them up. The plan they adopt shall be binding upon the present and all future councils. Also a protest against this petition. Several of the men named as commissioners are prejudiced and unfit to handle such large powers. Signed by Dennis Ramsay, John Lomax, Peter Wise, Andw. Wales, Edwd. Sanford, James Adam and 61 others. Signatures not now present with petition. No note on action. Box A.

Sundry Freeholders and Inhabitants of Alexandria.
1784, 2 DEC. A466-1. Petition of sundry freeholders and inhabitants of Alexandria investing five persons with absolute powers irrevocably to determine and order how and by what ways the water that falls in the said Town shall be conveyed from thence to the River, where the streets are to be raised with Dirt, where to be dug down and how much.

Robert Fairfax died childless in 1793, leaving his five-sixths of the Proprietary to Denny Martin.
[14] Thomas, Second Lord Culpeper, had by July 1681 bought out all the proprietors of the Northern Neck except his cousin Alexander, and on 10 September 1681, he bought out Lord Arlington [Kilmer and Sweig, p. 7].
[15] On 11 APR 1745, an order in Council at the Court of St. James, determined the bounds of Lord Fairfax's lands in Virginia, and fixed the tenure of those lands within his grants which had settled under grants from the Governor of Virginia [Douglas Southall Freeman, George Washington, A Biography (New York: Charles Scribner's Sons, 1948), Vol. 1, pp. 520-25, citing original document in England's Public Record Office, London, C.O. 5, 1326, f. 293-304].
[16] The Virginia Journal and Alexandria Gazette, 18 AUG 1785, p. 3, reported the death of Dr. Shubael Pratt, formerly of Connecticut. He resided on Fairfax Street.
[17] Hening, Vol. 12, 1785-1788, Chapter XCI, pp. 205-06, "An act for regulating the streets in an adjoining to the town of Alexandria."

Legislative Petitions of the Town and County of Alexandria, Virginia

Signed by Dennis Ramsay, John Lomax, Wm. Hepburn, Peter Wise, Andw. Wales, Edwd. Sanford, James Adam, John Dundas, James Parsons, John Stewart, William Ownbread, Joseph Wilson, Andrew Hays, Wm. Martin, Gerrard T. Conn, Je. Jett, William Ward, Jno. Oliphant, Wm. Ramsay, Patrick Murray, Baldwin Dade, Wm. Hunter, Joseph Robinson, Thomas Machen, Henry Stroman, Wm. Bushby, Saml. Arell, Hen. B. Deman, Jacob Butts, Thos. Wilkinson, George Thrift, Jacob Bontz, John Short, William Bromley, Michael Thorn, Washer Blunt, John Bogue, Philip Webster, Tobias Zimmerman, John Longden, Roger Chew, Windel Bright, Joel Cooper, Colin MacIver, Thos. Kirkpatrick, John Allison, Wm. Duvall, John Hendricks, Sam. Monty. Brown, Edward Harper, William Ellis, A.W. Maxwell, Wm. Wilson, John Murray, John Jolly, Wm. Warden, Cyrus Copper, John Sanford, John Wise, James Halliday, Lawrence Hooff, Wm. McKnight, R. McKnight, Alexander Couper, Jacob Hess, and Saml. Simmonds. No note of action. Box A.

Inhabitants of Virginia and Maryland.
1784, 4 DEC. A467. Navigation of Potomac River should be improved by joint action of Virginia and Maryland. Petitioners met at Alexandria and think that navigation can be perfected from Great Falls to a good distance beyond Fort Cumberland and also through the Great and Lower falls, at a moderate expense. Virginia should pass an act for formation of company, or two States should act jointly. Signed by Wm. Hartshorne, Chairman. *Referred.* Box A.

Merchants, Traders, and Other Inhabitants of the Town of Alexandria.
1785, 5 NOV. A468. New commercial regulations. Petitioners ask whether it would not be for the general welfare of the United States if Congress were vested with certain rights over the foreign trade and commerce.[18] At present foreigners are freely admitted to American ports and to export therefrom, with few restrictions, while citizens of United States are absolutely prohibited from carrying into foreign ports and taking therefrom some of the most important articles of trade. The merchants of the United States should be put upon equal footing with merchants of foreign nations trading with them.

Signed by Wm. Tyler, James Kirk, Wm. Hartshorne, R. Hooe, D. Arell, John Potts, Junr., Samuel Arell, Jas. Craik, Junr., John Saunders, William Abbott, John Reynolds, James Lawrason, John Gretter, Alexander Smith, David Pancoast, Aaron Hewes, Enoch Morgan, Thos. Thomas, Joseph Fullmer, William Finley, Robt. Whitain, Samuel Wright, Chas. MacIver, Michael Greghagan, Jeremiah Mahony, Charles Thruston, William Wilson, Ephraim Edwards, James Fletcher, Peter Wise, James Eakin, Augustus Delarue, Adam Lynn, Philip Webster, James Hendricks, Jacob Bontz, William Ferguson, John L. McLor?, Joshua Spiers, John

---

[18] The conflict between the States in regard to duties led to the establishment of the United States Constitution, adopted 17 SEP 1787. This was the occasion; there were many causes.

Legislative Petitions of the Town and County of Alexandria, Virginia

Dundas, William Armstrong, Lawrence Hooff, William T. Leech, Thomas Conn, Robt. Conn, Alexander Couper, James Adam, Robert Allison, John Muir, Edward Ramsay, Robert Adam, Edwd. Sanford, Willm. Loury, Dennis Ramsay, Hiram Chapin, W. Brown, John E. Ford, Richd. Duvall, John Wise, Wm. Hunter, H. Leigh, Thomas Reed<u>or</u>, Chs. Mortimore, Jr., George Richards, John Lomax, Lewis Weston, Wm. Ward, Valentine Uhler, Jonah Thompson, <u>Wm.</u> Dalton, John Lo<u>u</u>dan, Danl. McPherson, Isaac McPherson, Jas. Keith, and John Fitzgerald. *Referred.* Box A.

Common Council of Alexandria.
1785, 5 NOV. A469. Act for laying off the lands adjoining the town of Alexandria agreeable to the plan prepared by John Allison and Robert Adam.[19] This is very important, in order to preserve the uniformity and regularity of the town, as well as for other reasons. If the owners of property take the matter into their own hands, these will not be considered. Signed by Oliver Price, Clk. *Reasonable.* Badly damaged. Box A.

David Griffith, Clerk (d. 1789).
1785, 15 NOV. A470. If Washington Street is opened through its whole extent and widened to 100 ft.,[20] the petitioner will sustain a loss of £200 annually. He prays Legislature if it should decide to open Washington Street, that it will provide that compensation be made him proportionate to the injury done. Signed by David Griffith. *Reasonable.* Box A.

John Harper, Charles Simms, Leven Powell and James Keith.
1785, 15 NOV. A4831. Fairfax County. Box A.

To the Honorable Speaker and other Members of the House of Delegates. The Petition of John Harper, Charles Simms, Leven Powell and James Keith, Humbly Sheweth:

That the Executors of John Alexander, Gent., deceased, in the month of October 1784, laid out a number of Lotts of ground adjoining the Town of Alexandria with Streets calculated for the Convenience of the Inhabitants and for the Ornament of the Town and that among

---

[19] It is not surprising that these two gentleman would have been involved in developing a survey, as they were two of the town's leading citizens. Each was a respectible merchant; Allison of "Notley Hall" and "Bellemont" outside of Alexandria conducted his store on King Street, while Robert Adam who resided near the Potomac River maintained a line of food, beverages and dry goods on Water Street near Oronoco. Notice to this effect appeared in the <u>Virginia Journal and Alexandria Gazette</u>, 18 AUG 1785.

[20] <u>Hening</u>, Vol. 12, Chapter XCI, p. 205, October 1785, "An act for regulating the streets in and adjoining the town of Alexandria." Most streets were to be 66 feet wide, while Washington Street shall be one hundred feet wide in every part, and be extended to the limits of the aforesaid distance except that part of Washington Street laid out sixty-six feet wide, which shall continue that width, unless the Mayor and Commonalty of the town choose to widen it to one hundred feet, in which case on or before April 1 next, the sheriff of Fairfax County shall impanel a jury of twelve good and lawful men to assess the damages...

Legislative Petitions of the Town and County of Alexandria, Virginia

others two Streets were laid out of the Breadth of one hundred feet each upon the western & Southern Limits of the Town the one distinguished by the name of Washington the other by the name of Franklin Street.

That Franklin Street runing in an Eastern and Western Direction strikes the River Potomack at Union Street (which runs nearly parallel with the River) at High water mark from whence if it should be extended It must be done by the Labour and at the Expence of those persons who purchased the Lotts of Ground lying upon it and who might have an Interest in extending it beyond the Limits set to it by the River.

That the Executors in laying out the Street aforesaid and the Lotts of Ground adjoining it sensible that the same coud [sic] not be continued to the Eastward of Union Street unless the Purchasers of those Lotts adjoining would do it at their own expence and being fully aware of the heavy expence attending such an undertaking concluded that the Street would never be extended by them beyond high water mark if it shoud [sic] be continued [Page 2] of the same Breadth beyond it which was given to [ ] the main Land and therefore contracted it on the East Side of Union Street to fifty feet and in laying out the ground upon the north and south sides of Franklin Street and upon the east side of Water Street threw the whole into two Lotts in order to furnish the Purchasers with a sufficiently quantity of earth to run out wharves and to extend the street as far with the River as they should conceive it to be their interest to run [ ].

That your Petitioners at the sale aforesaid purchased the two Lotts of ground lying upon the North and South sides of Franklin Street and east side of Water Street at a very extravagant rate and as soon as the Season woud [sic] permit began to construct a Frame to include the street as laid out by the Ers. and and [sic] that part of the said Lotts of Ground as conveyed by them by the Executors which lay below high water mark within it which they have extended four hundred feet forward into the River and are now engaged in filling it in with Earth at a very heavy expence.

That at the time of the sale of the lotts aforesaid the principal inhabitants of the Town attended the same and were purchasers of different lotts in different situations and did not at that time in any manner testify their disapprobation of the manner the addition was made to the Town neither did they at the time your Petitioners began to construct a Frame which was to enclose the Street and the Lotts of ground below high water mark to the manner in which the said Street was laid out by the Executors but seemed to consider it as highly ornamental to the Town and beneficial to the Inhabitants.

[Page 3] That some months after your Petitioners had constructed their Frame and thrown in a large Quantity of Dirt and were advancing with their work in such a manner as to leave do Doubt of their compleating it in a reasonable time some persons began to complain of the contraction of the street as a measure that would destroy the uniformity of the Town and have prepared a Petition to be laid before your Honorable House praying for an act to compell your Petitioners to enlarge the street through their wharfs to one hundred feet which your

Petitioners cannot but consider as a most unjust and unwarrantable attack upon their Rights and Property.

That your Petitioners do in the most solemn manner assure the Honorable House that they woud [sic] not have taken the [damaged] upon the east side of Water Street at the extravagant Price they gave for them but from the single consideration of the Benefits which woud [sic] arise from a Spacious Street leading through the Town to the wharf which they intended to run out and be Right of contracting that street through the ground which should be made at their Expence. That upon this Principle they purchased conceiving that the Proprietors had a right to dispose of their own Property in the manner which would best suit their Purposes and that after purchasing your Petitioners had an absolute Right vested in them and that no person or persons ought to interfere [Page 4] with them in their manner of improvement.

That your Petitioners are now filling in the street fifty feet wide and four hundred feet [long] which they have nearly compleated and which will cost them one thousand pounds a Sum which your Petitioners conceived to be fully sufficient for them to advance for the Convenience & Benefit of the Town at large that if your Honorable House shoud [sic] grant the request of the petition it now not only be doubling that expence to them for a public [---]ment without any particular advantage resulting from it either to your Petitioners or the Town at large but will be depriving them of a Piece of Ground four hundred feet long and fifty feet wide taken out of the River at an enormous Expence and the Privilege of doing it purchased at a very extravagant rate and m[---] will prevent them from constructing commodious Piers and Docks in the Front of their wharf for the Reception of Shipping, That the street as laid out is sufficiently wide to answer for the Transaction of every kind of Business and as wide as the two principal streets in the Town runing parallel with the River where all the shipping business must be transacted, Union & Water Streets.

That the contraction of the street will not in any manner injure the regularity of the Town it being at the side and under a Bank at least thirty feet high. Your Petitioners therefore humbly pray that the Honourable House will reject the Petition of the Town & permit your Petitioners to possess unmolested the Property which they have so dearly purchased and improve it in such manner as they shall conceive most to their interest. And they shall ever pray &c. Signed by Leven Powell, Jas. Keith, John Harper and Ch. Simms.

Subscribers, Members of the First Presbyterian Church in Alexandria.

1786, 30 OCT. 1520. Religious Petition, No. 227. Petitioners have a lot on which they have erected a *convenient house for the public worship of God*, wish to document clear authorities, a Committee, and certain rights and responsibilities. The present minister and Committee of the church are the Revd. Isaac Stockton Keith [1755-1813], minister, and Messieurs Robert Adam, James Hendricks, Robert McCrea, Josiah Watson, Jesse Taylor, Robert Allison, William Hunter and William Hunter, Junr.,

Legislative Petitions of the Town and County of Alexandria, Virginia

Committee members. The church's lot was conveyed by Richard Arell[21] to the Revd. William Thom, deceased,[22] first pastor of the church, together with the house for public worship now built on the lot and all heredititaments and appurtenances, and also books, plates and furniture appropriated. Request for the incorporated minister and committee to have full power and authority to take, receive, acquire, purchase, use and enjoy lands, etc., to demise, alien, improve and lease the said lands if their judgment deems necessary, and apply monies, goods or chattles of the church toward reparations. Beginning the first Monday in May 1787, an election will determine the minister and committee members, keeping records thereof in minutes or records of the Corporation. Alexandria, Octber 2nd 1786. *Referred.* Box A.

Signed by[23] Isaac Stockton Keith, Robert Adam, Robert McCrea, James Hendricks, Jesse Taylor, Robert Allison, Peter Wise, John Hendricks, Jas. M. McKea, Wm. Paton, John McClenachan, James Irvine, Thomas Conn, Robert Mease, William McWhir, John Dunlap, Alex. Buchan, Josiah Watson, Andrew Wales, W. McKnight, Charles Little, John Allison, Daniel Roberdeau,[24] Wm. Hunter, Colin McIver, Peter Dow, John McIver, Wm. Ward, Wm. Wilson, James Wilson, Will. Hunter, Jr., George Bowie, Robt. Lyle, Junr., Robert Lyle, and George Irvin Hull.

Inhabitants of the Town of Alexandria.
1786, 30 OCT. A471. Incorporation of the Alexandria Academy,[25] with George Washington, William Brown, David Stewart, John Fitzgerald, Charles Lee, William Baker, Isaac Stockton Keith, Samuel Hanson, James Hendricks, William Hartshorne, Josiah Watson, Benjamin Dulany and Charles Simms as trustees. George Washington approves of an academy and has made a donation. Also that revenue arising from billiard tables and tavern licenses to be given to the academy. *First part reported, second part rejected.* Box A.

Signed by Wm. Brown, Isaac S. Keith, John Fitzgerald, Robert McCrea, Jesse Taylor, Ch. Simms, Robert Adam, John Allison, John Murray, Thomas Barclay, James Lawrason, Benjn. Shreve, Jos. Greenway, Jonah

---

[21] Fairfax County Deeds, Bk. L, p. 215.
[22] Pennsylvania Gazette (Philadelphia, 8 SEP 1773), *On Thursday the 5th of August last, departed this life at Alexandria, Va., Mrs. Mary Thom, and on the Sabbath following [i.e. 8 AUG 1773], the Rev. William Thom. They both died of an ardent fever and were decently intered in the burial ground of the Presbyterians in that Town. Mr. Thom, the son of a worthy clergyman, entered into the sacred office of the ministry in the 21st year of his age and was removed by death in the 23rd year of his age.*
[23] Most of these represent founding families of Alexandria from whom many area descendants are known.
[24] General Daniel Roberdeau removed to Frederick County, Va. where his will dated 29 APR 1794/5, was proved in JUL 1795 [Frederick County Wills, Bk. 6, 1795-1802, pp. 50-4].
[25] Hening, Vol. 12, 1785-1788, Chapter C, pp. 392-93, "An act for incorporating the Academy in the town of Alexandria." A structure for the Academy was erected on Wolfe Street, the cornerstone for which was laid by the Worshipful Master of Lodge No. 39, on September 7, 1785 [Virginia Journal and Alexandria Gazette, 15 SEP 1785].

Thompson, Peter Wise, Wm. Paton, John Butcher, Jona. Swift, Wm. Lowry & Co., Wm. Lyles, Josiah Watson, Will. Hunter, P. Marsteller, James Hendricks, Wm. Ramsay, David Griffith, Wm. Herbert, Wm. Duvall, John Hendricks, Wm. McKnight, Thomas Conn, Robert Mease, Cleon Moore, Wm. Hartshorne, and S. Hanson of Saml.

Baldwin Dade, Jr. (1760-1809).[26]
1786, 3 NOV. A472. Repeal of so much of an act of the last Assembly as relates to the narrowing of Washington Street between Queen and Oronoka streets, so that Washington Street will again be uniform and the private contracts of individuals will be undisturbed.[27] Not signed. *Reasonable.* Box A.

Alexandria Merchants.
1786, 14 NOV. A628. Trade of South Potomac is declining and petitioners believe it is caused by higher duties charged upon articles of commerce in Virginia than in Maryland. No action noted. Box A.

Petition and Memorial of the Merchants of the Town of Alexandria humbly sheweth:
That your Petitioners have for some time past observed with uneasiness the declension of the Trade of South Potomack in general and more especially of the Town of Alexandria and have endeavored to Discover what have or still may be the causes of that event--and they are humbly of opinion that they ought principally to attribute it to this, that the duties imposed by the Laws of Virginia on some of the leading articles of Commerce are much higher than the duties on the same Articles in the State of Maryland and that drawbacks of the whole duties area allowed there under certain regulations.
Though on comparing the duties in the two states, they will appear in many instances different, yet it is the intention of your Petitioners to call the attention of the Legislature only to such of them where the inequality is most oppressive to the Trade and consequently most injurious to the revenue of the Commonwealth, for it must be admitted that the well being of the latter must wholly depend on the prosperity of the former.
Salt, sugar, coffee and distilled spirits may properly be called leading articles in commerce, because they are in general nay almost universal use and are therefore consumed in the greatest quantities. Where these are to be had on the easiest terms, there every one will go, and at the same time that any of these are purchased such other things will naturally be laid in as may happen to be wanted. Thus the importation of these articles having an effect on Trade in general deserves particular encouragement.

---

[26] In 1782, Baldwin Dade was appointed surveyor of streets for the lower district, that closest to the Potomac River.
[27] Hening, Vol. 12, 1785-1788, Chapter LXXIII, p. 362, "An act to repeal in part the act intitled An act for regulating the streets in and adjoining to the town of Alexandria."

Legislative Petitions of the Town and County of Alexandria, Virginia

In Maryland there is no duty on Salt, in Virginia it is subject to a duty of Nine pence pr. Bushell.

In Maryland the duty on brown sugar is one shilling for each one hundred & twelve pounds weight. In Virginia the duty on brown sugar is four shillings & two pence, equal to five shillings & two pence half penny Maryland Currency for each one hundred pounds weight.

In Maryland the duty on distilled spirits is three pence for each gallon, and in Virginia the duty is fourpence, equal to five pence Maryland currency for each Gallon.

In Maryland the duty on coffee is five shillings for each one hundred & twelve pounds weight, in Virginia it is Eight shillings and four pence equal to ten shillings & five pence Maryland Currency for each one hundred pounds weight.

While these differences subsist some place or places on the north of Potomack River in the state of Maryland, will become the object [page 2] or objects to which trading people whither citizens or foreigners will turn their attention and wherever on Potomack River, salt, sugar, coffee and distilled spirits may be had on the cheapest terms, that will be the greatest place of trace and whither this will be on the north or south side of the River must depend wholly on the Laws of each State, not withstanding the natural advantages of Alexandria....

Signed by John Harper, James Lawrason, Josiah Watson, P. Marsteller, R. Hooe, Wm. Hartshorne, Richard Arell, John Saunders, Jona. Swift, Wm. H. Powell, Wm. Ward, George Richards, Robert Lyle, Hugh McCaughen, Robert Sim, James Purdy, Robt. Lyle, Junr., Francis Brooke, Alexr. Buchan, William Hunter, Junr., Wm. Wilson, John Potts, Junr., Richd. Conway, Wm. Duvall, Thos. Porter, Isaac Roberdeau, Daniel Roberdeau, Richd. Ratcliff, Jno. Hawkins, Edward Ramsay, Joseph Bryan, Saml. Monty. Brown, Wm. Herbert, O. Winsor, John Hendricks, Robert Donaldson, Baldn. Dade, Philip Dalby, Jonah Thompson, John Reynolds, Wm. Anderson, Francis Peyton, John Jolly, Gurden Chapin, George Gilpin, Jesse Tayler, Saml. Murray, Benjn. Shreve, Wm. Paton, George Hunter, Wm. Warden, John Sutton, Evan McLean, James Patton, S. Hanson, Colin MacIver, Philip Boyer, Benjn. Hunt, Thomas O. Ryan, Perrin & Brothers, Peter Wilke, Peter Beill, Henry Budd, Thomas Conn, John Crowch, James Hendricks, Rd. McCrea, Robert Allison, Robert Mease, Isaac McPherson, Danl. McPherson, Augustus Delarue, J'ph. Delarue, Jean Gibe, Jacob Hess, Peter Wise, James McKenna, John Dundas, Wm. Hepburn, Alexandr. Smith, Rob. Coupar, Wm. O'Landry, Edward Harper, John Dunlap, John McClenachan, Jonathan Cartwright, Ja. Woodard, Wm. Harper, George Triplett, Ichabod Hunter, William Cox, Michael Thorn, Washer Blunt, Philip Dawe, John Korn, Andw. Wales, Jacob Cox, Jno. Minchin, C. Ferguson, John Collins, Thos. Low, George Wilson, Lewis Wisendahl, Robinson Sanderson & Rumney, Williams Cary & Co., Benj. A. Hamp, A. Maxwell, George Opleteler, Edwd. Sanford, Joseph Greenway, John Tobin, Aaron Hewes, Othniell Tripp, Benjamin Smith, W. Brown, John Harper, Jo. Kempff, Michael Greghagan, Peter Iratzcalf, Geo. Croft, William Freeman, *, John Earnshaw, Wm. Bushby,

Legislative Petitions of the Town and County of Alexandria, Virginia

Jos. Bushby, Richd. Boyce, John Murray & Co., Richd. Pickrell, Adam Butt, John Hickman & Co., R.W. Ashton, Andrew *, Andw. John, Joseph Wilson, Ephraim Evans, John Stewart, Patrick Murray, Pettit & Power, John Chew, William Bromley, M. Lutz, Wm. Findley, Wm. Shakspear, Josha. Jacobs, James Boyd, Alexr. Hunter, Caleb Whitacre, George Heale, *, *, John Burns, George [his mark] Rutter, Richard Jenkins, *, George Williams, H. Thompson, Wm. Pope, George Herbert, Gabriel Slacom, George Coryell, John Moore, Samuel Smith, Samuel Harper, Jas. Keith, Zach. Shugart, Philip Conn, Edwd. K. Thompson & Co., Wm. Lowry & Co., Joshua Merryman, Sebastien Schiese, Thos. Machin, and Wm. Wright.

Sundry Inhabitants of the County of Fairfax.
1786, 15 NOV. A473. New tobacco inspection at Alexandria. Convenient place to load, as vessels come there in great numbers and give good prices for tobacco. So much tobacco comes to Alexandria by way of Potomac and other routes that it cannot be warehoused. That your Petitioners are assured a Lott of Ground may be had (with consent of the owners thereof) on the South end of Alexandria upon the Bank of the River, which they conceive the most propper place for erecting a new sett of Ware Houses on, it being upon the edge of the water will be the most convenient place for Tobacco coming down the River to be landed and inspected at and will be equally convenient with the present ware Houses for all Tobacco which may be brought by Land and at the same time will save the shipper the charge of Drayage to the Landing which for the greatest part now is and must continue to be paid on all Tobacco inspected at the present ware Houses... Your Petitioners therefore humbly pray that a new Inspection under a different sett of Inspectors may be established on the Lott abovementioned. With 15 accompanying papers dealing with tobacco warehouses. *Rejected.* Box A.

Signed by George Gilpin, *, Jno. Hawkins, Natt. Twining, Sam. Hanson of Wm., Saml. Jones, Sam. McPherson, Wm. McConchie, Robert Throckmorton, Townd. Dade, Wm. *, Ben Reeder, Nathaniel Clagett, Walter S. Chandler, Rd. Goodrick, Nathl. C. Weems, Henry D. Hooe, Wm. Horner, R. Hooe, John Keith, W.H. Terrett, G. Chapman, Charles Jones, Philip Stuart, Benj. Payne, Walter Johnson, Gray Douglass, Benj. Dulany, Nathl. C. Hunter, John Courts, Jo. Marbury, Wm. Darrell, John Hooe, Junr., A. Conkling, Peter Dow, Roger West, Jno. C. Hunter, Nathan Smith, Saml. Arell, William Smith, Townshend Dade, Walter Brooke, Robt. Alexander, Thomas Barclay, Michael Reynolds, Edwd. Washington, Jr., Jno. Grimes, * Payne, Thom. Johnson, James Collins, Robt. Smith, Sampson Darrell, Willm. Bowling, Whaley Violet, Gilson Whaley, William Simpson, John Hunter, John Brent, Laurence Ashton, Ben. Gwinn, Henry Washington, Wm. Skinker, Charles L. Broadwater, Motley Young, Joseph Powell, Edward Harding, Richard Fitzhugh, N. Fitzhugh, W. Stuart, Daniel McCarty, Junr., Lewis Weston, Tempel Smith, Charles Polk, Elisha C. Dick, John Powell, Willm. Gates, Coleman Duncan, Robert Lawson, John West, Jno. Casey, Henry Davis, Edward

Legislative Petitions of the Town and County of Alexandria, Virginia

Conner, William Boyd, Benjamin Stone, James Greenlees, William Smith, McKinzey Talbot by R.H., James Fletcher, John Mills, Laurence McGinnis, Henry Brent, Zachariah Fergeson, John Ratcliff, Th. McIntosh, John Robertson, Samuel Fairbank, Saml. Baggit, Geo. Summers, Zachariah Ward, Samuel Weedon, Benoni Price, Benja. Davis, Thomas Pool, Gerard Sprinks, Joshua Jorden, Hy. Reardon, Hez. Fairfax, Elijah Wood, Wm. Reardon, William Crump, Jun., Manery More, Fra. Gray, Thoms. Alliston, Willm. Jurden, Robert Boggess, Joshua May, Francis Spencer, Hugh Voylet, John Wren, William Jones, Caleb Earp, Will. Price, Jno. Graham, Hugh Fleming, Hiram Chapin, Abel Willis, Moses Milton, Elijah Milton, French Simpson, Timothy Carrington, James Henney, Lancelot Johnston, Thoms. Simmons, Henry Hatcher, R.H., Val. Peers, Jacob Storm, Michael Delarouche, J. _farsall, John Hawderfer, Adam Stohr, *, Thos. Dove, R.H., James Young, Hezekiah Williams, John Edwards, Wm. Rogers, Samuel Lightfoot, John Butt, James McCardall, John Spencer, James Conner, Charles Jones, Nehemiah Nevitt, Hensley Reas, James Officer, Raphel Hodgkin, Wm. Stone, Daniel Carril, Jos. W. Harrison, George Wood, Jno. Carnicle, Philip Alexander, Philip France, Josiah Emmet, Henry Lowe, Frederick Whitman, John Hufman, William Merchant, Richard Dickson, William Gray, Philip Ferno, Thomas Hedrick, Saml. Hull, *, Thoms. Simmons, John Lang, John Lewis, Nathan Wheeler, Moses Wilson, James Young, James Richards, Thos. Johnson, William Steele, Isaac Davis, John Peacock, John McIntosh, Bennett Hill, Lewis Sanders, Charles Noland, ~~Lewis~~ Thomas Winn, William Mitchell, John Odaniel, Isaac Halbert, Charles Davis, Jas. Wren, Junr., William Presgraves, Bartin Martin, James Conner, William Askin, Bennett Johnson, Nicholas Sebastien, William Sisson, John Horseman, John Wilson, James Moxley, Joseph Powell, Senr., Jesse McLaughlin, and Charles Smith.

Duplicate signed by Jonathan Cartwright, Levi Talbot, Philip Coyer, Thoms. O'Ryan, Jesse Simms, Peter Wilke, Daniel O'Sullivan, James Wells, Frederick Weaver, Isaac McPherson, Danl. McPherson, Jr., Alexandr. Smith, Edward Harper, John Dunlap, Ja. Woodard, George Triplett, *, Wm. Harper, Philip Dalby, Josiah Thompson, John Reynolds, Joseph Brown, Wm. Anderson, Wm. Baker, Gideon Snow, Gurden Chapin, Benjn. Shreve, Saml. Murray, T.M. Paton, George Hunter, Robert Little, James Bo____, William Taylor, Evan McLean, P. Wanton, Colin MacIver, R. Hooe, Wm. Hartshorne, Josiah Watson, Richard Arell, P. Marsteller, James Lawrason, John Harper, John Saunders, Wm. H. Powell, Jona. Swift, James Purdy, Daniel Roberdeau, Isaac Roberdeau, Jno. Hawkins, Buckner Stith, Thos. Porter, Robert Donaldson, Baldwin Dade, Ichabod Hunter, William Cox, Michael Thorn, Washer Blunt, Philip Dawe, John Thorn, Andw. Wales, Jno. Minchin, Cumberland Ferguson, John Collins, Thos. Low, George Wilson, Lewis Wisendahl, Robinson Sanderson & Rumney, Williams Cary & Co., Benj. Aug. [Hamp], Joseph Greenway, John Tobin, Aaron Hewes, Othniell Tripp, Benjamin Smith, John Harper, Jo. Kempff, Wm. Barkley, Jos. Bushby, Rd. W. Ashton, Antoine Cayol, Andw. John, Ephraim

Legislative Petitions of the Town and County of Alexandria, Virginia

Evans, John Stewart, Nath. Spooner, John Chase, William Bromley, Mi. Lutz, Wm. Findley, Wm. Shakspear, Joshua Jacobs, James Boyd, Alexr. Hunter, Caleb Whitacre, George Heale, Ludwig *, George Fletcher, Michael Greghagan, [ink blot], William Freeman, Thoms. Jones, John Earnshaw, Richd. Boyce, Richd. Pickrell, Wm. Lyles, Adam Butt, Joseph Wilson, Patrick Murray, *, John Burns, George Rutter, *, William *, George Williams, Wm. Pane, George Herbert, Gabriel Slacom, George Coryell, John Moore, Samuel Smith, Samuel Harper, Ja. Keith, Zach. Shugart, Philip Conn, Edwd. K. Thompson, Wm. Lowry & Co., Joshua Merryman, Sebastien Schiese, Thos. Machen, Wm. Wright, Jacob Cox, John Aug. Washington, John Murray, Jas. Swoope, A. Swope, James Grimes, D. Arell, Wm. McWhir, John Short, Jacob Butts, Jacob *, John Black, Willm. *, Michl. Swoope.

Second duplicate signed by Michael Shore, Benjamin Lanston, Jas. Morrison, Jno. Potts, Lewis Cook, John Allan, Joseph Smith, William Fraser, Thos. T. Humfreys, P. Howe, Jr., Thomas Beach, Abraham S. Beach, Chandler Sprinks, Joseph Smith, William Richards, William Summers, John Summers, John Summers, Jr., Edward Davis, John Davis, Samuel Johnston, John Moss, Richard Lane, Samuel Adams, and James Hardage Lane.

Inhabitants of the Town of Alexandria and County Adjacent.

1786, 15 NOV. A474. Protest against establishment of new tobacco inspection. Only about 1,500 hogsheads of tobacco have come to town annually since the peace with England.[28] New inspectors must be paid by Commonwealth or their salaries taken from present inspectors, who receive only £60 per annum. Place proposed for new inspection is in uninhabited part of town, while proprietors of present inspection are willing to build new warehouses if necessary. Because one set of Inspectors has heretofore been adequate to the Inspection of all the Tobacco brought to the said town of Alexandria and in the opinion of your memorialists will continue for some years to come, to be adequate to that business, the number of hogsheads brought to the said town having been upon an average in each year since the peace only about fifteen hundred, and for the present year not having exceeded seventeen hundred and thirty from the 1st of October 1785 to the 10th of August 1786... *Reasonable.* Box A.

Signed by Charles Lee, John Potts, Jun., James Hendricks, Walter Brooke, Thomas Herbert, Charles Little, Wm. West, Robert Lyles, Alex. Beecham, Thomas Moxley, Edw. Sanford, Thomas Conn, Robert Lyle, Junr., D. Griffith, Hugh McCaughen, Fran. Brooke, Jesse Moore, Junr., Saml. Montgomery Brown, John Dowdall, Garrard Trammell, Robert Adam, Moses Ball, John Banninger, John Fitzgerald, Phil. Rd. Fendall,

---

[28] Refers to final treaty of peace with Great Britain which was signed September 25, 1783, ending the Revolutionary War.

Legislative Petitions of the Town and County of Alexandria, Virginia

Richd. Conway, Wm. Herbert, Will: Hunter, Jr., Dennis Ramsay, M. Madden, John Allison, Lawrence Hooff, Peter Wise, Robert Mease, Wm. Wilson, Roger Chew, John Lomax, Neill Moon<u>ey</u>, Arthr. Maxwell, John Jolly, James Irvine, James Thompson, Christopher Barr, Charles Bryan, Bryan Allison, Thos. Richards, Henry Turnbaugh, William Alliston, Peter Piles, Peter Wilke, John Wise, Robert Sim, George Mason, William Woolls, Nicols. Bryce, Robert E<u>vans</u>, Patrick Hagerty, Alexr. Couper, John Hendricks, Moses Tandy, Alphonsus Surratt, John Crowch, Jacob Fort<u>t</u>ney, George Darling, Oliver Price, Francis Peyton, Henry Budd, Cleon Moore, Jno. Graham, Wm. Worden, John Shaw, Richard Weightman, Edmd. Warriner, Ninian Anderson, Henry Stroman, Michl. Gretter, Saml. Whiteford, Andrew MacMasters, Joseph Turner, Andw. Jamieson, Jacob Heinemann, John Smith, Peter Wil<u>li</u>ams, Jno. Oliphant, James Meyler, Edmund Edmonds, Thomas Ramsay, Thomas [his X mark] Thedrick, Patrick Byrne, James Rattle, Alexander Keith, Jacob Hess, Jean Gi<u>be</u>, John Wren, Joseph Cary, James McKenna, Willm. Lowry, Perrin & Brothers, J. Simms, Levi Talburt [Talbot], John Hickman & Co., George Bowie, Richd. Ratcliff, John Longden, William Bromley, Jacob Vallentine, Morris Worrell, Thomas Redman, Edward Ramsay, Conrad Doyle, James Halliday, Alexander Perry, George [torn], Joseph [S]pinks, Saml. Simm[s], Augustus Delarue, Petit en gloudelet, Caleb Earp, Thos. Lindsay, Wm. Anderson, Philip Dalby, James Balfour, Thomas West, George Summers, Valentin Uhler, Charles Thrift, Hambleton Thrift, Robert Alexander, John C. Marteni, John Gretter, William Warrick, James Meredy, Guy Evans, Wm. Allison, George Grimes, Robt. Greeves, James Somervill, Adam Ebert, William Halley, *, Saml. Howard, Gray Douglass, Alexandr. Smith, Wm. Haycock, Thomas Reed, Grafton Kirke, Jos. Broders, John Steel, Alexr. Hannah, Alexander Taylor, John Jackson, Junr., Wm. Ramsay, Benjn. Hunter, Wm. Duvall, Jas. M. McKea, Rob. Coupar, John Sutton, John Mandeville, William Ward, Richd. Sanford, Robt. Sanford, Sanford Potter, David Jones, Charles Alexander, W. Brown, William Peake, Wm. Triplett, Enoch Morgan, Sampson Cockerille, Jarvis Hammond, *, Wm. Darrell, Philip Alexander, John Jackson, Senr., Jno. Evans, W. McKnight, Robert McCrea, Jesse Taylor, William Taylor, James Tyler, Jas. McCliesh, Jeremiah Clifford, Nehemiah Clifford, Wm. Hepburn, John Dundas, Geo. Mason, Henry Peake, [S.] Hanson of Saml., Robert Allison, Giles Cooke, G. Deneale, Wm. Triplett, Junr., Elie Stone, Daniel Lewis, William Keith, Chas. MacIver, James Scot, Henry Gardner, John Devaughn, Arran Johnston, Geo: Fielder, Robt. Conn, James Coleman, and William Gunnell 3d.

1786, 15 NOV. See A461 at page 5. Sybil West. Signed, S. West. No action noted. Box A.

<u>Sundry Inhabitants of the Town of Winchester and the County of Frederick.</u>
1786, 20 NOV. A6341. Establishing an additional inspection in the Town of Alexandria might be a means of removing some of the complaints at this time made and inducing the planters in general to carry their crops to that Inspection as the most convenient to them. *Referred.* Box A.

Signed by Richard Blanton, Samuel Kercheval, N. Fasson, B. Rice, Jas. Baker, Senr., Jas. Baker, Junr., Tho. S. Williams, Archibald McDonald, Wm. Glascock, William F. Sydnor, John M'Ginnis, John S. Williams, Wm. Elzey, John Jones, Tho. Lancaster, William McLeod, Burgess Barkley, David Catlett, W. Taylor, Saml. Earle, C. Earle, Geo. Murray, J. Berry, Peter Epp, Saml. Baker, Elias Earle, Philip Helphinstine, James Cochran, A. Jennings, Robert Smith, Robert Alten, Montgomery Allen, James *, *, Jno. Grove, Daniel Mytinger, Jacob Neswanger, Anw. Pitman, Joseph Stevens, Tho. Vaughan, Dennis Bush, James Hening, David Wilson, John Catlett, Francis McKenny, Jas. Kercheval, Jno. Smith, Jr., John Bryan, Enoch Berry, Joseph Berry, Ben. Berry, Geo. Blakemore, Corns. Livingston, Henry Catlett, Eppa. Hubbard, Page Dixon, James Ware, Collin Campbell, George Carpenter, Matthew Carpenter, and David Castleman.

John Fitzgerald, Mayor (June 1786-February 1787).
1786, 24 NOV. A627. Jurisdiction of Hustings Court Enlarged. John Fitzgerald, mayor of Alexandria, petitions that the trade & business of the town have increased since the restoration of peace and with it the number of inhabitants have been nearly doubled, that it would be adding greatly to the advantage of the town if the jurisdiction of the court of hustings was enlarged, and it be done in the same manner as the hustings of Richmond, and that in like manner two more aldermen may be added to the court and that one half or two thirds of the members of the said court may be of the quorum. Signed by John Fitzgerald, Mayor, and Oliver Price, C. Council. *Reasonable.* Box A.

John Hoomes.
1787, 6 NOV. A476. Exclusive right to run a stage line between Alexandria, Richmond and Hampton, for a period of three years.[29] *Reported, Bill Drawn.* Box A.

That the time being nearly expired during which your petitioner [John Hoomes] was bound by law to keep up several lines of stage carriages, he is induced to apply to this honorable house for a continuance of an exclusive right to run carriages on the north side of James River only between Alexandria, Richmond and Hampton during the further time of three years, for the following, among other, reasons:

1st. The utility of such an establishment is never fully ascertained, and your petitioner hopes he has given sufficient proof of his attention and [ability] in conducting the business with propriety.

2nd. The proffits resulting from it are now very moderate, and too low to admit of competition, but if no exclusive right is established, sundry adventurers will set up temporary carriages at those seasons only when most business of that kind is to be had and which alone produce a proffit

---

[29] Hening, Vol. 12, 1785-1788, Chapter LXXIX, pp. 618-19, "An act giving John Hoomes the exclusive privilege of conveying persons in stage carriages between certain places for a limited time," passed December 4, 1787.

Legislative Petitions of the Town and County of Alexandria, Virginia

to a standing line of stages: a partial competition therefore will defeat every one in an attempt to keep up a standing line because at certain seasons of the year it is attended with a considerable loss instead of proffit.

3rd. That the line between Alexandria and Fredericksburg is kept up by others, but the business hath been so indifferently managed & conducted as greatly to disappoint Travellers and materially injure the lines under the direction of the Petitioner, who otherwise would hot have applied for an exclusive right of runing stage, between these places.

For the purpose therefore or preventing an utter abolition of this useful institution, which will eventually take place, if no regulation is made. Your petitioner humbly prays that a Law may pass in conformity to his petition. Not signed.

William Hepburn and John Dundas, Merchants of Alexandria.

1787, 20 NOV. A477. Protest against establishment of a new tobacco inspection until the quantity of tobacco shall be double what it is at present, as another warehouse would be an unnecessary public expense and a burden and a great private loss and injury to the memorialists... That some few years ago your memorialists became purchasers of the Tobacco warehouses in the said Town for which they gave a very valuable consideration, being induced to do so from conceiving them so well established as not to admit of any alteration or rivalship. The place where they are established being occupied as a Rolling house[30] previous to the year 1730. That in that year they were established as warehouses and Inspectors appointed. That so they remained untill the establishing the said Town in 1749. That the Trustees of the said town in its original plan and survey appropriated to the use and purpose of the said warehouses the Lotts No. 8 & 9, to which plan and survey the memorialists beg leave to refer. That each of these Lotts contain half an acre and upon No. 9 all the warehouses at present stand; yet No. 8 remains appropriated to the same purpose and was included in the memorialists purchase, who are prohibited from making any other use of it... Signed by Wm. Hepburn and John Dundas. Contains plat of tobacco warehouse at the corner of Oronoko and Water streets, showing also the public wharf and warehouse at the foot of Oronoko Street at Potomack River. *Rejected.* Box A.

A477-1. Accompanying petition signed by Robert Adam, James Hendricks, George Irvin Hull, Moses Tandy, Thomas Conn, James McKenna, Robert Mease, Perrin & Brothers, Cleon Moore, John Hendricks, R. Peyton, Wm. Duvall, Wm. Wilson, Rogr. Coltart, John Wise, John Sutton, Robt. Lyle, Junr., Wm. Herbert, John Potts, Junr., John Allison, Jesse Taylor, Dennis Ramsay, John Edwd. Ford, M. Madden, James Kennedy, Jas. M. McKea, William McKea, James Balfour, Alex. Buchan, James Patton, Charles R. Scott, Philip Webster,

---

[30] So called because tobacco hogsheads were rolled into these public warehouses.

Legislative Petitions of the Town and County of Alexandria, Virginia

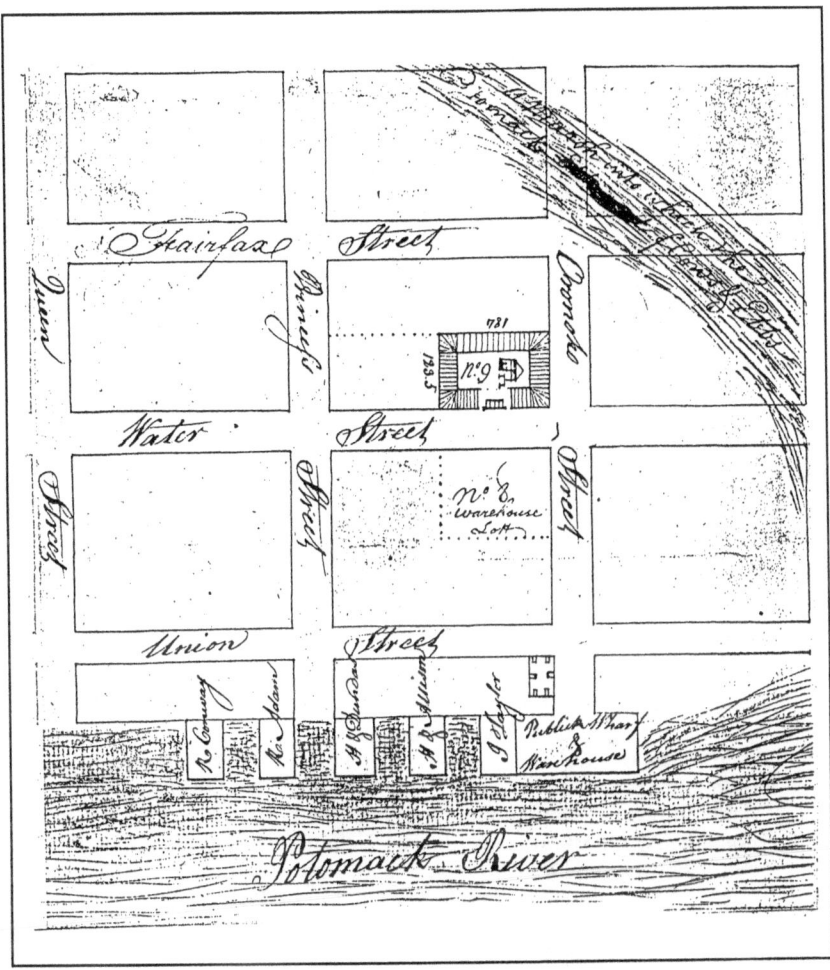

Wm. Allison, George Bowie, John Gretter, Jno. Thos. Knight, Thos. Prather, John Sutton, Junr., William Lyle, Roger Chew, William Ward, Edwd. Whiteside, Robt. Groves, Levi Talbot, Robert Lyle, Senr., Charles Turner, Charles Drum, Samuel Bowling, Jacob Beery, Edwd. Sanford, Patrick Hagerty, George Darling, Neill Mooney, Leonard Reeves, Maurice Herlihy, John McGee, John Foushee, Robert Evans, Thomas Glover, James McRedy, James [his mark] Cochran, Chas. MacIver, Jeremiah Clifford, Nehemiah Clifford, George Mason, Wm. Miller, Alexander Couper, Tobias Zimmerman, Guy Evans, Joseph Turner, Chas. Abrams, Jacob Heinemann, Hugh Barr, Tho. West, Michl. Gretter, Wm. Triplett, Jr., Richard Weightman, Ninian Anderson, Mungo Dykes, Edmd.

Legislative Petitions of the Town and County of Alexandria, Virginia

Warriner, David Jones, Baldwin Dade, Joseph Birch, Owing Corfield, Geo. Summers, Jos. Broders, John Parsons, John Mason, James Thompson, Stephen Shehee, Samuel Tillet, Adam Felser, Martin Shemes, Frederick Weaver, Hugh McCaughen, Henry Stroman, Gilbert Harrow, Samuel McLean, Wm. Warden, Peter Pil_es_, Peter Wilke, * (German script), Valentin Uhler, William Young, Thomas Richards, Henry Warner, Bartholomew Duffy, Jacob Fort_t_ney, W. McKnight, David Young, Charles Bryan, Wm. Dalton, W. White, George Grimes, Jno. Dowdle, John Jolly, James Smith, Michael Geoghegan, Hiram Chapin, Wm. Compton, Hendley Barron, John Su_ll_ivan, John Stewart, Dixon & [Littlepage], Alexander Keith, Jeremiah Williams, James Rattle, Adam Ebert, Michael Hoke, Christifer Walder, James Fr_e_nd, H.J. Potten, Lewis Traiseler [Tressler], Robert Smith, Lewis Cook, Philip Conn, Benjamin Bassel, Jno. Ramsay, Wm. Anderson, James Purd_e_y, Reuben Winterhouse, James McCliesh, Archd. McCliesh, Isaac Fouch, Junior, Thomas Ramsay, Samuel Fairbank, Samuel Hu_ll_s, John Evans, William Moxley, Hector Moxley, Younger Hardwick, Thos. Herbert, Jona. Mandeville, John Graham, Robert Sims, Saml. Bristill Fazan, Edmund Edmonds, John Kean [or Korn], John Steel, Thos. Stewart, Diedric_h_ Sch_e_kel [Shekle], Andrew Fleming, Duncan Niven, Bernard McLean, Thomas Reed, Jno. Mandeville, George D_uress_, John Wanenmacker, Joseph Fullmer, Matthew Earp, Alexr. Hannah, James Henney, George Clements, James Scot_t_, Grafton Kirke, John Robertson, William Mitchell, Benjamin Wigganton, John Mathews, Griffin Matthews, James Hooff, Chas. Eckridge, William Read, Thomas Neale, William Eckridge, Thomas Harris, Geo. Trunnell, Th. Newman, Gabriel B_ebe_, John Buckley, James Burke, Joshua Buckley, Samuel Jackson, John McIntosh, William Johnson, James Taylor, Francis Taylor, Sylvester Hall, John Patton, Bennit Johnson, John Per_r_yman, Charles Turley, John Ashford, Geo. Moxley, Thomas Wilcoxon, Benja. Davis, Jno. Cozzens, Robt. Gunnell, Joshua Coffer, Thos. Black, H. Hurst, Jno. Jackson, Junr., William Harrison, Robert Love, John Hurst, Jr., David Johnson, Peter Gullatt, Edward Adams, Theron Finkens, M.R. Beckwith, William Smith, Jas. Wiley, Frank Stone, Patt. McCarthy, James Love, Charles Broadwater *signs the above petition because there is sufficient warehouse room for all Toba_c_o that will come to the Town of Alexandria for many years and one sett of Inspectors is sufficient to Inspect all the Toba_c_o, without any further charges of warehouses or Inspectors*, Benja. Talbott, Thos. Palmer, Oliver Burch, E. Cotton, Charles Lowe, Walter Lowe, Eliza More, William Henderson, John Wren, Lewis Sanders, Benja. Sanders, Barneby Weelbright, Daniel T. Co_x_en, Edward Brown, Thomas Brown, John O'Daniel, William Pres_s_grav_es_, Richd. Bennett, James Dove, John B. Finley, Sarah Monroe, Wm. H. Monroe, John Oliver, Henry Gant, Michael Weller, Strother Johnson, John Edmons, John Balinger, Spenc Monroe, William Richards, Mathew Bozell, Sampson Talbott, Thomas Kidwell, William Stevens, John Stephens, Samuel Thompson, Daniel Hodgkin, O. Nalley, Jun., Samuell Tompson, John Tompson, Michelhines Robey, Michelhines Robey, Jun., Elisha Robey, Benjamin Beeder Davis, Simon Davis, Wm. Triplett, Jas. Deneale, Henry Wiginton, Thos. Sangster,

Legislative Petitions of the Town and County of Alexandria, Virginia

Francis Summers, William Fresher, Edward Davis, John Hepburn, M. Beckwith, T. Ellzey, John Simpson, Ewd. Ratliff, Jno. Grimes, William Ferguson, H. Steuart, Basil Stonstreet, Thomas Williams, Spencer Donaldson, John Horseman, Jno. Erskine, Caleb Richards, Thos. Pollard, Francis Coffer, John Tillett, Josiah Ferguson, Edwd. Ford, David Loefbournes, Richard Clarke, Thomas Johnson, John Sanders, James Turley, Daniel Kincheloe, John Manley, John Femister, Ch. Smith, William Lightfoot, Thomas Dove, John *, George Simpson, John Dawson, James Lyles, Abednego Adams, James Keith, Jr., Peter Martin, John Keyth, Anthony Wright, Thomas *, James McIntosh, and Daniel Hurley.

Duplicate signed by Thomas Hedrick, Andw. Jamieson, Andrew McMasters, William Peake, Edwd. Watkin, John Wren, Junr., W. Payne, John Hague, Thos. Triplett, John Moss, S. Hanson, of Saml., Will. Hunter, James Irwin, Thomas Tyler, Peter Wise, M. McDonald, W. Brown, Josias Clark, John Clark, Thos. West, Felix Duffel, *, Samuel Smith, W. Bird, Benjamin Gwinn, Thos. Winser, Edwd. Dulin, William Whaley, Richard Jenkins, Mathew Croughon, Andrew Allen, William Boling, Henry Peake, George Selmon, Joseph Gant, Jacob Hall, Geo. Minor, James Hurst, Jno. Mills, Gerrard Tramell, Rezin Offutt, Thos. Allison, Frances Poston, Nathen Wheler, Wm. Rogers, John Azman, Gervus Hammond, Jr., Benjamin Bailey, George Williams, Thomas Tramel, John Scott, Zacrahia Scott, William Violett, Lewis Hipkins, Char. Lewis Broadwater, John Hooe, J. Wagener, William Follan, Enoch Smith, Richard Blackburn, Wm. Darne, Gilbert Simpson, Daniel Jinkins, Wm. Haycock, Jas. Kinsey, Henry Turnbaugh, Thomas Duckett, William Crump, Junr., John Harper, John Garlen, James Chatham, Michael Albert, Robert Boggess, Robert Boggess, Jr., Wm. Aylett Lee, John Ratliffe, James Coleman, Caleb Earp, Joseph Nickelson, James McHenry, Richd. Wheeler, Nehemiah Davis, Saml. Adams, Junr., Wm. Wren, Simon Adams, John Jones, Henry Jones, Benjn. Britton, Wm. Keating, John Alliston, Thos. Pooll, Henry Wingate, John Davies, William Ogdon, Richard Freeman, John Ballenger, Benoni Price, Henry Husey, Thomas Ogden, Henry Ogdon, William Keith, Peter Williams, Daniel Thomson, *, Israel Wright, Alexr. Gordon, Morris Worrell, Benjn. Worrell, Samuel Howard, William Robison, Thomas Chatter, Stephen Daniel, Edward Jacobs, James Collins, John Daniel, Ignatius McFarling, John Whitney, Alexander Perry, Benjamin Ogle, Ambros Cox, William Dun, Webster Little, John Ogle, Geo. Slatford, John Smith, And. Payne, Thomas Sherwood, William Jones, Wm. Halley, William Summers, James Valendeham, Jr., Joseph Bennett, James Tyler, Thomas Simmens, Jesse Morgan, Wm. Drummond, John *, Richd. Clark, McKinsey Talbot, Arthur Carnes, Will: Shreve, Dennis Leahy, Augustus Delarue, William Williams, Jerem. Jeffrey, Will: Watson, Doras Neill, *, Thomas Woodward, Stanford Potter, Thomas Baker, John Clark, William Woolls, Joseph Powell, Junr., John C. Robinson, George Basall, Andrew Monroe, Nathaniel Parker, William Darrell, Giles Cooke, Gervus Hammond, Sen., William Johnston, Robt. Broket, John Dulin, John Jackson, Thomas

Legislative Petitions of the Town and County of Alexandria, Virginia

Lewis, James Gill, William Pool, Edwd. Tayler, Jr., James Richards, Thaddeus Dulin, John Devaughan, Daniel Sanford, John Gess, Lindores Lucas, John Morey, Daniel Summers, Benjamin Balinger, George Fielder, Michael Hall, William Cash, John Gladding, William Simmons, Thomas Simmons, John Javins, William Trirvey, Chas. Craig, Joseph Cockerill, James Moxley, John Moore, David Black, Thos. Lindsay, William Turner, Jr., Henry Stots, Denise Carrell, Saml. Smitherman, Hugh Conn, Ralph Longden, Charles Hooff, John Harrison, Thomas Jenkins, Thos. Fransess, Robert Wright, Danl. Rush, James Reves, Constantine Hughes, Andrew Orison, John Hurst, John Moreland, Enos Moreland, John Moreland, Junr., Hezekiah Kidwell, Richd. Warden, Wm. Lewis, John Smith, Luke Frizell, Thomas Taylor, William Davis, Joseph Longley, Joshua Skidwell, William McDowell, James Carrel, Hodson Bennett, John Dalgarn, Merryman Harroway, James Marten, Sandford Payne, Bennett Hill, Thomas Love, Terrence Burn, William Cleveland, Gideon Smith, Daniel Bradley, Dozier Bennett, John Harrison, Benjn. Dixon, George Smith, John S. Prather, John Shortridge, Beel Green, George *, James Fenley, Sanford *, John Anderson, Junr., William Grimes, Morris Fox, Thos. Sinclair, George Williams, Junr., Richard Halley, Levi Simson, James Balch, Jas. Lane, Jun., Robert Thomas, Sen., John Jest, *, Francis Keen, Joseph Walker, Jebob Shiveley, John Hutchinson, Charles Poessey, Jas. Cleveland, Michl. Ashford, Robert Athey, Adam Mitchel, Tho. Bennett, Mason Johnson, John Go____, James Lane, Sen., John Allison, Benjamin Stone, John Burnes, Samuel Black, Laurence Southward, William Powell, Francis Summers, Senr., John Park, Thos. Burnes, Wm. Hany, John Giles, Cors. Ford, John Lawrence, James Fox, William Bucher, Frederick Nichols, Chrisr. Neale, Robert Thomas, Junr., Benjamin Cockrell, Benjamin Hutchenson, Geo. Hutchenson, Alexander McKim, John Shed, Daniel King, John Whaley, Wethers Smith, Wm. Baker, Joseph Asbury, Daniel Sanders, Coleman Brown, *, Peter Mauzey, William Dunbar, George Thomas, Isaac Hutchinson, Solomon Cassett, Stephen Grimes, Sampson Kent, Jonathan Ward, William Ward, John Curtis, Joseph Bennett, Thos. Daley, * Garnett, John Ryan, Richard Wesley, James Harriss, Frederick Marmontell, William Steel, William Rogers, Jerimiah Bonham, Charles Alexander, Jas. Waugh, Richd. Conway. Edwd. Blackburn, Richd. Sanford, Robt. Sanford, Drummond Wheeler, Abraham Lay, David Davies, Charles Thrift, Charles Noland, John Barker, Alexr. McDonald, James Rowland, Hezekiah Williams, Charles Charters, Philip *, Enoch Ward, Lancelot Johnston, William Hall, John Peake, Wm. Simms, Drummond Wheeler, Senr., Sampson Turley, Coleman Duncan, Wm. Ramsay, John Hunter, Thomas Hornbuckle, John Wiggs, Nicholas Grimes, Charles Beach, Allen Davis, William Cockerille, Caleb Earp, Junr., Saml. Smuderman, Charles Gardner, Joseph Balinger, Hargess King, Bazel Williams, Daniel Michael, Peter McKenna, Bartin Martin, John Muir, Wm. Adams, George Thrift, and John Whitesides.

Second duplicate petition marked A477-1, signed by R. Hooe, Joseph Cary, Thomas Williams, Nicholas Hannah, Francis Peyton, Danl. McPherson, Benja. Hamp & Co., Ch. Simms, Wilfrid Johnston, Lawrence

Hooff, John Saunders, Aaron Hewes, Wm. Harper, Jno. Contee Keith, Saml. Harper, John Dunlap, John McMoory, B. Pettit, Jas. Keith, George Hunter, Caleb Earp, Paton & Butcher, George Wilson, Jonah Thompson, John Reynolds, Thomas Barclay, Josiah Watson & Co., Gurden Chapin, Benj. C. Payne, Jeremiah Cockerill, John McIver, Jno. Hickman & Co., Thomas Hickman, William Newton & Co., Jos. Caverly, Robt. Alexander, Robt. Coupar, W. McKnight, Adam S. Swope, Robert Donaldson, James Prather, John Brent, Richard Sanford, Junr., Levin C. Wailes, Jonathan Swift, Wm. Mounsher, Wm. Lyles, Wm. Hartshorne, Robinson Sanderson & Rumney, David Finlay, Archd. Dobbin, R.W. Ashton, Elie Vallette, Joseph Lewis, John Murray, John Wheaton, Thomas Rogerson, Edwd. K. Thompson & Co., A. & Jacob Swoope, P. Marsteller, John McClinachan, Benjn. Shreve, William Shreve, Michl. Clarke, Ja. Woodard, Theodorick Lee, John Pleasants, Colin MacIver, Andw. Wales, Jos. Greenway, Michael Reynolds, D. Arell, Philip Webster, E. McLean, Samson Darrell, Wm. Baker, William Lowry & Co., George Heites, Jno. Winterbery, Barton Baker, Jacob Leap, Saml. *, Jacob Moore, Jno. C. Hunter, James Lawrason, Ichd. Hunter, Edward Ramsay, Jacob Cox, Zach. Shugart, *, Flenoy Smith, John Potts, Jas. Bushby, Henry Budd, Benj. Dulany, Roger West, William Smith, John West, Jno. Hankins, * Ansley, Walter Brooke, John Robertson, Tho. Swann, Philip Dalby, Wm. Bowling, John Harper, John Bronaugh, Samuel *, Jno. Hannah, Jacob Butts, Jas. Campbell, Wm. Smith, Philip France, Robt. Greeves, Wm. Hunter, Adam Bence, Abel Willis, John C. Lewis, Alexandr. Smith, Michael Thorn, Edward Harper, George Taylor, Wm. Bushby, Solomon Hornbuckle, Michael Pepper, Thos. McVale, John Allan, Thomas West, Daniel Roberdeau, Oliver Price, John Jolly, Henry Preston, Junr., Peter Peterson, Robert Fulton, Israel S. Wright, John Korn, Richard Arell, John Short, Thos. Low, John *, Washer Blunt, Jno. Minchin, *, Wm. Smull, James McCormick, Thos. Wilkinson, Richard Jenkins, John Burrs, William Bromley, William Wright, John Hunter, Robert Hunter, Ephraim Evans, Joseph Fullmer, James Gra__bury, Seth Starr, John Harper, and Wm. H. Powell & Co. *Reasonable.* Box A.

Inhabitants.
1787, 24 NOV. Fairfax County. Overseers of the Poor. That under the Act to provide for the Poor of the several countys within this Commonwealth, the said County of Fairfax hath been laid off or divided into two nearly equal distinct Districts, for electing Overseers of the Poor, in the upper of which District is the town of Alexandria. That the Overseers elected for the lower District having refused to serve, and their places not having been supplyed by other appointments, the business devolved upon the three overseers elected in the upper district, two of which three are inhabitants of the said town of Alexandria in consequence of which most of the poor in the lower district have remained unprovided for and have had no other means of subsistence but the contributions of private charity... Signed by 617 persons. Oversize. Box 5A.

Legislative Petitions of the Town and County of Alexandria, Virginia

Inhabitants.
1787, 24 NOV. Fairfax County, Alexandria Town. Overseers of the poor and execution of the poor laws. Oversize. *Referred*. Box 5A

....The County of Fairfax having been originally divided into two parishes,[31] the same division was contained in an upper and lower district; the lower Parish having no glebe and employing no Minister, their vestries had been negligent in meeting, and their church wardens for a while declined acting at all whereby their poor were not regularly provided for and consequently at the time of the abolition of vestries considerable arrearages were due on their account which the county court was then directed by law to levy for and did levy for on the county at large. This rendered the levy of last year higher than it would otherwise have been; however, the said lower district did appoint overseers of the poor under the new law, which overseers have acted, and in August last made their levy on the county at large for their poor rates of last year according to law, as well as did the upper district, with this difference that the vestries of the lower district provided only for each of their poor as were boarded out privately or received partial [damage] in the upper district where in a poor house had been provided such as they judged for only for that [ ] of provision.

With regard to the election of overseers of the poor in the upper district, it was made in a centrical part of the county under the direction of a county magistrate living very remote from the town of Alexandria, only four persons from the town of Alexandria and its vicinity were present at the election and three of those having been formerly church wardens and now threatened with being appointed overseers of the poor attended for the sole and declared purpose of preventing their being elected, and getting the business of the poor shifted on some other hands. Nevertheless the aforesaid superintending magistrate finding none willing to serve that were competent to the business, did finally prevail on two of the said old churchwardens (who unfortunately happened to live in Alexandria) to agree to serve, he himself undertaking to serve with them as overseers of the poor, and they were appointed accordingly, not by themselves, but by the votes of the county, people assembled at the election.

The three overseers thus constituted, knowing from experience (as they had charge of the poor formerly as churchwardens) that wheresoever in the county the poor originate the town is the place they resort to and present themselves, whether led thither by the hopes of getting some suitable employ by which they might earn a pittance for themselves, or for the greater convenience of asking and probability of receiving alms of the people; and having also found many impositions, inconveniences and superfluous expences to result from having places to seek for the reception of the poor wherever they fall on hand, and

---

[31] When Fairfax County was formed, it embraced Truro Parish which was founded in 1732. Fairfax Parish was created from Truro Parish in 1765.

means to provide for their transportation thither, as well as because the purchase of provisions is always more difficult and the price generally higher in every part of this county than in Town, and in consideration of the frequent seizure of provision of every kind at the market in Town for the use of the poor, of the low price of the [ ] of the markett and their getting fish out of the Potowmack gratis during the season of seine hauling and without much labour & other times; for all these considerations your petitioners beg have to inform your honours that the said overseers of the poor did rent a plantation in the neighborhood of Alexandria and on Potomack river for the purposes of a poor house, with the privilege of cutting and using what quantity of wood they pleased for use thereof and all the other appurtenances for the same of £12 per annum (which sum your petitioners are persuaded is as low a rent as the same plantation would be let for, if situated in the most remote and interior part of the county) and that the poor persons accommodated in the said poor house have always raised for themselves on said plantation an abundance of garden vegetables and roots and have also been employed (as far as they were able) in fishing and picking oakum, to assist in defraying the expences of their maintenance... Mentions tithables.

Signed by *, Hugh McCaughen, Jo. Kempff, Robt. Lyle, Junr., Thos. Stewart, Saml. Simmonds, Andw. Wales, Richard Arell, Ja. Woodard, Michael Thorn, Danl. W. Sherron, Junr., Isaac McPherson, P. War. Miller, Lawrence Hooff, Levi Talbot, John Smith, Peter Williams, Wm. Fisher, Jacob Heinemann, Beal Howard, Michl. Gretter, J.J. Delawar, John Danenmarker, Henry Stroman, Samuel McLean, Christian Perth, Valentine Uhler, John Kean, Dennis Ramsay, John Hendricks, Robert Mease, John Saunders, John Jolly, Wm. Williams, John Tonsdall, Washer Blunt, Jas. McCliesh, Philip Conn, Oliver Price, Jonah Thompson, Benj. A. Hamp, John Short, George Coryell, Aaron Hewes, John Gretter, Wm. Hartshorne, Charles Little, Wm. Herbert, John Fitzgerald, Ch. Simms, Richd. Conway, W. Brown, Robert McCrea, George Muir, Benj. Shreve, Wm. Lowry & Co., Patrick Murray, Wm. Bushby, George Hunter, George Hayes, Wm. Duvall, Jas. M. McKea, Chas. Turner, Thos. Conn, William McRea, Thos. Coltar, Wm. Ramsay, Moses Tandy, Gilbert Harrow, George Richards, Robert Lyle, Junr., Andw. Jamiesson, Ninian Anderson, Adam Bloss, Andr. Black, Hugh Baylor, Richd. Weightman, Aaron Hougland, Jacob Lee, John Spurr, Ths. Stodd'rd, Andw. Fleming, James Bell, Roger Chew, Patrick Hagerty, George Darling, Mungo Dykes, Neil Mooney, James Douglass, William Ward, Archd. McCliesh, John Graham, Jacob Weismuller, John Wise, James Kennedy, John Harper, Thos. Hedrick, Elisha C. Dick, Wm. Lyles, Samuel Smith, Thomas Ramsay, Jona. Swift, Anthy. Maxwell, John B. Fouche, Wm. Wright, Wm. Paton, John Butcher, Lewis Weston, John Dunlap, Wm. Harper, Wm. Chew, Jos. Bushby, Peter Tertzbach, Baldwin Dade, James Grimes, Robert Fulton, Jacob Cox, James Lawrason, Valentine Bontz, John Murray, Thadw. Bowen, Chas. B. Finley, Alexandr. Smith, Edwd. Sanford, D. Arell, John McClenachan, John Rumney, Wm. Mounsher,

Legislative Petitions of the Town and County of Alexandria, Virginia

Wm. Hunter, Andw. *, John Longden, Jacob Forttney, W. McKnight, Robt. Conn, Jno. McKnight, Tho. Richards, John Harper, John Hunter, Jacob Butts, Wm. H. Powell, *, Mich'l Clarke, Edward McGwin, Fraser *, Adam Ebert, Philip France, John Smith, Thos. Copper, Mathis Syfort, Conrad Miller, Jos. Watkins, J. Pettit, Thomas Barclay, John Reynolds, Peter Wise, Jno. Winterbery, John Pettigrew, Michael Hoke, James Smith, William Shakespear, John Hamilton, Guy Evans, Jas. Morrison, John Evans, Edmund Edmonds, Saml. Montgomery Brown, Will: Hunter, Jr., Jesse Taylor, John E. _ford, Geo. Clements, John Allison, Peter Piles, Jesse Simms, Jerome *, Stephen Holmes, Chas. McIver, Robt. Broket, Patrick Byrne, R.T. Hooe, Joseph Cary, Gerrard S. Conn, John Muir, Wm. Wilson, S. Hanson of Sam., Thomas Reid, James Rattle, Joseph M. Perrin, James Lownes, and Peter Vilke.

Merchants, Traders and Other Inhabitants of Alexandria.
1788, 5 NOV. A478. Establishment of an inspection of flour and bread. That the good designs of the Legislature in passing the Act for Regulating the Inspection of Flour & Bread on the 23rd of November[32] last will be entirely Defeated, without speedy remedy to the last paragraph of said Act for recovery of the penalties and forfeitures, Particularly as they respect deficient weight of flour & bread brought to market for sale, an enormity common to at least one sixth part of all the flour brought to this market. No defauls of twenty five shillings [are] recoverable for a single magistrate, but exceeding that sum in almost every instance of seizure, all which are entirely fruitless as our judges refuse condemnation alledgeing [sic] that they are not authorized to do it on motion. Consequently defaulters have hitherto passed with impunity, otherwise than their transgression being marked by the officer in desiring the purchaser of such light flour to retain in their hands the millets prescribed by said act until he could effectuate the punishment of such defauls.... *Reported.* Box B.

Signed by Wm. Hartshorne, Jonah Thompson, Francis Peyton, Jonah Thompson, Francis Peyton, John Fitzgerald, Will. Hunter, Jr., Benj. A. Hamp, Dav. Finley, Gurden Chapin, Jas. Kennedy, Jos. Greenway, William Hickman, Jr., Joseph Cary, John Murray, John Reynolds, Benjn. Shreve, Andw. Jamiesson, Joseph Gilpin, Ninian Anderson, Job Green, Danl. & Isaac McPherson, P. Marsteller, N. Marsteller, Jr., R. Hooe, Wm. Lowry & Co., Robinson Sanders, Adam S. Swope, Jno. Miller Carson, John McIver, John Muir, John Hendricks, Robert Allison, Strayer & Heidey, Darling & Earp, Adrien Tellier, Alexr. Buchan, Wm. Ramsay, Dennis Ramsay, William Duvall, Peter Wise, Jenckes Winsor & Co., Saml. Packard, Samuel Monty. Brown, Wm. Paton, Saml. Craig, Wm. Lyles, Jacob Bedinger, John B. Dabney, Tho. Rogerson, John E. Ford, John Allison, John Wise, Mitchell Donaldson, S. Hanson of Saml.,

---

[32] Hening, Vol. 12, 1785-1788, Chapter XXX, pp. 515-20, "An act to regulate the inspection of four and bread," passed November 23, 1787.

Edward Harper, Philip Webster, Andw. Wales, Robt. Coupar, Robert McCrea, Josiah Watson & Co., Washer Blunt, Edwd. K. Thompson, Jas. Craik, Jas. Craik, Junr., I. Roberdeau, Robt. Mease, Thomas Irwin, George Taylor, Baldwin Dade, George Hill, Daniel Roberdeau, Jesse Taylor, William Halley, Wm. Herbert, John Potts, Junr., Robert Donaldson, Cleon Moore, James Irvin, James Wilson, Rog: <u>Coltart</u>, William Summers, W. McKnight, J. Love, Thos. Williams, Mordecai Miller, and Alexandr. Smith.

James and John Hendricks.
1788, 6 NOV. A479. Renewal of military certificates which were stolen from petitioners. That on the night of the 8th of September last their store in the Town of Alexandria was broke open, Rob'd of much property & set on fire by some evil dispos'd persons, that amongst the property missing is a considerable number of Military Certificates issued by this State, some of which was issued in the name of James Hendricks one of your Petitioners, your Petitioners therefore pray that your Hon'ble House will order renewal of the sd. certificates as are now suppos'd to be burn'd under such restrictions as to your Hon'ble House may think reasonable and your Petitioners as in duty bound shall ever pray &c., Alexandria 25th October 1788. Signed by James & John Hendricks. *Reported.* Box B.

Fairfax County Inhabitants.
1789, 3 NOV. Fairfax County.[33] Also see 11 NOV 1790. Location of Fairfax County Courthouse. That the court house of the said County is so much out of repair, and gone to decay, that it is hardly fit for the purpose of holding courts, and not worth repairing, having been so badly built at first, that the charge of repairing or rebuilding the same would be almost as great as building a new court house... that the county must immediately or very soon incur the charge of building a new court house, Your petitioners are induced to hope that the general interest and convenience of the inhabitants will be consulted, in fixing the place for holding the county courts in future as near the center of the county as the publick road and other circumstances will admit... That the present court house in the Town of Alexandria being situated on the extream edge of the county and within two hundred yards of the boundary of the state of Virginia is extremely inconvenient to the bulk of the inhabitants of the county; who are obliged to attend court, at more than double the distance they would have occasion to do if the court house was fixed (as of right it ought to be) near the center of the county; from whence the greater part of the inhabitants when obliged to attend court, could conveniently return to their own homes, every night; and thereby save the charge of posting use of taverns and publick houses; an expence grievous to them all, and ruinous to many of the poorest sect of

---

[33] <u>Hening</u>, Vol. 13, 1789-1792, Chapter LVII, p. 79, "An act for altering the place of holding courts in the county of Fairfax," passed December 4, 1789.

Legislative Petitions of the Town and County of Alexandria, Virginia

people... That since the jurisdiction of the corporation court of the town of Alexandria hath been by law extend to any sum in controversy between the citizens and inhabitants thereof, the removal of the county court to the center of the county can be attended with little inconvenience to the inhabitants of the town compared with the benefits resulting from it to the county in general. That the reasons usually urged for establishing county courts in town, however, distant from the middle of the county, in preference to some place near the center, vizt. that it is necessary to promote trade and commerce-- and that it is a matter of convenience to the people, in affording them an opportunity of transacting their business with the merchants, at the same time they attend court, are your petitioners conceive ill founded and erroneous... Oversize. *Reasonable.* Box 5A.

Gives names (not signatures) of the following petitioners: Thomas Bayliss, Junr., John Gladding, John Wiggs, Joseph Ballenger, Edward Worthin, Samuel Stone, Thomas Simpson, Thomas Halley, Thomas Windsor, William Deneale, Peter Mauzey, Junr., Thomas Fr[tear], *, John Hickey, Thomas West, John Simpson, Thomas Hunt, James Tascoe, John Simpson Read, David Loefbournes, Lewis Pritchard, Michael Rooney, Tapley Fryer, William Buckley, Merryman Harrower, William Harrower, John Harrower, Richard Wheeler, William Reardon, John Powell, James Rowland, Gilbert Rowland, James Sallmon, Tylor Waugh, Benjamin Suddeth, George West, Spencer Simpson, William Ogden, George Wyley, George Mason, Junr., Daniel McCarty, Junr., William Donaldson, William King, Francis Mason, Jeremiah Woodyard, Lee Massey, Martin Cockburn, Michael Rooney, George Halley, French Simpson, William Essex, George Mason of Pohick, Samuel Green, Gilbert Simpson, Terrence Conner, Junr., Jeremiah Atcheson, William *, Josiah Boggess, George Reardon, Henry Hunt, William Eaton, John Hunt, Robert Speake, Jacob Moreland, Senr., Charles Wright, Junr., Gilbert Deavers, Senr., Gilbert Deavers, Junr., William Deavers, Richard Deavers, James Grimsley, James Smith, John Cranford, Jacob Moreland, Junr., John Atchison, Samuel Bayley, John Saxton, Joseph Potter, John Short, Isaac Rogers, William Carico, Abel Carico, Lewis Tressler, Henry Pell, Leonard Smith, Charles Reed, William Johnson, Senr., William Skinner, Rezon Wilcoxon, Jonathan DeVaughn, John Hewitt, Sr., Edward Bates, James Henderson, Nicholas Garrett, Michael Grush, Felix Duffil, Thomas Pain, David Allen, William Sisson, John Harrison, William Crump, Senr., William Crump, Junr., George Crump, Stephen Crump, James Ballenger, Ignatious Luckett, Thomas Dove, Walter Johnson, Edward Davis, Junr., John Pearson, Benjamin Thomas, John Gooding, William Dawson, Thomas Birch, Joshua Gist, Sampson Cockerill, Merryman Haryway, Joshua Gorden, Bastin Martin, * Martin, Thomas Parmer, Abednego White, Nicholas Morris, Aaron Simpson, John Buckley, James Taylor, William Harrison, John Skinner, James Simpson (son of George), John Brumback, Wm. Simpson (son of George), Sanford Payne, James Martin, James Dove, George Simpson, Peter Mauzey, Samuel Smith, Sylvester Halley, Samuel Weedon, James Halley, George Williams, John Dawson,

Legislative Petitions of the Town and County of Alexandria, Virginia

Edward Hylor, Thomas Johnson, Timothy Carrington, James Halley, Junr., William Dawes, John Simpson, Peter Hermon, Noah Morton, Sampson Talbott, Benoni Price, Thomas Gossom, Drummond Wheeler, Junr., Samuel Hampton, Michael Ramy, John Jackson, Walter Johnson, Edward Ford, Sampson Turley, Junr., * Eales, Daniel McCarty, Senr., George Mason, Senr., Thomas Pollard, John Alliston, Thomas Alliston, Junr., Lawson Parker, Josiah Clark, James Gloster, Benjamin Riley, Rubin Kirk, Henry Loyd, Henry Worthin, Joseph Davenport, William Gilpin, Aquilla Davis, Thomas Dodson, Charles Smith, John Violett, Daniel *, John Allison, Junr., John Devaughan, George Mills, Hezekiah Price, James Jenkins, William Hall, Richard Hornbuckle, John Kent, John MacIntosh, William Bladen, Junr., Alexander McDonald, John Stone, Junr., Grafton Kirke, Sanford Potter, Zebedea Compton, James Grimsley, Samuel Smitherman, Samuel Smitherman, Junr., Abednego Adams, Daniel Stone, Henry Herman, William Essex, Charles Birch, Richard Scrivener, Enoch Ward, Josiah Boggess, Edward Potter, John Vernon, Zechariah Morris, George Fielder, William Reardon, John Alton, Daniel Linch, James Richards, John Jones, Henry Davis, Andrew Allen, William Richards, Allen Davis, Thomas Trammel, John Fraser, William Price, William Mills, Thomas Kirby, John Peacock, John Mitchell, Benjamin Rogers, Daniel McCarty, Junr., George Moxley, John Harrison Manly, Edward Pool, Daniel Javins, Michael Ashford, William Ward, Hugh Smitherman, Thomas Johnson, William Gooden, Junr., William Mason, John Scott, Thomas *, Henry Gunnell, John Gunnell, Junr., Solomon Cassett, Joshua Kidwell, Michael Webber, Andrew Monroe, Strother Johnson, John Moreland, Francis Eaton, Stephen Lomax, John Moreland, Junr., Michael Roby, Junr., Archibald Moreland, Enos Moreland, Hezekiah Kidwell, John Robinson, John Ballenger, Samuel Thompson, James Thompson, William Monroe, Aaron Nalley, William Thompson, Charles Low, John Thompson, Daniel Thompson, Michael H. Roby, Elias Roby, Levi Roby, <u>Lish</u> T. Roby, John Wren, Frank Hagen, Hopkin Rice, John Rand, James Halley, James Wren, Junr., William Barry, William Turner, Thomazin Ellzey, Thomas Turner, John Mansell, James Gill, Joshua Jacobs, James Ford, Thomas Sangster, Samuel Stone, Junr., George Harley, Charles G. Holden, Josias Ward, William Kern, James Kern, Thomas *, John Rogers, Leonard Barker, William Barker, Moses Barker, John Barker, Jonathan Denty, Richard Procter, John M. Clark, Josias Clark, Junr., Thomas Dodson, John Ward, John Dodson, Joshua Coffer, William Ferguson, James Hurford, James Sudd<u>e</u>th, James Riley, John Harrison, Thomas Harrison, John Harrison, Junr., George Harrison, Caleb Stone, Sampson Turley, Thomas Dye, James Prichard, Nehemiah Morris, Solomon Jackson, Harry Jackson, Thomas Gossom, William Barker, Junr., John Harley, John Allen, John Powell, Henry Wingate, William Hicks, John Clark, Junr., <u>Prince</u> Bayliss, William Simms, John Askin, George Askin, Eli Stone, William Stone, John Dulin, Atwell Dulin, John Towers, James Bosswell, Thomas Atkinson, Matthew Boswell, John Boswell, William Boswell, James Hurst, John Hurst, Richard Presgraves, William Presgraves, Junr., William Presgraves, Senr., William McPherson, Alexander Simms, Thomas Burger, Henry Richards, Joseph

Legislative Petitions of the Town and County of Alexandria, Virginia

Condon, Richard Chichester, John Hereford, Junr., William Payne Bayliss, Thomas Mason, William Rogers, Junr., Joseph Potter, Joseph Warner, Thomas Bayliss, William Bayliss, John Johnson, Junr., William Carico, Junr., Cornelious Thompson, John Thompson, Marmaduke Beckwith, William Turner, James Conner, Lancelot Johnson, John Love, Richard Halley, A. Winn, John Tillett, Joshua Coffer, Henry Hurst, J.H. Manly, William West, Stephen Daniel, J. Simpson, William Johnson, Junr., William Potter, John Meara, Bryan Alliston, Stephen King, John King, Laurence King, Lewis Suddeth, Hugh West, William Simpson, Joab Reid, Henry Griffin, Jesse Chapple, John Chapple, Joseph Jackson, James Hunt, John Clarke, Abednego Adams, Daniel Stone, Henry Hermon, William Essex, Charles Birch, Richard Scrivener, Enoch Ward, Josiah Boggess, Edward Potter, Daniel McCarty, Thomas Athey, Henry Rowland, Thomas Rowland, William Moon, Thomas Reid, Joseph Reighley, Joseph Jacobs, Junr., John Young, William Holemon, George Nickolls, Mordecai Jacobs, John Marshel, William Simpson, Senr., Joseph Blansett, John Blansett, John Jackson, Junr., John Hampton, Junr., Edmond Bostick, William Hampton, William Keen, John Phillips, Henry Russan, Cornelious Kincheloe, William Eaton, Senr., Hargess King, Gerard Barnett, Zachariah Ward, William Gunnel[l], Jacob Woolbright, Bazzel Williams, William Simpson, Senr., James Rowland, John Stone, Robert Molchen, Leonard Atkinson, Bennett Atkinson, Terrence Conner, Senr., Walter Atchison, Thomas Church, George Mason, Junr. (Pohick), French Mason, Jacob Hoakes, Richard Hall, John Simpson, William Weston, Junr., William Baily, William Potter, William Green, Jeremiah Fugate, William McAtie, James Athey, Whaley Violet, Alexand. Voss, Daniel McCarty Chichester, Doddridge Pitt Chichester, Presley Gunnell, Thomas Gunnell, John Shortridge, George Smith, Daniel McCarty, Thomas Oisens, John Gunnell, Robert Gunnell, Alexander Marcey, John Anderson, Junr., Daniel Jenkins, Joseph Powell, Junr., John Davis, Edward Davis, Samuel Johnson, William Lewis, Francis Summers, John Summers, Thomas Lombard, Thomas Johnson, Thomas Blackburn, Henson Jenkins, Thomas Biddle, William Lightfoot, Richard Fremon, Daniel Story, Thomas Kirby, Junr., Reuben Potter, James Rattle, John Murry, John Johnson, Thomas Kirby, John Jackson, William Smith, Joseph Davis, Jacob Rooksley, Joseph Simpson, Raphel Hodgkin, William Harrison, James Gill, Edward Lanham, James Bigwood, George Simpson, Daniel Hodskin, James Daviss, John Phillips, William Phillips, Spencer Moxley, Gibson Whaley, George Smith, Weathers Smith, James Smith, George Williams, John Anderson, John Vallindigham, John Shortridge, Reuben Rookley, James Dyer, Thomas Dyer, William Simms, Senr., John Owens, Thomas Owens, John Lewis, Junr., John Moxley, Spencer Jackson, John Jackson, Junr., Hambleton Thrift, William Summers, Bennett Hill, E.D. Ratcliff, Atwill Dulin, John Kent, Francis Keen, Daniel Kent, Joseph Wood, James Tillett, Richard Simpson, Thomas Sangster, George Manley, Francis Coffer, William Ferguson, Zechariah Morris, Lewis Sanders, John King, Joseph Powell, Junr., Richard Ratcliffe, William Jacobs, Zechariah Dove, John Hampton, Francis Stone, Robert Church, Terrence Conner, Senr., Thomas Church,

Legislative Petitions of the Town and County of Alexandria, Virginia

Senr., Jesse Church, William Harrison, William Bryant, Charles Broadwater, Benjamin Talbott and Charles Lewis Broadwater.

<u>Citizens of Alexandria.</u>
1789, 14 NOV. A480. Lottery for Raising Funds to Pave Streets.[34] That your Petitioners as well for their own advantage as for the convenience of those who trade to the said town are desirous of paving some of the most frequented streets therein, and being unable to raise a sum sufficient for the purpose by subscription are induced to apply to your Honorable body to authorize them to raise the sum of fifteen hundred pounds by Lottery, your petitioners are apprized that the Legislature have wisely prohibited Lotteries in general but for usefull and beneficial purposes have frequently permitted them, your Petitioners being well convinced that the object they have in view is Laudable and if accomplished will be of Public utility are emboldened to Petition your honorable body to pass an act to enable the Inhabitants of Alexandria to raise the sum of fifteen hundred pounds by Lottery under the management of Charles Simms, Charles Lee, Richard Conway, William Hunter, Junr., George Gilpin, Philip Marsteller, William Herbert, Robert Townsend Hooe, Jesse Taylor, William Brown, Thomas Porter, John Fitzgerald, and John Dundas, or any seven of them. *Referred.* Box B.

Signed by Ch: Simms, Richd. Conway, Will: Hunter, Jr., Dennis Ramsay, O. Winsor, John Murray, Thomas Rogerson, Nathl. Ingraham, Jesse Taylor, Wm. Hepburn, John Dundas, James Wilson, John Allison, Jona. Mandeville, Gurden Chapin, Lewis Weston, Absal<u>e</u>m Wroe, P. Marsteller, W. Farrell, Robert McCrea, Wm. Summers, John Gretter, Shedrick Shumaker, Luke *, Saml. Montgomery Brown, Robert Jamiesson, Wm. Duvall, Jesper Is<u>er</u>loan?, Oliver Price, Hugh McCaughen, David Finlay, John Burns, J.M. Carson, Michl. Gretter, James Balfour, Roger Chew, Lanty Crowe, Benja. Lanston, Ralph Longden, William Young, Thomas West, Robert Sim, Robt. Coupar, Peter Williams, Andrew <u>Slowen</u>, Nicholas <u>D</u>ills, Jeremiah Fervall, John Chew, Thos. Stewart, Wm. Morgan, Edwd. Sanford, R. Harrison, John Korn, Jacob Wiesmuller, Gilbert Harrow, Alexandr. Smith, Henry McCue, George Rutter, Philip Heide, Patr. Byrne, Adam Butt, Washer Blunt, *, Thos. Jewell, John McClinachan, John Reynolds, Jas. Keith, Samuel Harper, Adam Bence, Robert Fulton, George Mason, Vincent Kelly, Edward M'Gwin, Chas. Abrams, Wm. Worden, William Page, Joseph Gilpin, John Harper, Alex. MacKenzie, Paterson Taylor & Co., John Hunter, William Rhodes, George Goodes, Michael Thorn, George Gilpin, John Boyer, Hugh Dempster, Jacob Butts, Frederick Weaver, Henry Fletzer, George *, Val. Peyton, W. Hodgson, Geo. Coryell, Samuel Simmonds, Jacob Price, Hugh Jorden, Richard Weightman, John Umb<u>e</u>reit, William Farrell, James Murray, James Plowman, William Dunlap, Michael Grimler, Edward Ramsay, John

---

[34] <u>Hening</u>, Vol. 13, 1789-1792, Chapter LXXV, p. 94, "An act to authorise the raising of a sum of money by lottery, for the use of the town of Alexandria," passed December 9, 1789.

Legislative Petitions of the Town and County of Alexandria, Virginia

Longden, James Kellyham, Smith Keith, Joseph Jackson, Jacob Fortney, Peter Krouse, John Steel, Michael Reynolds, Jacob Resler, Peter Wise, George Darling, Caleb Earp, Peter Wise, Jr., Peter Tatsapaugh, Phillip France, James M. McRea, Wm. McRea, Robert Mease, Neil Mooney, Thomas Sly, William Woolls, Erasmus Welch, Cleon Moore, Joseph Thomas, Jno. Dalton, Archibald Swain, Charles Jones, Patrick Hagerty, Wm. Miller, Richard Sanford, Junr., John Harrison, Andrew Reed, Jacob Shuck, Andw. Reintzell, Tobias Zimmerman, Wm. Norris, James McReady, John Tonsdall, Saml. Sheobalds, Jr., Josias Williams, Philip Webster, Park Muny, *, Richard Arell, D. Arell, John Wise, Andw. Jamiesson, Ninian Anderson, John Snider, Ephraim Weylie, Saml. Arell, Valentin Uhler, Wm. Bird, and John Fitzgerald.

Inhabitants of the Town of Alexandria.
1789, 16 NOV. A481. Permission to hold a lottery for the purpose of raising £5,000 to complete paving streets of town.[35] The sum raised by former lottery is inadequate; also that Wm. Brown, Richard Conway, Jno. Potts, Jr., Josiah Watson, Olney Winsor, Jonathan Swift, and Wm. Hodgson be appointed trustees of the lottery. Alexandria, Nov. 12th 1790. *Reasonable.* Box B.

Signed by Lemuel Bent, John Fitzgerald, James Patton, Josiah Watson, James McDonald, Thos. Porter, O. Winsor, Jonah Thompson, Jesse Taylor, Will. Hunter, Bushrod Washington, Thomas Rogerson, John Foster, Thomas Irwin, R. Prescott, John Potts, Junr., Wm. Wilson, R. Harrison, Benj. Hamp, George Taylor, A. Browne, Richd. Conway, W. Brown, P. Marsteller, James Lawrason, Isaac McPherson, Daniel McPherson, John Murray, Obadh. Bowen, G. Deneale, George Gilpin, and John B. Dabney.

Sundry Inhabitants of the Town of Alexandria.
c.1790. A629. Aid in repairing roads from mountain passes to Alexandria. They are in such poor condition that farmers cross the river and go to Baltimore rather than travel them. No note of action. Box B.

Signed by James Kirk, William Lyles, Jos. Greenway, Edward Harper, Jas. Woodard, Robert Sanderson, Jona. Swift, Wm. Hartshorne, Geo. Hollingsworth, Thos. Williams, John Clark, T. O'Ryan, Ch. Mortimore, petit en gloudelet, John Butcher, George Wilson, Wm. Hickman, Junr., Wm. Baker, David Henley, William Taylor, Philip Dalby, Arth. Maxwell, Gurden Chapin, William Abbott, William Mounsher, Robt. C. Newton, Randle Mitchell, Hugh Mitchell, George Gilpin, Josiah Watson, Obadh. Bowen, Jos. Caverly, John Brent, Alexandr. Smith, Danl. McPherson, Isaac McPherson, Edwd. K. Thompson, Thos. Tobin, Oliver Price, James Lownes, Joseph Janney, P. Marsteller, James McKenna, John Muir, W. McKnight, Edwd. Blackburn, R. McKnight, Charles Bryan, John Allison,

---

[35] Act authorized, Virginia Journal and Alexandria Advertiser, 23 SEP 1790.

Thos. Conn, Robt. Conn, Lawrence Hooff, John Dundas, Wm. Hepburn, Benj. Dulany, James Hendricks, Augustus Delarue, Adam Lynn, Peter Wise, Jesse Taylor, Jas. M. McKea, Alexander Couper, Robert Allison, Thomas Whiting, Wm. Bird, Ben. Shreve, John Jolly, Roger Chew, W. Keith, James Adam, Richd. Sanford, Robert Sanford, Robert Lyle, Senr., Robert Lyle, Junr., John Graham, Joel Cooper, Hugh McCaughen, Cleon Moore, John Sutton, Thomas *, John Wise, Chas. Lewis Broadwater, Saml. Arell, Wm. Duvall, Wm. Triplett, Daniel Roberdeau, Robert Adam, Michl. Gretter, Godfrey Miller, Grafton Kirke, *, Baldn. Dade, Rd. Ratcliff, Geo. Summers, Wm. Carlin, Joseph Powell, Jr., Dennis Ramsay, John Hendricks, Wm. Ramsay, Henry Lyles, S. Hanson of Saml., Will. Hunter, Jr., Robert Donaldson, Thomas Porter, B. Beeler, *, John Potts, Junr., Thos. Wilkinson, Colin MacIver, George Richards, John McTrue, Alexander Thomas, John Lomax, Wm. Dalton, Thos. McSavage, Richd. Conway, Thomas Moxley, George Mason, Levi Talbot, Val. Peers, Perrin Brothers & Co., Henry Budd, Wm. Paton, W.H. Terrett, Aaron Hewes, John Hickman, R. Hooe, Jacob Harman, * Johnson, Lewis Weston, Jacob Butts, Wm. Hunter, Richd. Arell, William Knight, Jacob Cox, William Bromley, George Herbert, *, James Halliday, D. Arell, Wm. Bushby, John B. Finley, Michl. Thorn, William Cox, Andw. Wales, William Buddicom, Samuel McLean, Will. Glass, Junius Corryell, Robt. Brocket, John Johnston, John Reynolds, Robert Fulton, Jno. Hawkins, John Fitzgerald, A. Skinner, Joseph Robinson, Jonah Thompson, Washer Blunt, and James Lawrason.

Inhabitants.
1790, 11 NOV. Inhabitants of Fairfax County.[36] Also see 3 NOV 1789. Location of Fairfax County Courthouse. That upon the petition of a great number of the inhabitants of the said County of the last Session of Assembly, setting forth the inconvenience and hardships they laboured under by having the county court held in the town of Alexandria, and praying that the same might be removed to some place near the center of the county (a copy of which petition is hereunto annexed, to shew the reasons upon which the application was founded; and which, therefore, your petitioners pray may be taken as part of this their present petition), an Act of Assembly was passed for their relief; altering the place of holding the County Courts from the town of Alexandria to such place as should be found most convenient, near the center of the County, within one mile of the cross roads at Price's Ordinary; and expressly directing the justices of the said County, before the first day of June then next ensuing, to levy on the tithable persons within their County, a sum sufficient to erect the necessary buildings, and to purchase two acres of ground, whereon to place them, &c., as by the said act (to which your petitioners refer) will more fully appear... And in direct contrast to the Act of the General Assembly, an Act of the Corporation of Alexandria (as if their authority too was paramount to the Laws of the State) was

---

[36] Virginia Gazette and Alexandria Advertiser, 21 OCT 1790.

passed on the 20th day of January 1790, for making some additions or improvements to their market house, and appropriating the same to the purpose of holding the County Courts; a copy of which remonstrance, and Act of the Corporation of Alexandria are hereto annexed, to shew that they were manufactured out of the same materials with the petition, since set on foot to the General Assembly, for repealing the said "Act for altering the place of holding Courts in the County of Fairfax," These were the preparatory steps taken to frustrate and defeat a positive law, and the arguments used in the progress of the business... The circumstance mentioned in the Town petition, of the great number of suits lately instituted in the District Court (if the fact be true) is owning, not to an apprehension of the delays which will be occasioned by the removal of the County Court to the center of the County, but to the procrastination and delay which the suitors have already experienced, by the County Courts sitting in the Town of Alexandria, and to the incompetence and partiality of the Town juries. Some of your petitioners will remember the removal of the County Court into the Town of Alexandria, near forty years ago,[37] and know that it was done by the then Governor of Virginia, in virtue of the Crown's prerogative, very contrary to the interest and inclination of the people... Oversize. Box 5A. Names (no signatures) 563 Fairfax County inhabitants.

David Arell, d. 1792.
1790, 16 NOV. A482. Divorce from his wife, *nee* Phebe Caverley.[38] That he was married in Alexandria in this state in the year [blank] to Phebe Caverley the daughter of Joseph Caverley of that Town who [has] after the marriage discovered signs of infidelity, that in the course of the five years in which he has inhabited with her he has been frequently under the necessity of parting with her in consequence of her adulterous and infamous practices, and that at length she became to base a prostitute that he found it absolutely impossible to live with her any longer... Signed by D. Arell. *Rejected, then Reported.* Box B.

First Presbyterian Church.
1790, 16 NOV. X1-4, Religious Petition No. 337. Presbyterian Church of Alexandria petitions for lottery to raise funds with which to complete church.[39] On behalf of the congregation, your petitioners anxious to

---

[37] The first session of the Fairfax County Court in its new location at Market Square in Alexandria was conveyed May 3, 1752 [Virginia Gazette, 30 APR 1752; Alexandria Trustee Minutes, 21 FEB 1753, p. 19]. William Anne Keppel, Earl of Albemarle, Virginia's Governor from 1737 to 1754, never went to Virginia. He was represented by deputies: Thomas Lee (1747-1750), Lewis Burwell (1750-1751), and Robert Dinwiddie (1751-1758).

[38] The Virginia Journal and Alexandria Gazette, 12 MAY 1785, p. 3, announced the recent marriage. Alexandria Hustings Court Deeds, Bk. G, p. 312, and the Alexandria Gazette, of 1 MAR 1796, p. 3, show that Mrs. Phoebe Arell was married 29 FEB 1796, to Capt. Stephen Moore.

[39] Hening, Vol. 13, 1789-1792, Chapter XLVI, pp. 173-75, "An act for authorizing several lotteries, and the sale of certain lots in the town of Portsmouth," at p. 174, 'for building a church in Alexandria.' Virginia Gazette and Alexandria Advertiser, 13 SEP 1792, pp. 1-2, "The Managers of the Alexandria Preſbyterian Church Lottery inform the public that the drawing of the 4th Claſs of ſaid Lottery will

promote the public worship of the Supreme Being, and impressed with a sense of their obligations to him, as well as of the influence of religion on civil society, were induced some years past to undertake to build an House in which they with others of their Christian Brethren might assemble for Public Worship. Unhappily for them, notwithstanding their utmost exertions, their House remains in an unfinished state and the funds generously contributed for the purpose exhausted, at the same time some demands against them are yet unsatisfied... that they may be enabled by Law to raise a sum of money not exceeding five hundred pounds by Lottery[40] of one or more classes for the purpose of discharging the demands against them finishing their church and erecting a steeple for a bell already provided the want of which has long been felt in this place... Alexandria, November 12, 1790. Signed by James Muir,[41] Wm. Lowry, John Dundas, Jesse Taylor, Robert McCrea, Will. Hunter, Jr., John Murray, and Andw. Jamieson. *Reasonable.* Box B.

Hannah Griffith (d. 1811).
1791, 21 OCT. B482. *Reported.* Box B.
   The humble petition of Hannah Griffith, widow and administratrix of the Reverend David Griffith, deceased.[42] In behalf of herself and children, humbly sheweth: That the said David Griffith in his life time being possessed of sundry tracts of land in the District of Kentucky and also of several lotts in the Town of Alexandria and being indebted to the executors of Mrs. Ann Colville in or about the sum of six hundred pounds Virga. cury., and also to Mr. Thomas Lewis in or about the sum of eight hundred & forty pounds, for several bonds given by him to Mr. Baldwin Dade and assigned by him to the said Thomas Lewis, to secure the payment of said debts, mortgaged his lotts in the Town of Alexandria to the Executors of the said Ann Colville, and also the said Baldwin Dade, which said last mentioned mortgage is assigned to the said Thomas Lewis. That the said David Griffith conceiving that it would be more for the interest of his family to dispose of as much of his Kentucky lands as would be sufficient to discharge said debts rather than suffer the mortgage on his town property to be foreclosed, or the property sold. On the eighteenth day of June one Thousand seven hundred and eighty nine made and executed a power of attorney to Christopher Greenup, Esq., authorizing and empowering him to sell and dispose of his Kentucky lands under the limitations and restrictions

---

commence on Tuesday the 20th day of November next..."
[40] Alexandria Hustings Court Minutes, 25 MAR 1794, p. 176, the Presbyterian Church Lottery trustees are discontinued.
[41] Following Isaac Stockton Keith, Rev. James Muir served the First Presbyterian Church from March 1789, until his death in 1820. The son of Rev. Dr. George and Tibbie Wardlaw Muir, he was born 12 APR 1757, in Catrine, Scotland, married in Bermuda on 28 FEB 1783, to Elizabeth Wellman, and died 8 AUG 1820, at "Bel Air" [later "Colross"], the spacious home of one of his parishioners, Jonathan Swift [William Randolph Sengel, Can These Bones Live? (Kingsport Press, 1973), pp. 39-46].
[42] David Griffith, born in New York City, died 1789, appears as a minister of Christ Episcopal Church in 1780. Hannah Griffith qualifies as administratrix of the estate of David Griffith, deceased, 19 OCT 1789, in Fairfax County records [Fairfax County Wills, Bk. E, 1784-1791, p. 347].

contained in a letter of instructions, which at the same time he wrote to the said Christopher Greenup and which power of attorney and letter of instructions are hereunto annexed, and to which your petitioner refers, but unfortunately for your petitioner and his children, he soon after departed this life, before the power of attorney or letter of instructions were received by Mr. Greenup...

Griffith's power of attorney letter, in part. Fairfax County, 22nd June 1789. Sir, I herewith enclose you a Power of Attorney, to dispose of all my patented lands in the district of Kentucky agreeably to the instructions herein contained. I also enclose you the copy of a patent for 1,000 acres on a treasury warrant and four copies of patents for 500 acres each on a military warrant. There is another patent ready to issue for 5,160 acres, a copy of which I will transmit you as soon as I receive the original. One half of the 1,000 acres, Treasury right, is the property of Mr. Isaac Hite, who located and surveyed it, which part is not to be disposed of the person purchasing from me is to have his choice, after Mr. Hite has divided it, agreeable to Powell's bargain, a copy of which I believe you are possessed of. The military patents are entirely my own: they were located by Col. Powell on his first journey into the western country and previous to any entries made after the opening of the land office. You are to dispose of the military rights altogether, or in single patents, as you may find most for my interest, on a credit for not longer than two years, and for a price not less than six shillings Virginia money per acre. You will observe to take bonds with sufficient security and conditioned to pay interest from the date if the principal is not punctually paid when due... Mr. Thomas Lewis, later of this county, and now living at or near Lexington, is possessed of two bonds given by me to Baldwin Dade, on one of which there is a balance of about £230 due... Signed, Your most humble and obedt. servt., David Griffith.

Moses Tandy.
1791, 12 NOV. A483. Compensation for storage and reshipping on board the ship "Custis" at Alexandria, in 1778, of 238 hogsheads of tobacco belonging to the State, agreeable to orders from Thomas Smith, Esq., then State agent. Petitioner never received pay. Itemized account; note from Robt. Todd, justice of the peace for Fayette Co. *Rejected.* Box B.

Alexandria Lodge No. 22.
1792, 6 OCT. A484. Act authorizing petitioners to raise money by way of lottery to the amount of $6,000 for the building of a Mason's Hall, in which will be situated a hall for a circulating library,[43] and another hall

---

[43] Those who were desirous of establishing a circulating library in Alexandria were requested to meet at the tavern of Mr. [John] Wise, Virginia Gazette and Alexandria Advertiser, 24 NOV 1791, p. 3, *Circulating Library. Gentleman defirious of establifhing a Circulating Library in Alexandria, are requefted to meet at Mr. Wife's Tavern, to-morrow evening at 6 o'clock, November 27, 1791;* Virginia Gazette and Alexandria Advertiser, 13 SEP 1792, p. 2, *A PETITION will be prefented, by the Lodge of Alexandria, to the next General Afsembly of this State, praying to be authorized to raife, by*

Legislative Petitions of the Town and County of Alexandria, Virginia

for the use of public meetings. *Reported.* Box B.

Signed by Jesse Taylor, Jr., Secy., John Dunlap, Treasurer, Jas. Taylor, Senior Deacon, Charles Turner, Junr., Deacon, Elisha C. Dick, Master, Benjamin Hamp, Warden, James Taylor, Jr. Warden, Joseph Thomas Tyler, John Donnell, Richd. Hannah, W. MacRea, Thos. Porter, John Allison, Guy Atkinson, Jonathan Swift, W. Payne, James Gillies, Dennis Ramsay, John Dalrymple, Joseph Cury [or Cary], Robert Allison, Ch. Simms, G. Deneale, Baldwin Dade, John Harper, Will. Hunter, Jr., Charles Little, W. Bird, George Gilpin, W. Hodgson, Richd. Conway, Jno. B. O'Kelly, Michael Flannery, G. Douglas, Jr., Robt. Wagener, Samuel Harper, Jos. Greenway, * Gray, Jno. Carson Seton, Chas. Gus. Sinclair, and Geo. Stovin.

Merchants and Others.
1792, 9 OCT. A485. Establishing of a bank in town, the capital of which is not to exceed $150,000.[44] A bank has become necessary to the commerce of the town and the State. The banks at Baltimore and Philadelphia draw to those towns all the trade of the fertile back country of Virginia and also of Maryland and Pennsylvania, which naturally should come to Alexandria through the channels of Potomac and James Rivers. Document is very faint. *Referred.* Box B.

Signed by Jesse Taylor, Phil. Rd. Fendall, Hartshorne & Donaldson, Charles Lee, John Fitzgerald, Jas. Keith, Wm. Herbert, John Donnell, Wm. Wilson, John Foster, Hodgson Nicholson & Co., Jonathan Swift, Josiah Watson & Co., *, Lewis Hipkins, Rogerson & Dabney, Isaac McPherson, George Gilpin, Fletcher Otway & Co., Steph. Cooke, Jas. Wilson, Jonah Thompson, Geo. Deneale, William Newton, John Hickman & Co., Dunlap & Craig, J. Levyson, Jr. & Co., Andw. Wales, Dennis Ramsay, Jesse Taylor, Jr., Samuel Harper, James Douglass, Joseph Riddle & Co., James Lawrason, G. Mason, Elisha Janney, John Potts, Junr., James H. Hooe, George Hunter, Casenove & Walker, George Slacum, Moore & Young, Adam Bence, Thos. Porter, Chs. Turner, P. Thomas, Wm. Bushby, Alexandr. Smith, Robert B. Jamiesson, Wm. Bird, Richd. Conway, Murray & Wheaton, Geo. Coryell, Williams & Cary, Francis Peyton, Andrew Peyton, Richd. Hannah, Jacob Cox, Prichd. Newby, Paton & Butcher, Jas. Kennedy, Andrew & William Ramsay, John Janney, Philip Wanton, Benjn. A. Hamp & Co., George Taylor, John Edwd. Ford, Gurden Chapin, Jno. Bealle, Norwood & Warfield, Jona. Mandeville, Wm. McKnight, Charles *, Darling & Earp, Alexr. Gordon, Hepburn & Dundas, Jas. & Jno. Camock, Elisha C. Dick, James Kerr, Forrest & Seton, Thomas & James Irvin, Henry Piercy, Perrin Frères,

---

way of Lottery, a fum of money for the purpofe of building a Mason's Hall in faid Town. *Alexandria, Auguft 1, 1792.*

[44] Hening, Vol. 13, 1789-1792, Chapter LXXVI, October 1792, pp. 592-98, "An act for establishing a Bank in the town of Alexandria," passed November 23, 1792; 3WM(2), pp. 207-08; first situated at 305 Cameron Street.

Legislative Petitions of the Town and County of Alexandria, Virginia

Saml. Craig, Wm. Duvall, Peter Wise, Jesse Simms, John Wise, Wm. Mendinhall, Jas. M. McRea, Lawrence Hooff, Adam S. Swope, Baldwin Dade, D. Casey, D. Stuart, Edwd. Stabler, Benjn. Shreve, Walter Brooke, Wm. Gunnell 3d, James Hurst, David Easton, J. Mason, James Coleman, Thos. Gunnell, Robinson Sanderson & Co., P. Marsteller, Korn & Wisemiller, R. Hooe, Robt. Hamilton & Co., John Gill, Robert Mease, John Hooe, Charles Alexander, N. Fitzhugh, Stump & Ricketts, Ricketts & Newton, James Craik, Junr., John S. Stone, John Jackson, Richd. Simpson, James Halley, Charles Little, Wm. Bayliss, Jas. Craik, and Andw. Jamiesson.

Sundry Merchants, Traders, Dealers in Flour, and Manufacturers of Wheat Upon the Waters of Potomack.
1792, 13 OCT. A486 and A486-1. Reduction of the rate of inspecting flour in Alexandria and other places where large quantities are collected for exportation, from two pence to one penny ha' penny per barrel, and that the charge of inspection may in the future be imposed upon the exporter of the commodity. That another grade of flour (in addition to the flour enumerated in the Act of 1787[45]), between fine and middling may be distinguished by the inspector, and branded for exportation with the words "seconds." Also that some proper person be appointed by law to call the inspectors of flour to an account, as well for the fines which they have heretofore collected, as for those which they shall hereafter collect, and to receive from them the part due to the State. *Reported.* Box B.

Signed by Joseph Finall, manufacturer of flour, Thos. Stribling, Wm. Snickers, John Smith, John Donaldson, Thos. Williams, James McDonald, Elijah Milton, Adam Douglass, C. Beeler, Robt. McMunn, Geo. McMunn, James Simsall, Thos. Edmondson, Micajah Rock, Joseph Holmes, John Brady, Smith Slaughton, William Groverman, Jno. Kercheval, Archd. Dick, Fredk. Com___, H. Holmes, Wm. Johnston, Wm. McGuire, Robert Gray, Thos. Berry, Robert Wood, John Gilkerson, C.M. Shurton, merchant of flour, Thomas Cantwell, James A. Vance, Jno. Bell, manufacturer of flour, John McAlister, John Dowdall, Jno. Conrad, Jno. Brown, William Ball, Obed. Waite, J. Peyton, Archd. McCagill, Abraham Neill, Edmd. Smith, William Holliday, Matthew Wright, William Stribling, P. Dougherty, Jon. Drinker, Samuel Dowdall, J. Milton, Robt. Haines, Geo. Barnett, Jos. Turley, David Lupton, Ban. Berry, Junr., Wm. Throckmorton, Thos. Throckmorton, and Thomas McCormick.

Duplicate signed by Dd. Stuart, Stump & Ricketts, Wm. Hartshorne, Wm. Bird, Fendall & Hipkins, Isaac McPherson, Joseph Kirkbride & Co., Alexr. Henderson, and one illegible.

---

[45] Hening, Vol. 12, 1785-1788, Chapter XIX, October 1787, pp. 517-20, "An act to regulate the inspection of flour and bread," passed 23 NOV 1787; *Virginia Gazette and Alexandria Advertiser*, 13 SEP 1792, p. 2, *NOTICE IS HEREBY GIVEN, That a petition...*

Legislative Petitions of the Town and County of Alexandria, Virginia

Sundry Persons.
1792, 13 OCT. A487. Great increase in quantity of flour inspected at Alexandria-- 24,400 barrels in 1784, and 60,000 in 1791. At the same time, tobacco cultivation is rapidly decreasing, and wheat and flour will soon become principal exports. Wheat, however, sells about six pence a bushel higher at Baltimore and Philadelphia than in Virginia, which fact tends to draw all grain towards those centers. This difference in price is due to great number of mills around the cities, which bid for wheat. Remedy is for State to encourage Virginia millers and relieve them of disabilities. Price of flour inspection is too high-- two pence a barrel-- while in Maryland and Pennsylvania it is one penny. Alexandria inspector, from salary and perquisites, made about £535 last year, of which he pays only £30 to his assistant and also the charge of a small boy and horse to carry around town the forge for heating branding-irons. His extravagant salary is constantly increasing. Besides, the fee for inspection is paid by the miller instead of exporter. There should also be some new designation of flour brands, as millers lose greatly because of having two different brands marked "middling." Petitioners ask that rate of inspection be reduced one penny ha' penny and that the charge may be imposed upon the importers, and that the grade of flour between full and middling be branded "seconds." Signed by David Stuart, Stump & Ricketts, William Hartshorne, William Bird, and five others. Box B.

President, Directors and Company of Bank of Alexandria, and Others.
1793. A488. Dated 3 SEP 1793. The bank needs to be enlarged. Petitioners request an increase of capital stock of bank to the sum of $300,000, and also that bank be allowed to issue notes as low as one dollar. *The late General Affembly impreffed with a conviction of the propriety, and utility of having a Bank eftablifhed in the town of Alexandria, for the purpofe of affifting its commerce, arrefting the exportation of fpecie from this ftate, to aid in the fupport of Banks eftablifhed in the other ftates eaftward of us; and keeping up the price of our contry's produce, by the aids at once given to the merchants' capital, and the regular flow of a circulating medium upon a well eftablifhed paper credit-- Incorporated by law the Bank of Alexandria.* No note on action. Box B.

Signed by Thomas Chinn, Andrew Henderson, Alderson Wilkes, William Elliott, Jas. McClenachan, William Debill, Richd. Weedon, Francis Linn, James Lewis, John McConnekey, Robert Patterson, Charles Monday, W. Powell, James Wornald, Thomas Weeks, Jas. McCormick, Leven Powell, W. Harrison, James Henretty, John Monday, Saml. Pearle, John Lake, Josiah Dillon, Henry Peyton, Robert Fulton, Jesse McVeigh, Samuel Evans, George Faris, Jno. T. Harrison, Simon Triplett, Saml. Skinner, Samuel Kearshall, Jacob G. Pierce, Danl. Cummins, Charles Metcalfe, James McDawney, James McClenachan, James Harris, Robt. Smarr, David Bishop, James White, Joshua Owens, Robert Combs, John White, Robert Johnston, Jacob Ruder, Robt. Garrett, George Crosby, Thomas Ammon Herreford, Jacob Moore, John Crupper, Henry Wey, Charles Barker, Burr Powell, Wm. H. Powell, P. Harrison, Jr., James Lawson,

Legislative Petitions of the Town and County of Alexandria, Virginia

Reuben Murray, Lewis Danham, Thomas Lewis, James Fitzsimmons, Owen Sullivan, Reuben Triplett, Daniel John, Mattw. Kennedy, Joshua Fletcher, Simeon Haines, Thomas Tippett, Samuel Henderson, John Wilson, Cornelia Reynolds, Cha. Peyton, John Robinson, Wilfrid Johnston, Hezh. Shacklett, Denise Carrell, Jonathan White, Edward Carrell, John Carrell, Danl. Jackson, John Crane, Benjn. Carpenter, John Glascock, Phily Dyson, Cuthbert Musgrove, George Barr, Hugh Barr, William Vanhorn, Amos Niles, Joseph Cummins, Andrew Beaty, Mason Owens, Simon Triplett, Jr., Henry Hieronymus, John Huff, Thos. Phillips, Linus Massey, Joseph Green, Joseph Jeffries, Jun., Archabald Glasscock, William T. Taylor, Ephraim *, John Thomas, George Gibson, Joseph Pomer, Thos. Lewis, Jr., Thos. Triplitt, Benjamin John, James Johnson, Gerrard Vanhorn, Sam. Bartlett, William Pearle, Sanford *, Elisha Marks, John Field, Benja. S. Strother, Jonathan McVeigh, John Wood, John Sullivan, Thos. Priest, Spencer Walker, Jno. Walker, Peter Glasscock, William Rector, Greenberry Triplitt, Ralph Murray, James Sinkler, Thomas Clarke, Henry Penkstone, Jesse Attrill, Chas. Dulin, Randle Biggs, Charles Stovin, Thomas Blake, Robert Thomas, Thos. Wren, Anthony Owsley, Wm. Young, Wm. Singleton, Jesse *, Thomas Shields, Jonathan Tof__, Thos. Middleton, Saml. Boggess, Wm. Cummins, Jeremiah Hampton, John Garrett, John Dulin, Hezekiah Glasscock, Joseph Fuller, William Eaton, George Dulin, Uriah Fox, William Shrophshire, Jno. Kelly, Joshua Singleton, Samuel Singleton, David Battson, Saml. Baker, George Thrift, Edward Feagan, Henry Rector, Senr., Jeremiah Hampton, Senr., James Grigsby, Benjamin W__ & Son, John Bowie, Thomas Squires, Jesse Humphrey, John Dennis, John Luke, James McCaffrey, Thos. Leech, Wm. Bronaugh, Jr., William Thomas, Abel Battson, William Garner, James Downs, Jas. Carter, Cornelius Kings, James Reed, John Beale, Gregory Glasscock, Henry Owsley, Thomas Russell, Adam Hagerman, Reuben Franck, Edward Martin, John Marlende, Christopher Hoofman, Hugh Henderson, Caleb Squires, George Eskridge, John Parry, Ignatius Hazell, John Francis, John Walker, Henry Downy, and Jesse Glinn.

Duplicate signed by C.M. Thruston, Charles Thruston, John Smith, Nathl. Burwell, Dan. Morgan, Hugh Scott, Wm. McGuire, Jno. Keith, H. Daingerfield, Edwd. McGuire, Junr., J. Tinball, F. Daugherty, and one illegible.

Second duplicate signed by Phil. Rd. Fendall, John Fitzgerald, Jonah Thompson, Wm. Herbert, Wm. Wilson, W. Hodgson, Wm. Hartshorne, John Muir, Josiah Watson, Jos. Forrest, Thos. Herbert, Richd. Conway, William Halley, Wm. Paton, Robert Patton, Jr., Williams & Cary, John Muncaster, Robt. Alexander, Gerrard Alexander, Jr., Geo. Gray, Joseph Riddle, Jas. Keith, Francis Peyton, Mordecai Miller, Robert B. Jamiesson & Co., Bryan Hampson, Thos. Vowell & Sons, Ricketts & Newton, Jesse Simms, Jas. Patton & Davd. Finlay, Henry Walker, Luke Shortill, Rogerson & Dabney, Jesse Wherry & Co., G. Deneale, J. Mason, George Moore & Co., James Douglass, Saml. Craig, Sparhawk & Jarvis, Vincent

Legislative Petitions of the Town and County of Alexandria, Virginia

Gray, Ephraim Evans, John Butcher, Jesse Taylor, Wm. McKnight, Thomas Davis, John Dunlap, James Wilson, John Foster, Robert Young & Co., Chas. Young, Jr., James Watson, Elisha C. Dick, Jas. B. Nickolls, Geo. Coryell, Jas. M. McKea, Isaac McPherson, Nicholas Hannah, Jno. B. Dabney, Bernd. Ghequiere, James & Jno. Camock, Leml. Bent & Co., Robert Mease, Andrew Payton, David Easton, Murray & Wheaton, John R. Wheaton, Thos. Patten & Co., Cazenove & Walker, Laurence Muse, John Potts, Jun., Jacob Heinemann, John Janney, Fletcher & Otway, Wm. Bayly, Val. Peers, Wm. MacKenzie, Wm. Gunnell 3d, Rob. Hamilton & Co., M. Flannery, Jas. Kennedy, Thos. Gunnell, John Martin, Andw. Jamieson, B. Dade, James Coleman, Elisha Janney, S. Hanson, of Saml., Jesse Taylor, Jr. & Co., Ludwell Lee, George Taylor, Scudamore Nickolls, J. Gilpin, MacIver & MacKenzie, Patk. Byrne, R. Hood, James Hamilton, Wm. Thompson, Jno. Beatty, John Dundas, William Hepburn, D. Sutton, Mark Edgar, Dan Casey, Henry Piercy, Allen Gordon, Matthew Robinson & Co., George Darling, Caleb Earp, Peter Wise, Lanty Crowe, Wm. Bird, Lewis & Stover, Guy Atkinson, Wm. Duvall, Wm. Mendinhall, Thomas White, Jesse Simms, Lawrence Hooff, Gurden Chapin, Charles Love, James McKenna, John Langden, Alexr. McConnell, Daniel Roberdeau, John Harper, Thomas Irwin, Samuel Harper, John Neill, Josiah Faxon, George Hunter, Charles Bennett, Chas. R. Scott, Alexandr. Smith, D. Douglass, Chas. Finley, B. Pettit, Peter Slimmer, Oliver Price, Jonathan Mandeville, John Brent, Wm. Brent, Will. Smith, Mattw. Sexsmith, James Martin, Wm. Summers, John Love, John [his mark] Limrick, William Casey, Edwd. Sanford, Adam Lynn, John White, Aaron Hewes, Adam S. Swope, George Halley, Geo. Clementson, B. Rawlings, Wm. Bushby, P. Marsteller, Edwd. Stabler, Benjamin Weir, James McCready, Junigel, Ebenezer Vowell, Wm. Hoye, Seth Cartwright, Jacob Cox, Michael Thorn, Isaac Andrews, Charles Page, Andw. Waley, William Harper, Mungo Dykes, James Taylor, John Rozier, Benjamin Lanston, John McIntosh, Cornelius Falvey, John Reynolds, Joseph Curtis, John Madden, Thomas Jacobs, Waitmon Sipple, George Gilpin, *, Jno. Winterbery, Nathaniel J. Magruder, John James Neblon, Nathl. Spooner, James Chattam, Jno. Lockwood, * M. Latruite, John Burke, Alexander Greer, William *, Jo. Kempff, Thomas Redmon, Archd. J. Taylor, Andrew Reintzel, John Horner, Jacob Reintzel, Peter Pyles, Wm. Reynolds, Samuel Simmons, Geo. [his 2 marks] Hoomes, Jacob Gallentine, John McFarland, Thomas Brock, James McGill, John Sommers, Edward Ramsay, Matthew Rust, Jesse Moore, James Wiley, Rd. Ratcliffe, T.A. Broder 2d, Chas. McKnight, Carles [sic] Bryan, David Griffith, Charles Richter, John Wise, Hugh Morrison, Jno. Abert, Tho. Whittaker, Tho: West, Thomas Lancaster, Geo. Sweeney & Co., Peter Hauck, Peter Goretz, Paul Arnold Cherus, French Vice *, Wm. Wilson, Thomas Richards, Thomas Conn, Thos. Stewart, Philip Webster, J. Baden, *, Edmund Edmonds, Andw. Wales, Geo. Washington Dent, John Kitten, Michael B__, Robert Evans, and Abrm. Forst.

Legislative **Petitions of the Town and County of Alexandria, Virginia**

President, Directors and Company of Bank of Alexandria, and Others.
1793, 3 SEP. No number. Same as A488. No note of action. Box B.

    Signed by Moses Hunter, Phil. Pendleton, Elisha Boyd, Robert Stephen, James Wilson, John Cook, James Ash, Jas. Starkey, Alexr. Straith, Michl. W. Keenan, Joseph Swearingen, Fa. Maxwell, Winn Winship, Abraham Morgan, Saml. Reed, Everard Beeson, James Stephenson, A. Waggener, Jas. Swearingen, Wm. Shinn, Wm. Craghill, Jr., Jas. Graham, Joshua Riddle, Jno. Of___, James T. Pollock, Robert Hastings, Robt. Cookburn, Amos Nichols, James Jordan, and James Miller.

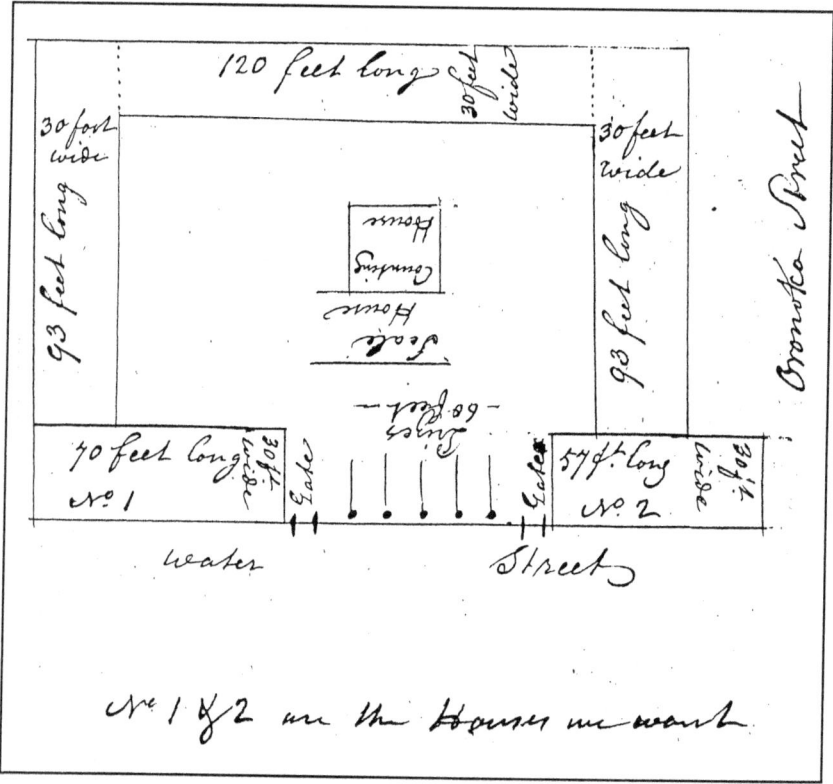

William Hepburn (d. 1817) and John Dundas (d. 1813).[46]
1793, 26 OCT. A489. Permission to use the two tobacco warehouses facing on Water Street as store houses until such time as they may be needed for tobacco. Thomas Graffort is shown as the first inspector. Alexandria 17th Octr. 1793. Signed by Wm. Hepburn, John Dundas.

---

[46] Notice given in Virginia Gazette and Alexandria Advertiser, 11 JUL 1793.

Legislative Petitions of the Town and County of Alexandria, Virginia

Contains diagram of tobacco counting house and scales at corner of Oronoka and Water streets. *Reported.* Box B.

Thomas Graffort and Jacob Cox, Tobacco Inspectors.
1793, 2 NOV. A490. Payment of the deficiency in petitioners' salaries by the State. The inspection does not receive enough tobacco to provide salaries for inspectors. Two documents accompanying. *Reported.* Box B.

Jacob Michael.
1794, 22 NOV. A491. Act vesting the house and lot of the late Frederick Henninger, a native of Germany, in petitioner, in consideration of the sum of 1,200 gilders which he paid Henninger's heir, residing in Germany, who he supposed would be legally entitled to estate. He did not know that property descending to aliens escheated.[47] Not signed. *Rejected and Reported.* Box B.

Mayor,[48] Common Council, and Others.
1794, 24 NOV. A492. Change in time of holding Alexandria Court[49] to the fourth Monday in each month and the quarterly session to March, June, August and November. Present terms conflict with Fairfax County Court and District Court. Signed by Charles Lee and Saml. Arell. *Reported.* Box B.

Sundry Merchants and Traders of the Town of Alexandria.
1795, 12 NOV. A493. Act compelling millers to brand "superfine" upon each barrel that they judge to be of that quality, and directing inspectors to merely stamp each barrel with the initial letters of the port and state wherein they act. *Reasonable.* Box B.

Signed by Wm. Hartshorne & Sons, Jonah Thompson, Wm. Wilson, Bennett & Watts, Wm. Hodgson, Ricketts & Newton, Robert Hamilton, Francis Peyton, Fletcher & Otway, Jesse Taylor, Janney & Irish, George Taylor, Jno. & Thos. Vowell, Leven Powell, Jr. & Co., Jno. Norwood, Abram Hewes, John Gill, Saml. Craig, Archd. L. Taylor, James Cavan, Andrew & William Ramsay, Joseph Riddle, Williams & Cary, R. Young, Will. Armistead & Co., Alexandr. Smith, Phil. Rd. Fendall, Korn & Wisemiller, R. Hooe, Ford Patton & Co., Robert Allison, Jas. Wilson, Jos.

---

[47] The British term signifies any lands or tenements that casually fall to a Lord within his Manor, by way of forfeiture, or by the death of his tenant, leaving no heir general or special. [Giles Jacob, A New Law Dictionary: Containing The Interpretation and Definition of Words and Terms Used in the Law, etc. (Savoy: Henry Lintot, MDCCLVI). In Virginia, escheated land is that forfeited to the state because a man died intestate or for want of an heir or claimant; also the forfeiting thereof. [Richard M. Lederer, Jr., Colonial American English (Essex, Conn.: Verbatim, 1985), p. 80.
[48] Robert Mease was Mayor of Alexandria between February 1794 and February 1795.
[49] Shepherd, Vol. 1, Chapter 28, pp. 310-11, "An ACT for altering the court days and quarterly sessions of certain counties," passed December 12, 1794, language reading "that a court of hustings, in the town of Alexandria, shall be held on the Friday after the third Monday in every month."

Legislative Petitions of the Town and County of Alexandria, Virginia

& Sam. Harper, James Porter, John Mandeville, Josiah Faxon, William Harper, John Foster, John Dunlap, Andw. Jamieson, John McIver, Leml. Bent, Thomas Rogerson, Matthew Robinson & Co., Dennis Ramsay, Jas. Keith, George Hunter, Jesse Wherry, W. Hall, and John Neill.

William Hepburn (d. 1817) and John Dundas (d. 1813).
1795, 16 NOV. A494. Discontinuance of tobacco warehouses at Alexandria[50] and return of them to the petitioners, proprietors of the same. They own the lot on which houses stand, and have spent large sums of money in the improvement of them, and the present amount of business done at Alexandria does not justify the maintenance any longer of an inspection for tobacco there, especially as two other warehouses are in the county. Affidavit from Thos. Graffort and Jacob Cox, former inspectors, that the tobacco inspected for the last two years amounted to only 391 hogsheads. Alexandria, 10th November 1795. Signed by Wm. Hepburn, John Dundas. *Bill drawn.* Box B.

Citizens of Fauquier.
1795, 16 NOV. A495. Increase of capital of Bank of Alexandria to $300,000.[51] Since establishment of bank, trade and prosperity of town have increased greatly, but the inadequacy of the capital caused a rival bank to be established at Georgetown, with a capital of $1,000,000, which threatens to affect the prosperity of Alexandria banks and of that section of the state. Signed by Charles Duncan, Wm. Brent, Thos. Roy, Thornton Buckner, and 18 others. *Reasonable.* Box B.

Inhabitants of the Town of Alexandria.
1795, 16 NOV. A496. Authority for common council to pay justices of the peace. Owing to rapid increase in town's population, justices must devote one-third of their time to their office, which they cannot afford to do without compensation, as there is not a single man in town who lives upon his fortune alone. Document in poor condition. *Reported.* Box B.

Signed by Jas. Keith, Steph. Cooke, Edw. Stabler, Thos. Patten, Alexandr. Smith, Leml. Bent, Thomas Rogerson, James McGaw, Jacob Clingman, Thomas Irwin, Wm. Wilson, Jas. Wilson, George Taylor, John W. Fletcher, William Harper, George Slacum, Benj. Shreve, Seth Cartwright, D. Douglass, Abram Hewes, Samuel Harper, Elisha Janney, John Reynolds, *, Washer Blunt, Jacob Leap, Joseph Coleman, Isaac McPherson, Joseph Harper, Andw. Estave, Thos. Vowell, Jun., Robert Allison, Thomas Preston, Wm. Wright, * Young, James Taylor, John Harper, Josiah Watson, Jno. Norwood, John Muncaster, Joseph Cary,

---

[50] Shepherd, Vol. 1, Chapter 39, p. 404, "An ACT to discontinue the inspection of tobacco in the town of Alexandria," passed December 4, 1795.
[51] Shepherd, Vol. 1, Chapter 21, pp. 373-74, "An ACT for augmenting the capital stock of the bank of Alexandria." passed December 5, 1795.

Legislative Petitions of the Town and County of Alexandria, Virginia

Cleon Moore, Geo: Drinker, Jonathan Swift, Aaron Hewes, Saml. Craig, [R]obt. Dobbin, Geo. Coryell, Josiah Coryton, Mordecai Miller, John Dunlap, Richard Veitch, Bryan Hampson, J. Thos. Ricketts, John Fitzgerald, Wm. Hartshorne, Wm. Newton, Lawrence Hooff, Matthew Robinson, John Neill, Mungo Dykes, James Cavan, Joseph Riddle, Guy Atkinson, Charles Jamieson, John Butcher, John Jefferson, Philip Wanton, Wm. Hodgson, *, John Janney, John Foster, Jesse Wherry, Will. Armistead, Jonathan Mandeville, Gurden Chapin, John Smith, Jno. Abert, James Patton, James Gillies, John Wise, Richd. Conway, J. Nickolls, Jesse Simms, Philip G. Marsteller, and R. Hooe.

Citizens of Fairfax.
1795, 21 NOV. A497, see A495. Increase of capital of Alexandria Bank to $350,000. Duplicate of A488. *Reasonable.* Box B.

Signed by Wm. Hartshorne, Wm. Herbert, Wm. Wilson, Andrew Ramsay, John Fitzgerald, James Patton, Robert Mease, J.B. Nickolls, Ch. Simms, Josiah Watson, John Janney, Jonah Thompson, Benj. Grayson, R. West, John Hickman & Co., Elisha C. Dick, Jas. Keith, Richd. Conway, Wm. Hodgson, John Dunlap, Joseph Riddle, T. Cooke, James Wilson, * Young, Leven Powell, John B. Wheaton, James Porter, Jesse Wherry, James Kennedy, Phil. Rd. Fendall, Benjn. Dulany, Jesse Taylor, T. Fairfax, Jesse Simms, Bryan Hampson, Alexr. Smith, Chas. Jones, Philip G. Marsteller, W. Wall, John McIver, Saml. Craig, Edmund J. Lee, Leven Powell, Jr., Mordecai Miller, Thos. Vowell, Jr., Jonathan Mandeville, John Mandeville, William Harper, Alexr. MacKenzie, William Newton, William Armistead & Co., Ricketts & Newton, James Cavan, Andw. Wales, Fletcher & Otway, Andw. Jamieson, Elisha Janney, Gurden Chapin, Richd. Flannery, John Potts, Abram Hewes, William Bayly, George Drinker, Vincent Gray, Geo. Coryell, Zacharias Lyles, Ber. Ghequiere, Jno. Norwood, Charles Love, James McKenna, P. Marsteller, Chas. & Andw. Jamieson, John Lemoine, David Easton, Denis Ramsay, Henry Rose, Battaile Fitzhugh, John Muncaster, Robert B. Jamiesson, Jas. Murray, A. Dobbin, * Gordon, John Wise, Jonathan Swift, Giles Fitzhugh, G. McMunn, Allison & Young, N. Fitzhugh, * & Triplett, Peter Murray, Jo. Kempff, Thos. Mezarvey, Jeremiah Moore, W. McKnight, Joseph Mandeville, Francis Peyton, *, Thomas Murray, Wm. Summers, B. Gwinn, Charles Turner, Cleon Moore, Wm. Mendinhall, George Taylor, Peterson & Taylor, Peter Peterson, Josiah Faxon, Edmund Edmonds, John Burton, John H. Belcher, Jno. V. Thomas, George Slacum, Richard Sanford, Jun., F. Jeffrey, Archd. Taylor, Henry Piercy, Thomas Rogerson, Henry Walker, John Foster, George Gilpin, Williams & Cary, Lud. Alberts, Joseph Thornton, Isaac M. Johnson, Martin Cochburn, Gerrard Tramell, John Winterbery, Jun., William Hickman, George Mason, Wm. Gunnell, Jr., Robt. Brocket, G. Deneale, Jas. Wren, F. Patton, Thos. Gunnell, Tempile Smith, R. Hooe, Caleb Earp, Geo: Darling, Diedrick Shekle, J. Watts, John *, Benja. Shreve, Robt. Henderson, Samuel Harper, Wm. Paton, Jas. M. McKea, Philip Wanton, Thos. Kirby, Guy Atkinson, John Harper, Matthew Robinson & Co., James Kennedy,

Legislative **Petitions of the Town and County of Alexandria, Virginia**

Jacob Leap, Cavan Boa, Ignatius Junigel, William Crech, Bar. White, William Bushby, Carne & Slade, Jno. Mason, Jos. Bushby, Wm. Carne, Wm. G. Marks, George W. Slatford, Wm. Cunningham, Josiah Coryton, Andrew Taylor, Tho. White, Bernard Bryan, Mattw. Sexsmith, Theophilus Harris, John Duffey, Thomas Davis, Henry Gird, Wm. Sample, Henry F. Lowe, Lanty Crowe, Jno. Dalton, *, *, John D. Orr, James Graham, Robert Allison, Perrin Brothers, John Dundas, John Terrall, Thomas White, Hugh O'Neal & Co., Pomery & Isabell, Foster & May, Thos. Harrison, Jr., *, John MacLeod, Thomas Crandell, Wm. Pomery, Henry Polkinhorn, Richard Andrews, Luke Shertell, Willm. Richards, J. White, John Johnston, Philip Conn, John Lumsdon, Daniel MacLeod, Timothy Sullivan, Jno. Bryan, Samuel McCloud, Ephraim Weylie, Richd. Hewitt, Andw. Estave, Jacob Forttney, Joseph N____, Wm. Sheppard, Bennett & Watts, Joseph Harper, Lawrence Hooff, Jacob Heinemann, William Bowie, Stephen Alley, W. McKnight, Walter Dodson, Walter Lyon, James Muir, James Irvin, John Limrick, James Taylor, F. Vivent, *, *, Oliver Price, Geo. H. Gloyd, Will: Smith, Elisha Janney, and John Gill & Co.

Mayor and Commonalty.
1796, 1 NOV. A498. Nuisances.[52] Incorporation of each improved half acre lot in the area lately added to town, bounded by Montgomery Street, [Great] Hunting Creek, West Street, and Potomac River, and every other half acre lot within said limits whenever a tenantable dwelling house shall be erected upon it. Also that the mayor and commonalty be enabled to compel the proprietors of the lots to remove all nuisances from such lots not incorporated as may injure the health of the inhabitants. Signed by Jonah Thompson, mayor. *Reported.* Box B.

Andrew Wales (d. 1800), Executor of Samuel McLean.
1796, 12 NOV. A499. Permission to sell lot in town of Alexandria belonging to late Samuel McLean, in order to pay, as far as possible, his debts. Samuel McLean died greatly in debt and left but little other property. He directed in his will that his just debts be paid. Copy of will of Samuel McLean mentions wife Isabella, son Thomas, daughters Jane and Margaret, and appoints friends Andrew Wales, Robert McCrea and Charles Little as executors, dated 2 AUG 1785. *Reported.* Box B.

Mayor and Commonalty.
1796, 16 NOV. A500. Change of day of holding the hustings court of the town of Alexandria from the Friday after the 3rd Monday to the 4th Monday in each month.[53] Great inconvenience is now experienced from practice of holding hustings court in the same week as county court, as the attorneys find it impossible to attend to all their business, and it is difficult to procure juries and witnesses. Signed by Jonah

---

[52] Shepherd, Vol. 2, Chapter 32, pp. 40-1, "An ACT concerning the town of Alexandria," passed December 16, 1796; Columbia Mirror and Alexandria Gazette, 29 OCT 1795.

[53] Shepherd, Vol. 2, Chapter 29, p. 37, "An ACT for altering the day of the court of hustings of the town of Alexandria," passed November 30, 1796.

Thompson, Mayor. *Reported.* Box B.

Mayor and Commonalty.
1796, 16 NOV. A501. Authority to levy taxes upon all landed property in town to pay for the paving of streets,[54] and also right to bring distress proceedings against owners of lots which contain stagnant water or other nuisances. Signed by Jonah Thompson, Mayor. *Bill drawn.* Box B.

Peter Caverly, Guardian of Richard and Christiana Arell.[55]
1796, 18 NOV. A502. Authority for petitioner during minority of said orphans to grant their lands in manner directed by the will of the late David Arell, subject to the payment of an annual rent. The testator provided lands to be granted by his brother Samuel Arell, for the benefit of such children, that the said Samuel Arell hath since died. A502-1 is a copy of will of David Arell of the parish and county of Fairfax, dated 15 AUG 1789, proved 17 APR 1792. *Reported.* Box B.

Frances Ryan.
1796, 23 NOV. A503. Grant to petitioner of the title to lot of land in the town of Alexandria, of which the late Col. Michael Ryan, her husband, died seized. He died intestate, and the daughter of a former marriage, who by the laws of the State inherited his property, also died without issue, and the lot devolved on the Commonwealth. The petitioner is left almost destitute, and as the lot is unimproved, she derives no benefit from her right of dower.[56] A note indicates that sale of the lot was published in The Herald from the 11th of Octr. to 11th Nov. *Reported.* Box B.

The petition of Frances Ryan humbly sheweth that her late Husband Colo. Michael Ryan being possessed of a Lott of land in the Town of Alexandria departed this life intestate leaving only one child, a daughter

---

[54] Shepherd, Vol. 2, Chapter 31, p. 40, "An ACT concerning the town of Alexandria," passed December 16, 1796. Also see William Munford, Reports of Cases Argued and Determined in the Supreme Court of Appeals of Virginia (New York: I. Riley, 1814), p. 228, "Mayor and Commonalty of Alexandria against Hunter." In this case a judgment of the county court of Fairfax, in favour of the mayor and commonalty of Alexandria, upon a motion in a summary way, against John Chapman Hunter, was reversed by the district court held at Haymarket, and the motion dismissed with costs. This judgment (which corresponded with the notice) was for £73.19.3, 'being the amount of the assessment imposed on the property of the aforesaid John C. Hunter, in Alexandria, for paving the streets of the said town.' Under the act of 1796, Chapter 31, the mayor and commonalty of Alexandria are not authorized to recover by motion money due for the town taxes; but only for paving the streets.
[55] Shepherd, Vol. 2, Chapter 77, p. 65, "An ACT authorizing Peter Caverley to lease, for the benefit of the orphans of David Arell, certain lots whereof he died seized, in the town of Alexandria," passed December 10, 1796.
[56] Simply, property owned by a bride at the time of her marriage. It is a portion which a widow has of the lands of her husband after his decease, for the sustenance of herself, and education of her children.

by a former marriage, who by the laws of this state inherited the lott above mentioned. But soon after the death of her father, she also died of the yellow fever in Philadelphia, leaving no person capable of inheriting her property, in consequence whereof the property to which she was entitled will escheat for want of heirs; Your petitioner further sheweth that by the death of her husband, she is left almost destitute of the means of subsistence, for as the lott is unimproved. She derives, nor can derive no benefit from her right of dower in it, wherefore she humbly prays that your honourable body will do what she is assured her husband would have done had he made a will, give the said lott to your petitioner, it will much relieve her and be of no sensible detriment to the state, and your petitioner will ever gratefully remember the favour conferred on her. Signed by Fran. Ryan, November 17, 1796.

Merchants and Other Inhabitants of the Town of Alexandria.
1797, 13 DEC. A504. The Marine Insurance Company of Alexandria.[57] Incorporation in the town of a company for making insurances upon shipping and merchandize and exports and imports of every species. The trade of the town has greatly increased, exports for past year amounting to $1,222,900, and a great deal of the insurance belonging to the town is taken out in the North or in Europe, with inconvenience and additional expense, which would be avoided if it were taken out at home.

Signed by Wm. Herbert, Wm. Wilson, Wm. Hodgson, George Taylor, John Potts, Jas. Dykes, Jas. Kennedy, A. Ramsay, Francis Peyton, John Ramsay, Frances Cavan, Wm. Ramsay, Thos. Williams, James Wilson, Wm. Byrd Page, Saml. Craig, T.M. Vanhavre, James Patton, C.J. Stier, Robt. Fergurran, Junr., Jesse Simms, Steph. Cooke, John Gill, Benj. Dulany, George Irish, Jno. G. Ladd, Elisha Janney, Philip Magruder, Benja. Shreve, George Gilpin, Wm. Harper, Saml. Davis, James Porter, Alexr. MacKenzie, Wm. Hartshorne, Senr., Wm. Hartshorne & Son, James Lawrason, Seth Cartwright, James Keith, Jun., Abram Hewes, Jno. Thos. Ricketts, Wm. Newton, *, James Taylor, John Muncaster, R. Hooe, Richd. Richards, Guy Atkinson, Joseph & Samuel Harper, Thos. Vowell, Junr., Jno. Vowell, James Gillies, Joseph Riddle, Jas. Keith, John Janney, Jonathan Swift, Vincent Gray, N. Fitzhugh, Jas. M. McKea, John Foster, Wm. Paton, John Butcher, Charles Bennett, Jno. Watts, Jacob Clingman, Robt. & Jas. Hamilton, Isaac M. Johnson, Joshua Riddle, Bernard Ghequiere, Jonah Thompson, Richd. Veitch, J.B. Nickolls, and Cleon Moore. *Reasonable.* Box B.

---

[57] Shepherd, Vol. 2, Chapter 20, pp. 89-92, "An ACT to incorporate a company for marine insurances, and other purposes, in the town of Alexandria," passed January 10, 1798.

Legislative Petitions of the Town and County of Alexandria, Virginia

Inhabitants of the Town of Alexandria.
1797, 16 DEC. A505. The Library Company in the Town of Alexandria.[58] Incorporation of a library company in Alexandria, with power to make by-laws, &c., choose a president and 12 directors and appoint a treasurer and librarian with proper salaries. Petitioners have already associated themselves to raise the necessary funds, and have collected more than 1,000 volumes.

Signed by Jas. Keith, Archd. McClean, Jas. Muir, Abram Hewes, James Oldden, James Lawrason, Leml. Bent, Wm. Harper, Henry Woodrow, Saml. Davis, Jno. C. Vowell, Thos. Vowell, Junr., Wm. Milnor, Jr., Robert Mease, Dennis Ramsay, Ellis Price, Edmund Edmonds, Henry Gird, Junr., Jonathan Swift, Jas. M. McRea, Mordecai Miller, Aaron Hewes, Elisha C. Dick, Wm. Hartshorne, Bernard Ghequiere, John Janney, Wm. Paton, Saml. Craig, Samuel Stansbury, Geo. Drinker, Thomas Rogerson, Bartemus White, Thomas White, K. Hurst, Wm. Newton, Geo. Coryell, G. Deneale, James D. Westcott, John Longden, John Lloyd, Wm. Talbott, and John Hunter. *Reported.* Box B.

Mayor and Commonalty.
1797, 18 DEC. A506. Amendment of law incorporating within town certain lots "such as are built upon,"[59] and exempting all intermediate lots from such regulation as others are subject to, so that mayor and council may exercise the same jurisdiction in those parts of town and along the Potomac River as in the incorporated section. Mentions jurisdiction over vessels passing to wharves. Signed by Francis Peyton, Mayor. *Reported.* Box B.

Joseph and Samuel Harper.
1797, 23 DEC. A507. Act making null and void an order of town council extending Washington and Queen streets through the rope walk[60] of the petitioners. Council is acting out of its province, as the land included in the streets has not been incorporated, and it proposes to destroy a valuable industry without advantage to anybody. Signed by Joseph Harper, Samuel Harper, Jas. Keith, Wm. Hartshorne, R. Hooe, Ch. Simms, and 240 others.

Counter-petition demonstrating the inconvenience and hardship caused by the division of the town by Joseph and Samuel Harper's rope walk. All seven streets parallel to Potomac River and westward of Washington

---

[58] Shepherd, Vol. 2, Chapter 82, p. 133, "An ACT to incorporate the library company in the town of Alexandria," passed January 11, 1798. The Alexandria Library Company was organized 24 JUL 1794 [James Randall Caton, Legislative Chronicles of the City of Alexandria (Alexandria: Newell-Cole Co., Inc., 1933), p. 34.
[59] Shepherd, Vol. 2, Chapter 60, pp. 122-23, "An ACT extending the jurisdiction of the mayor and commonalty of the town of Alexandria, and for other purposes," passed January 8, 1798.
[60] Lederer, p. 198. A shed in which twine was twisted into rope. Some were more than 1,000 feet long.

Street are obstructed and people must go past fourteen streets to get around obstacle. The injury and hardship sustained by the lower end of the town, will be made more evident, when it is observed that there are no stores or warehouses used for the reception of produce on Oronoko Street, where the Leesburg and Georgetown turnpike roads are let in, and that five-sixths of the business is done with the back country below King Street, three squares to the south of Oronoko; and, of course, the public are obliged to cross three streets to the south and then to proceed back to the westward in order to get to that part of the town where the business begins, and when they could go in a direct line, if the obstruction could be removed. Signed by Wm. Willington, John Powers, Joseph Thornton, John Brown, Peter Wise, Jr., Jas. Miller, and 375 others. Brittle and fragmented copies are wrapped in plastic in Oversize Box A. *Rejected.* Reported.

John Dundas (d. 1813), Mayor and Commonalty.
1798. A630. Means of making quarantine regulations effective. At present, vessels are required to lie a quarter of mile below town, whence one man escaped into town and died of fever. Suggestion that Craney Island, twenty miles below Alexandria, be selected as quarantine station. Signed by John Dundas, mayor.

Inhabitants of Fairfax and Loudoun.
1798, 6 DEC. A508. Reestablishment of the tobacco inspection at Alexandria.[61] Owing to the high price of wheat and flour during the European war, tobacco cultivation decreased greatly and inspection was closed in 1793. Now price of tobacco has risen again and it is to be extensively planted, the crop this year exceeding the crops of many former years. Oversize Box 5A.

Signed by A. Janney, Gabl. Smither, Sm. Harper, William Isabel, Ch. Douglas, Jas. Case, and 278 others.

Sundry Inhabitants of the Federal District, and of the State of Virginia.
1798, 6 DEC, No Number. That your petitioners are strongly impressed by information, as well as their own knowledge, that there is a necessity for a great leading road, as direct as the ground will admit of, from the City of Washington, thro' the middle Counties of the different states, south-westward to the seat of Government, in Georgia; and are of opinion, that such a road would have a tendency to facilitate information, promote the progress of the said City, and be to it and the inhabitants of the counties thro' which it would pass, of the greatest utility... we observe there is now a petition signed by a great number of very respectable characters, praying your honorable body to grant them a road from the town of Alexandria, to Norman's Ford, on the north branch of Rappahannock;

---

[61] Shepherd, Vol. 2, Chapter 17, p. 156, "An ACT to revive the inspection of tobacco at certain places," passed January 14, 1799; <u>Columbia Mirror and Alexandria Gazette</u>, 17 SEP 1799.

Legislative Petitions of the Town and County of Alexandria, Virginia

and as we humbly conceive that the purpose of a great national communication aforementioned, may be effected by continuing the same road from Norman's Ford, by, or near the Raccoon Ford in Orange, Boswell's in Louisa, Martin Key's Ford on the Rivanna, the mouth of the Slate river in Buckingham, the high bridge on the Appomattox, and thence along accustomed roads, by Prince Edward court-house, Charlotte court-house, Coles' and Dix's Ferries, Guilford court-house, Salisbury, Criswell's, on the Saluda, Ninety-Six and Augusta; shortening the present general rout from fifty to one hundred miles, and carrying it over the principal cross-ridges of the water courses... Printed. Box C.

Signed by James Hume, Junr., Hancock Eustace, Dan Casey, James Strother, Lewis Shumate, Barley Shumate, Daniel Shumate, Britain Lewis, Richd. E. Beal, Beverly R. Wagener, John Tredel, Fran. Boyle, Edwin Eustace, William Mon<u>es</u>, James Gillison, Senr., Jas. Gillison, Junr., Charles Hume, John Shumate, Junr., George Shumate, Jery. Evans, John Shumate, Nimrod Young, Toliafer Shumate, Robert Kerns, Senr., Benjamin Bronaugh, Saml. Blackwell, Hancock Eustace, Wm. Eustace, Sr., Wm. Eustace, Junr., John Mozea, Wm. Gunyon, Wm. WestBrook [or West Brook], Thos. Thornton, Wm. Kearns, Britain <u>Lewis</u>, John Shumate, Jr., Joseph Shumate, Joseph George, Thos. Shumate, Bailey Shumate, Lewis Shumate, Benja. Shumate, Benja. James, Jno. Ross, Jas. Seaton, Jonathan Brown, Wm. Seaton.

Inhabitants of the Town of Alexandria.
1798, 7 DEC. A509. Exemption of tithables from the payment of that part of Fairfax County levy which is to be used for the erection of public buildings.[62] These buildings will be of no service to the town and Fairfax County contributes nothing for the Alexandria public buildings. *Bill drawn.* Box C.

To the Honorable Speaker and the other Members of the House of Delegates of the Commonwealth of Virginia. The Petition of the Inhabitants of the Town of Alexandria, sheweth:

That the Justices of Fairfax County, and those in that part of Loudoun, lately added thereto, in compliance with an act passed at the last session of assembly, have fixed upon and procured a piece of ground for erecting a courthouse; and other necessary public buildings upon those buildings have been undertaken, and are to be finished and paid for in the court of the next year to defray this charge a levy of one dollar and seventy seven cents, on each tithable in the said county has been directed of whom those of the Town form a considerable part.

That your Petitioners so long ago as the year 1786 at the sole expence of the Town prepared a Courthouse which from that time has been used

---

[62] <u>Shepherd</u>, Vol. 2, Chapter 85, p. 191, "An ACT to exempt the tithables in the town of Alexandria, from a certain part of the county levy," passed December 31, 1798; Fairfax Harrison, <u>Landmarks of Old Prince William, A Study of Origins in Northern Virginia</u> (Richmond: Old Dominion Press, 1924), pp. 691-96.

by the Justices of the County without any Cost or charge of any kind, not even that of repair, this might still have answered every purpose without any inconvenience to the Inhabitants of the County whose private business frequently calling them to Town, that as well as Court business could and was generally transacted at the same time.

That by the Cession made by the State of a portion of it to compose the district for the residence of Congress, the Town of Alexandria lying within that portion will probably in the year 1800 be separated from the County that it appears to your petitioners extremely hard to be called on to bear a part of the expence of public buildings from whence they can claim no benefit, and in case of a Sale of them after such separation can have no proportion of the proceeds, and now especially when they had at their sole expence provided an house which for twelve years has answered every purpose.

That upon every occasion there a charge has arisen from causes within the Town that charge has ever been born by the Town, without any contribution from the County, it being always urged as unreasonable that the County should be called upon to contribute to an expence, which arose from causes without the Town that the poor in Town in proportion to the Inhabitants is more numerous than in the County. Upon an application from the Inhabitants of the County, the Honorable Assembly passed a law obliging the Town to support their own poor, from this princible [sic] laid down by the County our petitioners conceive they ought to be exempted from the charge of the public buildings, having no Interest in the buildings, and they being at present unnecessary, at least as far as respects the Inhabitants of the Town, and if those of the County have occasion for them, it appears but just that they should be at the sole expence.

That the courthouse built by the County when the pleas were transferred to the Town of Alexandria, fell to pieces in the year 1786, at which time the Town of Alexandria furnished the Courthouse for the use of the County, that the Goal built by the County is at this time in such a ruinous state that the Town as soon as the pleas of the County are removed out of it will be obliged to erect a new one at their own expence, to this, the Inhabitants of the County will make no contribution, can it then be just or reasonable that the Inhabitants of the Town should be taxed to build the public buildings, for the use of the County when the County does not contribute anything towards the public buildings necessary for the Town.

Your Petitioners therefore pray the Honorable House to take the same into consideration and pass an act to exempt the Tithables of the Town of Alexandria from the payment of that part of the County Levy which is to be appropriated to the erecting of the public buildings, which exemption your petitioners are encouraged to hope will be readily granted by your honorable body, as a similar exemption was granted to the Citizens of Richmond at the last Session of Assembly.

Signed by Benj. Davies, Wm. Grimes, Wm. Wilson, John G. Davies, Thos. Stewart, George Brown, Saml. Long, John Stewart, Junr., Joseph

Legislative Petitions of the Town and County of Alexandria, Virginia

[Vale?], James L. Orr, Jno. V. Thomas, George Darling, Jno. Harrison, Charles Pascoe, Guy Atkinson, Wm. Bowie, Joseph Stimer, Thomas Jefferson, Mickel Dooren, Peter Cottom, John A. Stewart, John Livingston, W. McKnight, Joseph Thornton, Wm. Cash, Junr., P. Marsteller, *, Samuel McCloud, [Reuben?] Demuth, James Newton, Mike Rutter, George Hartley, William Manum, James Gale, John Morris, Edward Davies, Willm. Gird, John Wright, Jno. Limerick, John Thornton, Coats Ridgway, Andrew Taylor, Thomas Shreve, Jonathan Butcher, Reuben Shreve, Bernard Ghequiere, Robt. Fergurron, Junr., David Richards, Jonathan Swift, Dan. McClean, Joseph Dean, Wm. Paton, Francis Peyton, George Gilpin, John Dundas, Wm. Hepburn, Nicholas Voss, Richd. Brooke, John Richter, Joshua Clarke, William Wiggins, Wm. Halley, Isaac Bigson, Jr., Alexr. Smith, Theophilus Harris, Bernard Bryan, John Kincaid, Andrew Dumax, Richd. Buckner, James Kennedy, Senr., Samuel Kirk, Isaac Butler, Benjn. __nston, Jno. Mason, Hanson Reno, Hugh O'Neal, Jno. Bryan, Jno. Horwell, Samuel Cooper, Patrick McCanne, Wm. Billington, Wm. Newton, M. Walton, Walter Pomery, Jonah Isabell, A. Faw, Jesse Taylor, R.J. Taylor, David Henderson, John Norsbrough, John Higginbotham, Robt. Guest, Robert Clarke, Michael Mackay, Danl. Douglass, Joseph Varden, Adam Lynn, Wm. Paton, Junr., John Cranston, Jno. Jamieson, Beal Howard, Friederick Treidle, * Zimmerman, Robt. Brocket, Alexr. Latimer, Going Lanphier, Joseph Dudley, Henry T. Vernon, Daniel Mullin, Thos. Graffort, Robert G. Lanphier, Samuel Lewis, Ignatius Ratcliff, George Clingan, John Frewel, Hugh O'Donald, Andrew Wood, John Boyd, John Mating, Mic'l. Derry, James McGahan, Jacob Fortney, James Card, Garret Doyle, Edward H. Cuiter?, Joseph Harper, James Dixon, Ephraim Weylie, Wm. Tyler, James Gallat, David Mankins, Walter Hodgkin, William Woolls, Henry Finly, John Schmidt, Davey Shirley, Thoms. Frankland, John Potts, Jno. Albert, Edward Redmond, Mordecai Miller, Wm. Herbert, James McKenna, Gurden Chapin, Joseph Paul, Michl. Flannery, Cleon Moore, Henry Moore, James Gillies, Saml. Adams, Hugh Smith, Jona. Faw, William Myers, Jms. McGuire, Robt. Smith, Henry Lewis, Richd. Lewis, Danl. Bishop, William Cummings, Ephraim Miller, Joseph Miller, Thos. Patten, Geo. Coryell, George Heal, Henry Stroman, G.H. Lanham, Alexr. Perry, Charles Richter, P. Javain, Thomas Magruder, Hugh Wallace, Albion Gibson, John Scott, James L. Scott, Joseph Ingle, Daniel MacLeod, John Lumsdon, John Janney, Joseph Janney, Jno. Watts, Charles Bennett, Andrew Heath, Jr., Jas. Dykes, William Cohen, Timy. Ryan, J.R.M. Lowe, Chrisr. Gird, Patk. Byrne, John O'Connor, John Buchan, Mattw. Sexsmith, John Craferd, Thos. Mezarvey, John Gadsby, Stephen Stephens, Jas. Campbell, John Hunter, Jas. Russell, Matthew Robinson, John Gretter, D. C__the, Thos. Mullan, Wm. Turner, Jacob Shuck, Law. Hooff, John Hayes?, Geo. Wm. Slatford, Allen Davis, Thos. White, John Wise, Robert Mease, Jh. M. Perrin, Mathzarin Perrin, T. Commargill, James D. Westcott, Phil. Rd. Fendall, Joseph Mandeville, Robert B. Jamesson, J.A. Sutton, N. Fitzhugh, James Cavan, John Green, Jonathan Mandeville, John G. Fentham, John Gildea, Hugh Carolin, Richard Quirk, Bernard Crook, W.B. Hodes, John Hodgkin, Daniel

Legislative Petitions of the Town and County of Alexandria, Virginia

Mc.A. Coles, Richd. Masters, Patrick K. Hendy, Thomas West, James Young, John Gordon, John Boyier, Chas. Page, Joseph Riddle, Absolem Wroe, Wm. Hunter, Elisha Bagby, Zacharias Lyles, George Bayly, W.M. Jenkin, Thos. Porter, Geo. Clementson, R. Hooe, Thomas Preston, Anty. Chs. Cazenove, Philip Wanton, Clement Greir, Wm. Lowry, John Muncaster, John Hubball, James Foy, Hugh Barr, Nobert Garden, John Korn, Thos. Triplett, Charles Love, Jac. Geiger, Ludwig *, Joseph T__, Philip Ferneau, Smith Keith, James Patton, Lewis Cooke, Thomas Jacobs, Tho: Redman, Philip Ferno, David Hesse, William Follin, Jos. Bowling, Fredrick Kerchner, Nathaniel Webster, James G. McAlister, Nicholas Reintzel, John Harper, Thos. Foster, Dennis Foley, Ch. Simms, Thos. Evans, Ephraim Evans, James Muir, John Brooks, Jas. Kennedy, Jr., John Wood__, Saml. Craig, Jno. Winterbery, C.H. Coffey, Gabriel Slacum, Ch: Douglas, Wm. Milnor, Adam Bence, Wm. Sanford, Thomas Sanford, Peter Vassoy, Rob. Hamilton, Jas. Hamilton, Benjn. Shreve, Benjn. Shreve, Jnr., Jno. G. Ladd, S.M. Casteen, Jr., Leml. Bent, Michael Cleary, Charles Harper, H. Woodrow, Alexander Keith, Hezekiah Smoot, James Brandon, Abel Janney & Geo. Graham, Jacob Wisemiller, Michl. Carley, Duncan Charles, George Hill, John Reardon, Edward Lewis, Thomas White, Jr., Edward Gray, Thos. Locke, Daniel Campbell, Cumberland Ferguson, George Drinker, James McCleish, Wm. Hartshorne, Senr., James H. Hamilton, Jno. Lemoine, Dennis Ramsay, Aaron Hewes, Edm. J. Lee, John Slacum, Richd. S. Yeaton, Thomas Clark, Richd. Clark, Joshua Riddle, Amos Alley, Amos Allison, Ellis Price, Jacob Hoffman, Allan M. Chapman, Ben. Locke [or Eicke], James E. Marshall, Wm. McMechen, Edwd. Stabler, Nicho. Kingston, John Johnston, William Everard, Thos. Steal, Cor. Colwell, James Hanna, Jos. Martin, William Wood, William Shropeshire, Enoch Sullivan, J.A. Taylor, Jonah Thompson, T.W. Peyton, Richard Taylor, Bryan Hampson, Flavius Millon, Alexr. MacKenzie, Jos. Bowden, Obadiah Clifford, Enoch M. Lyles, James McMechen, Jr., G. McMunn, George Jest, George Trisler, John Duffy, Charles McClaghen, John Austin, James Smith, Thos. Brocchus, John Talton, John Ramsay, Maurice Herlihy, Thomas Irwin, Edward Harper, John Dunlap, George Sutter, Cl. Maxwell, Andw. Wales, Thos. Low, John Crawford, Samuel Cather, John Boyer, Jacob Hookes, Geo. Pomery, Francis Sherd, George Slacum, Wm. Groverman, John Bolte, Charles Foeke, Wm. Bartleman, Chas. Jamieson, Samuel Harper, William Isabel, William Pomery, John Walkom, Peter Toffler, Samuel Hilton, John Fadely, Jas. Brown, Adam S. Swope, Ignatius Junigel, Thomas Beedle, Josiah Faxon, Wm. V. Hall, John McIver, David Wren, Fras. Foster, Edwd. Burke, Willm. Gird, James Grimes, William Halbert, Henry McGough, Wm. F. Noble, Jacob Resler, John Pittman, John Hill, John Backus, Enoch Pelten, John Johnson, John Muir, Daniel McDougall, William Bray, Danl. C. Puppo, John Harper, John Wallace, Chas. Smallwood, Saml. Hatton, M'h. Gressller, A.M. Deale, Wm. Kelly, Alexr. Bryman, Diedrick Sheckle, John Jacobs, Andrew Reintzell, Geo. M. Chapman, Peter Hauck, William Fraser, Samuel Evans, David Morgan, John Horner, Jr., Joseph Cary, John Foster, Andrew Ramsay, Duncan Niven, Wm. Ramsay, John Oswald, Jas. Kenner, Jno. Thos. Ricketts, M.

Alexander, and Wm. Newton.

Library Company of Alexandria.
1798, 10 DEC. A510. Repeal of act passed at last session incorporating a library company in Alexandria, as it was inadequate. Petitioners ask for the incorporation of the Alexandria Library Company with power to own and convey property and to sue and be sued.[63] Signed by James Muir, President, Robert Mease, Jas. M. McRae, Francis Peyton, Philip Wanton, Jno. V. Thomas, Wm. Milnor, Abram Hewes, and Arch. McClean. *Reported.* Box C.

Inhabitants of Fairfax County.
1798, 13 DEC. A511. Act empowering corporation of Alexandria to lay off two acres to be used for the holding of fairs twice a year, in April and October.[64] Fairs are of great advantage to farmers and mechanics in enabling them to sell surplus stock, to learn how to improve breeds, to buy provisions at lower rates and in other ways. *Reported.* Box C.

Gives the following names (no signatures) of petitioners: Benj. Dulany, Phil. Marsteller, Lawrence Hooff, John Hooper, Robt. Gordon, J. Davies, Wm. Lowry, Joseph Milbourne, A. Faw, Peter Piles, Christr. Gird, Jno. Abert, Thos. Herbert, Jacob Shuck, James Foy, John Kincaid, Edm. Hogan, Jh. M. Perrin, Wm. McKnight, Cleon Moore, Henry Moore, Chas. Jones, John Gadsby, Saml. Love, Wm. Lanphier, Wm. Tyler, John Longdon, Elias Dearing, Robt. Clarke, Adam Lynn, Chas. J. Stier, G. DeNeale, John Dunlap, J.B. Nickolls, John Janney, Bryan Hampson, Phil. Magruder, Jas. Dykes, Jas. Miller, George Taylor, Thos. Irwin, Jacob Hoffman, Wm. Herbert, Isaac McPherson, Wm. Ramsay, Jas. Wilson, Wm. Groverman, Thos. Williams, Jesse Simms, Rd. Veitch, Chas. Bennett, Jos. Mandeville, Ed. Stabler, Amos Alexander, John Korn, Ja. Wisemiller, John Dundas̲s̲, John T. Ricketts, Jonah Thompson, Thos. Davis, Wm. Newton, Robt. Hamilton, Jas. Hamilton, John Foster, J.M.A. Vanhavre, Jas. Kennedy, Ludl. Lee, Jas. Patten, Jas. Gillies, Francis Peyton, George Coryell, J. Faw, P. Wise, Jas. McRea, C.R. Scott, Rd. Conway, Chs. Si̲m̲s, Rd. Boggess, Jesse Moore, D. Foley, Andw. Jamieson, and Jas. Lawrason.

---

[63] Shepherd, Vol. 2, Chapter 44, pp. 171-72, "An ACT to incorporate a library company in the town of Alexandria," passed January 9, 1799. *Be it therefore enacted*, That the said library company be, and they are hereby made and constituted a body politic and corporate by the name of "The Alexandria Library Company," and by that name shall have perpetual succession and a common seal, with capacity to purchase, receive and possess goods and chattels, lands and tenements, in fee or otherwise, and the same to grant, let, sell, or assign...

[64] Shepherd, Vol. 2, Chapter 63, p. 183, "An ACT for holding fairs in the town of Alexandria," passed January 12, 1799.

Philip Wanton	Lewis Ford
Joseph Harper	Jesse Taylor
Thomas Janney	Richd Latham
Joseph Cary	John Harburgh
Saml Craig	Benj Moody
Wm Wilson	John Richards
T. Dreale	Josiah Langston
John Potts	Jno Bryan
Chilwel Dick	Jonan Farr
W. Sitherly	A. Face
Charles Bennett	John Foster
W. Watts	Jacob Steinemann
William Bowie	Samuel Kirk
Henry Ingle	Edwd May
John Harper	Robt Evans
P. Wise Jr	Gleen & Co
Wm Groverman	Alexr Kerr
Isaac Hell	Jarvis Ward
William Myers	Wm Park Junr
Joseph Thornton	John Richter
	H. Mustellee
	Adam Lynn
	Geo Wise

John Overall
Wm Ramsay
Bernard Hooe(?)

Jno. G. Ladd
Thos. Janes(?)
Thomas M Locke
Elisha Janney
Thomas Crandell
Samuel Crandell
Thos Vowell Junr
John C Vowell
Bolles(?) Locke
Jos Harton(?)
Clement Green
Chs Larmore(?)
James H Hooe
R. Hooe not doubting but that the law is unconstitutional.
Thos Smith
Ch. Douglas

David Wilson Scott
Rich Howell(?)
Alex Mackenzie
Warner Hunter(?)
James Huthrian(?)
Benj. Shreve Junr
L. Gardner
Cuthbert Meeks(?)
Benjn Shreve
John Lloyd
Joseph Coleman
Wm Hoye
Hezekiah Smoot
James Porter
Geo Graham
Abel Janney
John Moore
James Brandon
Abel Willis
Dunn(?)
Jacob Leap
Arch. M'Cleod

John Gould	John Ritton
Thomas Simms	John Duffey
Adam S. Swope	James Lawson
Ignatius Junigel	Wm Shropshire
William Isabell	James Wilson
John Pittman	Bryant Hampson
Joseph Dyer	John Butcher
Josiah Hay or Co	Jon a Butcher
John Pegg	Morris Worrell
Wm Bartleman	Joshua Riddle
Wm Mitchell	Amos Allison
Amos Alexander	Edwd Stabler
Wm S. Hall	Wm Lanphier
Wm Hodgson	John Johnston
Mathew Robinson	Samuel Wheeler
Jas Craik	Ambrose White
John W Bronaugh	Jacob Resler
Jas Russell	Ann Gray
	John Moir
	James Lowe

W. M. Tripp
Geo: Darling
Thos. M. Scott
James D. Westcott
Char Gullatt
Josiah Roby
Thos. Williams
Daniel MacLeod
John Lumsdon
John Homor
Wm. Fletcher
James Patton
Wm. G. Marks
Hugh Barr
Robert Gordon
Walter Boyels
Robert Stewart
William Erwin
Jacob Niremiller
John Korn
Wm. C. Newton
Wm. Paten
Aaron Reves
Chs. Slade
Richd Libby
Wm. Cone

Philip Wanton
Henry S. Earl
John Sloan
Nicholas Kingston
Geo. Toub Jr.
George Flamm
Davd Douglass
Josiah Emmet
Chas. Paweson
John Mills
John Janney
Jacob Hoffman
Abram Hewes
Henry S. Miller
Robert H. Watson
Jesse High
Geo Pomery
William Pomery
Math. Ellicott
Joseph Janney

Legislative Petitions of the Town and County of Alexandria, Virginia

Sundry Inhabitants of the Town of Alexandria.
1799, 4 APR. Original not found.[65] It is advised that the 60th Regiment of the Militia of this Commonwealth be Divided, and that the said Town of Alexandria form a complete Regiment of two Battalions, to consist of four companies to each Battalion, which Regiment is to be Numbered (106).

Merchants and Others.
1799, 14 DEC. A512. Protest against the injustice of act passed in 1797[66] imposing a tax of $40 upon wholesale vendors of foreign articles and $15 upon retail. The law is unconstitutional and injurious both to the merchants and the community at large. Virginia laws are unfavorable to commerce and often prevent merchants of large means from settling in the state. Petitioners trust that Legislature will allow the above mentioned law to expire without renewal. *Referred.* Box C.

Signed by Dennis Ramsay, Robert Allison, Jas. Keith, Wm. Hartshorne, Wm. Hartshorne, Junr., Jno. Thos. Ricketts, William Newton, Mark Alexander, George Taylor, George Gilpin, Samuel Harper, George Campbell, R.B. Jamesson, Jonathan Mandeville, Samuel McCloud, Saml. Adams, Wm. Hepburn, Peter Wise, John Kincaid, Thos. Harris, Saml. Bishop, Henry Ingle, Henry Gird, Junr., Ellis Price, J.B. Sullivan, Gurden Chapin, Joseph Paul, Jno. V. Thomas, John Dunlap, John Dundas, John Stewart, Peter Cottom, L. Labiltz, Walter Pomery, Jonah Isabell, Saml. Foudray, Charles Love, James Kennedy, Jr., David Davy, T.W. Peyton, Frans. Peyton, Lanty Crowe, Jonathan Swift, John Wyl<u>ie</u>, John Green, Close Maxwell, James Bacon, Philip G. Marsteller, Guy Atkinson, Danl. McClean, George Drinker, Jno. Roberts, Saml. G. Griffith, Andw. W. Jamiesson, Thomas Dempsey, Peter Sherron, Philip Wanton, Joseph Harper, Thomas Janney, Joseph Cary, Saml. Craig, Wm. Wilson, G. Deneale, John Potts, Elisha C. Dick, N. Fitzhugh, Charles Bennett, Jno. Watts, William Bowie, Henry Ingle, John Harper, P. Wise, Jr., Wm. Groverman, Isaac Kell, William Myers, Joseph Thornton, James Ford, Jesse Taylor, Richd. Latham, John Hasbrough, Benj. Moody, John Richards, Josiah Coryton, Jno. Bryan, Jona. Faw, A. Faw, John Foster, Jacob Heinemann, Samuel Kirk, Edwd. May, Robt. Evans, Gleese & Co., Alexr. Kerr, Zach. Ward, Wm. Cash, Jr., John Richter, P. Marsteller, Adam Lynn, Geo. Wise, John Overall, Wm. Ramsay, Bernard Ghequiere, Jno. G. Ladd, Thos. <u>Lore</u>, Thomas M. Locke, Elisha Janney, Thomas Crandell, Samuel Crandell, Thos. Vowell, Junr., John C. Vowell, Rolle & Foeke, Jos. Martin, Clement Green, Anty. Chs. Cazenove, James H. Hooe, R. Hooe, not doubting but that the law is unconstitutional, Thos. Smith, Ch. Douglas, David Wilson Scott, Richd. Horwell, Alexr. MacKenzie, Washer Blunt, James Keith, Junr., Benja. Shreve, Junr., L.

---

[65] Flournoy, H.W., ed., <u>Calendar of Virginia State Papers and Other Manuscripts, From January 1, 1799, to December 31, 1807, Preserved in the Capitol at Richmond</u>, Vol. IX (Richmond, 1890), p. 16.
[66] <u>Shepherd</u>, Vol. 2, Chapter 1, pp. 73-5, "An ACT laying taxes for the year one thousand seven hundred and ninety-seven," passed January 22, 1798.

Gardner, Catlett & Meeks, Benjn. Shreve, John Lloyd, Joseph Coleman, Wm. Hoye, Hezekiah Smoot, James Porter, Geo. Graham, Abel Janney, John Moore, James Brandon, Abel Willis, J. Dean, Jacob Leap, Archd. McCliesh, John Gould, Thomas Simms, Adam S. Swope, Ignatius J. Junigel, William Isabell, John Pittman, Joseph Dyson, Josiah Faxon & Co., John Clegg, Wm. Bartleman, Wm. Mitchell, Amos Alexander, W.J. Hall, Wm. Hodgson, Matthew Robinson, Jas. Craik, Joseph Riddle, Jas. Russell, John Ritson, John Duffey, James Lawrason, Wm. Shropshire, James Wilson, Bryan Hampson, John Butcher, Jona. Butcher, Morris Worrell, Joshua Riddle, Amos Allison, Edwd. Stabler, Wm. Lanphier, John Johnston, Samuel Wheeler, Ambrose White, Jacob Resler, Ann Gray, John Minor, James Lowe, W. McKnight, Geo: Darling, Richd. M. Scott, James D. Westcott, Chas. Gullatt, Josiah Robey, Ths. Williams, Daniel MacLeod, John Lumsdon, John Horner, Wm. Fletcher, James Patton, Wm. G. Marks, Hugh Barr, Robert Gordon, Peter Payels, Robert Stewart, William Erwin, Jacob Wisemiller, John Korn, Wm. C. Newton, Wm. Paton, Aaron Hewes, Chas. Slade, Richd. Libby, Wm. Carne, Philip Wanton, Henry S. Earle, John Sloan, Nicholas Kingston, Geo. Irish, Jr., George Slacum, Danl. Douglass, Josiah Emmet, Chas. Jamieson, John Mills, John Janney, Jacob Hoffman, Abram Hewes, Hewes & Miller, Robert T. Watson, Jesse Pugh, Geo. Pomery, William Pomery, Nathl. Ellicott, and Joseph Janney.

<u>Merchants, Tradesmen, and Other Inhabitants of the Town of Alexandria.</u>
1799, 16 DEC. A513. Extension of charter of Bank of Alexandria for twenty years.[67] Without a bank, commerce of town would be diverted to Baltimore, and besides, as the circulation of bank notes cannot be prevented, the notes should be Alexandria notes and not issued of Northern banks. Printed. *Referred.* Box C, also see A515, no date.

Signed by Jas. Campbell, Jno. V. Thomas, R.B. Jamiesson, Francis Murphy, Alexr. Berry, Richd. Conway, Wm. Herbert, John Dundas, Alexr. Smith, Amos Alexander, Henry Moore, Jesse Carter, Andw. Jamieson, Walter Pomery, Jonah Isabell, George Kilton, Hanson Reno, Samuel Cooper, Henry L. Yeatman, Andrew Dumax, John Kincaid, Wm. Billington, James Kennedy, Davey Dewery, Michael Solomon, Alexander Williams, John Richter, Joseph Harper, William Myers, William Cash, Junior, John Gibson, Robt. Evans, Thomas Allen, Samuel Kirk, Delius & Weidemeyer, Jno. Bryan, Josiah Coryton, John Horsburgh, Saml. Adams, Mathew Eakin, Jonathan Mandeville, Jno. Watts, John Lumsdon, Daniel MacLeod, Andw. & Wm. Ramsay, Jesse Simms, John Ramsay, Alexander Kern, Bernard Ghequiere, Henry Ingle, Benjn. Mitchell, Thos. Clark, Richd. Clark, John Stewart, Wm. Yeaton, Dennis Ramsay, John Rielly, Thos. Clarke, Robert Mease, James Gillies, Mattw. Sexsmith, Guy Atkinson, James Bacon, John Morris, Phil. Rd. Fendall,

---

[67] <u>Shepherd</u>, Vol. 2, Chapter 57, p. 292, "An ACT concerning the bank of Alexandria," passed January 21, 1801. *That the charter of the said bank shall be and the same is hereby continued until the fourth day of March, one thousand eight hundred and eleven.*

Legislative Petitions of the Town and County of Alexandria, Virginia

Cuthbert Powell, Thom. Frankland, James Murray, Jo. Kempff, Patk. Byrne, Chris. Gird, Jesse Taylor, John White, James Young, Neal Mooney, Hugh McCaughen, Joseph Milburn, James McCliesh, Jas. Carolin, Bernard Crook, Hugh Carolin, Leonard Reeves, Clo. Maxwell, Thomas White, Robt. Brocket, Jacob Fortney, Edm. J. Lee, John Throop, Tho. Swann, Wm. Wilson, John Potts, John Wyld, Wm. Hepburn, *, P. Heiskell, David Henderson, Joseph Thornton, Thos. Patten, W. McKnight, Peter Cottom, Richd. M. Scott, *, John Gadsby, Thomas Davis, and L.B. Mikells.

Duplicate signed by George Gilpin, Jno. Thos. Ricketts, John Janney, Wm. Hodgson, J.M.A. Vanhavre, R. Hooe, James H. Hooe, John Muncaster, Wm. J. Hall, Joseph Cary, Jona. Swift, Catlett & Meeks, John Foster, Jas. Kennedy, Jr., Thompson & Veitch, Bryan Hampson, Thos. Vowell, Junr., Saml. Craig, John Kitson, John Duffey, Thos. Williams, Wm. Paton, John Butcher, Jas. Keith, Amos Allison, Jacob Hoffman, Wm. McMechen, Edwd. Stabler, Samuel Wheeler, Hiram *, Isaac McPherson, John T. Brooks, Ch. Douglas, Roberts & Griffith, James Keith, Junr., Benjn. Shreve, Edward Harper, Benja. Shreve, Junr., Z. Gardner, Alexr. MacKenzie, George Coryell, Geo. Graham, John Stewart, Jun., Jo. Kempff, Bolte & Foeke, Jno. C. Vowell, John Boyer, Thos. Mezarvey, Rob. Hamilton, Jas. Hamilton, Sam. Allen, Joseph Riddle, Jas. M. McRea, Ja. R. Riddle, Wm. Hartshorne, Junr., Elisha C. Dick, Jno. Lemoine, Jas. Craik, George Drinker, Wm. Bartleman, Josiah Faxon & Co., John Clegg, Thos. Smith, Washer Blunt, J. Lawrason, J. McGuire, Geo. Pomery, John Harper, Samuel Harper, Jno. G. Ladd, Geo. Darling, John Longden, John MacLeod, G. McMunn, Josiah Robey, Levi Talbot, Jacob Wisemiller, Benj. Moody, Robert Gorden, Hugh Barr, George Rutter, Aaron Hewes, Ignatius Junigel, Richard Horwell, David Wilson Scott, Joshua Riddle, Josh. Dyson, Robert Watson, John Winterbury, Jr., John C. Love, James Wallace, John Korn, Dan. McClean, Philip Magruder, James Richardson, Jno. Harper, Wm. Kelly, Geo. Baldwin, Chas. Grater, Joseph Wooden, Thos. Moore, *, P. Wise & Co., Scudamore Nickolls, Jh. M. Perrin, Matzurin Perrin, Saml. Bishop, Daniel McDougall, George Taylor, Hezekiah Smoot & Co., Geo. Irish, Anty. Chs. Cazenove, Richd. Walsh, John Gould, Zachariah Muncaster, Chas. R. Scott, John Mackintosh, Mordecai Miller, Thomas Irwin, James Irvin, Stephen Moore, Wm. Paton, Junr., John Johnson, Joseph Dean, Harper & Davis, James Brandon, Philip G. Marsteller, John Woodrow, Charles Love, Thos. Porter, Philip Wanton, Wm. Groverman, and Charles J. Stier.

Jesse Taylor (d. 1812) and Inhabitants.
1799, 16 DEC. No number. Ferry Across Potomack River.[68] To the

---

[68] Shepherd, Vol. 2, Chapter 30, pp. 221-22, "An ACT for establishing several new ferries, and increasing the rates of a former one," passed January 20, 1800, "...and from the land of Jesse Taylor, in the town of Alexandria, across Patowmac river, to the opposite shore, in the state of Maryland, the price for a man seventeen cents, and for a horse the same."

Legislative Petitions of the Town and County of Alexandria, Virginia

Honorable General Assembly of the Commonwealth of Virginia the Petition of Jesse Taylor humbly sheweth that your petitioner is the owner of land situated in the upper part of the town of Alexandria and lying on the River Potomack very well calculated for a Ferry for the accommodation of persons desirous of passing into Maryland or travelling to the northward-- That people travelling from the southward or westward in the direction above mentioned usually stop at Alexandria which lies directly in their road, and it would be very inconvenient for such persons to be compelled to cross the Potomack at a ferry at any distance from that town. Your petitioner further begs leave to represent that there is at present but one ferry established by law from Alexandria to the Maryland shore. That from the increasing trade of the town and from the road thro' it to George-Town the Federal City and Baltimore having of late become more frequented than formerly, that Ferry is by no means sufficient for the quick and ready transporting of passengers. Your petitioner suggests that by authorizing the establishment of another ferry a competition would be created which would be productive of the most beneficial consequences to the public. Your petitioner has already contracted with a person of responsibility on the Maryland shore for providing everything which may be necessary for the accommodation of passengers, provided your Honorable body should think proper to grant this petition. The number of respectable signatures annexed hereto fully evince that the public concur in your petitioner's request. Your petitioner therefore prays that a law may be passed by the honorable general assembly of this commonwealth authorizing your petitioner to establish [page 2] a ferry from his land in Alexandria to the corresponding part of the Maryland shore. Box C.

Signed by A. Faw, Jno. Watts, Charles Bennett, P. Marsteller, Peter Sherron, Dennis Ramsay, Sprague Yeaton, Thos. Williams, Wm. Chapman, Wm. Emmons, Wm. Mitchell, Jas. Kennedy, Jr., Thos. Vowell, Jr., Saml. Dunlap, James Laurence, John Korn, George Gilpin, George Taylor, Jno. C. Vowell, Benj. Shreve, Junr., Z. Gardner, Abram Hewes, Wm. Harper, Benj. Shreve, Samuel Harper, Aaron Hewes, Thomas Irwin, Hezekiah Smoot, Joseph Mandeville, William Cash, Jr., George Rutter, Dennis McCarty Johnson, Wm. Hartshorne, John Muncaster, Leonard Cook, Catlett & Meeks, Bryan Hampson, Jno. G. Ladd, Danl. Douglass, John Dundas, P. Heiskell, Lawr. Hooff, Jacob Cox, Thos. Cook, Jonathan Mandeville, Chas. Love, James Davenport, John A. Stewart, Peter Cottom, Isaac Kell, Richard Walsh, Samuel McCloud, Robert Young, David Henderson, Alexr. Smith, Jonah Isabell, John Gordon, Charles McKnight, Jonah Thompson, Amos Alexander, G. Deneale, Stephen Cooke, Jona. Faw, John Towers, David Graham, Matthew Robinson, W. Yeaton, Joseph Thornton, Thos. Peterkin, Wm. Moss, John Johnston, Henry S. Earle, Henry Moore, Jas. Campbell, William Myers, Wm. Lanphier, Wm. Turner, F. Marsteller, John MacLeod, Thomas Rogerson, Walt: Jones, Jr., Bartleman & White, Edm. J. Lee, Saml. Hilton, Chas. Turner, Jesse Simms, Coats Ridgway, Ch. Simms, J.H. Hooe, J. Summers, Jh. M. Perrin, Mathzurin Perrin, Saml. Bishop,

Legislative Petitions of the Town and County of Alexandria, Virginia

Frs. Neale, Jos. Neale, Richd. Lewis, Jno. McKnight, William Carrington, Chas. Page, Jno. Lemoine, Robert Anderson, Walter Pomery, Samuel Cooper, *, Ellis Price, Allan M. Chapman, James D. Westcott, John Ramsay, Henry Woodrow, Jas. Keith, John Richter, John Harper, Adam Lynn, Geo. Danbury, Jonathan Swift, Geo. Wise, Thomas Lawrason, P. Wise, Jr., Josiah Coryton, Jno. Bryan, David Wilson Scott, Jacob Wisemiller, Jac. Geiger, *, Richd. Libby, Wm. Carne, Elisha Janney, Geo. Irish, Jr., Joshua Riddle, Jas. Russell, Daniel Dowling, George Wily, James Patton, Rob. Smock, James Richardson, Thomas Dempsey, Thos. Casey, Joseph Riddle, R.B. Jamiesson, Robert Edie, Francis Murphy, Wm. Groverman, Henry Gird, Junr., John Smith, George Forteny, John Wyld, Lewis Gordon, Peter Wise, William Higgins, Thomas Otway, Robt. Evans, Jno. Evans, John Richards, John Johnston, Hugh Adrain, John McRea, John Watson, Henry Keppell, Gurden Chapin, Michl. Flannery, J.A. Sutton, Jos. Paul, James McKenna, James Baron, John Wright, Mattw. Sexsmith, Bernard Bryan, Josiah Emmet, Patk. Byrne, Henry Nichols, Thomas Darne, Jr., Diedrick Shekle, R.J. Taylor, Ephraim Evans, John Hubball, [German, Anthony Inatzcouf?], *, Jno. Harrison, Geo. W. Craik, John Decker, Jo. Kempff, W. O'Brian, Tho. Steel, Wm. Friend, John Green, Isaac Gibson, Jacob Leap, Abel Janney, Geo. Graham, John Moore, James Keith, Jr., Thomas Crandell, John Dunlap, J.B. Nickolls, Robert Smith, William Isabell, William Pomery, Robert Watson, Adam S. Swope, Alexr. MacKenzie, Philip G. Marsteller, Nathaniel Wattles, Charles Alexander, Thos. Smith, John Lynd, Wm. Bartleman, Jas. MacKenzie, John Borrowdale, Josiah Faxon, John Clegg, David Davy, Wm. Newton, Wm. J. Hall, Benj. Moody, John Watson, John Janney, Joseph Harper, Thomas White, Joseph Janney, Thomas Preston, Andrew Heath, James Porter, Jas. M. McRea, Theo. Hume, Jno. Norwood, John Kincaid, Thomas Cruse, Geo. Pomery, And. Bryson, Thos. Herbert, John Sutton, Jno. V. Thomas, Robt. Brocket, Thos. Patten, John Butcher, James Wilson, John Foster, J.A. Taylor, Saml. Craig, Ch: Douglas, Wm. Wood, Guy Atkinson, Nicholas Voss, John Winterbury, Geo. Coryell, Henry Ingle, John Horsbaugh, Saml. Adams, Richd. Latham & Co., Hugh McCloud, and Wm. Byrd Page.

<u>William Hodgson, John Hunter and Joseph Thomas, Proprietors of the Ferry From Alexandria to the Landings Upon the South and North Sides of Oxen Creek in the State of Maryland.</u>
1799, 16 DEC. No number. Petition of William Hodgson, John Hunter and Joseph Thomas, proprietors of the ferry from Alexandria to the landings upon the south and north sides of Oxen Creek in the State of Maryland sheweth: That the assemblies of Virginia have in order to procure a ready and certain passage over those waters which were not fordable established at different times Ferries over the most of those waters at those places most necessary granting the same to the proprietors of the ground where established with certain rates of ferriage and other privileges to encourage and enable them to encounter the expenses attending upon a Ferry, among other privileges a punishment of such as should intrude upon the business to deprive them of the profits, and a

Legislative Petitions of the Town and County of Alexandria, Virginia

careful attention not to establish other ferries so near as to deprive the one first established of a sufficient support. That among other ferries so established by the Assembly is the Ferry from the Town of Alexandria to the above landings in the state of Maryland which is established upon the lands formerly belonging to Hugh West in whose Family it continued for many years, that the lands have been sold[69] by one of his descendants together with the Ferry attached thereto, which has come to the possession of your petitioners, that it has been a received opinion with all those possessing ferries and others acquainted with the subject, that the grant or establishment of a ferry rests in the proprietor as absolute a right therein as to a piece of land granted him, so long as he continues to fulfill the terms of the grant by keeping a ferry in a proper manner at all times for the accommodation of the public, under this impression your petitioners made the purchase, your petitioners William Hodgson, John Hunter & Joseph Thomas, having the interest of the ferry and the said John Hunter and Joseph Thomas having the land to which the ferry is attached, that this opinion appears to your petitioners bounded in justice and with a view to the public convenience and could not be expected that any person would lay out his money in procuring the necessary articles for keeping a ferry and encounter the heavy expense of it if he was not to have a permanent interest in it, that large sums of money have been expended in tending the landing place commodious by running out or there forming a dock and a convenient method of getting carriages in and out of the boat, building a house for ferrymen upon the [shot] and providing boats and keeping ferrymen always in readiness, that your petitioners have a lott of ferrymen and boats to attend to those whom to land upon the north side of Oxen Creek and two setts of ferrymen to attend to those who want to land upon the south side of the Creek that being the most public landing, on the management of the land it is the constant [ ]tree as soon as the boat leaves the shore for a boat from the opposite shore to set off to replace it to prevent those wanting to cross meeting with delay... your petitioners do assure the honorable [body] that they would not with a monopoly if the profits were sufficient to support two ferries in a proper manner, the application of Mr. Baldwin Dade to establish a ferry over the river from his land about three quarters of a mile above the town at the last sessions met with no opposition from your petitioners nor would they oppose the present application from a consciousness that the public will be as greatly injured by the establishment of another ferry at this time as your petitioners. *Rejected.* Box C.

Michael Jacob.
1799, 19 DEC. A514. Act vesting in petitioner right in fee simple to houses and lots owned by John Frederick Henninger, deceased. Decedent had only one daughter, Mary Magdalena Henninger, a native of Germany,

---

[69] Also see Fairfax County Deeds, Bk. O, 1763-1784, pp. 452-58, dated 1 MAY 1784, between Thomas West and Anne his wife, and William Hunter, Junr., and John Allison, for grounds of Sybil West together with a ferry landing annexed thereto.

Legislative Petitions of the Town and County of Alexandria, Virginia

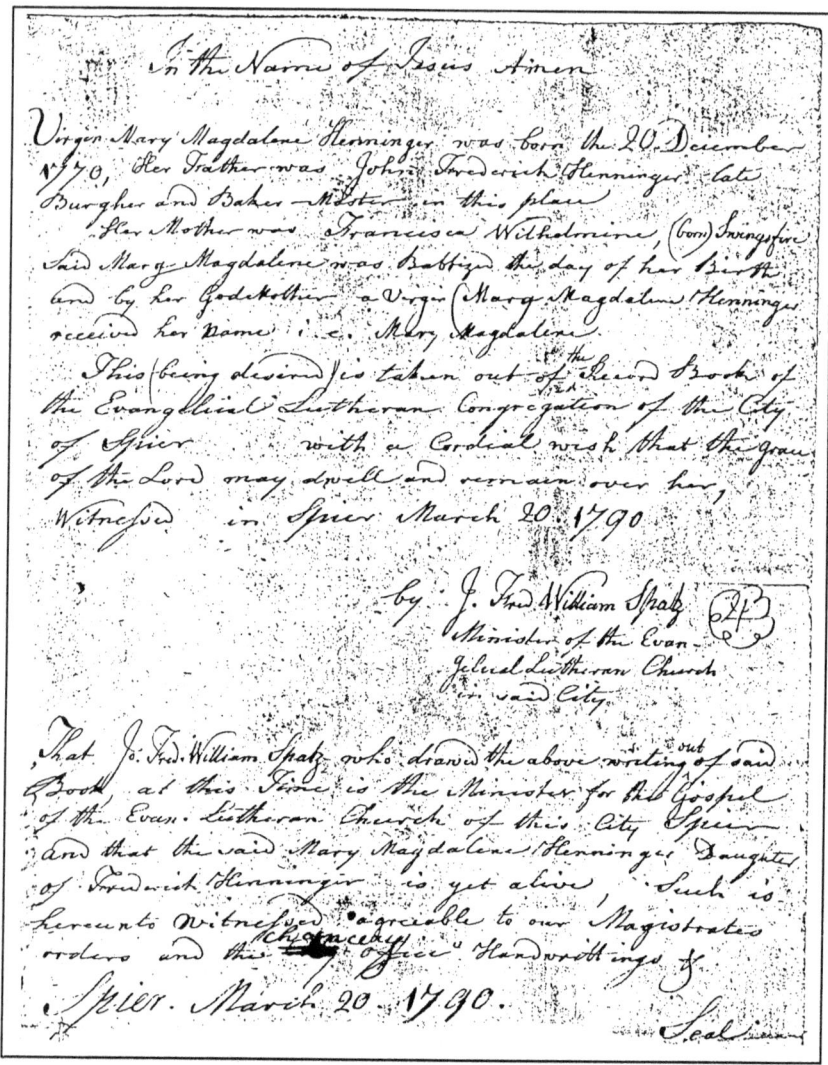

who by laws of Virginia is an alien and cannot inherit property in State. Petitioner has purchased her claim to estate. Copy of power of attorney in German and English. Included in the record [marked A1499-2] is a certified copy of baptism record for Mary Magdalene Henninger, who was born the 20 DEC 1770, her father was John Frederick Henninger late burgher and baker, master in this place. Her mother was Francisca Wilhelmine (born Swingsfire) said Mary Magdalene was baptized the day of her birth and by her god mother a virgin Mary Magdalene Henninger received her name, i.e. Mary Magdalene. This being desired is taken out of the record book of the Evangelical Lutheran Congregation of the City of Spier with a cordial wish that the grace of the Lord may dwell and remain over her, witnessed in Spier, March 20, 1790. *Referred.* Box C.

Be it known unto all persons particularly to those whome it concerns, that we the subscribers (John Bartholomew Dines authoritatively constituted guardian for Mary Magdalene Heninger [sic], daughter of Frederick Henninger, late of Alexandria Virginia, deceased, and John Michael Henninger, uncle to said Mary Magdalene), have to our true and lawful attorney entrusted and constituted and by these presents to entrust, ordain, constitute and authorize Jacob Michael (born in the Dukedom Leiningen at the Haardt and in the county of Falkenburg and the Village Hettenhousen, son of Henry Michael (Shultheis), justice for the peace) and now of the state of Virginia and county of Frederick. That he for us, and in our name and in our head, is to act demand and receive such portion or legacy left to said Mary Magdalene Henninger by her father ~~John~~ Frederick Henninger, late inhabitant, a baker master in Alexandria and the state of Virginia, amounting to about twelve hundred gilders according to the rhineish value, for which said Jacob Michael hath paid down the quantum to the said guardian &c. according to their agreement between them made (and upon receipt of such agreed quantum) we make over all our right and title of the said twelve hundred gilders to our said Attorney Jacob Michael to demand, receive and keep the same for himself and his own use forever... Transcript of document in German which is also in the file.

President and Directors of Bank of Alexandria.
1799. A515. Extension of charter of bank for twenty years, as the present charter will expire on January 1, 1803.[70] "Certain it is that should the Bank of Alexandria be put down, the profit of money lending, must either accrue to the Northern Merchants and Banks from whom it must be borrowed, or to a certain set of greedy usurers who fatten upon the spoils of others." Signed by Wm. Herbert, Pres. Box C.

Sundry Merchants, Traders, Mechanics and Other Citizens of the Town of Alexandria.
1799, 19 DEC. A516. Extension of charter of Bank of Alexandria for twenty years, with an amendment increasing number of directors from nine to fifteen, and making one-third of them ineligible for reelection for three years after expiration of their term of service. *To lie on table.* Box C.

Signed by Abel Janney, Joseph Dean, <u>Wm.</u> Smithson, Richard Lewis, R. Burford, James Lawrason, Benj. Shreve, Junr., Wm. Harper, Catlett & Meeks, Aaron Hewes, Theo. Hume, C. Martin, Saml. Adams, Jno. V. Thomas, Henry Lewis, James Westcott, John MacLeod, Bernard Bryan, Thomas White, Henry Nicholson, Edm. J. Lee, William Myers, Arch. J.

---

[70] <u>Shepherd</u>, Vol. 2, Chapter 57, p. 292, "An ACT concerning the Bank of Alexandria."

Taylor, Lewis Summers, John Gadsby, Mattw. Sexsmith, Arch. McClean, John Duvall, James McGuire, Jesse Green, John Foster, John Mandeville, Thos. Gunnell, Leonard Cook, John Stewart, Thos. Peterkin, H. Gunnell, Joseph Neale, William Bowie, Thomas Durhill, Francis Neale, Saml. Watts, Lanty Crowe, Walter Pomery, Josiah Coryton, A. Faw, Joseph Thornton, John Rhodes, William Cash, Junior, Gleese & Co., Saml. Sangster, Henry Burford, John Kincaid, Jno. Evans, Jonah Isabell, Chas. Jones, Walt. Jones, Jr., Wm. Billington, Jno. Lemoine, Stephen Stephens, Clotworthy Stevenson, Bart. White, Nicholas Voss, Robt. Harrison, George Pomery, Francis Murphy, Thomas Cruse, Thos. Smith, Josh. Dyson, Samuel Smith, John Courtenay, Richard Libby, William Carne, Jno. Bryan, Hanson Reno, Samuel Cooper, William Cummings, Richd. Brooke, Wm. H. Bartl[eman], Wm. Lanphier, Jos. Varden, Alexr. Baggott, Saml. Johnson, Wm. Tyler, J. Thomas, D. Campbell, Patk. Byrne, C.F. Schewe, Jas. L. Orr, Thomas Drown, Wm. Friend, Benj. Davis, John Sloan, Henry McCue, Thomas White, Junr., James Young, Hugh Maxwell, Jno. Cranston, John Hodgkin, James McCliesh, Joseph Birch, Allen Davis, Nehemiah Clifford, William Mitchell, Alexander Baggett, William Higgins, Thomas *, David Dick, Bryan Cook, Alexander Malone, Michael Solomon, Henry Davis, Barnabas Brooke, Meshack Tucker, John Bicksler, William Stoops, Absolem Wroe, Solomon Cassidy, Jno. Weylie, Amos Alexander, James Martin, Wm. Martin, John Martin, Robt. Gray, John Gray, William F. Gray, T.F. Jones, James McFadon, John Kent, Jno. Horwell, Chas. Horwell, John Johnston, John Richards, Hugh Adrain, and Abel Blakeny.

Inhabitants of the Town of Alexandria.
1800, 9 DEC. A517. Act opening a road from Norman's Ford to Alexandria, and regulating manner of building the same. This road would be of great benefit to petitioners, as it would open a new market. *Rejected.* Box C.

Signed by Wm. Herbert, John Muncaster, Walt. Jones, Jr., John Richter, Wm. Hartshorne, Philip Magruder, Geo. Drinker, Michl. Flannery, Gurden Chapin, J.A. Sutton, Scudamore Nickolls, George Taylor, N. Fitzhugh, Jas. M. McRea, P. Wise, Junr., George Slacum, W. McKnight, Robt. Lyle, Allan M. Chapman, Charles McKnight, Wm. Myers, Robert Black, Jonathan Mandeville, Thos. *, Jacob Fortney, Jonathan Swift, John Oswald, Duncan Niven, John Ramsay, Chas. Jones, John Dunlap, Bryan Hampson, Jas. M. Steuart, Robert Mease, David Wilson Scott, Peter Catlett, John Mandeville, Thomas Irwin, Philip G. Marsteller, Joshua Riddle, John Stewart, Junr., Wm. Paton, J. Butcher, Jno. Watts, C. Bennett, Bernard Bryan, R.B. Jamiesson, W. Halley, John Dundas, Rd. Weightman, A. Faw, Peter Wise, Thos. Hume, Thomas White, George Rutter, Aquila Janney, Philip G. Marsteller, Joseph Harper, Smith & Bartleman, Samuel Smith, John Clegg, Josh. Dyson, Daniel C. Puppo, Cuthbert Powell, Wm. Billington, Robert Young, James D. Lowry, Robert K. Lowry, Jno. Roberts, * Griffin, Thomas Swann, John Walkom, William Isabel, Samuel Harper, Alexr. Smith, Danl. McClean, Joseph Dean, Zachariah Gardner, Benjn. Shreve, Benja. Shreve, Junr., Abel

Janney, Jacob Leap, Wm. Harper, Wm. Newton, Jno. Thos. Ricketts, Jas. Caran, Jr., James Richardson, James Keith, Jr., Chas. Slade, Wm. Carne, Elisha Janney, Geo. Irish, John Hunter, George Gilpin, Ch: Douglas, John Gould, J. Lawrason, Danl. Douglass, Thos. Vowell, Junr., Jno. C. Vowell, Thos. Low, Jas. Campbell, and Thos. Mezarvey. Duplicate.

Merchants and Others.
1800, 11 DEC. A518. Increase of salary of tobacco inspectors at Alexandria to $200. Warehouses were reestablished at last session of Legislature, which fixed inspector's salary at inadequate sum of $75 a year. ...*increasing the salary to Two hundred Dollars for each acting Inspector (which was formerly allowed and is now allowed to the Inspectors of the other warehouses in this County) but that additional compensation would be made them for the time they have acted. It must be verry [sic] evident to every member of your Hble. body that no Man can pofsibly support a Family even in the Meanest way and pay House Rent on the verry [sic] small sum of Seventy five Dollars p. annum which in fact is hardley [sic] sufficient to pay House Rent alone...* Bill drawn. Box C.

Signed by D. Stuart, Wm. Wilson, A._.W. Ramsay, John Foster, Wm. Groverman, R. Hooe (who will always give more for Tobacco in Alexa. Warehouse than any other on Potomack River), Joseph Riddle & Co., Jacob Hoffman, Amos Allison, Wm. Triplett, Peter Algeron, R.B. Jamesson, Thompson Stark, E. Myers, Joshua Riddle, Jno. Watts, C. Bennett, Jno. Watts, David Wilson Scott, James Patton, John Ramsay, Thos. Janney, Jas. Russell & Co., James Wilson, Charles Alexander, Jonathan Mandeville, Thomas White, Jonah Isabell, Giles Cooke, Wm. Hepburn, Lewis Summers, Robt. Black, Charles McKnight, Campbell Wilson & Co., Thomas Lawrason, Robert Young, Dennis Ramsay, Hewes & Miller, John & Thos. Vowell, Smith & McClean, Thos. Cook, Joseph Dean, Zach. Gardner, Benjn. Shreve, A. Janney, Alexr. MacKenzie, Daniel C. Puppo, G. McMunn, Smith & Bartleman, Bryan Hampson, P. Marsteller, George Irish, Jr., Aquila Janney, John Janney, John McClenachan, Anth. Chs. Cazenove, Wm. Paton, Sm. Sommers, Wm. Stuart of W., Geo. Pomery, W. McKnight, Saml. Craig, Wm. Mitchell, A. Faw, George Gilpin, and N. Fitzhugh.

President and Directors of Bank of Alexandria.
1800, 19 DEC. A519. Extension of charter of bank ten years from January 1, 1803, on which date it expires. Branch of the Bank of the United States is established at Norfolk and if charter of Bank of Alexandria is not renewed, this bank will establish a branch in town. Citizens of Alexandria prefer the continuance of Bank of Alexandria, of the stock of which they hold the great part, to the establishment of a bank whose stock is owned by citizens of other states and foreigners. Signed by Wm. Herbert, President, Jonah Thompson, Richd. Conway, George Gilpin, Ch. Simms, John Dunlap, John Janney, Jno. Thos. Ricketts, and John Dundas. *Reasonable.* Box C.

Legislative Petitions of the Town and County of Alexandria, Virginia

President and Directors of the Little River Turnpike Company.
1802, 21 DEC. A632. Little River Turnpike.[71] Directors of the Little River Turnpike Company petitioners complain that a recent act[72] has set the width of proposed road too narrow. That the Honorable Assembly at their last session passed an act to incorporate a company for the purpose of making a turnpike road from that part of the line of Columbia District where Duke Street crossed to the Ford on little river, the road proposed, if made, will be productive of extensive profits to a great body of the citizens of the state, and making it will be attended with a very heavy expense, when these circumstances are taken into consideration a plan which may procure the advantages looked for and justify the expense which will certainly be incurred seems a first an principal point in the business... roads much frequented require a breadth proportioned to the use made of them... kept in a tolerable state of repair... That the Lancaster turnpike road when first established was extended to fifty feet, twenty one feet of which was to be artificial the residue side ways or summer road, this was afterwards augmented to sixty eight feet in certain parts of the road if the company should incline to increase it to that breadth. That the subscribers to the little river turnpike road having considered the subject maturely and the impractability of keeping in repair and the inutility to the public of a road of the breadth limited in the said act... Your petitioners further shew that by the act incorporating the company, provision is made to present the tolls from exceeding fifteen percentum, they respectfully submit to the honorable house as the tolls cannot at any future day give them an enlarged interest to compensate for many years deficiency of a legal interest whether justice does not seem to require the means of a common interest to those advancing their money for a great and national purpose. Signed by James Keith, President, Leven Powell, George Gilpin, Richd. M. Scott, and Jno. Thos. Ricketts. *Reasonable.* Box C.

President and Directors of Bank of Potomac.
1805, 19 DEC. A520. Grant of charter to Bank of Potomac on condition that it establishes its office in Virginia contiguous to Alexandria. File contains a printed copy of "Articles of Association of the Bank of Potomac, Established at Alexandria," printed in Alexandria by Samuel Snowden. Alexandria, Decr. 16, 1805. Signed by Thos. Vowell, Jr., President, N. Fitzhugh, Robert Young, Wm. Hartshorne, Jno. G. Ladd, E. Janney, James Patton, Jas. H. Hooe, Jacob Hoffman, Cuthbert Powell, J. Riddle, and James Keith, Jun. *Referred.* Box C.

---

[71] Shepherd, Vol. 2, Chapter 52, pp. 452-55, "An ACT to amend the act, entituled, 'An act to incorporate a company for establishing a turnpike road from the intersection of Duke street, in the town of Alexandria, with the south-west line of the district of Columbia, to the ford of Little river, where the turnpike road now crosses it,'" passed January 19, 1803.

[72] Shepherd, Vol. 2, Chapter 83, pp. 383-86, "An ACT to incorporate a company for establishing a turnpike road from the intersection of Duke street in the town of Alexandria, with the south-west line of the District of Columbia, to the ford of Little river where the turnpike road now crosses it," passed January 28, 1802.

Citizens.
1805. A521. Thornton Gap Road.[73] Act opening a road from Thornton's Gap to Alexandria, thereby shortening the distance from Staunton by 35 miles. Petitioners have suffered inconvenience and loss in selling their produce for want of a road, and trade of a most fertile part of the state has been diverted to Baltimore. Signed by Wm. S. Mayre, Joshua Ruffner, Wm. Almond, Thomas Corbin, and 31 others. Original not found.

Little River Turnpike Company.[74]
1807, 18 DEC. A522. Permission to charge toll on every five miles of the new road instead of on every ten miles, according to the present law. The road is now being built and is much impaired by the passing of wagons from the upper country over it and expense of construction is much greater than was estimated. *During the time that their new road kept in the direction of the old one fo that the waggoners & travellers were compelled to use it, the company fubmitted to this heavy expence without a murmur, hoping that as foon as the new road left at the old one altogether it would fustain no further injury from the waggons until it fhould be completed, but in this they have been disappointed for by means of bye roads and by opening to them it is pafsages through the woods, the waggons face their way into it, and the injury is found to be nearly as great af at first. Your petitioners beg leave to ftate that roads made of ftone & gravel require time to fettle, and are not only more fubject to injury when new but the repairs much more expensive; they further ftate that their new road is entirely off the tract of the old road, and will not again touch it till it comes to the concluding point at the ford of Little river--Under these considerations it is thought fair that if the waggoners and travellers will make use of the new road that they fhould contribute by tolls to the repairs which they themselves make necefsary, especially when they have it entirely in their option to use the old road...* Signed by Leven Powell, Pres., Ch. Simms, Phineas Janney, Jacob Hoffman, August. J. Smith, Directors. Copy of proceedings of meeting of stockholders. *Reported.* Box C.

---

[73] <u>Shepherd</u>, Vol. 3, Chapter 29, pp. 225-27, "An ACT appointing commissioners to view and mark out a way for a road from Thornton's gap in the Blue Ridge to the Little river turnpike road leading to Alexandria, and to raise a certain sum of money by lottery for opening the said road," passed January 3, 1806.

[74] <u>Acts Passed at a General Assembly</u>, 1808, Chapter LXXVIII, p. 72, "An act to amend an act entitled 'An act to incorporate a company for establishing a Turnpike Road from the intersection of Duke Street in the Town of Alexandria, with the west line of the District of Columbia, to the ford of Little River, where the Turnpike Road now crosses it,'" passed January 27, 1809. Refers to a previous act passed January 28, 1802, and requests additional time for completion, the further period of five years, and additional stock; refers to act passed January 19, 1803, which permitted to raise by subscription in similar manner a further sum not to exceed $50,000; also <u>Acts Passed at a General Assembly</u>, 1808, Chapter LXXXVIII, p. 78, "An act to Incorporate a Company to establish a Turnpike from the Town of Leesburg in Loudoun County to the Little River Turnpike," passed February 3, 1809.

Legislative Petitions of the Town and County of Alexandria, Virginia

President and Directors of Little River Turnpike Company.
1808, 16 DEC. A523. Permission to issue $50,000 worth of new stock, in shares of $100, and also to collect toll on any part of the road as it is finished, in proportion to the toll allowed on ten miles. And farther, an extension of time allowed for completion of road to five years. Petitioners claim operations have proceeded at an unexpected expence, and under circumstances, the most discouraging, the Company have completed twenty miles of the road, which they were authorized to pave, and have advanced within five or six miles of the point where the contemplated pavement will intersect the road leading from Wormley's and Keys' gaps in the Blue-ridge, by Leesburg and the Gum-spring, to Alexandria. *That, at this state of their progrefs they find their funds exhausted, and that without further Legislative aid, they will be compelled to suspend, or abandon an enterprize on which the Commerce of the City of Alexandria and the agriculture of a large and flourishing portion of Virginia materially depend.* Signed by Leven Powell, Pres., Ch. Simms, Jacob Hoffman, Phineas Janney, Charles Fenton Mercer, Directors. *Reported.* Box C.

Little River Turnpike Company.
1809, 13 DEC. A524. Act vesting in the president and directors the power to value material used in building the road; also an increase in the amount of stock not to exceed 150 shares. The road will cost more than the whole amount of stock the company is at present authorized to issue. Signed by Leven Powell, Pres., Ch. Fenton Mercer, Jacob Hoffman, and Hugh Smith, Directors. *Reported.* Box C.

Citizens.
c.1810. A631. Modification of act passed at last session, the object of which is to prevent the circulation of private bank notes. Without calling in question, the policy of said act or condemning the principle, petitioners ask for such amendment as will preclude them from the peculiar hardships they now experience. Signed by Gerard Alexander, John J. Fitzhugh, Thomas Harrison, Geo. Fitzhugh, William C. Fitzhugh. Two duplicates signed by 64 persons. Original not found.

Frederica Augusta Beeler (d. 1822), Wife of Christian Louis Beeler.
1810, 20 DEC. A525. Act vesting in petitioner, who is a native of Germany, the Commonwealth's right to a lot in Alexandria left by her late husband, Matthew Eakin [d. 1807], a citizen of Virginia. *Reasonable.* Box C.

To the Hon'ble The Speaker and House of Delegates of the Commonwealth of Virginia.

The petition of Frederica Augusta Beeler, wife of Lewis Beeler but formerly the wife of Matthew Eakin, respectfully represents:

That your petitioner is a native of Germany and at a very early period of her life intermarried with the said Matthew Eakin, also a native of Germany, and shortly after their marriage that is to say about fifteen years ago, they left their native Country and came to the Commonwealth of Virginia and fixed their residence in the Town of Alexandria. They came to that Town in great poverty, destitute of friends, and with nothing to depend upon but their industry; they accordingly applied themselves to personal labour, and by their exertions and frugality in the course of a few years acquired some property. Matthew Eakin became a citizen of the Commonwealth of Virginia and some time afterwards he became a purchaser of a lott of six acres of land in the vicinity of Alexandria but within the County of Fairfax. Upon this lott he made some improvements and he possessed and held the same untill the time of his death which happened somewhere about three years ago. He died intestate and left no child or connexion in this Country other than your petitioner. Your petitioner is advised that under the 14th section of the act of this commonwealth concerning descents, she became entitled to the said lott of land in consequence of the death of the said Matthew Eakin intestate and without heirs as aforesaid, but if she should not have been truly advised upon this point, she has been encouraged to hope that the assembly would relinquish to her the right which the Commonwealth may have to the said lott of land. Your petitioner therefore respectfully entreats that a law may pass granting to your petitioner the Commonwealth's right to the said lott of land.

And your Petitioner as in duty bound, shall every pray &c.

Signed, Frederica Augusta Beeler.

Certified as to knowing Matthew Eakin: Thos. Swann, N. Fitzhugh, G. Deneale and Thomson Mason.

William Thomas Swann (d. 1820).

1811, 9 DEC. No number (also see A528). Fairfax County. To the Hon'ble the General Assembly of the Commonwealth of Virginia. The petition of William T. Swann, respectfully represents-- That your petitioner was born in the state of Maryland and removed from thence to the Town of Alexandria some time about the year 1797, during your petitioners residence in Alexandria his father a resident of the state of Maryland bequeathed to him after the death of your petitioner's mother, sundry slaves. Your petitioner after the death of his father was desirous of settling in Virginia and his mother would have permitted him to have taken possession of the slaves devised to him and to have removed these into Virginia, if the laws then in force would have authorized such removal. But at that time the laws of Virginia did not admit of such removal in consequence of which in the year 1807 your petitioner returned to Maryland and continued in that state until the death of his mother which happened some time in the year 1810. Immediately after this your petitioner removed with most of the slaves devised to him into the District of Columbia where they have lived ever since. Since your petitioner's return to the District of Columbia he is the more desirous of removing into Virginia for the right of his wife he is now the owner of lands in different places in Virginia, and the very tract upon which he now resides is situated partly in Virginia and partly in the District of Columbia. Your petitioner saith that if at the time of the passage of the law of the last session of your humble body he had resided upon that

Legislative Petitions of the Town and County of Alexandria, Virginia

part of the land situated in Virginia he presumes he would have been entitled to have removed the said slaves into the said state, But as he resided at the period aforesaid within the District of Columbia he is not embraced by the law. Your petitioner has been encouraged to hope that as his interest as well as his wishes lead him to a residence in Virginia that your humble body would permit him to remove with himself at least such of his slaves as he shall have acquired by devise. Your petitioner would be ready to give such proof touching the requirement of his said slaves by devise as aforesaid as shall be deemed necessary by your humble body. The slaves which he holds of this description are: Jack, Harry, Frank, Ned, Henson, Old Harry, Sall, Nace. Your petitioner holds several others in the District of Columbia connected with one of his aforesaid slaves, that is to say Henny the wife of Harry herein before mentioned, and her four children James, Harry, Oswald and Frank. Your petitioner also holds several slaves in right of his wife whom he married in the District of Columbia and which said slaves have always resided within the District of Columbia, and if a removal of these slaves with your petitioner should be consistent with the interests of the Commonwealth he humbly requests that he may be permitted to remove them with those devised to him as herein before mentioned. Your petitioner therefore humbly requests that a law may be passed authorizing him to remove the slaves above mentioned into the Commonwealth of Virginia. And your petitioner as in duty bound shall ever pray. Signed, Wm. Thos. Swann. No note on action. Box C.

Cuthbert Powell (1775-1849).
1811, 19 DEC. A526. Permission to bring into State a slave, Jenny, with her children. Petitioner is about to return to his home in Loudoun and under the act of January 21, 1804, he is allowed to bring with him into the State only such slaves as he formerly took out of it. He purchased this woman, a native of Virginia, in Alexandria. *Reasonable.* Box C.

Cuthbert Powell (1775-1849).
1812, 2 DEC. A527. Same as A526. Note signed by Joseph Riddle. *Bill drawn.* Box C.

William Thomas Swann (d. 1820).
1812, 11 DEC. A528. Permission to bring fifteen slaves from Alexandria County into Virginia. The real estate of Charles Alexander [1737-1806], decd., is situated partly in the District of Columbia and partly in Virginia, and as no division of the said estate has been made among the children of the said Charles Alexander, your petitioner and his wife have resided at the mansion house[75] of the said Charles Alexander in the District of Columbia... *Reasonable.* Box C.

---

[75] The home of this Charles Alexander was named "Preston," and situated on the south side of the Four Mile Run estuary.

The petition of Wm. Thos. Swann of the County of Alexandria in the District of Columbia respectfully represents: That your petitioner married the daughter of Charles Alexander, late of the County of Fairfax and Commonwealth of Virginia, and in right of his wife became entitled to a share of his real estate. Your petitioner saith that the real estate of Charles Alexander decd. is situated partly in the District of Columbia and partly in Virginia and as no division of the said estate has been made among the children of the said Charles Alexander, your petitioner and his wife have resided at the mansion house of the said Charles Alexander in the District of Columbia. Your petitioner saith that a division of the said estate is now about to be made and the portion will be allotted to his wife will as your petitioner verily believes be situated in Virginia. Your petitioner also has land of his own in the County of Fairfax upon which he is very desirous of settling but as he cannot remove his slaves upon either of the said estates, he will be exposed to great inconvenience in the use of the said property. The slaves which your petitioner wishes to remove into Virginia are all in the County of Alexandria and have been there for a considerable time past. They are slaves of good character raised in the families of your petitioner and his wife attached to and anxious to continue with them. Your petitioner indulges the hope that your Hon'ble body will permit him to remove his said slaves upon his lands in the County of Fairfax. The names of his slaves are: Harry, Frank, Ned, Jack, John, Joe, Hanson, Nace, Lucy, Henny and her children, viz. James, Harry, Ozzy, Frank, Mary. The slaves in right of his wife cannot be yet ascertained the division not having yet taken place. Signed, Wm. Thos. Swann. Cert. Abraham Faw, J.P.

Henry King.
1815, November Term. No number. District of Columbia, to wit: Henry King who was committed by a Justice of the Peace of the County of Alexandria on the charge of stealing from the waggoner of Mercer & Cooke, sundry Bank notes of the Merchants Bank of Alexandria was this day brought before the Court upon a Writ of Habeas Corpus and it appearing upon the examination of James Anderson, William Cooke and Elijah Chenault that the offence was committed in the County of Fairfax and State of Virginia, it is ordered that the said Henry King be remanded to the jail of this County and be there detained until otherwise disposed of according to law. A copy, test. G. Deneale. <u>U.S. v. Henry King</u>. Box C.

Little River Turnpike Company.
1818, 23 DEC. A531. Same as A529, below. *Bill reported.* Box C.

Little River Turnpike Company.
1819, 22 DEC. A529. Company has, according to charter, completed the road from the intersection of Duke Street in Alexandria to the ford of Little River. Charter required the road to be fifty feet wide, with which regulation company has complied, and the space beyond the paved road has been fixed up as a dirt summer road. This has been used, however,

at all seasons and has been cut to pieces by heavy wagons, much to the detriment of the paved road. Expenses of keeping dirt road in repair consume the profit and petitioners ask that they may be allowed to discontinue said road. Signed by Phineas Janney, Pres., Jonah Thompson, Secy. *Rejected.* Box C.

Citizens of Fairfax and Loudoun.
1828, 16 DEC. A530. Act requiring Little River Turnpike Company to charge only half toll on return wagons carrying loads of all weights, instead of charging, as at present, full toll on return wagons carrying loads of five hundred pounds and no toll on those wagons carrying less. The Turnpike Company is willing to make the change, which is in accordance with the general turnpike law. *Reasonable.* Box C.

Signed by Robert Allison, Gabriel Fox, Jno. H. Halley, Henry Fairfax, Stephen Murphy, John W. Ashton, Elijah Hutchison, W.B. Butler, Henry Shacklett, P.B. Bradley, Benjn. F. Higgs, Ely Hutchison, R.H. Cockerille, George Whaley, Joshua Hutchison, Gus. H. Scott, James Williams, Robt. Bayly, Henry Duncan, Alexander Stuart, Chas. Stewart, Peter Gooding, and W.H. Gooding. Duplicate petition from Little River Turnpike Company.

Alexandria Canal Company.
1834, 1 FEB. A532. Grant of aid, either by subscription to company's stock or in other ways, to carry through petitioner's undertaking, which is the bringing of the Chesapeake and Ohio Canal to Alexandria. Commencing on the line of the Chesapeake and Ohio Canal a short distance above the Town of George Town, the proposed Canal will cross the [Potomac] River by an Aqueduct one thousand and fifty feet long to an embankment or causeway connecting it with the Southern Shore, and proceeding thence for the most part on an elevated plane, will at the distance of seven miles reach the Harbor of Alexandria." Signed by Thomson Mason, President, Phineas Janney, Wm. Fowle, Robert H. Miller, Alexander Hunter, Hugh Smith, and B. Hooe. *Reasonable to subscribe for 1,000 shares.* Box C.

Alexandria Canal Company.[76]
1835, 6 JAN. A533. Company was organized to connect Chesapeake and Ohio Canal, via Washington and Cumberland [counties], with Alexandria. The canal will be carried across the river by aqueduct 1,050 feet long and thence to Alexandria. Cost has been estimated to be $372,204. Sum of $231,200 has been raised, of which $150,000 has been spent, and $213,190 has been secured, leaving $18,010 to be called in. Chesapeake and Ohio Canal is 100 feet broad and seven deep; it stops at Georgetown. Potomac River from Georgetown to Washington Bridge,

---

[76] Congress chartered the Alexandria Canal Company on 26 MAY 1830. The canal existed from 1843-1886.

a distance of three miles, has a narrow sinuous channel, varying from nine to eleven feet in depth at different tides. Below Washington the channel is impeded by sand bars, so that only vessels of light draft can navigate it. On the other hand a boat entering the canal at Washington will be carried seven miles to Alexandria, where river is 1,200 feet wide and 40 feet deep, giving an unimpeded passage to the ocean. Work is important and petitioners ask aid from Virginia. Signed by Thomson F. Mason, pres., Phineas Janney, Wm. Fowle, Robert H. Miller, John Cohagan, Hugh Smith, and B. Hooe. *Reasonable.* Box C.

William Wedderburn.
1835, 12 DEC. A534. Grant of aid by State. Petitioner saw service in the Revolution, both as a militia man and as an assistant to his father, who was a surgeon in the Williamsburg hospital. Petition relates an incident of the siege of Yorktown. *Resolution reported.* Rejected on 30 DEC 1835. Box C.

The petition of William Wedderburn, of Alexandria, D.C. (a native of Virginia), respectfully shows:

That he was drafted from King & Queen County, Va. about the first of May 1781, to serve for two months under Capt. John Bayliss in a company of Col. Harrison's U.S. Artillery, commanded by Capt. Samuel Eddons, & stationed at Gloucesterton; which he accordingly did in two days after he was called upon. His duty while in this service, was very arduous; the number of men being small & the stations to be guarded numerous, every man had to mount guard eight hours in every 24. After Lord Cornwallis got to Williamsburg with his army from the south, it was expected that a part of his force would be send from Williamsburg across the York river to surprise us; and we were consequently kept most vigilantly on duty. On Sunday, the 4th day of July 1781, about 10 o'clock a.m., Lord Cornwallis came down with a company of horse & one of infantry from Williamsburg. The horse dismounted under a shady cover near Windmill Point, waiting it was supposed the coming up of the rear guard. Before this, however, Capt. Edd<u>e</u>ns ordered a fire from our fort from three long 24# cannon, which caused them to remount immediately & make for to York, which not being defended by any armed force, they entered without opposition. Their rear having heard our firing, also entered York by a more southern route. About 4 o'clock p.m. their horse[s] were seen proceeding southwardly, it was supposed to Hampton. Capt. Edd<u>e</u>ns immediately ordered a long barge to be manned, armed & equipped, & to proceed as quick as possible to York. At the same time your petitioner was ordered to mount guard at the extreme end of Gloucester Point & to keep a vigilant look out. Soon after he took his station, he saw several men come from the town, disguised by turned coats, with trailed arms, & secrete[d] themselves behind some long wooden buildings; & shortly after, several squads of from 20 to 50 men, proceeded in the same manner to the same spot. At this time (our barge being opposite the lower part of York), several women on the hill opposite the barge, waved their white handkerchiefs as signal for the barge to return, which signal they continued as the barge rowed off & on. Lieut. Camp now put the barge about & stood up the river; and, when he got opposite the wooden buildings before mentioned, began to put in for the shore. When he had arrived within about 50 yards of it, the petitioner fired an alarm gun for him to return, upon which the men who were secreted behind the buildings ran out & fired upon the barge, the crew of which returned their fire, altho' the balls flew hotly around them. A part of the crew, however, continued rowing & carried her out of the reach of the fire to the place from whence she set out. As she approached the shore, your petitioner advanced to meet her. Lieut. Camp sprung ashore, seized my hand & declared that I had saved him & his crew from death or capture. The crew were much rejoiced at their narrow escape-- not one of them having been wounded.

After serving out this tour, we were dismissed with the thanks of our Captain for our conduct, while under his command, and returned to our homes. After your petitioner had been at his father's some 8 or 10 days, Lord Cornwallis came with his fleet & army up York river, & took and fortified York & Gloucesterton. Your petitioner was then warned to join Capt. Richard Anderson's company, which he did the same day. After being under his command about two weeks, he was dismissed, as he had just served out his turn in Gloucesterton.

Soon after this, a hospital was established near the residence of your petitioner's father, who was appointed Assistant Surgeon thereof, under Dr. Anthony Gardner, its Surgeon. To this hospital your petitioner repaired & assisted in preparing & distributing the medicines to be administered to the sick, of whom the house was generally as full as it could hold. He remained in this service several weeks.

Your petitioner has used every exertion to find out some person who served with him, but without success. Lieut. Camp died about eighteen years after the war, & his widow remembers nothing of the occurrences above detailed. Capt. Eddens has been dead more than 30 years.

All the compensation your petitioner ever received for his services was a certificate worth about $2.50 or $4, in the year 1783. He is now 71 years old, in feeble health, in straitened circumstances, & with two persons (a wife & child) to support besides himself.

Your petitioner prays your Honorable Body to grant him such assistance as may seem just; & he as in duty bound, will every pray. Signed, W. Wedderburn.

District of Columbia, Alexandria County. William Wedderburn, the within named petitioner, personally appeared before me a Justice of the Peace, for the County aforesaid, & made oath in due form of law, that the matters & things in his annexed petition contained are truly set forth. Given under my hand this [blank] day of November 1835. Not signed.

Heirs of Dr. William Rumney (d. 1783).[77]

1836, 23 JAN. A535. William Rumney, a surgeon in Virginia Continental line from March 1778, was director of hospital at Alexandria for some time before the close of the war. Petitioners ask for grant of bounty land last year, but were refused. They again apply to legislature. Signed by John Adam, James Dade, Robert Adam, and heirs of Honoria McClean, by Thomas Hord, their attorney. *Referred.* Box C.

To the Senate and House of Delegates of the Virginia Assembly--

Your petitioners, John Adam & Jane Dade of Alexandria, Robert Adam of Ohio, and the infant children of Honoria McClean, decd., formerly Barry of Loudoun County, being the devisees of the late Robert Adam of Fairfax Co., who was sole devisee of William Rumney, decd., late of Alexandria-- Respectfully beg leave to represent that said William Rumney was duly appointed Senior Surgeon in the Virginia Line on Continental Establishment in the War of the Revolution, as early as the month of March 1778, and in that Capacity continued to serve till the end of said War, and for some time before the close of the War had the direction of the Continental Hospital at Alexandria-- That in former times as well as of late years as your petitioners are informed and believe, Surgeons of the Rank & pay of Doctr. Rumney received Virginia Land bounty of the same amount that officers in the Line were entitled to, receiving the same pay & rations & believing that they as the representatives of Dr. Rumney might lawfully claim said land, they have in the course of the last year petitioned His Excellency the Governor for its allowance, which from some cause unknown to your petitioners was rejected--

The claim of your petitioners it will be perceived is founded upon record proof extracted from the Revolutionary Archives of the State, and the testimony of several respectable persons who have a perfect recollection of Dr. Rumney and his services-- This being the case they confidently hope and believe that the same measure of justice will be awarded to them in this case as other have received under like circumstances-- It further appears from the Auditor's certificate that Dr. Rumney's pay pr. day was at the rate of 24/-- and rations accordingly, which your petitioners believe will entitle them to the same amt. of bounty Land that officers of the same pay & rations in the Line received, and that according to that rate the amount would be such allowed to a full Colonel-- All these matters they submit to the judgment and tender consideration of your Honorable bodies, and pray that the Register may by law be authorized to issue warrants to them accordingly & they will

---

[77] Margie G. Brown, *Genealogical Abstracts, Revolutionary War Veterans, Script Act 1852* (Decorah, Ia.: The Anundsen Publishing Co., 1990), p. 18, Dr. William Rumney served in the Virginia Continental line, then became a surgeon in the Continental hospital at Alexandria, Va. He died 9 JAN 1783 in Fairfax Co., Va. without issue and left his estate to his friend Dr. Robert Adam who died in 1789. Robert Adam had four children: (1) John Adam, in Alexandria in 1856; (2) Robert Adam, in Ohio in 1856; (3) Jane Adam Dade, widow in 1856; and (4) Mary Adam, died before 1838, widow of Daniel Darry, and who had a daughter Honoria Barry, wife of John McLean [sic] of Loudoun County.

Legislative Petitions of the Town and County of Alexandria, Virginia

ever pray.
Signed by John Adam, Jane Dade, Robt. Adam, the heirs of Honoria McClean by Thomas Hord, their agent attorney in fact.

The petitioners respectfully ask that the copies of papers herewith filed may be sufficient to refer your Hon. bodies to the originals on file in the Secretaries office-- The proc'ss of business at the present time is such that certified copies can scarcely be made out. Doctors Fouchee & Julian & Doctr. Walter McClurg have recd. land from Va. and numerous others under similar circumstances.[78]

Heirs of William Ramsay.
1836, 23 JAN. A536. Petitioners Eliza Blacklock, Robert T. Ramsay, Anne McCarty Blacklock, Jane A. Ramsay, George W.D. Ramsay, of Alexandria, and Amelia Barry [Mrs. Robert], of Baltimore, and Daniel Porter, Sarah R. Porter, Betsey Porter and Sally Cawood, of Washington, and Ann Allison and John Allison, of Frederick, Maryland, ask for a bounty land grant in right of William Ramsay.[79] The latter was commissioned a surgeon's mate in 1777 and was in service until the end of the war. Signed, Thomas Hord, attorney for the heirs. *Referred.* Box C.

President and Directors of Fauquier and Alexandria Turnpike Company.
1843, 19 DEC. A537. Modification of the act of 1834 regarding lotteries in so far as said act concerns the grant made to the Fauquier and Alexandria Turnpike Company in the act of 1829. Lottery is only means of saving road from ruin. By the original act passed, no time limitation placed on lottery; however by another act passed 25 FEB 1834, the drawing of lotteries was limited to the first day of January 1840. The road lies wholly in the Commonwealth, commencing at Warrenton and terminating at its junction with the Little River Turnpike road a little to the westward of Fairfax Courthouse. Signed, Thomas Smith, Treas.

---

[78] Hening, Vol. 10, 1779-1781, Chapter IX, p. 141, "An act for giving a bounty of lands to the chaplains, surgeons, and surgeon's mates of regiments or brigades raised by this state, and upon continental establishment."
[79] Margie G. Brown, Genealogical Abstracts, Revolutionary War Veterans, Scrip Act 1852 (Decorah, Ia.: Anundsen Publishing Co., 1990), p. 356, references Application 1513, 1542; Alexandria, D.C. Court, 15 JAN 1835, and Washington, D.C. Court, 6 JUL 1837. File seems to indicate that Dr. William Ramsay of Alexandria, Va., son of Dr. William Ramsay, died during the Revolutionary War at Brooklyn, New York. We know he was alive on 14 JUL 1785, when as *William Ramsay (the late William Ramsay's eldest son)*, he leased a lot in Alexandria to Dennis Ramsay [James D. Munson, Alexandria, Virginia Alexandria Hustings Court Deeds, 1783-1797 (Bowie, Md.: Heritage Books, Inc., 1990), p. 15; Alexandria Hustings Court Deeds, Bk. B, p. 168]. By his will dated 21 JUL 1787, proved 21 SEP 1795, Dr. Wiliam Ramsay made provision for his natural son/heir William Ramsay alias Tucker [Wesley E. Pippenger, Alexandria, Virginia Wills, Administrations and Guardianships, 1786-1800 (Westminster, Md.: Family Line Publications, 1994), pp. 39-40]. A notice of his death appeared in the Alexandria Gazette, 22 NOV 1787, p. 2. He was unmarried, and his estate went to his eldest brother, Colonel Dennis Ramsay of Alexandria, Va. and his heirs. Munson, p. 101, shows exerpt from the will of David Arell: *if both die, then to brother Samuel except the property in Town Devised to my Daughter in which case I give to William Ramsay natural Son of Doctor William Ramsay of Alexandria.*

Legislative Petitions of the Town and County of Alexandria, Virginia

Box C.

Citizens of the Town and County of Alexandria.
1846, 29 JAN. A538. Passage of provisional act by Legislature accepting the retrocession to Virginia of portion of the District of Columbia south of Potomac River.[80] *Referred.* Box C.

Signed by Jos. Eaches, Robt. Jamieson, R. Johnston, Thos. E. Baird, Wm. Veitch, James English, Lewis McKenzie, Wm. N. Mills, John B. *, Edgar Snowden, Geo. R. Adams, C.C. Bradley, Wm. R. Ball, Benj. Thomas, Thos. A. Waters, Thos. Burrage, R.T. Ramsay, Mark E. Masterson, D. Wright, George Johnson, William D. Price, E. Burchell, Geo. O. Dixion, Thos. Smith, Charles Neale, J.I. Thomas, Wm. N. Brown, James Entwisle, Samuel Jones, George Davis, James D. Bryan, John E. Henderson, M. D. Corse, Richd. C. Smith, William Boswell, Ellis L. Price, E.C. Horwell, A. Lammond, Benj. H. Lambert, Robt. Bell, W.C. Johnston, Wm. Fountain, William N. McVeigh, Wells A. Harper, James L. Chamberlain, W.H. Marbury, A. Fleming, Robt. Wilson Wheat, James Irwin, Francis A. Marbury, John Hart, Geo. W. Maxwell, Saml. Evans, *, Emanuel Francis, John P. Whitmore, Richd. Y. Cross, Robert J. Nash, Thomas Travers, W.H. McKnight, James Young, Ebenezer Bacon, James H. McVeigh, Jesse H. McVeigh, Isaac *, Henry L. Stuart, John F. Dyer, Wm. C. Bontz, Benoni Wheat, Thos. Marbury, Matthew Baird, G.W.D. Ramsay, Isaac Kell, P.G. Uhler, Chs. B. Shirley, Charles H. Cowman, James Spinks, Wm. H. Irwin, Robt. Brockett, Thos. M. White, Jas. D. Kerr, R.J. Andrews, Geo. C. Harvey, Law. B. Taylor, J.T. Evans, Richard M. Scott, F.S. Brockett, Charles T. Stuart, B.T. Plummer, Charles S. Price, Louis A. Cazenove, John T. Johnston, Henry Mansfield, James F. Carlin, James Boyd, Francis Garcia, Benjamin Guy, Henry Simpson, Samuel H. Devaughn, Stephen Kent, Edward Short, Chas. Hawkins, S. Norflet, Milton Glasgow, Jas. T. Jenkins, Chs. W. Veitch, Wm. N. Berkley, R. Zimmerman, Wm. W. Adam, John L. Brown, Francis Stabler, John Parkins, Richard Robinson, Charles Tenesson, J.H. Higdon, John I. Norton, Thos. P. Brown, William Arnold, John W. Campbell, James W. Sears, T.A. Koones, Wm. A. Dean, James G. Carey, Thomas W. Wood, David Appich, Samuel R. Adams, C.C. Berry, W. Corse, Jno. S. Grubb, Leml. D. Harper, W.D. Massey, M.P. Veitch, John Reis, Jno. Clark, A. Lockwood, O.C. Hewes, S. King Shay, W. Rhodes, T. Gardner Preston, Geo. L. Deeton, Josiah H. Davis, Jr., W.J. Entwisle, Wm. R. Ball, George Bryan, Peter G. Henderson, John Arnold, William Page, Jas. C. Goods, Josiah B. Hills, Gunter Evans, Wm. Francis Lockwood, Wm. Rock, B.F. Willis, Daniel D. Herbert, Jas. E. Mankin, Jesse C. Green, Jr., John T. Skinner, E.R. Kiefer [or Kuhn], Robt. G. Violett, Geo. H. Smoot, George Allison, Wm. Phillips, Wm. Mersham, C.F. Brown, P.B. Vernon, Thos.

---

[80] See also *Acts of the General Assembly*, 1847-1847, Chapter 53, "An ACT to extend the jurisdiction of the commonwealth of Virginia over the county of Alexandria," passed March 13, 1847, pp. 41-48. Alexandria was retroceded in 1846. It had formed part of Fairfax County before the cession, but on its reunion to Virginia, it was made into Alexandria County, the smallest in the State.

Legislative **Petitions of the Town and County of Alexandria, Virginia**

Marbury, John T. Ball, John Ball, William R. Campbell, Henry Boyer, Jacob Piles, James Moody, James Loyd, William Ward, Henry Thompson, Joseph Plant, Wm. Padgett, Jr., Clo. Jefferson, Francis R. Davidson, Joseph Crook, Newman Cross, Jas. M. Darnall, Charles W. Nowles, Robert Murry, John Hutchinson, John W. Ba<u>ngs</u>, John Waymoth, R.E. Buchanan, Charles H. Cowman, William Robinson, William R. Larrence, John Simms, Nathaniel Goodwin, John Larrence, Samuel Sanderson, John Brooke, Thomas Cravin, William Devaughn, French Johnston, Wm. Pomery, George Tatspaugh, Gilmore Nowles, William Herne, Thomas Burns, W.A. Wharton, Truman Short, Judson Mitchell, James H. Robinson, Henry Peel, Marion Walker, Smith & Clark, James Walker, Thos. Whittington, J.G. Swaine, James W. Simpson, John Elliott, Samuel Benton, Charles *, Jno. B. McGlue, Joseph Lupton, Thomas M. Mills, David Williams, Thomas Webster, Sandy Beach, Stephen Ball, Chapin Lee, Wm. B. Massey, Edward Daingerfield, Alexander M. Rose, John Risdon, William Lanphier, D.C. Smith, John L. Pascoe, H.F. Zimmerman, John F. Williams, J.R. *, Wesley Avery, John Demain, Harrison Bradley, Geo. F. Huguety, Nailor Webster, Wm. C. Reynolds, Wm. Powell, James H. Devaughn, H.B. Whittington, James C. Clark, Francis L. Smith, P.E. Hoffman, John Taylor, J.D. Lakenan, David Rice, James L. Henderson, James Carroll, Wm. Mankin, George Fletcher, George H. Markell, George M. Bayne, S.M. Wilkins, Hugh C. Smith, John West, James Buchanan, Thomas Burrage, Thos. Williams, George Plum, Jacob <u>Fortney</u>, Jas. W. Sears, Edwin T. Allen, Benjamin H. Jenkins, James T. Jenkins, James F. Carlin, Washington C. Page, W.A. Miller, Ro. Crupper, James Gough, Daniel Cawood, John T. Armstrong, N. Hicks, John W. Violett, Wesley Summers, Lucien Peyton, Joshua Taylor, James A. Javins, William R. Emerson, Jas. E. McGraw, Luis Nolte, C. Mellius, Samuel Tucker, William Burge<u>ss</u>, N.D. Harmon, John Thompson, Jacob R. _lson, Thomas Baggett, O. Fairfax, John J. Blue, Alfred A. Blue, James Padgett, James Fortney, Charles Mankins, L.E. Skidmore, John Sherrer, Frederick *, John M. Monroe, Wm. _linstine, Henry Cryss, Nathan Kell, Richard Bell, Robert Jackson, John H. Griffith, Abel D. Warfield, Charles Belden, Frederick Daws, Nicholas Barry, John A. Williams, John Travis, George W. Nelson, Joseph Padgett, William Armstrong, Thomas Barney, James O.C. Hoskins, Paton Crouse, Aquila Emerson, James L. Adams, and Thos. Slatford.

Citizens of the Town and County of Alexandria.
1846, 30 JAN. A539. Same as A538, citizens are anxious for retrocession to Virginia. *Referred.* Box C.

Signed by Wm. D. Nutt, P.C. Claughton, Wm. W. Hoxton, Peter R. Burrly, John Lawson, *, Wm. Veitch, Law. B. Taylor, Winfred [his mark] Sidebottom, Thos. B. Creighton, William Jefferson, C.C. Smoot, Jr., Robison Johnson, William Webster, John Webster, Henry Pollard, T. McCormick, Henry Cook, Christian Folmar, Jesse Ro<u>se</u>, George Webster, John Pettit, <u>B</u>.C. Milburn, Tildon Easton, Robt. R. Snyder, William Pollard, Wm. Davis, John Welsh, James Davis, William Lyles, R. V<u>ernon</u>,

Legislative Petitions of the Town and County of Alexandria, Virginia

W. Hemsley, John Hatchell, W. Harris, James Vernon, James Quaid, John Sprague, Toby Nightingale, Peyton Clark, James Chatham, Henry Chatham, Robt. Allison, John T. Mills, J.T. Bladen, W. Fugitt, John Nightingale, M.C. Ewing, John Ward, William Geiseling, Joshua Grady, and Wm. Owens.

Duplicate signed by Robt. I. Smith, A.S. Willis, G. Harper, Jas. Stoop, Anth. Chs. Cazenove, James Fossett, Chas. A. Henderson, Clemt. B. Ellis, Jno. Going, Wm. N. Rowe, Charles C. Smoot, John Wood, William Gregory, J.M. Martin, John H. Brent, George Bryan, Rob. M. Larmour, W.G. Cazenove, Henry Daingerfield, Edw. B. Powell, Wm. L. Powell, Jos. H. Hampson, John T.B. Perry, Danl. F. Hooe, J.C. Swann, Jas. Douglass, Edw. S. Hough, Edmd. Green, Isaac Buckingham, J. Roach, Edw. C. Fletcher, John Richards, Turner Dixon, A.G. Newton, James Sheehy, C.W. Violett, Jno. White, Harrison, Bradley, John G. Breithaupt, A. McLean, Joseph Carson, John Stephenson, John Howell, Jas. D. Kerr, Jr., J. Muir, Wm. Morgan, E. Claxton, John A. Fields, John Brener, John Norris, Jas. H. Clarridge, E. Plummer, T. Ward, T.W. Ashby, Dennis R. Blacklock, C.M. & F. Taylor, Geo. K. Witmer, Saml. J. McCormick, and W.A. Miller.

Second duplicate signed by Wm. Mankin, R.B. Alexander, S. Handy, W. Ennis, R. Russell, John Burch, William Johnson, John Rundel, George Hill, Jr., David Cooley, J.W. Sewell, Charles Kirby, Wm. Nelson, and Thomas *.

A Portion of the Citizens of the County of Alexandria.
1846, 8 DEC. A540. Suspension of action on part of State in regard to retrocession of Alexandria until it is determined by the Supreme Court whether the retrocession is constitutional. Protest by citizens of Alexandria against retrocession on the ground that it is unconstitutional and also that the wishes of only a minority were consulted.

Retrocession of the County of Alexandria... That on behalf of ourselves and of a large majority of our fellow-citizens of the rural portion of the county of Alexandria, we solemnly and respectfully protest against the act of retrocession passed by the congress of the United States, at the first session of the 29th congress, retroceding, under certain conditions, the county aforesaid to the commonwealth of Virginia, for the reasons following namely: that the country portion of the inhabitants of the said county were not consulted upon the matter of retrocession, or advised of the intention to seek a change of our allegiance, the whole proceeding having been concocted and determined upon a secret meeting of the corporation of Alexandria, an irresponsible body, having no manner of right to act upon the subject; That we believe the legislature of the commonwealth have been misinformed with respect to the wishes of the citizens of the country portion of the county as well as many of the town of Alexandria itself... Dated 2 DEC 1846. Signed by Anthony R. Fraser, Wesley Carlin, Henry Hardy, Richard

Legislative **Petitions of the Town and County of Alexandria, Virginia**

Sothoron, Nicholas Febrey, Walter S. Alexander, Samuel Birch, Horatio Ball and Wash. T. Harper. House Document (Va.) No. 5. No note on action. Alexandria County Box.

President and Directors of Farmers' Bank of Alexandria.
1846, 12 DEC. A541. Grant of charter to bank. Retrocession of Alexandria will cut off banking facilities of town unless State charters are issued, as the Farmers' Bank and the Bank of Potomac are private institutions and as such prohibited from doing business under the laws of Virginia. Signed by Robt. Jamieson, Pres., Louis A. Cazenove, Francis L. Smith, Lewis McKenzie, Dennis Johnston, J.H. Hooff, G.W.D. Ramsay, Cassius F. Lee, and D. Minor. *Referred to Select Committee.* Box C.

President and Trustees of Bank of Potomac.
1846, 12 DEC. A542. State charter for bank. This bank and the Farmers' Bank are the only banks in territory given back to Virginia and, as private institutions, are prohibited from doing business under the State laws. Alexandria, Decr. 10th 1846. Signed by Phineas Janney, President of the Board of Trustees of the Bank of Potomac, Hugh Smith, W. Fowle, Wm. Gregory, Geo. H. Smoot, A.P. Gover, Robert H. Miller, and John B. Daingerfield. *Referred to Select Committee.* Box C.

Citizens of the Town of Alexandria.
1846, 12 DEC. A543. Grant of charters to Bank of Potomac and Farmers' Bank of Alexandria. That by the retrocession of the Town and County of Alexandria, the citizens thereof, and the adjacent country, will cease to enjoy any banking facilities, so soon as the jurisdiction and laws of Virginia shall be extended over said territory: that the Bank of Potomac, and Farmers' Bank of Alexandira (the only Banks within said territory), are private associates, and as such, prohibited from doing business, by the laws of Virginia. Signed by Jno. Corse & Son, James F. Carlin, Chas. McKnight, W.A. Taylor, Saml. Solomon, Edwd. Burchell, Law. B. Taylor, Jacob Roxbury, and A.G. Newton. *Referred.* Box C.

Duplicate signed by Geo. W. Johnston & Co., Francis Garcia, George H. Markell, Josiah B. Hills, James Entwisle, Joseph G. Carr, C.C. Berry, J.G. Cobbs, Robt. M. Minor, Hartly Crawford, R. Crupper, John D. Brown, J.J. Wheat & Bros., Thomas Sanford, George Fletcher, Geo. White, L.W. Hooff, J.N. Harper, J.I. Wheat, Wm. Mc__, Chas. A. Henderson, Edw. B. Powell, Richd. Y. Cross, John Lawson, John T. Ballenger, R.G. Violett, Benj. Thomas, Francis G. Murphy, Samuel Lunt, F. Ward, H.F. Zimmerman, Townsh. D. Fendall, Thos. Marbury, Charles Graham, C.B. Ellis, B. Wheat, Jr., Geo. R. Adams, Thomas H. Lathram, Jeremiah West, Saml. Lindsay, George Bryant, James E. Smoot from the county, C.M. & F. Taylor, *, Robt. Brockett, W.G. Cazenove, John R. Pierpoint, Thomas Burress, Wm. N. Berkley, Robt. Harper, J.W. Lockwood, C.G. Wildman & Co., A. Lockwood, Geo. G. Harper, J.M. Steuart, Saml. R. Adams, John Howell, J. Muir, Jno. McCormick, Saml. J. McCormick, Peyton Ballentine, Gottlieb Appich, William Pratt, Reid Cross, John E.

Legislative Petitions of the Town and County of Alexandria, Virginia

Henderson, Richd. W. Windsor, James Stoops, Caleb L. Richards, John Moore, J.W. Violett, James E. McGraw, Wesley Summers, Joseph Grigg, Wm. C. Richards, John Hodgkins, Jos. Grigg, Jr., William Morgan, Chas. Hawkins, Jno. J. Proctor, Robt. Bell, Jas. P. Coleman, Walter L. Pomery, R.E. Buchanan, C. Short, Henry Simpson, S.H. Devaughn, Jesse C. Green, Jno. Leadbeater, Jno. W. Green, Geo. W. Harris, Christopher Schafer, James H. Bicking, James Green, Richard Carne, A. Lammond, William Woolls, A.D. Harmon, Jabez Wheeler, J. Th. Weeks, John L. Creighton, Wm. D. Massey, Wm. Arnold, Benj. Barton, John Adam, John C. Warner, Wm. N. Brown, James B. Hall, Wm. C. Johnston, U.W. Barker, W.H. McKnight, Waters & Zimmerman, Charles C. Neale, Jos. H. Hampson, Geo. * & Co., Benj. T. Fendall, Thomas & Dyer, J.H. Grubb, Hugh Latham, James T. Middleton, James Dempsey, John Waddey, Edward Daingerfield, A.D. Collinsworth, Chas. *, T.W. & R.C. Smith, Ebenezer Bacon, Charles Price, Mark Mankin, James Campbell, Wm. Rock, C.B. Unruh, G. McCliesh, Jno. C. Vowell, Willis Henderson, Edward Owen, E.W. Kincheloe, * McCracken, Enoch Grimes, Geo. H. Bayne, William Price, Wm. Bayne, Wm. N. Rowe, Daniel Cawood, Wm. B. Price, Kinzey Griffith, Thos. Waring, Geo. Plain, Wm. Johnson, H.C. Smith, Andrew J. Fleming, Jas. M. Steuart, J. Ross, John Arnold, H. Peel & Co., Koones & Dean, Jas. Vansant, Wm. F. Padgett, Judson Mitchell, Henry Cook, J.G. Swaine, James H. Devaughn, Geo. Wise, S.W. Aubinoe, and F.L. Brockett.

Second duplicate signed by John L. Pascoe, Masters & Co., Isaac Buckingham, Walter Harris, John H. Janney, Thomas Davey, Pethen & Davis, John Creighton, T.M. McCormick & Co., Benj. Fugitt, T.M. McCormick, E.R. Violett, Arthur Lunt, Jacob Roxbury, Charles Koones, H. Bradley & Son, Daniel Bayliss, David Appich, F.L. Brockett, Richd. B. Lloyd, Geo. Duffey, Jno. S. Grubb, J.J. McFagin, Franklin W. Martin, * Whittington, Francis M. Weadon, John Shaw, John Grubb, Wm. H. Muir, Cornelius Jacobs, Wm. C. Spilman, Senr., A.J. Ogden, Thos. M. White, Clark & Brother, W.D. Walker, Robt. Nall, Presly Jacobs, * Grimes, John T.B. Perry, Wm. N. Mills, A.C. Cazenove & Co., Andrew Jamieson & Son, Lambert & McKenzie, Francis L. Smith, Cassius F. Lee, D. Minor, * Lee, Wm. B. Richards, Stephen Shinn, Hooe & Powell, Wm. Minor from this county, and Chr: Neale.

Citizens of the Town of Alexandria.
1846, 12 DEC. A544. Incorporation of a cotton factory[81] with capital not exceeding $200,000. Such an industry will increase prosperity of the town. Signed by Robert Jamieson, William Gregory, Wm. H. Fowle, Hugh C. Smith, Louis C. Cazenove, William N. McVeigh, and Lewis McKenzie. *Referred.* Box C.

---

[81] James Randall Caton, Legislative Chronicles of the City of Alexandria (Alexandria: Newell-Cole Company, Inc., 1933), p. 196. Acts of the General Assembly, passed March 11, 1847, the Mount Vernon Cotton Manufacturing Company is incorporated. The building still stands on the east side of Washington Street between Oronoco and Pendleton streets. Hereafter cited as Caton.

Legislative Petitions of the Town and County of Alexandria, Virginia

Citizens of the County of Alexandria.
1846, 12 DEC. A545. Establishment of an election precinct at Ball's cross road. The undersigned citizens of the county of Alexandria respectfully petition your honorable bodies to establish a precinct election at Balls X roads in the said county of Alexandria. Dated 2 DEC 1846. Signed by B.F. Shreve, Alfred Donaldson, Luke Osbourn, Geo. W. Thompson, and James T. Ball. *Referred.* Alexandria County box.

Citizens of Alexandria and Fairfax.
1846, 16 DEC. A546. Incorporation of a company to build railroad from Alexandria to Warrenton. *Committee discharged.* Box C.

Signed by Francis L. Smith, Samuel Lunt, James Sheehy, John D. Harrison, R. Crupper, Richard Windsor, Dennis Johnston, John Hooff, P.H. Hooff, Lewis Hooff, Wells A. Harper, McVeigh & Bro., J.H. Larmour, R.J. Sheehy, R. Young, Robt. M. Larmour, Geo. Plain, Thos. Smith, Geo. R. Adams, L.D. Harrison, Lewis McKenzie, and M.P. Corn.

Citizens of Alexandria and Valley of Virginia.
1847, 7 JAN. A547. Incorporation of the Alexandria and Potomac Railroad Company, to construct railway from Alexandria to Harper's Ferry; also subscription by the State of two-thirds of the company's stock. Since the completion of the Baltimore and Ohio Railroad the large proportion of trade of Alexandria has been diverted to Baltimore and it is believed that the proposed road to Harper's Ferry will bring trade back to Alexandria. Signed by Bakers & Brown, Wm. Miller & Co., W. Baker Miller, O.M. Brown, W.B. Baker, Wm. H. Mansfield, *, H. * Baker, D. Hollingsworth, D.W. Barton, * Clark, and others. Signed primarily by County residents, with signatures that are not easily readable. Multiple copies. Printed. *Bill reported.* Box C.

Citizens of Alexandria and its Vicinity.
1847, 14 JAN. A548. Incorporation of railroad company to build road from Alexandria to Harper's Ferry[82], and that the Commonwealth subscribe to two-fifths of the capital stock of the same. Such road will bring back to Alexandria trade of the Valley, which has been diverted to Baltimore

---

[82] Acts of the General Assembly, 1847, Chapter 111, "An ACT incorporating the Alexandria and Harper's Ferry Railroad Company," passed March 20, 1847, pp. 101-103. *That it shall be lawful to open books of subscription in the town of Alexandria, under the direction of John H. Brent, George H. Smoot, William L. Powell, Henry Daingerfield, Robert Jamieson, Benoni Wheat, Lewis M'Kenzie, Cassius F. Lee, Reuben Johnston and Thomas M. M'Cormick, or any two of them...* Acts of the General Assembly, 1848, Chapter 158, "An ACT to explain and amend the act passed March 20th 1847, incorporating the Alexandria and Harper's Ferry railroad company," passed April 1, 1848, pp. 192-193. *That the sixth section of the act, entitled 'an act incorporating the Alexandria and Harper's Ferry railroad company,' passed March the twentieth, eighteen hundred and forty-seven, shall be so construed as to inhibit the Board of public works, or any agent or agents of the state from fixing and regulating the rates of toll and transportation of the said company, unless the said company should be dividing more than fifteen per cent on their capital stock expended in making and completing the said railroad, and providing every thing necessary for transportation on the same.*

Legislative Petitions of the Town and County of Alexandria, Virginia

by the construction of the Winchester and Potomac Railroad. Signed by L.A. Cazenove, Robt. Jamieson, Turner Dixon, Henry Daingerfield, Cassius F. Lee, W.G. Cazenove, John F. Johnson, W. Arthur Taylor, R. Johnston, and Lewis McKenzie. *Referred.* Box C.

Citizens of the Town and County of Alexandria.
1847, 12-14 JAN. Same as A549 and A548. No number. Praying a subscription by the State to a part of the capital stock of the Alexandria Canal. "Under the superintendence of a distinguished and scientific member of the U.S. Topographcal Engineers (Major Wm. Turnbull), with a liberal aid from Congress of $400,000, in a depth of water exceeding 35 feet, without the light of experience to guide us in the construction of coffer-dams under such an immense pressure, after repeated disasters with these dams, and under discouragements, that had well nigh disheartened the most sanguine amongst us, this great work of nine massive piers, and two immense abutments of granite, laid in hydraulic cement, with a superstructure of 'Kyanized' or imperishable timber, was accomplished, after ten years of toil, and an expense of $575,381.43." Multiple copies signed by over 400 citizens. *Bill ordered.* Box C.

Citizens of Alexandria and its Vicinity.
1847, 18 JAN. A549. Same as A548. Signed by Lewis McKenzie, Benj. H. Lambert, Jas. McKenzie, John B. Daingerfield, George Fletcher, W.A. Harper, and 49 others. Two copies. Printed. *Bill reported.* Box C.

Citizens of Town and County.
1847, 22 JAN. A550. Remonstrance against the grant of priority to the magistrates of that part of Fairfax County which it is proposed to annex to Alexandria. The giving of such a preference to Fairfax magistrates is an injustice to the people of Alexandria. *Laid on table.* Box C.

Signed by James Stoops, John Moore, F.M. Weadon, John Howard, Peter G. Henderson, Francis Taterson, H.N. Steele, P.G. Uhler, Nathan Kell, J.T. Ramsay, Charles Koones, Joseph Grimes, James H. Pickin, Cornelius Jacobs, John Kell, William Walker, Chas. Hawkins, John Demain, T.C. [or J.C.] Swann, John W. Campbell, Isaac Kell, Robert Walker, John F. Lloyd, Isaac Buckingham, John Craven, Edwd. Green, Enoch Grimes, Saml. R. Slack, Nimrod H. Nowland, Theophilus Nowland, John S. Radcliff, Jonathan Tibbett, [J.] Smyth, James L. Henderson, James C. [Gamble], Robt. Young, Jess. Sisson, Wm. C. Spilman, Senr., A.J. Ogden, John Kisendaffer, R.S. Douglas, Henry Daniels, William Morgan, Jr., Levi Hurdle, Hugh Latham, Charles D. Rudd, Christian Hulspringer, C.H. Moore, James S. Douglass, Thomas B. Pickell, Peyton Ballenger, C.F. Wilson, R.A. Rudd, Harrison Javins, S. King Shay, Henry Brengle, Hiram Reese, Quintin Barker, Wm. B. Scearce, Charles Javins, James Thomas Monroe, Stephen Jones, James Nightgill [his mark], M.P. Corse, William H. Geisendaffer, John A. Rudd, John W. Rudd, Benj. Fugitt, Robert E. Buchanan, Geo. L. Deeton, J.H. Hampson, George Berry, Peter Hewitt, E.W. Kincheloe, Noble Berry, J. Travis, James

McLean, Barsilla P. Green, John Brown, W. McDaniels, Geo. T. Howard, J. Ross, John Butcher, J.D. Lakewan, J.L. Strider, James Biggs, Edward Flanagan, Milton Glassgow, William R. Campbell, Edw. S. Hough, Jno. Hollensbury, John T. Skinner, Daniel D. Herbert, John Adams, Joseph McLean, John Williams, Robert L. Murray, James Fadeley, John Mitchell, James H. Buchanan, Charles Lawson, Joseph Taylor, James W. Nalls, F.L. Brockett, Wm. Morgan, J.D. Javins, Daniel Baley, Joshua Y. Grady, Edward Jacobs, Saml. H. Devaughn, James S. Dudley, Jas. Douglass, Lewis Mothershead, L. Edwd. Greene, Stephen Chattom, John T. Johnson, William Hamersley, James Jefferson, Robert Jefferson, W.L. Geaslin, Hezekiah Patten, Edward Valentine, Henry Cryss, Peyton Crouch, and John T. Head.

Similar petition, entitled "The Memorial of Sunday Citizens of the Town of Alexandria," remonstrating against giving to such magistrates as live in that portion of the County of Fairfax which it is proposed to annex to Alexandria priority over the citizens of Alexandria in the commission which may be granted them. *Referred.* Dated 14 JAN 1847.

Citizens of Alexandria.
1847, 28 JAN. A551. Incorporation of the Alexandria Savings Institution.[83] Signed by Lewis McKenzie, Robt. Jamieson, John T. Johnson, R. Johnston, J. Roach, Cassius F. Lee, Robert Brockett, Wm. G. Cazenove, and Francis L. Smith. Accompanying note with additional signatures. *Bill reported.* Box C.

Managers of the Orphan Asylum and Female Free School of Alexandria.
1847, 13 FEB. A552. Grant of act of incorporation and also of a small donation to aid the institution. It has, during its struggling existence of fifteen years, sheltered forty orphans and educated 308 females. *Referred.* Box C.

Signed by Anne Clagett, 1st Directress, Sarah Griffith, 2nd do., Virginia Cary, Secty., Elizabeth H. Smith, Treasurer, and Managers: Mrs. Gardner, Mrs. Wise, Mrs. Douglass, Mrs. Daingerfield, Mrs. Stewart, Mrs. Morril, Mrs. Sandford, Mrs. Danforth, Mrs. Harper, Mrs. Cawood, Mrs. Gregory, Mrs. H.C. Smith, Miss E. Smith, Miss Berry; Consulting Committee: Rev. Elias Harrison, Mr. Gregory, Mr. Hugh Charles Smith, and Mr. Withers.

---

[83] Acts of the General Assembly, 1846-1847, Chapter 192, "An ACT incorporating the Alexandria savings institution in the town of Alexandria," passed March 20, 1847, pp. 184-185. *That Lewis M'Kenzie, Robert Jamieson, John T. Johnson, R. Johnston, J. Roach, Cassius F. Lee, Robert Brockett, W.G. Cazenove, Francis L. Smith, J.H. M'Veigh, Stephen Shinn, E. Snowden, A.J. Fleming, John Muir, George O. Dixion, John F. Dyer, Daniel F. Hooe, Benjamin H. Lambert, W.N. Berkeley, R. Zimmerman, C.C. Smoot, John B. Daingerfield, Ebenezer Bacon, James Breen, Benjamin Barton, David Betzold, Jacob Roxbury, W.D. Massey and Thomas M'Cormick, esquires, together with such other persons as are now or may hereafter be associated with them, shall be and are hereby constituted and made a body politic and corporate by the name and style of "The Alexandria Savings Institution..."*

Officers and Managers of the Alexandria Orphan Asylum and Female Free School Society.

1847, 19 FEB. A553. Request that the Alexandria Orphan Asylum[84] and the Free School Society[85] be separated and incorporated as two schools. The schools have been supported by a voluntary contribution of the benevolent, with the exception of $100 contributed annually by the town authorities. It is believed that the separation of the schools will make them more efficient and draw larger contributions for their support. *No action.* Box C.

Signed by Anne Clagett, 1st Dir., Esther Sanford, Eliza F. Gardner, Mildred W. Berry, Jane J. Danforth, Mary Morrill, Margaret B. Daingerfield, Mary D. Gregory, Eliza Douglas, Mary Cawood, Mary A. Harper, Isabella K. Smith, Ann L. Stuart, Sally W. Griffith, 2nd Dir., Virginia Cary, Secty., and Elizabeth J. Smith, Treas.

Tobacco Merchants.

1847, 29 NOV. A554. Reenactment of the laws regulating inspection of tobacco and the appointment of inspectors which existed in Alexandria at the passage of the jurisdiction act of March 20, 1847. Nearly all tobacco brought to Alexandria is grown in Maryland, is of a light quality and cannot be packed tightly without injury, so that the casks contain only from 600 to 900 pounds, while the Virginia laws require a weight of 900 pounds to the cask for a certificate of first quality. The Virginia laws also exact an inspection fee of fifty cents per cask and in Maryland no fee is charged. By the present law, the two inspectors receive such small compensation that it is difficult to procure services of competent men. Signed by A.C. Cazenove & Co., Lambert & McKenzie, John B. Daingerfield, John S.B. Perry, Thomas McCormick, and seven others. Printed. Four duplicates with 355 names. *Bill ordered.* Box C.

Dealers in Tobacco, Citizens of the Town of Alexandria.

1847, 9 DEC. A555. In consequence of extension of Virginia tobacco laws to Alexandria, tobacco trade has fallen from 800 hogsheads per annum to 150. Nearly all tobacco brought to Alexandria is light weight

---

[84] Acts of the General Assembly, 1847-1847, Chapter 180, "An ACT to incorporate the Orphan asylum of Alexandria," passed March 22, 1847, p. 169. *That Robert Jamieson, Hugh C. Smith, James H. M'Veigh, Lewis M'Kensie, James Green, Charles C. Smoot, William Gregory, Edgar Snowden, I.F.M. Lowe, Robert H. Miller, Robert Crupper, William N. M'Veigh, Stephen Shinn, William H. Fowle, John Withers, George J. Thomas, John F. Dyer and James M'Guire be and they are hereby constituted a body politic and corporate by the name and style of "The Trustees of the Orphan Asylum of Alexandria..."*

[85] Acts of the General Assembly, 1847-1847, Chapter 169, "An ACT to incorporate the Female free school of Alexandria," passed March 22, 1847, pp. 158-159. *That Robert Jamieson, Hugh C. Smith, James H. M'Veigh, Lewis M'Kensie, James Vansant, Charles M. Taylor, Orlando Fairfax, James Green, Charles C. Smoot, William Gregory, Edgar Snowden, J.F.M. Lowe, Robert H. Miller, William N. M'Veigh, James M'Guire, Stephen Shinn, William H. Fowle, John Withers, George J. Thomas, John F. Dyer and Louis Cazenove, be and they are hereby constituted a body politic and corporate, by the name and style of "The Trustees of the Female Free School of Alexandria..."*

Maryland tobacco.[86] It cannot pass the Virginia inspection tests. Petitioners ask that tobacco regulations which were in force when Alexandria was part of the District of Columbia be reenacted; otherwise Alexandria cannot compete with Baltimore for tobacco trade. Alexandria, 29 Nov. 1847. Signed by Lambert S. McKenzie, John B. Daingerfield, John T.B. Perry, Thos. McCormick, Thomas & Dyer, Benjn. T. Fendall, J.J. Wheat & Bro., Joseph Grimes, Charles P. Shaw, R.T. Ramsay, and one illegible other. *Referred.* Box C.

Citizens of the Town of Alexandria.
1847, 11 DEC. A556 (also see A557 at page 95). Renewal of acts directing a survey and appropriation for improvement of navigation of Shenandoah River. By this improvement the trade of the Shenandoah Valley, instead of being diverted from the State, will be brought to Alexandria and that town will become an important commercial center. No note on action. Box C.

Signed by James Green, R. Crupper, Geo. W. Harris, Richard Wright, Lewis Hooff, Wm. B. Price, Benjn. F. Gay [sic], Jno. Leadbeater, Rudh. Massey, Edward L. Sheehy, E.H.F. Tatsapaugh, S. Baggett, M. Johnston, Richard Ha<u>rue</u>, Hugh C. Smith, Warren <u>Teatum</u>, <u>D.C.</u> Greene, Daniel Cawood, Peter R. Beverley, William H. Triplett, A.C. Cazenove & Co., Wm. Bayne, Geo. H. Bayne, H. Grimes & Co., Charles C. Smoot, Geo. Dixion & Co., J.G. Cobbs, E.R. Keefer, J.J. Wheat & Bro., Lambert & McKenzie, R.T. Ramsay, G.W.D. Ramsay, * Blacklock, Joseph G. Carr, John T. Ball, E.W. Kincheloe, Geo. H. Smoot & Uhler, Waters & Zimmerman, U.W. Barker, John W. Lugenbeel, W.T. Harper, Richard R. Mason, John B. Hancock, P.C. Claughton, Wm. Boswell, Gilbert Simpson, Wm. *, R. Berry, John Laphen, Robt. Hall, Henry Mansfield, Geo. White, W.D. Corse, Jas. Young, W.M. Smith, M.P. Corse, Robt. Cash, B. Hooe, Koones & Dean, Jas. Vansant, John Shackelford, A.G. Newton, T.W. Ashby, P.E. Hoffman, E.C. Fletcher, John A. Shinn, Samuel A. Masters, Benj. Thomas, E. Burchell, Jos. H. Hampson, Hy. Daingerfield, McVeigh & Bro. & Co., Stephen Shinn, Samuel Lunt, W. Fowle, Charles P. Shaw, John Lawson, W.S. Bodkin, J.H. Wilson, Henry Winter Davis, Josiah H. Davis, Jr., Saml. H. Devaughn, Walter Harris, Henry L. Simpson, E. Short, Robt. D. Dwyer, John A. Washington, James English, G.B. Alexander, W.M. Atwell, W.H. McKnight, John L. Pascoe, Peter G. Henderson, Douglas L. Gregory, Samuel R. Adams, James English, W.J. Entwisle, Washn. C. Page, D. Fauntleroy, Thos. A. Waters, Thos. M. White, Wm. W. Harper, Charles B. Dana, Jno. C. Vowell, T.W. & R.C. Smith, J.R. Riddle, Wells A. Harper, and Chs. Wilson.

---

[86] See requirement to weigh each hogshead coming into warehouse before it is uncased, in <u>Acts of the General Assembly</u>, 1846-1847, Chapter 81, "An ACT to amend an act entitled 'an act to reduce into one the several acts now in force concerning the inspection of tobacco,' passed March 6th 1819," passed March 16, 1847, p. 68.

TO THE HONORABLE THE GENERAL ASSEMBLY OF VIRGINIA:

The memorial of the undersigned citizens of the town of Alexandria, respectfully represents:—

That the improvement of the Shenandoah River has long been an object of public solicitude, and its importance frequently acknowledged by legislative enactments. Your memorialists need not enter into details, to make this position clear and undeniable. They will leave to their representatives the task of presenting facts and arguments bearing upon the question. It is sufficient for the present, to state, that an extensive range of counties, East and West of the River, have no convenient outlet to market, and that the natural channel is the Shenandoah.

A satisfactory arrangement has been made with the New Shenandoah Company, by which all obstacles to an increase of stock are likely to be removed, and your memorialists now confidently rely, not only upon the liberality of the Legislature, but upon its sense of justice, for a renewal of the acts directing a survey, and making an appropriation, which acts were suspended in 1840.

They need scarcely call your attention to the fact, that the counties so deeply interested, from the mouth of the Shenandoah to its source, are among the largest tax-paying communities in the Commonwealth, whose contributions have been freely used, and for all improvements of a general character (like this,) have been freely voted by their representatives, with a view to the development of the resources of the State.

Your memorialists may be excused for reminding your honorable body, that since Alexandria has been restored to the Commonwealth, there is a new motive for improving the means of intercourse with that place—and the trade of the Shenandoah, instead of being forced out of the State, can be made tributary to the prosperity of that good old City, which for many years past has been in the keeping of a step-mother. Alexandria, by the fostering hand of the Legislature, can be rendered, as she once was, an important commercial point, a market for the products of the whole Shenandoah Valley, and thus be made instrumental in contributing largely to the revenues of the State.

With a confident hope that your honorable body will promptly recognize the claims of this portion of your constituency to an impartial consideration, your memorialists earnestly but respectfully invoke early legislation, in such amendments of the charter of the New Shenandoah Company as may be deemed necessary, and in a renewal of the acts directing a survey and appropriations.

And as in duty bound, your memorialists will ever pray, &c.

[Signatures:]

Lew. B. Taylor
Cazenove F. Lee
S. Kingsbury
G. F. Thomas
Chas. T. Stuart
B. T. Plummer
Wm. H. Irwin
Wm. G. Cazenove
Wm. N. McVeigh

R. J. Violett
Thos. E. Baird
William Page
J. H. Thomas
B. W. Clagett
Lewis McKenzie
Wm. Veitch
John West
John Arnold
Alexander Arnold

Henry Cryss
Geo. Plain
Thompson Tyler
Geo. W. Rock
Henry Tatspaugh
Ch. Nevett
Peyton Ballenger
C. A. Wilson
John Howell
G. Powell

E. H. Hamden
James Biggs
Gustavus Pugitt
Jas R Caleman
John W. Smith
James G. Auld
William W. Adam
Zachariah Wright
Thos B Creighton
Wm C Reynolds
Robt Hunter
Robt J Edelen
Aaron C Clark
W. D. Walker
J T McTague
JOHN STEPHENSON
James Sparks
E. G. Compton
James C. Carnell
E L Richards
C Hammadinger
Thomas N. O'neal
Henry Brengle
Robt Brown

Geo L. Peyton
James W. Simpson
John Eveleth
Wm Attwell
Henry Chattane
Thos H Scott
Thomas Kinsey
Thomas Warren
Judson Mitchell
J D Harrison
John F. Peyton
Saml N Chipley
Thos Parsons
J T Roby
Richard Haws
Peter Davis
William Price
Jno. Ward

Lucien Taylor
James D. Fisher
Walter L Penn
Charles L Neale
E. Horseman
Joseph Grigg
J E McCrary
A E Henderson
G Henderson
Charles Koons
Wesley Avery
John Demaine
James D. Bryan
John Wm Sinclair
Thomas Ross
John W. Brown
Thomas Ross
Jno McCormick
Thos. Murchant
T. Thomas

94

Legislative Petitions of the Town and County of Alexandria, Virginia

Citizens.
1847, 15 DEC. A557. Same as A556 at page 92. *Reported.* Box C.

Signed by Law. B. Taylor, Cassius F. Lee, S. King Shay, G.J. Thomas, Chas. T. Stuart, B.T. Plummer, Wm. H. Irwin, Wm. D. Nutt, Wm. N. Mills, R. Johnston, R.G. Violett, Thos. E. Baird, William Page, J.H. Shuman, R.H. Clagett, Lewis McKenzie, Wm. Veitch, John West, John Arnold, Alexander Arnold, Henry Cryss, Geo. Plain, Thompson Tyler, Geo. W. Rock, Henry Tatsapaugh, Jos. Nevett, Peyton Ballenger, C.F. Wilson, John Howell, Jno. *, E.H. Staunton, James Biggs, Gustavus Fugitt, Jas. P. Coleman, John W. Smith, James T. Rudd, William W. Adam, Zachariah Wright, Thos. R. Creighton, Wm. C. Reynolds, Robt. Hunter, Robt. J. Edelin, James C. Clark, W.D. Walker, J.J. McTague, John Stephenson, James Spinks, E.G. Compton, James C. Gamell, C.L. Richards, C. Hammadinger, Thomas N. O'Neal, Henry Brengle, Geo. L. Deeton, James M. Simpson, John Eveleth, Wm. Attwell, Henry Chatham, Wm. Rock, Zenas Kinsey, Erasmus Warren, Judson Mitchell, J.D. Harrison, John F. Peyton, Saml. N. Chipley, Thos. Parsons, J.T. Roby, Richard House?, Peter Davis, William Price, Jno. Ward, Lucien Peyton, James B. McNair, Walter L. Penn, Charles C. Neale, E. Horseman, Joseph Grigg, J.E. McGraw, J.E. Henderson, G. Henderson, Charles Koones, Wesley Avery, John Demaine, James D. Bryan, John Wm. Sinclair, Samuel Reese, John W.C. Bowen, Thomas Clowe, Jno. McCormick, Thos. Murchant, and T. Thomas.

Citizens.
1848, 3 JAN. A558. Establishment of a hustings court in Alexandria. *Rejected.* Box D.

Signed by C.C. Berry, Wm. Harper, C.G. Wildman, John D. Brown, Dennis H. Blacklock, Rudolph Massey, Douglas S. Gregory, J.M. Harper, A.D. Warfield, H. Jacobs, Geo. W. Harris, Robt. Young, William Johnson, Geo. W. Wiley, Thos. Waring, O. Fairfax, Geo. Swain, F. Taylor, M.D. Corse, Geo. R. Adams, Jas. H. Clarridge, Francis Garcia, James Dempsey, J.R. Riddle, John M. Monroe, Andrew J. Fleming, John Manery, Geo. H. Duffey, Samuel Tennison, William O'Neal, Geo. Bryan, R.C. Smith, Jas. P. Middleton, Th. Sanford, John W. Padgett, Andrew Kilst__, James Phillips, Thos. Jacobs, Benj. Thomas, Peter R. Beverley, Jno. F. McLowe, Joseph Grigg, Benj. T. Fendall, Townsh. D. Fendall, Josiah H. Davis, Jos. H. Larmour, Richard H. Stabler, Stephen *, Chas. McKnight, Koones & Dean, Joseph Jewett, C.A. Arnold, Charles L. Neale, Judson Mitchell, Stephen Field, Caleb S. Hallowell, William W. Adam, R.J. Andrews, Geo. H. Smoot, Jas. W. Sears, E. Burchell, and Robert J. Nash. Seven duplicates with 151 signatures.

Citizens.
1848, 7 JAN. A559. Charter for railroad with liberty to extend to the City of Washington, to be built from Alexandria to Gordonsville; it will make connection with the Louisa railroad and consequently bring Alexandria

Legislative Petitions of the Town and County of Alexandria, Virginia

in touch with the Ohio River. "To Alexandria this road will be of inestimable importance, when the Louisa Rail Road shall reach the Ohio River. Located at the head of navigation, for vessels of all classes, with a river front of two miles, along which extends a channel of 1400 feet wide, with a depth of water from 25 to 35 feet, furnishing a port perfectly sheltered from storms, and free from all shoals and other impediments, there seems scarcely to be a limit to which its shipping business may not be extended. By the completion of the Chesapeake and Ohio Canal, and by means of the Alexandria Canal, Alexandria must be the outlet for the trade of the whole range of the Counties on the northern portion of the State, which in a few years, as your memorialists believe, will furnish a coal trade, giving employment to an amount of tonnage perhaps equal to that now employed in the whole coasting trade of the State." Signed by R. Crupper, Wm. H. Rogers, A.D. Harmon, Stephen Woolls, Alex. Lammond, and 290 others. *Referred.* Box D.

Assessors.
1848, 8 JAN. A560. Increase of compensation for petitioners' services from $100 to $200.[87] In order to perform their duties they spend much time in country part of county; they were obliged to visit each piece of land and examine both land and improvements. They have finished work and have filed in Alexandria Court table of valuation. Signed by W. Yeaton, John Gibson Peach, L. Peyton, Geo. Wise, Turner Dixon, Wm. H. Irwin, Wm. T. Harper, R. Crupper, John H. Brent, J. Ross, Joseph G. Carr, and two other illegible signatures. Certificate. *Bill ordered.* Box D.

Lawyers of Alexandria.
1848, 10 JAN. A561. Remonstrance against the establishment of a hustings court in Alexandria, which matter is now before the Legislature. Petitioners consider court unnecessary. Signed by Chr. Neale, B. Hooe, Francis L. Smith, Wm. H. Semmes, J.T. Ramsay, J. Louis Kinzer, and one illegible signature. *Referred.* Box D.

Citizens.
1848, 10 JAN. A562. Establishment of hustings court in Alexandria. Before the separation of town from the State it had a hustings court, which had existed for many years and had been a great service. Now on retrocession of town to Virginia, petitioners request a renewal of a privilege which is granted the other towns in State. Signed by W. Fowle, Wm. H. Fowle, Geo. D. Fowle, Wm. Eaches, Stephen Shinn, Benoni Wheat, George Fletcher, Hy. Daingerfield, C.C. Bradley, William

---

[87] Acts of the General Assembly, 1848, Chapter 321, "An ACT allowing additional compensation to the assessors of the town and county of Alexandria," passed February 3, 1848, p. 336. *That the auditor of public accounts be and he is hereby authorized and required to issue his warrant on the treasury, payable out of any money therein not otherwise appropriated, in favour of William Yeaton, J. Gibson Peach and Richard Rudd, assessors of the town and county of Alexandria, for the sum of one hundred dollars each, being additional compensation for extra services in assessing the lots and land in said town and county in the year eighteen hundred and forty seven.*

R. Ball, E. Jones, George Davis, J.E. Henderson, James Quaid (who signed opposite petition under a mistake), * Wheat, and Robt. W. Wheat. *Referred.* Box D.

Citizens of the County of Alexandria.
1848, 10 JAN. A563. Remonstrance against establishment of hustings court in Alexandria. Alexandria County is very small; county courthouse is situated in town only an hour's ride from any part of county, and consequently another court is unnecessary. Furthermore, county could not bear expense of court without assistance of town, and so citizens of town will have to pay double taxes; conducting of two courts will require a greatly increased attendance upon court duties on part of citizens and will lead to rivalry for appointments to office. Citizens beg restoration of the flour inspector, as was done in Winchester. Dated 11 DEC 1847. *Referred.* Box D.

Signed by William F. Hodgkin, Joseph Fraser, Robert Hodgkin, Andrew A. Ball, Reazon P. Taylor, John Potter, R.B. Alexander, L. Cary Selden, John Casey, James Carson, J. Roach, William F. Taylor, Bazil Williams, Geo. Thompson, B.S. Donaldson, G.D. Surratt, John Birch, Jr., John Birch, Charles Payne, John Donaldson, Robert Birch, William Bowling, Robert Baker, Robert Harrison, Alex. N. Terrett, W.B. Berryman, Saml. D. King, N. Mullikin, James Birch, W.R. Birch, Wesley Birch, Robert Donaldson, E.S. Germain, T.E. Macy, W. Douglass, Wm. Minor, Chs. Newton, Samuel Birch, Benjamin F. Shreve, Nicholas Febrey, Moses A. Febry, S.L. Sommers, Jno. W. Sommers, A. Sommers, Daniel Wells, Richd. Southern, William C. Reynolds, John Howard, William H. Smith, Thomas J. Edelen, William S. Johnson, J. Saunders Dudley, Monroe Harris, Thornton Avery, Thomas Javins, George Carson, Michael Micky, H.N. Steele, John S. Walker, Jacob L. Clapdore, William D. Loyd, John Sherer, William Golatt, Charles Golatt, Edward Green, H.G. Davies, Enoch Ward, John Bladen, G.A. Barde, F.A. Noland, Jno. Brown, James Williams, Jno. Smith, Robt. Williams, John Williams, John Boyd, Henry Blish, Jno. Dix, John Dixion, Wm. Wolf, Henry Schuter, Saml. Hilton, Geo. Snyder, William Hutchins, John M. Monroe, John Tyson, James Emery, R.J. Davies, T.H. Jones, J.W. Dickin, Geo. Glish, J.E. Johnson, Jno. F. Clarvins, George Allen, W.F. Davis, Jos. Taylor, John Taylor, Thomas West, John J. Baggett, J.W. Jones, David House, John Johnston, Harrison Javins, William Allison, Peyton Ballenger, Charles F. Wilson, Daniel Bayliss, Barriella N. Greene, Stephen Kent, William Manley, William H. Bartle, W.U. Herbert, M. German, Richard Javins, James L. Henderson, James H. Buchanan, John D. Javins, Hiram Webster, Henry Gilbreth, Joseph Cash, John Cornbarger, T.W. Baggett, John Sheller, Jno. B. Sherwood, John Wells, William Ellis, John Hartshorne, John Hallslaugh, Robins. Fisher, William Fisher, J.W. Mills, G.W. King, John Shriner, J.W. Kidwell, Jno. Hurtt, Thomas Drowns, J. Simpson, James Evans, John S. Curtts, J.W. Skidmore, T. Payne, Harry Stokes, John Ducket, J.W. Wells, Saml. Bartle, W. Yeaton, T.W. Skidmore, John Powell, Lauren Peyton, Thomas B. Pickett, B.H. Berry,

Legislative Petitions of the Town and County of Alexandria, Virginia

E.G. Compton, Levi Hurdle, Robert Taylor, John E. Owens, Walter L. Penn, Wm. Attwell, Peyton Clarke, Elijah Horseman, James S. Rudd, Thompson Javins, J.T. Edd, S.C. Beach, N. Beach, John L. Smith, Robt. Jos. Sheehy, Geo. B. Lancaster, J.L. Lancaster, Geo. White, James D. Bryan, E. Short, A. Fleming, Geo. L. Deeton, Marion Walker, Geo. Wise, Turner Dixon, Edwd. Smyth, James Fossett, John Summers, Henry Miffleton, Robt. J. Edelin, George G. Harper, William Nolland, Christian Schafer, Edward S. Sheehy, Henry Cryss, William Shilts, Joseph Carson, N. Washington, Capt. John Grey, Thornton Arey, W.M. Atwell, James Walker, James Tuleman, Peter Hewitt, Robert Hunter, John Howell, Bartholomew Rotchford, Philip Rotchford, Richard Rotchford, J. Louis Kinzer, H. Carlin Dorsey, George Tatsapaugh, Henry Lloyd, Francis L.B. Lloyd, John Laphen, Jas. Irvin, R.E. Buchanan, John Reed, James Sheehy, Edward Sheehy, Thomas Kell, Hugh Latham, Thomas Burns, Charles F. Cox, H.F. Fisher, Jno. Browne, Joseph G. Carr, James Chatham, George F. Washington, John S. Preston, Thos. B. Creighton, Thos. A. Waters, James E. Mankin, Slighter S. Monroe, George H. Wright, Joseph K. Plant, John Bontz, James English, Robert Tomlin, James Cole, James T. Monroe, James H. McLean, George Berry, Edwin Monroe, John H. Gray, Wm. Mankin, W.C. Richards, Richd. W. Windsor, Henry Bontz, William Windsor, James A. Javins, Samuel S. Kidwell, William H. Triplett, William Javins, Quinton Barker, W.W. Goodrich, Jas. H. Dove, Ricd. C. Barton, John Hodgkin, Wm. B. Scearce, David House, Jesse Skidmore, Peter Davis, Jesse Rye?, James Carroll, Alexander Violett, Richd. B. Lloyd, George Kreist, Samuel L. Campbell, Wm. L. Reese, John Kisendaffer, John Gibson Leach, W.T. Harper, Willis Henderson, Cornelius Jacobs, Samuel Reese, Henry Brengle, Hiram Reese, S. French Simpson, Peter Simpson, John T. Audley, James Quaid, James W. Nalls, Eli D. Swann, Charles Hammer, Isaac Kell, Charles Koones, Joseph Lupton, C.C. Bradley (revoking the signature in favor other the husting court), H. Bradley, W.H. Devaughn, B. Hooe, Anthony R. Fraser, John Hooe, John Jones, W.B. Nixon, John Thos. Price, Wm. A. Wharton, Walter Gahen, John McCracken, Barth. Rotchford, Wm. H. Thomas, Wm. R. Laurance, John Johnson, J.G. Padgett, William Jenkins, K. Griffith, Daniel Griffith, William Sherwood, Joseph McLean, Samuel Armstrong, James Smith, John M. Clapdore, Thomas Dix, John Williams, A.M. Simpson, Thomas Nicholasson, Louis Tycen, George Price, John Whealen, and James H. McLean, and seven illegible signatures.

Lucien Peyton, First Commissioner of the Revenue.
1848, 11 JAN. A564. Additional compensation at rate of $2 per day for service of 200 days.[88] Commissioner has been obliged to collect all

---

[88] <u>Acts of the General Assembly</u>, 1848, Chapter 322, "An ACT concerning Lucien Peyton, commissioner of the revenue for the town and county of Alexandria," passed March 2, 1848, p. 336. That the auditor of public accounts be and he is hereby authorized and required to issue a warrant upon the treasury, payable out of any money therein not otherwise appropriated, in favour of Lucien Peyton, for the sum of one hundred dollars, it being allowed him for extra services as commissioner

information without formal assessment books and has consequently employed a clerk in order to complete work in required time. Accompanying certificates. Endorsements by Asa Rogers (Senate Chambers, 19 FEB 1848), and Jas. E. Heath. *Reasonable.* Allowed $100 on 20 JAN 1848. Alexandria County box.

Bar of Alexandria.
1848, 20 JAN. A565. Restoration of hustings court. Alexandria had hustings court before its cession to the United States and should again have the court again. Signed by Law. B. Taylor, Henry Winter Davis, R. Johnston, W. Arthur Taylor, Albert Stuart, Chas. W. Stuart, R.I. Andrews. No note of action. Box D.

Joseph Eaches (d. 1857), President, Alexandria Canal Company.
1848, 24 JAN. A566. Loan of $600,000 to the company.[89] Money to be used for building wharves and appliances for loading of ships. Chief benefit of Chesapeake & Ohio Canal and Alexandria Canal will be the coal trade, and appliances must be built at Alexandria for accommodating this trade. It is expected that $34,800 will be received in tolls, wharfage and rents, a sum sufficient to speedily pay off loan of $60,000. Signed by Jos. Eaches, Pres., A. Canal Co. Nine accompanying papers. *Bill reported.* Box D.

Citizens.
1848, 27 JAN. A567. Incorporation of a company to erect a hotel in the town of Alexandria, under the name of the Alexandria Hotel Company.[90] *Reasonable.* Box D.

Signed by R. Crupper, Samuel Lunt, Wm. N. Berkley, A. Lockwood, Jno. Lockwood, Wm. H. Rogers, Saml. R. Adams, John H. Brent, Francis Murphy, Jno. Leadbeater, R.H. Miller, H.C. Smith, Francis L. Smith, *, J. Humphrey McVeigh, Edward Daingerfield, Fowle & Co., McVeigh &

---

of the revenue for the town and county of Alexandria, for the year eighteen hundred and forty-seven.
[89] Also see Acts of the General Assembly, 1848, Chapter 125, "An ACT to authorize the guarantee by the state of certain bonds of the Alexandria canal company," passed April 4, 1848, pp. 168-169. *That the treasurer of the commonwealth be, and he is hereby authorized and required to underwrite the guaranty of the state to the bonds of the Alexandria canal company and the common council or corporation of Alexandria, to an amount not exceeding forty-three thousand five hundred and twenty dollars...*
[90] Acts of the General Assembly, 1848, Chapter 259, "An ACT to incorporate the Alexandria hotel company," passed March 27, 1848, p. 291. *That Robert H. Miller, Henry Daingerfield, William H. Fowle, James H. M'Veigh, George H. Smoot, Lewis M'Kenzie, James Green, William N. M'Veigh, Stephen Shinn, John H. Brent, Hugh C. Smith, Robert Crupper, William L. Powell, Louis A. Cazenove, George O. Dixion, John J. Wheat, and such other persons as may be associated with them, shall be and they are hereby made a body politic and corporate under the name and style of "The Alexandria Hotel Company," for the purpose of erecting buildings and making all the other necessary arrangements for the accommodation of travellers and other visitors, at some suitable location, to be selected by the stockholders of said company in the town of Alexandria...* Caton, p. 196, the "Alexandria House," for many years was the familiar name of the hotel at the southeast corner of St. Asaph and Prince streets.

Legislative Petitions of the Town and County of Alexandria, Virginia

Bro. & Co., G.J. Thomas, Lambert & McKenzie, John West, John B. Daingerfield, *, George Fletcher, Nathl. Boush, Steph. Shinn, George O. Dixion & Co., Robt. Wilson Wheat, Wm. Bayne, Cazenove Co., and Geo. H. Smoot.

Moses Hepburn (d. 1861).[91]
1848, 27 JAN. A568. The will of William Hepburn of the County of Alexandria, dated 28 FEB 1817, as an exhibit.[92] Mentions sale of Esther (whom I bought some years ago of Benjamin Dulaney, Esqr.) and her children Moses, Letty and Julianna Eliza, to Hannah Jackson, and the said Hannah Jackson has since manumitted and set free the said three children... I wish and desire that Moses be sent to Philadelphia, or some other place where coloured children are carefully educated... I give unto Moses the son of Esther aforesaid, the houses and lots where I now live (one of the aforesaid lots I bought of William Herbert Junr., trustee for the creditors of Robert Conway, and the other I bought of Joseph Mandeville), together with my fishing shore... else to my grandchildren... and a bond I hold of John McPhersons for ten thousand dollars which was due the first day of April last and is now on interest and secured by a deed of trust on eleven hundred acres of land which I sold him in Fairfax County... I also give unto Moses my ground rent of the lot No. 124 in the plan of Alexandria of one hundred and ten dollars payable on the 8th August every year, by Thomas Brocchus, the lot lies on Queen and Pitt streets. I also give him my house and lot on Princess Street, at this time occupied by Frederick Green & John Smith, which lies on the west of Mrs. Dougherty's garden, and on the east of a house at this time rented by Robert Anderson, and is 36 feet front on Princess Street, running back 88 feet 34½ inches... to Letty and Juliana Eliza, daughter of the aforesaid Esther, jointly the lots which I bought of William Herbert, Senr. and the other executors of Richard Conway, deceased... I further bequeath to Letty my houses on King Street now occupied by Robert Gray with all the back buildings and warehouses to Hooff's Alley. To Juliana Eliza I further give and bequeath my corner brick house on King and Pitt streets together with the warehouse on Pitt Street and the other houses back to Hooff's Alley. I give to the three sons of Doll Bell, Daniel, John & Anderson [Bell?], my one half of the eighty acres of land known by the name of Ruckey Cock, which is undivided between the heirs of the late John Dundass & myself, only my half is to be on the east end of the tract and where Doll Bell now lives, as was aggreed on by the executors and myself, before I built the house thereon. I also give them my lot call'd Dowdel's town with all the houses on it, lying on the north side of Princess Street and west side of St. Asaph's street in the town of Alexandria... It is my desire that Jerry shall serve his brother Moses until he come to the age of twenty one years. ...to William H. Dundass my grandson all my wharf and warehouses with the whole of

---

[91] Alexandria Wills, Bk. 8, p. 50, will of Moses Hepburn of Chester Co., Pa., dated 12 DEC 1860, proved in Alexandria on 4 FEB 1861.
[92] Alexandria Wills, Bk. 2, p. 186, proved 20 MAY 1817.

the lot on the east side of Union Street, I also give unto him my house and lots now occupied by Robert Anderson on Princess Street and west of Moses's lot and east of the lot I deeded some time ago to Eliza Dundass his sister... of the six thousand acres of land decreed by the Supreme Court of the United States to John Dunlap &c. ...to Thomas Dundass my grandson... ten shares of bank stock in the Bank of Alexandria... also one half of the lot rented to Going Lanphier, Robert Going Lanphier and Joseph Dudley in the town of Alexandria, also I give him a vacant lot on Water Street south of the house of the late Doctor Kennedy, which I had of Wm. Herbert, Junr., trustee of the creditors of John Potts, deceased, being about 60 feet in front & running back to Mr. Kerling's lot... To Nancy Keene, wife of Newton Keene, and her heirs, I give and devise my house and lot on Princess & Union streets. To Sophia Peyton, wife of Thomas West Peyton and her children I give my lot and houses on the north side of Princess Street and west side of Water Street, at this time occupied by Catharine Sheverlane... There is a large balance in the Company's books of Hepburn & Dundass due to me... amounting to about $5,000, due me from John Dundass my late copartner one half of the $10,350 which I had to pay to John Dundass & Co. by the decree of the Supreme Court. ...two shares of stock in the Bank of Alexandria standing in the name of Hepburn & Dundass, which I give and bequeath to my daughter Agness Dundass.... her late husband John Dundass. Lastly, I appoint Jonah Isabell of the town of Alexandria and Archibald McLean late of Alexandria, but at this time of Chester County in the state of Pennsylvania to be executors... Dated 28 FEB 1817. Wits. John A. Stewart, John Johnston, James Johnson, and John Ramsay. Proved 26 MAY 1817, by Alexander Moore, Register or Wills.

To the General Assembly of Virginia.

By the will of William Hepburn dated 8th February 1817, and recorded in Alexandria County Court, it appears that the testator gave to Moses, the son of Esther aforesaid, the houses and lots where I now live + + + + + + + + + + together with my fishing shore during his natural life, and to his children, if he should have lawful issue; if not, then I give the said lots and fishing shore, at this decease, to my grandchildren, equally, and their heirs forever.

By this clause of the will, exactly quoted from the original in this memorial, I am advised that I have only a life-estate in the fishing shore.

I have five children, lawfully begotten in wedlock, the eldest of which is now about 15 years of age, the youngest, about two years of age.

Thus, "fishing shore," lies immediately contiguous to the terminus of the Alexandria Canal, near the town of Alexandria, and is desirable and desired for the purposes of said Canal Company in accommodating the large expected canal trade to come by the way of said canal.

On account of the rights of the above named infants, my children, I am unable to make with said Company such contracts in regard to said fishing shore, as may be highly beneficial to the infants themselves. If the present opportunity is misused of advancing their interests in regard

Legislative Petitions of the Town and County of Alexandria, Virginia

to said property, it may be lost altogether by contracts of said Company with other persons.

I therefore, respectfully ask the legislature to grant me the privilege of leasing said property to the Canal Company or any other company or person, for twenty years, or of selling it, as in my judgment... Dated 25 JAN 1848. Signed, Moses Hepburn. Alexandria County box.

Citizens.
1848, 28 JAN. A569. Establishment of hustings court. "Among the motives of that application are the thorough belief and conviction that the majority of the original 13 members of the county court were appointed by a corrupt combination between the present clerk of that court, the governor of the State and certain of the members and officers of that court, for the purpose of appointing Mr. Berry, clerk of that court, and disposing of other officers in the gift of this court." Custom of Assembly to grant corporations hustings courts, and such a court is needed in Alexandria to supervise issue of tavern licenses and for general benefit of town. Paper giving added list of reasons. *Referred.* Box D.

Signed by *, Wm. D. Massey, Hugh C. Smith, Wm. H. Fowle, Chas. M. Taylor, Geo. D. Fowle, Wm. L. Powell, Steph. Shinn, Louis A. Cazenove, Lewis McKenzie, Edw. B. Powell, Thos. M. White, Jno. McCormick, Wesley Summers, Robt. G. Violett, W. Arthur Taylor, W.G. Cazenove, Law. B. Taylor, R. Johnston, Albert Stuart, Wm. Veitch, Jno. J. Proctor, James F. Carlin, Wm. B. Price, A. Lammond, John D. Brown, E. Burchell, J. Winston, Samuel R. Adams, Robt. Harper, G.W.D. Ramsay, Jas. P. Middleton, Chas. Stuart, Wm. Rock, Jacob Roxbury, Jas. P. Coleman, A. Lockwood, Jno. Slacum, B.T. Plummer, Benj. T. Fendall, Townsh. D. Fendall, R.T. Ramsay, John T. Creighton, Dan. Shryer, Benoni Wheat, Henry Winter Davis, and Henry Daingerfield.

President and Directors of Alexandria Canal Company.
1848, 5 FEB. A570. Authority to purchase or condemn as much land, and water front, at and near the terminus of the canal, as may be necessary for the Alleghany coal trade. To secure this is an object of great importance. Signed Jos. Eaches, Pres. A.C. Co. Three letters, resolutions, pamphlet of copy of act of incorporation. *Referred.* Alexandria County Box.

Joseph Eaches (d. 1857), President, Alexandria Canal Company.
1848, 19 FEB. A566. Additional authority to condemn additional river front lands.[93] Dated 15 FEB 1848. Signed, Jos. Eaches, Pres., A.C. Co.

---

[93] Acts of the General Assembly, 1848, Chapter 124, "An ACT concerning the Alexandria canal company," passed April 1, 1848, pp. 167-168. *That the Alexandria canal company shall be and they are hereby authorized and empowered to construct such wharves, piers, basins and other works on the Potomac river, at or near their present outlet locks, as they may deem necessary for the accommodation of the trade of their canal... That the said company be and they are hereby confirmed in the full use and enjoyment of the right and title to, all real property hitherto conveyed to or acquired*

One letter in file, Alexandria, 17 FEB 1848, to Mr. Snowden by R. Johnston, "I send herewith a resolution of the Council in relation to the grant of the exclusive use of a certain street to the Canal Co. which run through their proposed coal yards & wha[r]ves & which requires confirmation by the Sen., apparently, also a resolution expressing the intention of Council to appropriate by way of loan, their proportion of the funds required for the construction of the requisite wharves c. to accommodate the shipment of coal... No note on action. Alexandria County box.

D. Boyd Smith.
1848, 5 DEC. A571. Incorporation of the Alexandria Railway Co., with a capital not exceeding $20,000 in $50 shares.[94] The road is to be located on the Potomac at Alexandria for the purpose of affording facilities for repairing vessels. The company may purchase such land as they may deem necessary, not exceeding five acres, whereon to construct their necessary works and buildings. Signed, D. Boyd Smith. *Bill ordered.* Box D.

Executors and Heirs of William H. Foote (d. 1846).
1848, 7 DEC. A572. Authority for the Circuit Court of Alexandria to enter a decree for sale at auction of "Hayfield," estate of the late William H. Foote.[95] Foote left many debts and his executors believe that sale will be advantageous to all parties concerned, as the land is rapidly depreciating in value. Suit had been brought by heirs of Foote for the annulment of the residuary devise to the Female Free School. In view of all the circumstances of the case, it is desired that "Hayfield," be sold at

---

by them, for the same interests and estates as were so conveyed or acquired; and that the lands, privileges and other things now held by George H. Smoot for said company, at and near the Georgetown ferry, may be conveyed to them... Also see Acts of the General Assembly, 1848-1849, Chapter 281, "An ACT to confirm the grant by the common council of Alexandria of part of certain streets in said town to the Alexandria canal company," passed January 17, 1849, p. 208. Confirmed.

[94] Acts of the General Assembly, 1848-1849, Chapter 156, "An ACT to incorporate the Alexandria Marine Railway Company," passed January 13, 1849, pp. 109-110. *That D. Boyd Smith, Richard C. Smith, Stephen Shinn, Edward Daingerfield, Nathaniel Goodhan, John T. Johnson and Joseph P. Grimes, with such other persons as have been or may be associated with them, and their successors, are hereby incorporated into a company by the name and style of 'The Alexandria Marine Railway Company...'*

[95] Acts of the General Assembly, 1848, Chapter 305, "An ACT for the relief of the devisees and heirs of William H. Foote, deceased," passed December 14, 1848, pp. 238-239. *Whereas by a decree of the circuit superior court of law and chancery of the county of Alexandria, pronounced in the late June term of the said court, in a suit of chancery therein depending, in the name of William H. Foote's heirs and distributees, plaintiffs, against the said William H. Foote's executors and others, defendants, it was adjudged, ordered and decreed, that all the real estate in the proceedings in the said suit mentioned, of which the said William H. Foote died seized, should be sold upon the terms in the said decree set forth; and whereas after the said decree was pronounced, it was discovered that one of the plaintiffs, at the date thereof, was an infant, and another of the said complainants had departed his life, leaving sundry heirs under age, and residing in the state of Missouri...* Mary M. Foote, the widow, executrix and principal devisee of the said testator, Francis L. Smith, his executor, and Lawrence B. Taylor and Henry W. Davis, attorneys and counsellors at law of the other parties in interest.

auction, under certain requirements as given in the petition.

Your petitioners, citizens of the town of Alexandria respectfully shew, that William H. Foote of the County of Fairfax departed this life about the 20th day of November 1846, leaving a last will and testament (a copy of which is herewith presented marked A) which has been duly admitted... that the testator died seized of considerable real and personal estate, the latter of which except the slaves, whom he emancipated will prove largely insufficient for the payment of the testator's debts. The real estate lies in the County of Fairfax in a single tract called "Hayfield" and contains between twelve and fifteen hundred acres, of which some seven hundred acres are cleared, and highly improved. This portion of the estate is low flat land on which there has been very extensive ditching, requiring a large outlay of labor and money, and demanding much attention to keep the same in proper order. ...That a suit has been brought on the Chancery side of the Circuit Superior Court of Law & Chancery for the County of Alexandria, by the heirs at law of the testator, praying amongst other things, that the residuary devise to the "Female Free School" in said will mentioned may be set aside and declared void, and claiming that at the death of the widow and executrix they are entitled to said tract of land in its proceeds... That one of the complainants was an infant and another of the complainants is dead leaving several heirs, some of whom as your petitioners are informed are also infants residing in the state of Missouri... that Francis L. Smith, Henry Winter Davis and Lawrence B. Taylor are hereby appointed commissioners to effectuate said sale: that the expenses attending to the said sale are to be in the first instance borne by the Executor and Executrix of the said W. Haywood Foote out of the assets of the estate... Dated 2 DEC 1848. Signed by Mary M. Foote, Exctx., Francis L. Smith, Exor. of Wm. H. Foote, decd., Law. B. Taylor, for the Free School, Henry Winter Davis, Counsel for Haywood Foote, William Foote, James B. Thornton & Sally his wife, Elizabeth Chevis?, William H. Triplett & Catherine his wife, John Fitzhugh, Lycurgus Fitzhugh, Francis Fitzhugh, Cook Fitzhugh & Frances his wife, George Fitzhugh, William G.S. Fitzhugh, Fugus R. Fitzhugh, Mary Frances Fitzhugh & Lucy Fitzhugh an infant suing by her next friend George Fitzhugh. Copy of will of William H. Foote, dated 16 AUG 1846, codicil 20 NOV 1846. Copy of chancery suit William H. Foote's heirs & distributees v. William H. Foote's Executors & others, from June Term 1848. *Referred.* Alexandria County box.

John Tatsapaugh.
1848, 16 DEC. A573. Payment of $42.13 to petitioner for goods furnished by him to volunteers in the Mexican War.[96] Accompanying certificate.

---

[96] Acts of the General Assembly, 1849-1850, Chapter 319, "An ACT concerning John Tatsapaugh of the town of Alexandria," passed March 14, 1850, p. 226. *...in favor of John Tatsapaugh of the town of Alexandria, or his legal representative, for the sum of forty-two dollars and thirteen cents, the amount of an account for clothing and goods furnished to a company of volunteers raised by Captain Henry Fairfax during the war with Mexico, after the enrolment of the men and before they were*

Reasonable. Box D.

Tobacco Merchants.
1848, 30 DEC. A574. Act giving control of tobacco inspection to council of Alexandria as heretofore.[97] No Virginia tobacco is received for inspection at Alexandria, but all tobacco coming there is raised in Maryland and town laws are better adapted to local tobacco inspection than laws of Virginia. *Referred.* Box D.

Signed by Steph. Shinn, Lambert McKenzie, J.T.B. Perry, Thomas & Lloyd, Isaac Buckingham, James Irwin, G.W.D. Ramsay, J.J. Wheat & Bros., Geo. H. Smoot & Uhler, Danl. F. Hooe, *, W. Fowle, Cazenove Co., John B. Daingerfield, R.T. Ramsay, Wm. L. Powell & Son, Benj. T. Fendall, Wm. Bayne, Fowle & Co., and George Fletcher.

Members of Alexandria and Fairfax Bar.
1848, 30 DEC. A575. Change of Alexandria County Court session from first to fourth Monday in every month.[98] In June and November the quarterly courts for Alexandria fall on the same day as county courts; besides, the term conflicts with Prince William County Court. *Referred.* Box D.

Signed by Chr. Neale, T.H. Hanson, W.C. Yeaton, Law. B. Taylor, Wm. H. *, Robt. J. Smith, R. Johnston, W.L. Edwards, Wm. H. Dulany, *, Alfred Moss, Tho. J. Murray, F.R. Love, B.H. Berry, Clerk Alexa. Co., and J. Louis Kinzer.

Voters of Alexandria.
1849, 6 JAN. A576. Subscription of 2,000 shares by the Common Council of Alexandria upon certain conditions to the stock of the Orange and Alexandria Railroad Company. Lists 416 names of persons (no signatures) in favor of the action, and three against: Presley Jacobs, Con: Jacobs and George Price. No note on action. Box D.

---

mustered into service.
[97] Acts of the General Assembly, 1848-1849, Chapter 280, "An ACT concerning the tobacco trade in the town of Alexandria," passed February 24, 1849, pp. 280-281. Also see Acts, 1846-1847, pp. 47-48.
[98] Acts of the General Assembly, 1848-1849, Chapter 84, "An ACT changing the time of holding the county court of Alexandria county," passed January 10, 1849, pp. 46-47.

Citizens of the County of Alexandria.
1849, 16 JAN. A577. Authority for council to subscribe $100,000 to stock of Orange and Alexandria Railroad Company.[99] To the General Assembly of Virginia-- The undersigned citizens of the county of Alexandria, and owners of real estate and other property in the town of Alexandria, most respectfully petition your honorable body, to pass a law authorizing the common council of Alexandria to subscribe $100,000 to the stock of the Orange and Alexandria Rail Road. Dec. 28th 1848. Signed by C.A. Alexander, J. Roach, Jas. A. English, W.T. Harper, William Page and James Carson. *Referred.* Alexandria County box.

Dealers and Consumers of Flour
1849, 25 JUN. A580. Remonstrance against the passage into law of the proposition to make the inspection of flour optional with the buyer or seller, as leading inevitably to collusions & frauds, and to the great injury of the markets of the State. That of Alexandria, with much effort and care in the inspections, has been raised from a comparatively low grade to an equality with the best Southern markets; and we doubt not that the character so acquired will be soon lost if the measure proposed be adopted. Dated 25 JUN 1849. Signed by Fowle & Co., Daniel Cawood, Lambert & McKenzie, R.J.T. Wilson, Danl. F. Hooe, Jos. H. Hampson, S.S. Masters & Son, C.W. Wilson, Wm. L. Powell, and T.M. McCormick. Not note on action. Box D.

Susan Horwell.
1849, 3 JUL. A581. Susan Horwell of the Town and County of Alexandria, wife of Richard Horwell, claims that soon after her marriage she perceived coldness and indifference had usurped the place of affection so warmly professed by her husband with whom her fortunes were united, and that its place had been supplanted by all the angry and malignant passions of the human heart. He presented the most wanton and cruel treatment, often compelling her to abandon the home.

Deposition of Bernard Hooe, now of Washington City. Do certify and declare that I removed from the County of Prince William in Virginia in the month of April in the year 1822 to reside in the Town of Alexandria... where I continued constantly to reside for twenty years, that in the month of March in the year 1833, I was elected Mayor of the said Town of Alexandria... at the Election in March 1836, another gentleman was chosen to be the Mayor of the Town, who served until the next annual election in 1837, when he declined to serve longer in that office, and in March 1837, I was again elected Mayor of that Town, which office I continued to hold for the three succeeding years (under annual Elections) termination in March 1840, making the whole period

---

[99] Acts of the General Assembly, 1848-1849, Chapter 154, "An ACT to amend the act 'incorporating the Orange and Alexandria railroad company,' passed March 27th 1848," passed March 6, 1849, pp. 107-108; Chapter 155, "An ACT to authorize the common council of Alexandria to subscribe to the stock of the Orange and Alexandria railroad company," passed February 27, 1849, pp. 108-109.

of my service in that capacity six years. During those six years I had ample opportunity of knowing much about the evil propensities and dissipated habits of the citizens of that Town, which I was not infrequently called on to enquire into and to reprove, and among those whose misconduct demanded the application of wholesome restraint was Richard Horwell... On one occasion when I had committed the said Richard Horwell to the county jail in default of his giving security to keep the peace, some dissolute companions and associates, who alone seemed to have for him any commiseration, applied to a judge of the United States Circuit Court for the District of Columbia at Washington for a writ of habeas corpus, and had him brought before the said Circuit Court that the cause of his commitment by one might be enquired into, which was accordingly done, and that trial resulted in the said Richard Horwell's being remanded to jail and there detained until he should give the required security for the peace, and for his good behavior. Whilst under the influence of strong drink the passions of Richard Horwell were violent... On one occasion when I had committed the said Richard Horwell to jail as above stated [his wife] petitioned to me for permission to send to the jail a bed and furniture for his greater comfort...

Deposition of Henry Mansfield, who had been acquainted with Richard Horwell and his wife Susan for the last eighteen or twenty years... the character of Susan Horwell is unimpeachable... and he can only attribute the ill treatment of her husband to the effects of his free indulgence in spirituous liquors. *Laid on table, then referred.* Box D.

John Arnold.
1849, 5 DEC. A579. Reimbursement of John Arnold for supplying hats and caps to soldiers of the company of Captain Henry Fairfax in March 1847, amounting to $56.75, exclusive of interest. Signed, John Arnold. *Bill ordered.* Box D.

Alfred Jacobs (d. 1897).
1849, 7 DEC. A582. Divorce of Alfred Jacobs.[100] Alexandria County box.

> The petition of Alfred Jacobs to the General Assembly of Virginia for a divorce *à vinculo matrimonii*[101] from his wife, Margaret Ann Jacobs. Your petitioner respectfully shows that he desires the General Assembly to grant him an absolute divorce *à vinculo matrimonii* from his said wife, Margaret Ann Jacobs, and that, the grounds his application for such divorce, upon the causes set forth in a statement contained in the record from the clerk's office of the Circuit Superior Court of law &

---

[100] Acts of the General Assembly, 1849-1850, Chapter 328, "An ACT divorcing Alfred Jacobs from his wife Margaret Ann," passed January 23, 1850, p. 229.
[101] This type of divorce completely dissolves the marriage, and makes it void from the beginning, the causes of it being precedent to the marriage. The parties may marry again. Upon the divorce of a man and his wife, equity will not assist the wife in recovering dower, at the husband's death, but shall leave her to the law.

chancery for Alexandria County, Virginia, herewith inclosed. Dated 5 DEC 1849. Signed, Alfred [his mark] Jacobs. Wit. Albert Stuart. *Referred.* Alexandria County box.

Alfred Jacobs v. Margaret Ann Jacobs. Be it remembered that heretofore, to wit: on the 12th day of July 1848, in the clerk's office of the court aforesaid, came the plaintiff and filed in writing a statement of causes for divorce...He respectfully states, that he was lawfully married to his said wife Margaret Ann sometime in the month of December in the year 1841 that for several years after their marriage they lived together in the utmost harmony, that during that time he had issue by his said wife, two children, to wit: Ann Virginia born in the year 1843, and Sarah Elizabeth born in the year 1845, that during the said period of time he always treated his said wife with the utmost kindness, and provided her liberally with all the necessaries of life, that notwithstanding about three years ago, to wit: sometime in the year 1845, his said wife Margaret Ann deserted him and commenced a career of open and notorious prostitution, and that without the slightest cause or provocation on the part of the said Alfred, since the said Alfred avers and can prove that before the commencement of her criminal conduct, he had at all times after their marriage treated his said wife with uniform kindness and attention. And the said Alfred Jacobs further states, that even after his said wife Margaret Ann had begun to conduct herself as a prostitute, he exercised the utmost forbearance towards her and actually received her into his house; that after that she again deserted him and went to Washington City on a visit to some relations there; that whilst there she continued her course of prostitution, and as the said Alfred avers and can prove, contracted the venereal disease. The said Alfred further states, that his said wife has at all times utterly neglected her children, and that they are now under the care of his parents, with whom he himself resides, and also that his said wife still continues to conduct herself as an open and abandoned prostitute, by which causes, the said Alfred says, that his domestic happiness has been entirely destroyed, and his life rendered a burden to him. The said Alfred Jacobs, therefore prays the court, to cause a jury to be impaneled to ascertain the facts set forth in the above statement and that their verdict may be recorded. Witness my hand this 11th day of July 1848. Signed, Alfred [his mark] Jacobs. Wit. James Quaid.

In the matter of Alfred Jacobs against Margaret Ann Jacobs for a divorce it is certified by the court that there was evidence to satisfy the mind of the court that the offenses charged were not committed by the procurement or with the connivance of the complainant, and that the same had not been forgiven, and that they occurred within the period of five years before the institution of the suit, and that the complainant had not been guilty of the same offenses charged against the defendant within five years next before the institution of this suit.

At another day, to wit, at a session of the circuit superior court of law and chancery continued and held for the county of Alexandria the 14th November 1849, cause the petition by his attorney Albert Stuart,

Legislative Petitions of the Town and County of Alexandria, Virginia

Esq., and therein came a jury, to wit... We of the jury find that the facts of the within statement are true...

Citizens of Alexandria.
1849, 8 DEC and 15 DEC. A583 and A586. Charter for the proposed Alexandria and Valley Rail Road. *Bill Reported.* Box D.

Signed by J.H. McVeigh, John J. Johnson, Wells A. Harper, John Waddey, Danl. F. Hooe, Wm. C. Bontz, Charles C. Smoot, John H. Janney, Geo. Plain, G. McCleish, John Wood, Robt. B. Snyder, Robt. Bell, John Howell, Wm. Adam, Wm. D. Massey, Joseph Grigg, Jr., Jno. C. Vowell, Wm. Bayne, Wm. Wright, Jno. Roach, Geo. H. Payne, H.C. Smith, A. Lammond, J. Roxbury, E.J. Miller, C.C. Bent, Wm. Harper, Wm. N. Brown, R.Y. Cross, R. Zimmerman, James B. McNair, John T. Creighton, William Arnold, John A. Field, Saml. Lindsay, John Arnold, Samuel R. Adams, Wm. Gregory, James Entwisle, Jr., J.M. Steuart, Henry Cook, Wm. Baker, James *, C.M. & F. Taylor, A.P. Gover, Robt. Hunter, Caleb S. Hallowell, Samuel Baggett, A.D. Warfield, Emanuel Francis, Wm. N. Berkley, Robt. Harper, *, Fleming & Douglass, Thomas Sanford, Henry Peel, R.L. Brockett, John T. White, Robert Burnett, John Summers, James W. Nalls, William R. Campbell, R.G. Violett, Thos. M. White, John Creighton, Thomas Davy, Jno. Newton Harper, P.G. Uhler, Wm. Stabler, Jno. Leadbeater, Andrew J. Fleming, John T.B. Perry, John Perry, James Dempsey, John F. Dyer, and Wm. B. Price.

Constituents.
1849, 10 DEC. Citizens of Alexandria praying for the passage of a law in resolution of errors made by Commissioners of the Revenue, and other makers connected therewith.[102] The commissioner and not the party agrieved should be taxed with clerks fees. *Reported.* 14 JAN 1851. Alexandria County box.

Signed by E. Burchell, Cook S. Peel, Walter Harris, C.M.F. Taylor, Samuel R. Adams, William Davis, Robt. Hunter, John Arnold, Geo. W. Rock, Jas. A. English, J. Roxbury, A. Lammond, James B. McNair, John T. Creighton, Joseph Grigg, Jr., W.D. Corse, Jno. J. Proctor, Thos. E. Baird, John Cohagen, J.M. Stewart, John H. Monroe, L.D. Harrison, Henry Mansfield, P.C. Claughton, James Entwisle, Douglas S. Gregory, C.C. Berry, William B. Price, Saml. D. Harper, Wm. D. Massey, Cassius F. Lee, W.R. Ball, W.A. Taylor, H. Davis, William Gregory, Edward Snowden, Stephen Woolls, Chas. T. Stuart, W.W. Barker, R.Y. Cross, George Davis, Geo. W. Wiley, David Appich, Geo. Plain, Chas. C. Tatsapaugh, Judson Mitchell, Robt. W. Davis, J.L. Javins, B.T. Plummer, Samuel Lunt, Daniel Harmon, John T. Evans, Wm. Veitch, J.D. Corse, and Andrew J. Fleming.

---

[102] Acts of the General Assembly, 1849-1850, Chapter 1, "An ACT appropriating the public revenue," passed March 14, 1850, pp. 3-4.

Legislative Petitions of the Town and County of Alexandria, Virginia

Mary Ann Conway.
1849, 17 DEC. A585 (also see A597). Divorce *à vinculo matrimonii* from her husband A.J. Conway. That on the 28th day of April 1840, she was married to Andrew Jamieson Conway, a mate and since a sea captain, engaged in the merchant service, and that the marriage took place in the Town of Alexandria where both parties then resided, and where your petitioner has lived from her birth to the present time... Becoming unfortunate in his voyages, in about two years, after the marriage, his fortunes became totally wrecked. His conduct in the course of the transactions, which resulted in his ruin, as your petitioner afterwards learned, was not only highly indiscreet, but might be characterized in much harsher language, were not your petitioner restrained from so doing, in the reflection, that his exposure, further than is actually necessary for the purposes of this petition, may hereafter injuriously affect the innocent offspring of said Conway and your petitioner... About the month of August 1842, they went on a visit to Washington, after being there a few days, the said Conway, under the pretext of having business in Baltimore, left your petitioner with the promise to return in a few days, and take her back to Alexandria where they were then residing. Violating his promise, by failing to return, he has from that period, now upwards of seven years, totally deserted and abandoned your petitioner. Signed, Mary Ann Conway. *Referred.* Box D.

Merchants, Fisherman, and Planters of Alexandria.
1850, 2 JAN. No number. *Referred.* For a law to prevent any seine, except floating sturgeon nets, not less than eight inch mesh, from the mouth of the Potomac to Liverpool Point, inclusive, on the Maryland side and from mouth to Mrs. Waller's Landing on the Virginia side, from the 25th day of April, to the 1st of August, in each year, and from Liverpool Point to Indian Head on the Maryland side and from Mrs. Waller's to High Point on the Virginia side, from the 28th of April to the 1st of August each year; and from Indian Head to Fort Washington on the Maryland side, and from High Point to Sheridan's Point on the Virginia side, from the 1st day of May to the 1st day of August in each year; from Fort Washington to the head of navigation on the Maryland side, and from Sheridan's Point to the head of navigation on the Virginia side, from the 5th of May to the 1st day of August in each year. *Reported.* Box E.

Signed by James Irwin, Solomon S. Masters, G.W.D. Ramsay, D. & J. Blacklock, R.T. Ramsay, Peter Hewitt, T.H. Hoskine, John R. Collard of Fairfax Co., W.H. Smoot, Prince William Co., W.G. Cazenove, Wm. Payne, Geo. H. Payne, William Page, John A. Dixion, Fowle & Co., John B. Daingerfield, Lambert & McKenzie, R.T.J. Wilson, McVeigh & Bro. & Co., Anth. Chs. Cazenove, Jno. Withers, J.H. Wheat & Bro., John T.B. Perry, Chas. Wilson, Waters & Zimmerman, John A. Janney, Alfred Lee, Daniel Cawood, Geo. P. Wise, John Snyder, Joseph Cawood, Joshua H. Davis, Aquila Emerson, and Levi Hurdle.

Jane Dade (d. 1873).[103]

1850, 3 JAN. A592. Also see A535. Commutation of a land warrant held by petitioner, who is widow of Charles Stuart Dade of Alexandria, one of the heirs of Dr. William Rumney. Land warrant No. 8628 for 1,125 acres was issued to Rumney for his services in the Revolution, but land designated in warrant cannot be found and petitioner desires a commutation at rate of $1.25 an acre. Letter of Jane Dade. *Referred.* Box E.

J. Louis Kinzer (1824-1863).

1850, 3 JAN. A593. Grant to petitioner of a full title to a lot in Alexandria, which he purchased from Davis & Smoot for $475. Title is withheld on account of alienage of Elizabeth Donaldson, who originally owned the land. Papers. *Referred.* Box D.

John C. McCracken (d. 1890).

1850, 9 JAN. A578. Refund of a fine imposed on him by the County Court. In August 1847, a dispute between Joseph Frazier and James Cole, two persons of color, who had a trifling fist fight. Cole was an employee of McCracken, left town and went to Washington City, D.C., then was imprisoned in the Alexandria County jail for about three or four weeks. Letter of Francis L. Smith. *Bill Ordered.* Box E.

Committee.

1850, 17 JAN. A587. Committee of a convention in favor of the Alexandria and Valley Rail Road. Railroad to commence at Harrisonburg, passing through the fertile and populous counties of Rockingham, Shenandoah, Warren, and Fauquier, and uniting with the Orange and Alexandria Railroad at a point in Prince William, about thirty miles from Alexandria. The Valley farmer at or near Harrisonburg, is now under the necessity of transporting his flour by wagon to Winchester, thence by railroad to Baltimore. The area through which the projected road passes is rich in iron, manganese, copper, limestone, and lumber. Printed signature block of Edwd. C. Marshall of Fauquier, and Wm. H. Fowle of Alexandria, on behalf of the Committee. *Reported.* Box E.

George G. Harper (d. 1878).

1850, 17 JAN. A594. Payment of $167.93 for clothing furnished Capt. Henry Fairfax's company.[104] Petitioner was given Capt. Fairfax's note for amount, but Fairfax died in Mexico, leaving many debts. *Referred.*

---

[103] Wesley E. Pippenger, Tombstone Inscriptions of Alexandria, Virginia (Volume 1) (Westminster, Md.: Family Line Publications, 1992), p. 7. First Presbyterian Church Cemetery (1809) graves in the Adam family plot include: *Jane Dade, daughter of Robert and Anna Adam, died Jan. 23, 1873, aged 89 years, widow of Charles Stuart Dade who was lost at sea July 1811.* [Lot 41:14]

[104] Acts of the General Assembly, 1849-1850, Chapter 310, "An ACT for the relief of George G. Harper of the county of Alexandria," passed March 21, 1850, p. 223. *...for the sum of one hundred and sixty-seven dollars and ninety-three cents, for furnishing clothing to Captain Henry Fairfax's company of volunteers on their way to the Mexican war.*

Box E.

Richard Y. Cross (d. 1860).
1850, 19 JAN. A588. Payment for furnishing supplies for Capt. Fairfax's Company of volunteers for the Mexican War.[105] Richard Y. Cross of Alexandria, a manufacturer and dealer in boots and shoes in the town, between 16th March and 1st April in 1847, furnished men boots and shoes suitable for their use in Captain Henry Fairfax's Company of the Fairfax Company of Volunteers. *Referred.* Box E.

James A. English (1816-1868).
1850, 21 JAN. A589. Refund for a license tax.[106] In September 1848, English purchased from Robert Crupper, a regularly licenced merchant in the town of Alexandria, his entire stock of hardware, that a licence of the said Crupper was by order of the County Court regularly transferred to English who then commenced and has since continued to transact business in Alexandria. Rate charged by the Commissioner of the Revenue was based in inflated expected sales. *Referred.* Box E.

Thomas McCleland.
1850, 13 FEB. A590. Protest over the process to selection an artist to design a monument to George Washington, to be located in Capitol Square at Richmond. Requests reimbursement of $100 for sketches sent the Honorable Edgar Snowden. *Rejected.* Box E.

John and Sarah Dixon.
1850, 13 MAR. A595. Permission for Sarah Dixon, free negress, to remain in State. By terms of will of William Henry Fitzhugh of "Ravensworth," who died in MAY 1830, Sarah Dixon was to be freed in 1850. When will was made in Alexandria was not in State and free negroes could live there, but now they are excluded. If Sarah Dixon is compelled to leave State, she must take her young children and abandon her husband, who is a slave. Sarah Dixon, the wife of John Dixon. Two certificates: "Sally, was formerly one of my servants..." by A.M. Fitzhugh, March 1850; and "Sally Dixon wishes to become a resident and get employment in Alexandria. I take pleasure in commending her as an honest and industrious woman." Signed, George Burke, 15 FEB 1850. *Referred.* Box E.

---

[105] Acts of the General Assembly, 1849-1850, Chapter 306, "An ACT for the relief of Richard Y. Cross of the county of Alexandria," passed March 21, 1850, p. 223. *...for the sum of one hundred and eighty-three dollars and thirty-seven cents for goods, viz: boots, shoes &c., furnished to Capt. Henry Fairfax's company of volunteers when on their way to the Mexican war.*

[106] Acts of the General Assembly, 1849-1850, Chapter 307, "An ACT concerning James A. English," passed March 15, 1850, p. 223. *That the auditor of public accounts be and he is hereby authorized and required to issue a warrant on the treasury, in favor of James A. English, for the sum of twenty-five dollars... that being the amount overcharged by the commissioner of the revenue for Alexandria.*

Legislative Petitions of the Town and County of Alexandria, Virginia

Eliza Jane Baare.
1850, 2 DEC. A598. Divorce from her husband Ferdinand Rudolph Baare,[107] who deserted petitioner and returned to his home in Prussia, stating to his brother that he never expected to return to America and that he would apply to Prussia authorities for annulment of marriage on ground of being liable to Prussian military service when married. Letters show Eliza Jane Fisher, daughter of Charles Fisher, was married in FEB 1847 in Washington, D.C.,[108] to Ferdinand R. Baare, by birth a Prussian of the town of Minden, by Rev. Gillis, minister of the Protestant Episcopal Church of England. In 1848, the husband wrote that he was now an established grocer of St. Louis, Missouri, and requested her to join him there, which she did in the Summer of 1848, carrying with her their infant child about six months old, the issue of the marriage, who died shortly after her arrival at St. Louis. Certificates. *Referred.* Box E.

Mary Ann Conway.
1850, 2 DEC. A597 (also see A585). Divorce from her husband, Andrew J. Conway, because of desertion, leaving her and an innocent child to mourn with her the loss of a father's care.[109] Petitioner was married in 1840 and lived happily with her husband until 1842 when he left her and has never returned. Affidavits of Edgar Snowden, John Muir, W. Harper, F. Middleton, Wm. N. Berkeley. Letters of John H. Brent and Washington T. Harper show Mary Vansant,[110] daughter of James Vansant, intermarried with Capt. Andrew Conway, both then of the town of Alexandria. *Referred.* Box E.

Citizens of Alexandria.
1850, 3 DEC. No number, see 10 DEC 1849. Praying for passage of law in relation to errors made by Commissioners of the Revenue. Signed, Wm. D. Massey. Box E.

Arthur Waring D'Essex of Port au Prince, St. Domingo.
1850, 5 DEC. A596 (also see 21 MAR 1851 at page 120). Act removing certain defects of title to real estate inherited by petitioner's children. Richard Conway left property to Letty and Juliana Eliza Hepburn, the latter of whom married the petitioner and went with him to San Domingo. He thinks it is to his children's advantage to sell property but cannot give a clear title. Deed, power of attorney. *Referred.* Box E.

---

[107] Acts of the General Assembly, 1850-1851, Chapter 296, "An ACT divorcing Eliza Jane Baare from her husband Ferdinand R. Baare," passed January 20, 1851, p. 196.
[108] Wesley E. Pippenger, District of Columbia Marriage Licenses, Register 1, 1811-1858 (Westminster, Md.: Family Line Publications, 1994), pp. 18, 203, "Eliza Fisher to Ferdinand Rudolph Baare, 24 FEB 1847."
[109] Acts of the General Assembly, 1850-1851, Chapter 301, "An ACT divorcing Mary Ann Conway from her husband Andrew J. Conway," passed January 9, 1851, pp. 197-198.
[110] Thomas Michael Miller, Alexandria & Alexandria (Arlington) County, Virginia Minister Returns & Marriage Bonds, 1801-1852 (Bowie, Md.: Heritage Books, Inc., 1987), p. 68, "Andrew J. Conway & Mary Ann VanZant, 27 APR 1840, bondsmen Andrew J. Conway, Andrew J. Fleming."

"...that by the will of William Hepburn of Alexandria County, now among the records of the County Court of said County, a devise is made in these words: 'I give and bequeath to Letty and Juliana Eliza, daughters of the aforesaid Esther, jointly, the lots which I bought of W. Herbert, Junr. & the other exors. of Richard Conway, decd., to them during their natural lives and to their children after them, should they have any; but if either die childless, I will her share to her surviving sister & her children,' that said lots consist of three or four acres of land near the town of Alexandria, worth about six hundred dollars; that Letty, named in the above extract of Hepburn's will, died, leaving no child; that your petitioner, about the year 1830, was lawfully married to the said Juliana Eliza and had one child by her, now about 18 years old, born in the City of Washington, D.C., that about the year 1834 he removed with his family to the Island of St. Domingo where they now live, that he has had two children born in said island, and now alive, one of them about 12 years old, the other about five; that your petitioner is now in the United States with his second child, on a visit, leaving his wife and the two other children at Port au Prince in St. Domingo; that on the 26th day of August, 1850, in the County Court of Alexandria County, your petitioner was appointed guardian of his said three children and gave bond and security..."

File includes two deeds, one of 9 SEP 1850, between Arthur Waring of the Island of St. Domingo, of the one part, acting as well for himself as in his character of guardian for his children appointed by the County Court of Alexandria County at its August Term 1850 (who are the children of his wife Juliana Eliza Waring, late Juliana Eliza Hepburn), his said wife Juliana Eliza, by her said husband Arthur Waring acting as her attorney in fact under a power of attorney under hand and seal and acknowledged by said Juliana Eliza before G.T. Usher, the commercial agent of the United States at Hayti... Recorded Liber Y, page 513.

<u>Citizens of Alexandria, Fairfax, Prince William, Loudoun, Fauquier, Culpeper, Madison, Orange and Greene.</u>
1850, 12 DEC. A599 (also see 27 FEB 1851, page 119). Incorporation of company with capital of $300,000, to build branch railway from South Lowell at Great Falls of Potomac to most convenient point of intersection with Orange and Alexandria Railroad.[111] No aid is asked from the State. *Referred.* Alexandria County box.

---

[111] Acts of the General Assembly, 1850-1851, Chapter 84, "An ACT to incorporate the South Lowell Branch railroad company," passed March 21, 1851, p. 66. *That it shall be lawful to open books of subscription in the town of South Lowell in the county of Fairfax, under the direction of Thomas Ap C. Jones, William Bradley, William Neilson, Thomas R. Love, William W. Ball, Lawson Littleton and General Roger Jones... for the purpose of constructing a railroad from some convenient point on the Alexandria and Gordonsville railroad, not more than three miles west of the town of Alexandria, to South Lowell at the Great falls of the Potomac river...*

To the Legislature of Virginia:

The undersigned citizens of Alexandria, Fairfax, Prince William, Loudon [sic], Fauquier, Culpepper [sic], Madison, Orange and Green [sic], respectfully represent to the Legislature of Virginia now in Session, that the agricultural, mineral, and commercial interest of that portion of Virginia to which they belong, will be in their opinion greatly enhanced by the construction of a branch Rail Road from the Orange and Alexandria Rail Road to the Town of South Lowell at the Great Falls of the Potomac River, a charter for which has been granted to certain individuals by the Legislature of Virginia.

Your petitioners are fully impressed with the general importance to the agricultural, manufacturing and commercial interests of Virginia, with which the Town of South Lowell is by its peculiar geographical position and vast water power invested presenting a fall of seventy seven and a half feet in the most convenient form for use in a distance of less than two miles, thus guaranteeing an almost unlimited water power, at all seasons of the year to be used in the various departments of manufacturing, and in the the [sic] present disturbed condition of popular, and political excitement, between the north and the south, it is a matter of paramount importance to Virginia to develop to the greatest possible extent every internal resource at her command. Considering therefore the vast advantages of the position of South Lowell and its unrivaled water power, they feel every desire to suit rapidly built up, as a means of increasing the wealth, and independence of the State; similar improvements having added great strength, wealth and prosperity to many of the northern states, by which Virginia has been made tributary to a large and impoverishing extent, your petitioners ~~therefore~~ wish that in the incipient stages of the contemplated improvements, at the Great Falls of the Potomac River, the Company already chartered by the Legislature and such private persons as may feel an interest in the prosperity of South Lowell, and the adjacent Country, may have secured to them the right to construct at their own expense a branch Rail Road, connecting that important point, with the Orange and Alexandria Rail Road, and of course with all the adjacent country which is rich in agricultural and mineral productions, the value of which would be greatly enhanced by opening this communication and by it and Alexandria the manufactured articles would find a market in this district of country and south and west and by shipment to foreign ports.

In the present condition of the slave interest, they desire every facility which can be legitimately afforded, calculated to build up, and foster the domestic and internal relations of the southern states, having entire confidence in the successful rivalry of South Lowell, with the manufacturing interest of the north, when it shall have been fairly tested in its practical advantages, they ~~therefore~~ express the belief that every permanent interest in Virginia and every slave interest in the entire south will be promoted by the speedy erection and permanent operation of the contemplated improvements at the Great Falls.

They therefore pray that your body will Charter a Company with a capital of $300,000 duly impowered to contract for, and build a branch

Legislative Petitions of the Town and County of Alexandria, Virginia

Rail Road from the Great Falls of the Potomac River to the most convenient and eligible point, for intersection with the Orange and Alexandria Rail Road, without asking the State to contribute any part of the capital.

Name	Residence
Charles P. Moncure	Culpeper County
Francis Jordoun	Orange County
N.K. Wickes	Loudoun Co.
Ths. Newman	Orange --
B.H. Berry	Alexandria
Edwd. C. Marshall	Fauquier
Garr. A. Freeman	Culpeper
William Early	Madison
Anthony Thornton	Greene
G.R. Peake	Richmond
Richard H. Field	Culpeper
John Walden	Fauquier
Perry J. Eggborn	Culpeper
Geo. Ficklen	Culpeper
Wm. Hill	Culpeper
Ths. Ap. C. Jones, by H. Wilson, on authority of his letter 29th December 1850.	Fairfax County, Va.

Citizens of Alexandria.

1850, 12 DEC. A600. Remonstrance against incorporation of company to build railroad from Great Falls of Potomac to intersect Orange and Alexandria Railroad. Petitioners think proposed railroad would injure rather than benefit Alexandria, which has already the burden of debt of Orange and Alexandria Railroad. No action noted. Box E.

Signed by Ant. Chs. Cazenove, Wm. Fowle, Wm. H. Fowle, Norval W. Burchell, Benj. H. Lambert, Lewis McKenzie, Peter Hewitt, N.S. Wattles, Louis A. Cazenove, Thos. W. Smith, Wm. H. Irwin, James Entwisle, F.A. Marbury, Edw. S. Hough, and 164 others.

Koones & Dean.

1851, 6 JAN. A601.[112] Payment of $481.32, which is owing to petitioners for goods furnished Capt. Henry Fairbank's Company of volunteers in the Mexican War. Accompanying certificates. Koones & Dean were engaged in mercantile business in Alexandria, furnished sundry goods, including cotton, canvas, black thread, cord, buttons, blankets, 6 doz. white Berlin gloves, black velvet, canton padding, cambrill, wadding, silk, 2 gross bone buttons, 1 card hook & eyes, etc. Note that Thomas

---

[112] Acts of the General Assembly, 1850-1851, Chapter 286, "An ACT for the relief of Koons and Dean of the county of Alexandria," passed March 29, 1851, p. 194.

Legislative Petitions of the Town and County of Alexandria, Virginia

Moore was a lieutenant in Capt. James Thrift's (late Fairfax) Company of Virginia Vols. *Reported.* Box E.

J. Louis Kinzer (1824-1863).
1851, 6 JAN. A593. Title to lot at the southeast corner of Duke and Pitt streets in Alexandria.[113] Petitioner informed that the lot originally belonged to John Muir who departed this life in the year 1791, leaving the property by his will dated in December 1789 to his sister Elizabeth Muir, that Elizabeth was a subject of Great Britain [born in Scotland] and removed to the U.S. after 1783 and resided here until she married Robert Donaldson, a native of Scotland who was then an inhabitant of the U.S., until 1793 when he together with his wife removed to England where they resided until their deaths. Elizabeth Donaldson owned the lot, and subsequent to her arrival in England, executed a general power of attorney. In 1816, the lot was in arrears for taxes, a judgment for $65.01. Prior to 1820, lot was in possession of Elisha Talbot who erected a shop on the same and continued to occupy it for many years without let or hinderance. Talbot to have purchased interest of Elizabeth Donaldson, resided there until 1832 [Alexandria Deeds, Liber U No. 2, folio 231] when he conveyed it to George H. Smoot and Josiah H. Davis in trust for credits. After this Talbot died and Smoot and Davis took possession and held until Sept. 1850. Jury members for inquisition of escheat. Signed by John Summers, Jas. Coleman, Geo. Plain, William Arnold, John Tatsapaugh, Samuel Barnes, and Peter J. Henderson. Robert J. Smith is Escheator of the Commonwealth, inquisition document gives measurements of lot. Copy of will of John Muir, dated DEC 1789, proved 19 APR 1791 in Fairfax County. No action noted. Box E.

Merchants, Traders and Others of Alexandria.
1851, 7 JAN. A602. Establishment of bank in Alexandria on the free banking principle.[114] Its great feature of unquestionable security for note-holders should be a recommendation to Legislature and the fact that it

---

[113] *Acts of the General Assembly*, 1850-1851, Chapter 268, "An ACT releasing to J. Louis Kinzer of the commonwealth's right to a lot of land in the town of Alexandria," passed March 28, 1851, p. 188. That all the estate, right, title and claim whatsoever which has accrued, or may accrue to the commonwealth of Virginia, or to the president and directors of the Literary fund, in or to a lot of ground on the southeast corner of Duke and Pitt streets in the town of Alexandria, belongong originally to one John Muir, and lately conveyed by deed to J. Louis Kinzer by George H. Smoot and Josiah Davis, shall be and the same is hereby released to J. Louis Kinzer...

[114] *Acts of the General Assembly*, 1850-1851, Chapter 59, "An ACT to incorporate the Bank of the Old Dominion, the Bank of Commerce at Fredericksburg, and the Mechanics and Traders Bank of the City of Norfolk," passed March 29, 1851, pp. 45-47. Books of subscription for raising the stock aforesaid shall be opened on the first Monday in May next, and will remain open till the stock shall be subscribed, at Alexandria in the county of Alexandria, under the superintendance of Lewis McKenzie, Robert H. Miller, John H. Brent, George H. Smoot, Reuben Johnston, Andrew J. Fleming, C.P. Shaw, C.C. Smoot, W.G. Cazenove, John J. Wheat, John B. Daingerfield, George D. Fowle, Isaac Buckingham, John Withers, Benjamin H. Lambert, William N. McVeigh, R.G. Violett, D.B. Smith, Benjamin Barton, John F. Dyer and James A. English.

will enhance the value of State stocks by making them the basis of banking capital should recommend it to the advocates of State internal improvements. *Bill ordered.* Box E.

Signed by Lewis McKenzie, McVeigh & Bro. & Co., Stephen Shinn & Son, John B. Daingerfield, R.J. Wilson, Thomas & Dyer, Geo. O. Dixion & Co., W.W. Harper, J.H. McVeigh, Fowle Co., S.S. Masters & Son, Wm. H. Irwin, John T.B. Perry, James Irwin, J.J. Wheat & Bros., Lancaster & Gardiner, D. & S. Blacklock, P.G. Uhler, W.S. Bodkin, Wm. Bayne, Cazenove & Co., Samuel Lunt, Danl. F. Hooe, John H. Janney, Edward Daingerfield, J.C. McCracken, A. Lammond, Robert Bell, F. Kingston, J.B. McNair, Cook & Peck, F. & M. Taylor, Robt. Hunter, J. Muir, R. Stuart Douglas, Charles Koones, C.C. Bradley, Robt. G. Violett, E.L. Richards, L.D. Harrison, J.E. McGraw, Geo. White, Waters & Zimmerman, Creighton & Bodkin, Ant. Chs. Cazenove, Jno. Withers, Jno. C. Vowell, Wm. L. Powell & Son, Grimes & Kincheloe, John Wood, H.C. Smith, Chas. P. Shaw, E.J. Miller, James A. English, R.H. Miller, Saml. Miller, Creighton & McNair, G.K. Witmer, J. McCormick, Jr., John D. Easter, Wm. H. Muir, H. Bradley, Wm. C. Richards, J.D. Harrison, Joseph Grigg, Wesley Summers, J.E. Henderson, Lewis & Quigley, John R. Pierpoint, W.T. Harper, James D. Bryan, C.W. Wattles, James W. Green, Ashby & Herbert, Philip Rotchford, James Entwisle, James McCormick, Wm. H. Rogers, B. Russell Barbee, Douglas S. Gregory, C.C. Berry, W. Walton Harper, C.G. Wildman, John H. Brent, Wm. Stabler & Bro., B.H. Jenkins, J.H. Reid, D.H. Guinn, Jno. Newton Harper, Thomas Burns, Richd. S. Huck, G.W.D. Ramsay, Andrew J. Fleming, Fleming & Douglass, Daniel Cawood, R.T. Ramsay, Ebenezer Bacon, and Chas. T. Stuart.

Merchants, Traders and Others of Alexandria.
1851, 13 JAN. A603. Establishment of bank in Alexandria on free banking principle. Want of sufficient banking capital has long been a drawback to trade of town, as farmers and exchange banks have a capital of only $500,000, which is insufficient. *Bill ordered.* Box E.

Signed by Turner Dixon, James Green, A. Lockwood, Wm. Veitch, James Entwisle, Peter Hewitt, Thos. Anty. Brewis, Joseph Carson, John Lawson, Wm. L. Lee, Wm. B. Scearce, Jas. P. Coleman, Daniel J. Egan, James F. Carlin, Henry L. Simpson, A.D. Collinsworth, Chas. McKnight, Zenas Kinsey, Walter L. Penn, P.C. Claughton, Wm. Baker, Ashby & Herbert, T.W. Ashby, Jas. Vansant, Geo. L. Sherwood, Grimes & Kincheloe, J.C. McCracken, Jos. H. Hampson, John Tatsapaugh, *, D.R. Blacklock, Alfred Madden, Henry Mansfield, John Arnold, Saml. Beach, W.E. Atwell, F.G. Murphy, Geo. Duffey, Robt. Harper, Berkley & Harper, George Bryan, B.A. *, Robt. Joseph Sheehy, Wm. N. Brown, Wm. Harper, R.Y. Cross, R.B. Randolph, Saml. Lindsay, J.W. Lockwood, Wm. W. Adam, H.B. Whittington, Saml. D. Harper, Benj. Barton, Samuel R. Adams, Geo. H. Payne & Co., D.B. Smith, G. Burchell, Robt. Taylor, George A. Thomas, A.G. Newton, Saml. H. Devaughn, George Snyder,

Legislative Petitions of the Town and County of Alexandria, Virginia

O. Fairfax, John T. White, Robt. J. Smith, S.S. Sanders, Cassius F. Lee, John J.O. Wilbar, James C. Garnett, P.H. Hooff, R.H. Stabler, R.H. Gemeny, Peyton Ballenger, Samuel Baggett, Geo. R. Blacklock, David Appich, John Laphen, R. Johnston, John B. Hancock, John L. Smith, George Berry, George McCliesh, B.H. Berry, James Fossett, Thomas Kell, Robt. R. Snyder, Richard Wright, Wm. B. Richards, John Bright, Robert Hodgkins, Joshua Taylor, Henry Bontz, Wm. Bright, Jno. P. Emerson, James R. Smoot, W.H. Marbury, James Dempsey, T.J. Adam, Joseph Masters, Jno. W. Green, J.D. Corse, Jas. English, Stephen A. Green, S. King Shay, John Douglass, I. Buckingham, Hugh Latham, Richard L. Carne, Jno. Snyder, Robert Tomlin, William Page, John Jamieson, Harrison Emerson, T. Betzold, Harrison Emerson, Jr., Geo. L. Deeton, W.R. Ball, Edw. B. Powell, Geo. P. Wise, Saml. A. Masters, and Benjn. H. Lambert.

George H. Smoot (1801-1870), President of Orange and Alexandria Railroad Company, and Directors.
1851, 23 JAN. A604. Increase of stock of company for purpose of extending road from Gordonsville through Lynchburg, thereby traversing a fertile and thriving section. This link between Gordonsville and Lynchburg is all that is wanted to make railroad communication from Washington to southern Mississippi continuous. Petitioners beg leave to state they have that part of their road between Alexandria and Culpeper Courthouse, a distance of 62 miles, in course of construction, and the remainder, 27 miles to Gordonville, already located, and that their prospects are encouraging for its prosecution to completion at an early day. Gives distances via railroad links between other cities throughout the south and north. Signed by Geo. H. Smoot, pres. Mentions a place called "South Lowell" at the Great Falls of the Potomac River, a charter for which has been granted to certain individuals by the Legislature of Virginia. *Referred and Printed.* Alexandria County box.

Citizens of Alexandria, Fairfax, Prince William, Loudoun, Fauquier, Culpeper, Madison, Orange and Greene.
1851, 27 FEB. No number. Same as A599 at page 114. Additional signatures. *Laid on table.* Alexandria County box.

Orange and Alexandria Railroad Company.
1851, 12 MAR. A609. Act guaranteeing company's bonds to amount of $300,000.[115] Original capital $937,500; amount needed to extend road to Culpeper, $360,000; company can raise $60,000 on its own credit. Change from flat rails to heavy ones has greatly increased cost of construction. Statement of expenditures dated 1 MAR 1851, includes amounts for wooden bridging, iron rails, cross ties, chains & spikes, right

---

[115] For construction of their road through the public lot of Orange County (upon which the courthouse of the said county is located), see *Acts of the General Assembly*, 1852, Chapter 164, "An ACT to authorize the Orange and Alexandria railroad company to construct their road through the public lot of Orange county," passed May 29, 1852, pp. 129-130.

of way, engineering expenses, water stations, switches, platforms, and extra equipment. Signed by George H. Smoot, Pres., Alex. R.R. Co. *To be Printed as Doc. No. 69.* Box E.

Hugh Smith (d. 1853).
1851, 21 MAR. Also see A596 at page 113. Original not found.[116] That the conveyance executed to Hugh Smith of Alexandria, dated the ninth of November eighteen hundred and fifty, by Arthur Warring, of the island of Saint Domingo, acting as well for himself as in his character or guardian for his children, appointed by the county court of Alexandria, and as attorney for his wife, for two lots on the commons of Alexandria, numbered five and six, shall as effectually convey the title of the said infants to the purchaser, in and to the said real estate, as if the said infants were respectively of full age and had joined in the said conveyance.

Orange and Alexandria Railroad Company.
1852, 12 JAN. A605. Increase of $180,000 in company's stock. Company planned to lay light rails but finds it wisest to lay heavy and expensive rails. Signed, John S. Barbour, Jr., Pres., O.A.R.R. Co. *Bill reported.* Box E.

President and Directors of the Orange and Alexandria Railroad Company.
1852, 12 JAN. A606. Extension of road from Gordonsville to Lynchburg. Communication between Richmond and Alexandria will soon be completed and extension of road is needed for a continuous communication between north and south. Signed, John S. Barbour, Jr., Pres. *Bill reported.* Box E.

Citizens.
1852, 30 JAN. A607. Act setting apart portion of courthouse lot ceded by Federal government to State for the purpose of building a gunhouse, or an appropriation sufficient to buy suitable site.[117] Quarters of 175th Regiment of Alexandria are insufficient for properly housing four pieces of cannon and other equipment. Signed by Col. C.A. Alexander, 175 Regt. V.; Lt. Col. Wm. L. Powell; Major S. King Shay; Geo. Duffey, Capt. Artillery; and A. Lammond, Supt. Fire Dept. *Bill reported.* Box E.

William H. Muir (d. 1891).
1852, 4 MAR. Original not found. Reimbursement for supplies furnished a

---

[116] Acts of the General Assembly, 1850-1851, Chapter 274, "An ACT concerning Hugh Smith of Alexandria," passed March 21, 1851, p. 191.
[117] Acts of the General Assembly, 1852, Chapter 47, "An ACT providing for a site for a gunhouse at Alexandria," passed February 28, 1852, p. 33. It was located at the northwest corner of Queen and Columbus streets.

company of volunteers for the Mexican war.[118]

Citizens of the Town and County of Alexandria.
1852, 28 APR. A608. Mechanics and merchants who are engaged in erecting or repairing buildings and furnishing materials for some, for the better security and collections of our debts, request enactment of lien law such as exists in other states and existed in Alexandria prior to retrocession.[119] *Referred.* Box E.

Signed by R.A. Rudd, Jas. Green & Son, W.H. McKnight, G.W.P. Maxwell, Thos. M. White, F.M. Weadon, William H. Marckley, Creighton & McNair, Levi Hurdle, Andrew Carson, Waters & Zimmerman, Bernard Crook, W.J. Higdon, James Campbell, John Greenwood, W.T. Watkins, William Jenkins, James Fadeley, Mark Mankin, John T. Hill, Wm. W. Rock, Enoch Grimes, Kephart & Barker, Geo. H. Smoot & Uhler, W.R. Campbell, John T. Johnson, Joseph Masters, Nalls & Co., B.H. Jenkins, Burbon N. Carpenter, and James F. Carlin.

Francis Keys and Others.
1852, 3 MAY. A610. Pilots.[120] Act granting board of commissioners authority to examine pilots in Alexandria County and to grant licenses to pilots working on Potomac River in same manner as licenses are granted to pilots at Cape Henry. Ask for rate of $1.50 per foot for pilotage from the mouth of the Potomac to Alexandria. *Rejected.* Alexandria County box.

Signed by George R. Line, Abm. D. Powell & Son, Cuth. Powell, A.C. Cazenove (with the prayer that the law may be repealed requiring vessels to take or pay for a pilot from sea to the mouth of the Potomac River), Lewis McKenzie, John B. Daingerfield, McVeigh, Harper & Chamberlain, J.I. Thomas, James Dempsey, D.J. Blacklock, Fishburk & Broth., and Charles A. Swan, master of brig. L. P. Swan.

Citizens.
1852, 27 NOV. A611. Dated 20 SEP 1852. Alexandria Limits Extended.[121]

---

[118] Also see Acts of the General Assembly, 1852, Chapter 428, "An ACT for the relief of William H. Muir of the town of Alexandria," passed March 4, 1852, p. 314. ...for the sum of fifty-three dollars and twenty cents, for supplies furnished by said William H. Muir to a company of volunteers for the Mexican war, commanded by the late Captain Henry Fairfax.

[119] Acts of the General Assembly, 1852, Chapter 359, "An ACT to secure to mechanics and others pyament for labor done and materials furnished in the erection of buildings in the city and county of Alexandria," passed June 5, 1852, pp. 242-243.

[120] Acts of the General Assembly, 1852-1853, p. 127, "An ACT concerning pilots," passed February 21, 1853. The rates before prescribed shall be subject to the following qualifications: A pilot shall not be entitled to more than three dollars and fifty cents per foot from sea to Alexandria, nor to more than two dollars and fifty cents per foot from Alexandria to sea...

[121] Acts of the General Assembly, 1852-1853, pp. 314-16, "An ACT amending the 22d and 5th sections of the act entitled an act to amend the charter of the city of Alexandria," passed February 18, 1853.

Notice of application to amend act dividing Fairfax and Alexandria counties, so as to embrace tract of land east of Hooff's Run and between Great Hunting Creek, and to give Alexandria jurisdiction over same for purposes of health, police supervision and protection of burial grounds situated in it. Signed by W.D. Massey, W.W. Harper, Lewis McKenzie, John F.M. Lowe, R. Johnston, and E. Burchell. Accompanying notice to same effect. Alexandria County box.

NOTICE is hereby given that application will be made to the General Assembly at its session which will commence on the 22d day of November 1852, for an amendment of the "act to amend the charter of Alexandria," passed the 7 of May 1852, by substitution for the 22d section thereof a section in the following words, to wit:

Section 22. The limits of the City of Alexandria shall be extended on the north and west so as to embrace the territory within the following bounds: Beginning in the Potomac River at a point distant northerly, in the direction of Fairfax street, 419 feet 2 inches from the present north line of the corporate limits of the town in said River, & running westerly, parallel to said north line, to intersect the west line of said limits produced northerly 419 feet 2 inches; then southerly, with said west line produced, to the northwest corner of the said limits; then easterly, with said north line, into the river; thence northerly to the Beginning; -- Beginning, again, at the intersection of the western line of said limits with the north line of Cameron Street; thence southerly with said western line, to the county line; thence northwesterly with the county line to the point where it intersects the brick wall on the south side of the Little River Turnpike Road; thence northerly by a straight line to the east corner of John Hooff's lot on the south side of King Street extended; thence crossing King street extended to the west corner of the lot late of Col. Francis Peyton; thence with the west line of said lot & the course thereof, to the north line of Cameron street extended; thence by a straight line to the Beginning. And the City Council of Alexandria shall have power to make all needful police & sanitary laws & regulations in and over the territory extending ten feet west of Hooff's or Mushpot Run, & lying between the first of the above courses extended & the county line. The fifty fourth and fifty sixth chapters of the code of Virginia shall be applicable to the said City of Alexandria and its Council, so far as may be consistent with this act. Signed by W.D. Massey, W.W. Harper, Zenas Kinsey, Jno. F.M. Lowe, R. Johnston, and E. Burchell.

Harrison L. Monroe (d. 1899).

1852, 2 DEC. A612. Act legalizing petitioner's election and acts as constable of town and county since his removal from the second district, for which he was elected, to the fourth district.[122] *Referred.* Box E.

---

[122] Acts of the General Assembly, 1852-1853, p. 346, "An ACT to legalize the acts of Harrison L. Monroe of the city of Alexandria as constable," passed December 22, 1852. Monroe was not a resident of the second district of the city when elected.

Citizens of Alexandria and Adjoining Counties.
1853, 5 FEB. A613. Some test of validity of charter granted Baltimore and Ohio Railroad in 1847. Usefulness of Chesapeake and Ohio Canal is much impaired by action of B. & O. R.R. Memorialists are convinced that charter was obtained by misrepresentation and is therefore invalid. *Referred.* Box E.

Signed by J.W. Ashby, P.A. Clagett, E.T. Ashby, Edwd. Snowden, C.D. Kerr, G.B. Blacklock, George C. Armistead, A.H. Johnson, B. Rollins Fowle, Robert S. Ashby, John Howell, S. Schoolherr & Bro., S. Seldner, Wm. Baker, Wm. H. Fitzhugh, Edgar C. King, Jas. Entwisle, Jr., Geo. O. Dixion, R.A. Cox, John Brennen, P. Payne, F. Westwood Ashby, Warren Yeaton,[123] D. Greene, Isaac Kell & Bro., John Kell, John Hill, R.R. Snyder, S.H. Sherman, W.H. Marbury, Saml. A. Masters, Edw. B. Powell, Wm. Wright, John A. Dixion, J.A. Duncan, J.S. Masters, Hugh C. Smith, Wallace Masters, William McVeigh, Wells A. Harper, James H. McVeigh, Charles S. Price, Jas. L. Chamberlain, Jas. C. Nevett, Lewis McKenzie, W.M. Smith, Jas. L. Dyson, John W. Campbell, Burke & Herbert, Albert Fairfax, Wm. T. Powell, J.A. Shinn, G. Wise, James H. Grubb, John Perry, D.R. Wilson & Co., Fowle & Co., M. Marbury, Ebenezer Bacon, Geo. W. Dearborne, Thomas Travers, Wm. K. Masters, M. Burchell, Wm. H. Lambert, Jos. H. Davis, John T.B. Perry, Geo. W. Shacklett, J. Buckingham, Turner Dixon, Thomas Buckingham, Washington C. Page, Edwd. C. Fletcher, W. Fowle, Jas. McKenzie, J.W.D. Ramsay, Jno. Lockwood, Edgar Snowden, B.T. Plummer, J. Slimmer, James Green, Townshd. D. Fendall, James S. Hallowell, William Gregory, Thos. M. White, John Summers, Jno. A. Taliaferro, Henry Peel, Wm. H. Rogers, Robt. Bayne, Wm. Bayne, L.P. Bayne, Charles Boyer, Martin Maddox, J.R. Nicklin, C.C. Calvert, Cassius F. Lee, James P. Smith, Wm. N. Berkley, John H. Brent, Harper & Bro., J. Dixon Page, J.M. Stewart, C.L. Adams, Robert Harper, Geo. E. French, W. Walton Harper, Law. B. Taylor, F. & M. Taylor, Henry Cook, Creighton & McNair, E.J. Miller, Jas. A. English, and C.M. Castleman.

Citizens of Alexandria.
1853, 25 FEB. B481. [originally numbered with Jefferson Co.]. Support of Bill 280 for the charter of the Alexandria, Loudoun and Harper's Ferry Rail Road Company. Signed by Geo. H. Smoot, Saml. Baggett, Kinch & Washington, W.G. Cazenove, Creighton & McNair, and others. *Reported.* Box E.

Orange and Alexandria Railroad Company.

---

[123] Also see Acts of the General Assembly, 1852, Chapter 414, "An Act releasing to William Yeaton the right of the commonwealth to a lot of land in the town of Alexandria," passed May 3, 1852, p. 311. *That all the estate, right, title and claim whatsoever... in and to a lot of ground on the north side of Prince's street, east side of Pitt street, and west side of Royal street, in the town of Alexandria, recently escheated as the property of Edward Harris, shall be and is hereby released to William Yeaton...*

1853, 8 DEC. A614. Stock Subscription in Orange and Alexandria Railroad Company.[124] Subscription by State to company's stock to be issued for purpose of extending road to Lynchburg. When extension was projected, company believed sufficient capital could be obtained from without the State, but unexpected pressure in money market makes this impracticable. Connection is important, as without this link trade of a fertile section will be diverted to other states. Signed, John S. Barbour, Jr., Pres. Printed. *Bill ordered.* Box E.

Citizens of Alexandria.
1854, 12 JAN. A615. Charter for Alexandria Improvement Company, which has been organized to build houses in town.[125] Impossibility of supplying growing demand for houses has prevented large increase in population; the company will remedy this. Signed by John Summers, James M. Whaley, William Arnold, John A. Field, J.J. Campbell, Stephen Swain, Chas. S. Moore, Isaac Entwisle, J. Louis Kinzer, John T. Johnson, Geo. Davis, George H. Markell, Jos. S. Stansbury, James Henderson, John J. Proctor, A.W. Eastburn, John L. Pascoe, and Andrew J. Fleming. *Bill ordered.* Box E.

Stephen Shinn (d. 1863).
1854, 12 JAN. No number. Resolution asking payment $105.41 to S. Shinn for supplies to Capt. Fairfax's Company of Volunteers during the Mexican War.[126] *Reported.* Withdrawn 1856. Box E.

Citizens.
1854, 3 FEB. A616. Report of proceedings of large public meeting in favor of the Alexandria, Loudoun and Hampshire Railroad.[127] Benjamin Hallowell, chairman, Reuben Zimmerman, secretary, and Thos. M. Monroe and David Funston, speakers at a meeting of friend in favor of the railroad. Signed by Benjn. Hallowell, chairman, R. Zimmerman, secretary. *Referred.* Box E.

Citizens, Presented by Lawrence B. Taylor.
1855, 7 DEC. A617. Removal of Alexandria Courthouse to a more central and

---

[124] Acts of General Assembly, 1852-1853, p. 316, "An ACT to authorize a further subscription by the city council of Alexandria to the stock of the Orange and Alexandria railroad company," passed March 14, 1853.
[125] Acts of the General Assembly, 1853-1854, Chapter 154, "An ACT incorporating the Alexandria improvement company," passed March 3, 1854, p. 89. ...*for the purpose of erecting buildings for sale or rent in the city of Alexandria or its vicinity...*
[126] Acts of the General Assembly, 1859-1860, Chapter 432, "An ACT for the relief of Stephen Shinn for furnishing Supplies for Captain Fairfax's Company, previous to being mustered into the Service of the United States, during the Mexican War," passed February 25, 1860, p. 652.
[127] Also see Acts of the General Assembly, 1853-1854, Chapter 59, "An ACT to authorize a change of the western terminus of the Alexandria, Loudoun and Hampshire railroad," passed February 15, 1854, p. 40. Allowing extention of their road, should they deem it expedient, to any point in Hampshire county west of Paddytown.

Legislative Petitions of the Town and County of Alexandria, Virginia

convenient site.[128] That the situation of the Court house of Alexandria County is so remote from the centre of population & business of the City of Alexandria as to be a source of great inconvenience. Dated NOV 1855. *Ordered.* Alexandria County box.

Signed by John W. Tyler, Chr. Neale, Francis L. Smith, Law. B. Taylor, W.A. Taylor, Albert Stuart, George Wm. Brent, W.C. Yeaton, C.W. Wattles, Fendall Marbury, Chas. W. Blincoe, H.C. Claughton, Landon C. Alliason, Monroe & Funsten, Sam Chilton, Edwd. M. Spilman, Thos. S. Hill, R.E. Scott, John Janney, B.H. Berry, J. Louis Kinzer, Joseph C. Moore, C.P. Shaw, C.F. Smith, and one illegible signature.

Purchase of Site for Custom-House and Post Office.

1855, 18 DEC. Original not found. U.S. has appropriated funds for the purchase of a site and construction of a suitable building at the city of Alexandria for a custom-house, post-office and other offices of the United States, on the condition that the lot for these shall be exempt from taxation for state and city purposes. The state retains concurrent jurisdiction with the U.S. over the place.[129]

Committee of Citizens.

1857, 7 DEC. A618. "Memorial of a Committee of Citizens, Appointed at a Late General Meeting of the Stockholders of the Orange and Alexandria Rail-Road Company (Charlottesville: James Alexander, Printer, 1857)." Subscription by State to Orange and Alexandria Railroad Company's stock, in order to complete the connection with the Virginia and Tennessee Railroad.[130] Printed. *Reported.* Box E.

Names the following petitioners: W.D. Massey and L.B. Taylor of Alexandria Co., Alfred Moss and R.H. Whaley of Fairfax Co., B.E. Harrison and Eppa Hunton of Prince Wm. Co., B. Shumate and B.H. Shackelford of Fauquier Co., D.F. Slaughter (written over R.H. Field) and

---

[128] Also see Acts of the General Assembly, 1859-1860, Chapter 346, "An ACT to amend the act authorizing the erection of a New Court-house in the City of Alexandria," passed March 27, 1860, p. 568. Should there be any surplus funds after the purchase and furnishing, such proceeds shall be equally divided between the county and city.

[129] Acts of the General Assembly, 1855-1856, Chapter 6, "An ACT giving the consent of this state to the purchase by the United States of a lot of land in the city of Alexandria, for the purpose of erecting theron a building for a custom-house, post-office and other offices of the United States, and exempting said lot and building from state and city taxes," passed December 18, 1855, pp. 6-7; and Chapter 7, "An ACT to amend and re-enact the act passed December 18, 1855, entitled an act giving the consent of this state to the purchase by the United States of a lot of land in the city of Alexandria, for the purpose of erecting theron a building for a custom-house, post-office, and other offices of the United States, and exempting said lot and building from state and city taxes," passed February 28, 1856, p. 7; Caton, p. 206, Prior to the erection of the building under this Act, the Post Office of the City was located in a two-story brick building on the south side of Prince Street, near its intersection with Pitt Street, and the Custom House in a brick building then standing at the southwest corner of King and Union streets.

[130] Also see Acts of the General Assembly, 1857-1858, Chapter 106, "An ACT authorizing a loan to the Orange and Alexandria rail road company," passed March 25, 1858, pp. 87-88.

Legislative Petitions of the Town and County of Alexandria, Virginia

J.F. Strother of Culpeper Co., Z. Turner and J.W. Miller of Rappahannock Co., T.J. Twyman and Nath. Tatum of Madison Co., Jer. Morton and P.B. Jones of Orange Co., W.D. Hart and W.C. Rives of Albemarle Co., Wm. Massie and W.M. Cabell of Nelson Co., S.M. Garland and Jos. Pettyjohn of Amherst Co., and Wm. Daniel and Odin G. Clay of Campbell Co.

Residents and Proprietors in the County of Alexandria.
1857, 8 DEC. A633. Not calendared (see 11 FEB 1858). Timber and wood in the County has been sold off and demolished so as to render the County deficient in materials for fencing, and therefore the running of hogs at large has become a great grievance to the residents. Alexandria County box.

Signed by Anthony R. Fraser, S.B. Corbett, Robt. Ball, Senr., G. Vanderwerken, Edward Clements, W.B. Lacy, Philo Baldwin, A.G. Gardiner, Allan Pearce, Wm. C. Veitch, Geo. C. Jackson, Wm. D. Nutt, E.A. Whipple, Robert Cruit, F. & A. Schneider, V.P. Austin, Thomas Hughes, Jas. W. Jackson, Jas. Donaldson, J.R. Johnston, J.W. Bowin, Elijah C. Pearl, John R. Brown, H.M. Brown, A.W. Law, O.W. Andrews, Wm. Birch, Samuel Titus, Alonzo Hayes, W.R. Birch, John W. Travers, J. Roach, Richd. Southern, Edwd. P. Upton, Henry C. Jewell, Peter Riptler, Harvey Bailey, Randolph Birch, John R. Compton, Nelson Vorce, C.C. Weston, D.M. Todd, J.W. Kay, E. Yohe, A. Kipp, C. Kipp, D. Scott, and one illegible signature.

Shipping Merchants at the Port of Alexandria and Others.
1857, 9 DEC. A619. Amendment to the pilot laws, to grant licenses and enforce proper regulations for the business of piloting the Potomac River alone as low as Point Lookout. *That there is a number of experienced and capable pilots upon said River who are able & desirous of pursuing their calling thereupon, but who, in consequence of their great distance from the Capes of Virginia, are unable to compete for business there with the Hampton and Baltimore pilots, and cannot, therefore, provide & maintain the equipment required by law & necefsary for the prosecution of their businefs at that point; and that, for this reason, the Board of Pilot Commifsioners at Alexandria can not give that effect to the law respecting pilots upon said River which was intended in the creation of that Board... Shipping, particularly in the larger clafses is, consequently, subjected to great risks, delays, and lofses, many instances of which might be named.* Your petitioners show that an effectual remedy for these evils would be found in an amendment of the law so as to authorize the Board of Commifsioners at Alexandria to grant licenses, and enforce proper regulations for the businefs of piloting on the Potomac River alone, requiring the persons so licensed to cruis [sic] as low down as Point Lookout, and to take charge of vefsels there or at any other point or place on said River. *Referred.* Box E.

Signed by Benj. H. Lambert, Fowle & Co., F.A. Marbury, Ebenezer

Bacon, R.J.T. Wilson, J.W. McVeigh & Chamberlain, C.F. Suttle & Co., Hill, Brown & Patton, Wheat & Bro., Nevett & Snowden, Washington & Co., P.G. Uhler, Robert Taylor, G.W. Taylor, R.G. Violett, Daniel Cawood, Robinson & Payne, J. Buckingham, Andrew J. Fleming, B.H. Berry (Clerk of the Alexa. County Court), D. Funsten, Jno. Addison, D.R. Blacklock, D.S. Gwin & Son, Ford & Wickliffe, J.C. McCracken, Wm. G. Boothe, David A. Lowe, Thomas Travers, Saml. A. Masters, J.W.H. Wheatley, William H. Treakle, Judah Chase, Jr., Sylvester Chase, Theophilus Chase, Samuel Parritt, Saml. P. Bower, S.S. Wicks, Samuel Baker, Joseph C. Moore, John H. Bailey, Steven Dunton, James Hammond, Wm. H. Fowle, Turner Dixon, T.N. Bemis & Co., D.B. Smith, T.W. Ashby, R. Johnston, Powell & Co., John T. Johnson, John R. Masters, W.A. Duncan, Josiah H. Davis, Thos. B. Travers, Aron Wallace, John R. Wallace, Thomas Butler, Wm. P. Baxter, Richard Kirkney, Robert Markes, William H. Brown, Wm. E. Bell, W.H. Shutt, and Susan S. Page, and two illegible signatures.

Merchants and Tradesmen of Alexandria.
1858, 4 JAN. A620. Change in the next revenue act passed providing for the same taxation of capital employed in mercantile pursuits as for that employed in manufactures and agriculture. For some years past merchants have been taxed five or six times their due and this system hinders commercial development. Signed by Ford & Wickliffe, McVeigh & Chamberlain, W.M. Smith, P.H. Hooff, and 110 others. *Referred.* Box E.

Citizens of Alexandria County.
1858, 6 JAN. A621. Protest against any further legislation for Washington and Alexandria Railroad. Arrangement between railroad and Washington and Alexandria Turnpike Company, by which railroad was built on bed of turnpike, has produced great inconvenience. It is almost impossible to recover damages inflicted by railroad and stockholders of turnpike have suffered great loss because of construction of railroad on it. Signed by R.E. Lee, A.E. Addison, Frances Roach, Robert Ball, and 21 others. *Referred.* Alexandria County box.

Citizens of Alexandria County.
1858. 6 JAN. Duplicate of A621. Arrangement of the Washington and Alexandria Rail Road Company and the Washington and Alexandria Turnpike, by which one half of the bed of the turnpike has been occupied by a railway. *Referred.* Alexandria County box.

Signed by A.E. Addison, R.E. Lee, Anthony R. Fraser, Robt. Ball, James Roach, Bushrod W. Hunter, G. Jackinan, John Slater, W.T. Harper (as to injury of travel), John J. Lloyd (do.), John Hoover (*inconvenience getting into my farm, all the above petitioners are sufferers as well as myself, damage to myself individually $5,000 would not pay*), Nicholas Febrey, H.W. Febrey, Richard Williams, Asa Gladmon, George Barber, George Sarat, William Taylor, James T. Ball, Junius Shimaker, John Febrey, and

Wm. N. Brown.

Citizens of the County of Alexandria.
1858, 11 JAN. A622. Against any further legislation for the Washington and Alexandria Rail Road Company and complaining of the great injustice done them by permitting it to be constructed on the only turnpike road they have leading to Washington. *Referred.* Alexandria County box.

Signed by Nelson Vorce, Wm. J. Gary, Saml. [his mark] Birch, Jr., James Longron, Mark Hartley, John Brown, M.A. Febrey, C.M. Yohe, Francis A. Dickins of Fairfax Co., William Elliott, Harvey Bailey, Samuel Shreve, Septemous Brown, Noah Drummonds, J.L. Sisson, J.R. Johnston, W.B. Lacy, Amos Dye, W.H. Clampitt, H.S. Wunder, E. Yuler, C.C. Weston, Archibald Dyer, Samuel Birch, Reason Orm, John T. Birch, Wesley Carlin, William R. Birch, Richard L. Shreve, Robert Donaldson, Alfred Wells, J.W. Sommers, Benjamin Black, Malcolm Douglass, Edward Clements, John Massey, John Clark, Edwd. A. Dickins of Fairfax Co., Alonzo Hayes, James T. Clark, Geo. O. Wunder, James E. Murray, H.C. Thompson, William Shreve, Samuel Scott, John Disney, Robert Disney, Geo. W. Thompson, W.C. Lipscomb, John Hall, John C. Disney, Benjamin Dennison, J. Cromwell, John Terrett, George W. Ginnacom, J.W. Kay, A.F. Tennent, J. Drull, J.W. Sherwood, Wm. McLean, Jas. B. Azena, Benjamin A. Hummer, W.H.F. Carlin, and Joshua Crabbs, Jr., and one illegible signature.

Alexandria Merchants.
1858, 9 FEB. A623. Revision of revenue laws, which at present are unjust to merchants and tradesmen. Under present laws, two-thirds of taxes are drawn from trade and agriculture and have arisen from heavy expenditure in internal improvements, which chiefly benefit farmers. In Maryland and Pennsylvania, farmers and freeholders pay more taxes than merchants. Signed by J. McVeigh & Chamberlain, Cazenove & Co., John B. Daingerfield, Benja. H. Lambert, Wm. H. Fowle, Nevett & Snowden, Green & Tuttle, Robinson & Payne, Stephen Shinn & Son, Harper & Baruch, Wheat & Bro., and others. Printed. *Referred.* Box E.

Residents and Proprietors in the County of Alexandria.
1858, 11 FEB. A624. Act to prevent running at large of hogs (see 8 DEC 1857).[131] Demand for timber in growing cities has made a scarcity of fencing material; consequently hogs are running at large. *Referred.* Alexandria County box.

Signed by Bazel Williams, Edw. B. Powell, B.W. Hunter, James Roach, John B. Daingerfield, J.H. Brewer, Robert Dyer, Wesley Carlin, H. Hoover, Maria Hayes, Allen Pearce, R.C. Farnsworth, Robt. Ball, Geo. W.

---

[131] Acts of the General Assembly, 1857-1858, Chapter 259, "An ACT to prevent the running at large of hogs in the county of Alexandria," passed January 5, 1858, pp. 160-161. Hogs trespassing in Alexandria county may be distrained or impounded.

Thompson, Richd. Southern, Caleb L. Birch, Daniel Wells, Edward P. Upton, Mrs. W.D. Wallach, A.G. Gardiner, John Birch, Timothy Milburn, Thomas Thompson, Wm. D. Nutt, W.B. Lacy, G.C. Synier, Wm. Jenks, Cyrus Martin, Lewis Martin, Philo Baldwin, John B. Brown, Addison Brown, R.B. Alexander, Jos. W. Davis, Anthony R. Fraser.

Citizens of Alexandria.
1860, 5 JAN. No number. Clerks of Alexandria in favor of abolishing the tax on salaries. Clerks employed in the various branches of business feel oppressive the tax on their salary. No note of action. Box E.

Signed by Edwd. C. Fletcher, D.R. Semmes, Townsh. C.D. Fendall, J. McCormick, Jr., Peter Wise, J.W. Hooff, A.J. Humphreys, H.B. Taliaferro, R.H. Patton, R. Crupper, Frank Wise, John T. Hart, Francis J. Davidson, Wm. Perry, Eugene V. Fairfield, Frank T. Grady, Thos. W. Smith, Chas. R. Hooff, James Entwisle, Lewis Hooff, H.B. Clagett, Lyttleton Withers, R.W. Nalls, N.L. Huntt, Wm. W. Larkin, Wm. H. Hutt, W.H. Marbury, Wm. Gregory, James M. Beckham, John D. Javins, James E. Green, F. Westwood Ashby, Robert Kell, Jr., W.J. Entwisle, C.L. Adams, James M. Adams, Edmund Perry, George Taylor, E.M. McMurran, John B. Slaymaker, Charles W. Jett, J.R. Hunter, Edgar Snowden, Jr., Robt. L. Ashby, George W. McCleish, Hesselius Smith, S.M. Dent, Daniel Morgan, J.W. Lockwood, G.W.P. Ramsay, C.W. Wattles, W.E.H. Clagett, and R.H. Gemen.

James P. Smith (d. 1873), Executor of Hugh Smith.
1860, 6 FEB. A625. Relief in the case of a judgment obtained by Hugh Smith against the Fauquier and Alexandria Turnpike Company. Court gave instruction to use any surplus arising from toll after payment of said judgment for repairs. But up to the present time expenses have equaled the earnings and judgment has not been paid. Signed, James P. Smith, Exr. of Hugh Smith, decd. *Referred.* Box E.

Citizens.
1860, 23 FEB. No number. Support of law requiring prepayment of freights on the railroad, believing it will greatly benefit the general interest of the City by relieving very heavy taxation and placing an equal footing with other commercial cities.[132] No note on action. Box E.

Signed by Barley & Triplett, Peel & Stevens, Ridgely Hampton & Co., Albert W. Gray & Co., Knox & Brother, Gray Miller & Co., Jno. W. Stewart, Bayne & Co., Wheat & Bro., Pennybacker & Perry Bros., Isaac Paul, Partlow Hill & Co., C.F. Suttle & Co., R.R. Snyder, Markell & Co., D.S. Gwin & Son, H. Eldridge & Co., C.A. Baldwin & Co., Fowle & Co., Jas. C. Nevett, Robt. G. Violett, Geo. H. Robinson, J.N. Harper & Co.,

---

[132] Acts of the General Assembly, 1859 1860, Chapter 129, "An ACT to prohibit Rail Road Agents from charging more than regular Transportation Rates on Rail Road Freights," passed March 30, 1860, p. 276.

Kincheloe & [Swain?], Smoot Uhler & Co., Waters & Zimmerman & Co., J. English & Bro., A. Jamieson & Co., Addison Wallace & Co., C.C. Smoot & Son, Meade & Marye, Josiah H. Davis, Wm. H. Fowle & Son, George H. Markell, J.H. McVeigh & Son, Blacklock Marshall & Co., S. Hartley & Son, D.B. Smith, Danl. F. Hooe, Daniel Cawood, Douglas S. Gregory, J.W. Wrenn, L.A. Larkin, C.C. Berry, R.Y. Cross, Henry C. Field, Bryan & Adam, Wm. W. Adam, *, Jno. J. Evans, John Latouche, Wm. H. Rogers, John T. Creighton, Harper & Bro., W.D. Massey, Jas. Entwisle, Jr., J. Rosenthal, Simon Waterman, G.C. French, *, W.B. Richards, Jr., William Arnold, Geo. Taylor, W.A. Hart, C.W. Green, H.J. Gregory, Peyton Ballenger, J.H. Devaughn, Henry Schwarz, Lewis Baar, W.H. Muir, S.W. Meyersberg, John Ogden, J.M. Stewart, Jas. Entwisle & Son, G.K. Witmer & Bros., Henry Cook & Co., Isaac Eichberg, M. Trenman & Co., James Green, R.H. Miller & Son & Co., Robt. Bell, John A. Dixon, Chas. J. Wise, Lyttleton Withers, P.H. Hooff, Jno. T. Young, Steph. Shinn, Clemson & Cookson, and Wise & Co.

Merchants.
1861, 15 FEB. A626. Protest against repeal of act prohibiting sale of wood in Alexandria without license. Wood is bought in Maryland and Delaware and sold in evasion of the law. If law is repealed, dealers should not be required to pay license. Signed by J.H. Harper & Co., Wheat & Bro., C.F. Suttle & Co. No note on action. Box E.

INDEX

Unknowns

()
Andrew	15, 28
B.A.	118
Charles	39, 84, 87
Daniel	31
Ephraim	42
Fraser	28
Frederick	84
French V.	43
George	18, 24, 33
Hiram	64
Isaac	83
J.R.	84
Jacob	17
James	19, 109
Jerome	28
Jesse	42
John	23, 25, 47, 95
John B.	83
Ludwig	17, 56
Luke	33
Philip	24
Samuel	25
Sanford	24, 42
Stephen	95
Thomas	23, 31, 35, 70, 85
William	15, 17, 30, 43, 92
William H.	105
Willm.	17

__FARSALL
    J. 16

__FORD
    John E. 28

__LINSTINE
    William 84

__LSON
    Jacob R. 84

__NSTON
    Benjamin 55

A

ABBOTT
    William 8, 34

ABERT
    John 43, 47, 57

ABRAMS
    Charles 21, 33

ADAM
    Anna () 111
    James 3, 6-9, 35

John	81, 82, 87
Robert	1, 3, 4, 6, 7, 9, 11, 12, 17, 20, 35, 81, 82, 111
T.J.	119
William	109
William W.	83, 95, 118, 130

ADAMS
Abednego	23, 31, 32
C.L.	123, 129
Edward	22
George R.	83, 86, 88, 95
James L.	84
James M.	129
John	90
Josiah P.	6
Samuel	17, 23, 55, 62, 63, 66, 69
Samuel R.	83, 86, 92, 99, 102, 109, 118
Simon	23
William	24

ADDISON
A.E.	127
John	127

ADRAIN
    Hugh 66, 70

ALBERT
John	55
Michael	23

ALBERTS
    Lud. 47

ALEXANDER
Amos	57, 63, 65, 70
C.A.	106, 120
Charles	3, 18, 24, 40, 66, 71, 76, 77
G.B.	92
Gerard	74
Gerrard	42
James	125
John	1, 2, 5, 9
M.	56
Mark	62
Philip	1, 16, 18
R.B.	85, 97, 129
Robert	15, 18, 25, 42
Walter S.	86

Alexandria:
Academy	12
Aldermen	2, 3, 6, 7, 19
Boundaries	2, 9, 48, 121
Building houses in	124
Burgess from	6
Burial Grounds	122
City Council	122

131

Climate 4
Common Council   2, 3, 6, 7, 9, 19, 45,
        46, 48, 51, 52, 105, 106
Custom-House 125
Election of Town Officers 2
Erection of the Town 1
Establishment of a Naval Office at .. 4
Fairs in 57
Gunhouse at 120
Harbor 5, 78
Harbor/Port 126
Hospital 7
Hotel 99
Hunting Creek Inspection 5
Hustings Court .. 19, 36, 37, 45, 48,
                                 95-99
Incorporation of 2
Library 38, 51, 57
Lots in   1, 6, 9, 10, 15, 20, 37, 46, 48,
        49, 51, 67, 74, 75, 100, 101
Market 3, 27, 36
Market Square 36
Mason's Hall 38
Mayor ... 2, 3, 6, 7, 9, 19, 45, 48, 51,
                                    52
Nuisances in 48
Piers and Docks 11
Police 122
Poor House 27
Post Office 125
Quarantine Regulations 52
Recorder 2, 3, 6
Rope Walk at 51
Sales of Lots at 2
Settlement of 1
Shipping 11
Ships at 1
Streets 7, 9
Taxes 5
Time Restriction for Building 1
Trustees 1, 6, 20, 36
Warehouse at .. 1, 20, 44, 46, 71, 92,
                                    100
Water 7
Wharf at 1, 20, 51, 100, 102
Wharves 10
Alexandria and Gordonsville Railroad .. 114
Alexandria and Harper's Ferry Railroad
    Company 88
Alexandria and Potomac Railroad
    Company 88
Alexandria and Valley Railroad .. 109, 111
Alexandria Canal 89, 96, 99, 101
Alexandria Canal Company . 78, 99, 101,
                                    102
Alexandria County Jail 111
Alexandria Courthouse 124
Alexandria Gazette 36
Alexandria Hospital 81
Alexandria Hotel Company 99

Alexandria Hustings Court 102
Alexandria Improvement Company ... 124
Alexandria Jail 54, 77, 107
Alexandria Library Company 51, 57
Alexandria Lodge No. 22 38
Alexandria Marine Railway Company .. 103
Alexandria Orphan Asylum 91
Alexandria Railroad Company 120
Alexandria Railway Company 103
Alexandria Savings Institution 90
Alexandria Turnpike Company 127
Alexandria, Loudoun and Hampshire
    Railroad 124
Alexandria, Loudoun and Harper's Ferry
    Railroad Company 123
ALGERON
    Peter 71
ALLAN
    John 17, 25
ALLEN
    Andrew 23, 31
    David 30
    Edwin T. 84
    George 97
    John 31
    Montgomery 19
    Samuel 64
    Thomas 63
ALLEY
    Amos 56
    Stephen 48
ALLIASON
    Landon C. 125
ALLISON
    Amos 56, 63, 64, 71
    Ann 82
    Bryan 18
    George 83
    J. 3
    John   8, 9, 12, 18, 20, 24, 28, 31, 33,
                    34, 39, 67, 82
    Robert   3, 6, 9, 11, 12, 14, 18, 28, 35,
                39, 45, 46, 48, 62, 78, 85
    Thomas 23
    William 18, 21, 97
ALLISTON
    Bryan 32
    John 23, 31
    Thomas 16, 31
    William 18
ALMOND
    William 73
ALTEN
    Robert 19
ALTON
    John 31
ANDERSON
    James 77
    John 24, 32
    Ninian 18, 21, 27, 28, 34

Richard 80
Robert 3, 66, 100, 101
William 14, 16, 18, 22
ANDREWS
   Isaac 43
   O.W. 126
   R.I. 99
   R.J. 83, 95
   Richard 48
ANSLEY
   () 25
APPICH
   David 83, 87, 109, 119
   Gottlieb 86
ARELL
   Christiana 49
   D. 3, 17, 25, 27, 34, 35
   David 8, 36, 49, 82
   Phebe (Caverly) 36
   Richard . 3, 12, 14, 16, 25, 27, 34, 35, 49
   Samuel 6, 8, 15, 34, 35, 45, 49
AREY
   Thornton 98
ARMISTEAD
   George C. 123
   William 47
ARMSTRONG
   John T. 84
   Samuel 98
   William 9, 84
ARNOLD
   Alexander 95
   C.A. 95
   John 83, 87, 95, 107, 109, 118
   William . . 83, 87, 109, 117, 124, 130
ASH
   James 44
ASHBURY
   Joseph 24
ASHBY
   E.T. 123
   F. Westwood 123, 129
   J.W. 123
   Robert L. 129
   Robert S. 123
   T.W. 85, 92, 118, 127
ASHFORD
   John 22
   Michael 24, 31
ASHTON
   John W. 78
   Laurence 15
   R.W. 15, 25
   Richard W. 16
ASKIN
   George 31
   John 31
   William 16

ATCHESON
   Jeremiah 30
ATCHISON
   John 30
   Walter 32
ATHEY
   James 32
   Robert 24
   Thomas 32
ATKINSON
   Bennett 32
   Guy . . 39, 43, 47, 50, 55, 62, 63, 66
   Leonard 32
   Thomas 31
ATTRILL
   Jesse 42
ATTWELL
   William 95, 98
ATWELL
   W.E. 118
   W.M. 92, 98
AUBINOE
   S.W. 87
AUDLEY
   John T. 98
AUSTIN
   John 56
   V.P. 126
AVERY
   Thornton 97
   Wesley 84, 95
AZENA
   James B. 128
AZMAN
   John 23

B

B__
   Michael 43
BAAR
   Lewis 130
BAARE
   Eliza (Fisher) 113
   Eliza J. 113
   Ferdinand R. 113
   Infant 113
BACKUS
   John 56
BACON
   Ebenezer . . 83, 87, 90, 118, 123, 126
   James 62, 63
BADEN
   J. 43
BAGBY
   Elisha 56
BAGGETT
   Alexander 70
   John J. 97
   S. 92

Samuel 109, 119, 123
T.W. 97
Thomas 84
BAGGIT
   Samuel 16
BAGGOTT
   Alexander 70
BAILEY
   Benjamin 23
   Harvey 126, 128
   John H. 127
BAILY
   William 32
BAIRD
   Matthew 83
   Thomas E. 83, 95, 109
BAKER
   Barton 25
   H. 88
   James 19
   Robert 97
   Samuel 19, 42, 127
   Thomas 23
   W.B. 88
   William . 12, 16, 24, 25, 34, 109, 118, 123
BALCH
   James 24
BALDWIN
   C.A. 129
   George 64
   Philo 126, 129
BALEY
   Daniel 90
BALFOUR
   James 18, 20, 33
BALINGER
   Benjamin 24
   John 22
   Joseph 24
BALL
   Andrew A. 97
   Horatio 86
   James T. 88, 127
   John 84
   John T. 84, 92
   Moses 17
   Robert 126-128
   Stephen 84
   W.R. 109, 119
   William 40
   William R. 83, 96
   William W. 114
BALLENGER
   James 30
   John 23, 31
   John T. 86
   Joseph 30
   Peyton 89, 95, 97, 119, 130

BALLENTINE
   Peyton 86
Baltimore and Ohio Railroad 88, 123
BANGS
   John W. 84
Bank of Alexandria . . 39, 44, 46, 47, 63, 69, 71, 101
   Capital Stock 41
Bank of Commerce 117
Bank of Potomac 72, 86
Bank of the Old Dominion 117
BANNINGER
   John 17
BARBEE
   B. Russell 118
BARBER
   George 127
BARBOUR
   John S. 120, 124
BARCLAY
   Thomas 12, 15, 25, 28
BARDE
   G.A. 97
BARKER
   Charles 41
   John 24, 31
   Leonard 31
   Moses 31
   Quintin 89
   Quinton 98
   U.W. 87, 92
   W.W. 109
   William 31
BARKLEY
   Burgess 19
   William 16
BARNES
   Samuel 117
BARNETT
   George 40
   Gerard 32
   Michael 3
BARNEY
   Thomas 84
BARON
   James 66
BARR
   Christopher 18
   George 42
   Hugh 21, 42, 56, 63, 64
BARRON
   Hendley 22
BARRY
   Amelia 82
   Daniel 81
   Honoria 81
   Nicholas 84
   Robert 82
   William 31

BARTLE
   Samuel 97
   William H. 97
BARTLEMAN
   William 56, 63, 64, 66
   William H. 70
BARTLETT
   Samuel 42
BARTON
   Benjamin 87, 90, 117, 118
   D.W. 88
   Richard C. 98
BASALL
   George 23
BASSEL
   Benjamin 22
BATES
   Edward 30
BATTSON
   Abel 42
   David 42
BAXTER
   William P. 127
BAYLEY
   Samuel 30
BAYLISS
   Daniel 87, 97
   John 79
   Prince 31
   Thomas 30, 32
   William 32, 40
   William P. 32
BAYLOR
   Hugh 27
BAYLY
   George 56
   Robert 78
   William 43, 47
BAYNE
   Benjamin 15
   George H. 87, 92
   George M. 84
   L.P. 123
   Robert 123
   William . . 87, 92, 100, 105, 109, 118,
                                                      123
BEACH
   Abraham S. 17
   Charles 24
   N. 98
   S.C. 98
   Samuel 118
   Sandy 84
   Thomas 17
BEAL
   Richard E. 53
BEALE
   John 42
BEALLE
   John 39

BEATTY
   John 43
BEATY
   Andrew 42
BEBE
   Gabriel 22
BECKHAM
   James M. 129
BECKWITH
   M. 23
   M.R. 22
   Marmaduke 32
BEDINGER
   Jacob 28
BEECHAM
   Alexander 17
BEEDLE
   Thomas 56
BEELER
   B. 35
   C. 40
   Christian L. 74
   Frederica A. 74, 75
BEERY
   Jacob 21
BEESON
   Everard 44
BEILL
   Peter 14
BELCHER
   John H. 47
BELDEN
   Charles 84
BELL
   Anderson 100
   Daniel 100
   Doll 100
   James 27
   John 40, 100
   Richard 84
   Robert 83, 87, 109, 118, 130
   William E. 127
BEMIS
   T.N. 127
BENCE
   Adam 25, 33, 39, 56
BENNETT
   C. 70, 71
   Charles 43, 50, 55, 57, 62, 65
   Dozier 24
   Hodson 24
   Joseph 23, 24
   Richard 22
   Thomas 24
BENT
   C.C. 109
   Lemuel 34, 43, 46, 51, 56
BENTON
   Samuel 84

BERKLEY
   William N. . . 83, 86, 90, 99, 109, 113, 123
BERRY
   Alexander 63
   B.H. . . . 97, 105, 116, 119, 125, 127
   Ban. 40
   Benjamin 19
   C.C. . 83, 86, 95, 102, 109, 118, 130
   Enoch 19
   George 89, 98, 119
   J. 19
   Joseph 19
   Mildred W. 91
   Miss 90
   Noble 89
   R. 92
   Thomas 40
BERRYMAN
   W.B. 97
BETZOLD
   David 90
   T. 119
BEVERLEY
   Peter R. 92, 95
BICKING
   James H. 87
BICKSLER
   John 70
BIDDLE
   Thomas 32
BIGGS
   James 90, 95
   Randle 42
BIGSON
   Isaac 55
BIGWOOD
   James 32
BILLINGTON
   William 55, 63, 70
BIRCH
   Caleb L. 129
   Charles 31, 32
   James 97
   John 97, 129
   John T. 128
   Joseph 22, 70
   Randolph 126
   Robert 97
   Samuel 86, 97, 128
   Thomas 30
   W.R. 97, 126
   Wesley 97
   William 126
   William R. 128
BIRD
   W. 23, 39
   William 6, 34, 35, 39-41, 43
BISHOP
   Daniel 55
   David 41
   Samuel 62, 64, 65
BLACK
   Andrew 27
   Benjamin 128
   David 24
   John 17
   Robert 70, 71
   Samuel 24
   Thomas 22
BLACKBURN
   Edward 24, 34
   Richard 23
   Thomas 32
BLACKLOCK
   () 92
   Anne M. 82
   D. 110, 118
   D.J. 121
   D.R. 118, 127
   Dennis H. 95
   Dennis R. 85
   Eliza 82
   G.B. 123
   George R. 119
   J. 110
   S. 118
BLACKWELL
   Samuel 53
BLADEN
   J.T. 85
   John 97
   William 31
BLAKE
   Thomas 42
BLAKEMORE
   George 19
BLAKENY
   Abel 70
BLANSETT
   John 32
   Joseph 32
BLANTON
   Richard 19
BLINCOE
   Charles W. 125
BLISH
   Henry 97
BLOSS
   Adam 27
BLUE
   Alfred A. 84
   John J. 84
BLUNT
   Washer . . . 3, 6, 8, 14, 16, 25, 27, 29, 33, 35, 46, 62, 64
BO___
   James 16
BOA
   Cavan 48

BODKIN
  W.S. 92, 118
BOGGESS
  Josiah 30-32
  Richard 57
  Robert 16, 23
  Samuel 42
BOGUE
  John 8
BOLING
  William 23
BOLTE
  John 56
BONHAM
  Jerimiah 24
BONTZ
  Henry 98, 119
  Jacob 8
  John 98
  Valentine 27
  William C. 83, 109
Books: 12, 51, 99
BOOTHE
  William G. 127
BORROWDALE
  John 66
BOSSWELL
  James 31
BOSTICK
  Edmond 32
BOSWELL
  John 31
  Matthew 31
  William 31, 83, 92
BOUSH
  Nathaniel 100
BOWDEN
  Joseph 56
BOWEN
  John W. 95
  Obadiah 34
  Thadw. 27
BOWER
  Samuel P. 127
BOWIE
  George 12, 18, 21
  John 42
  William 48, 55, 62, 70
BOWIN
  J.W. 126
BOWLING
  John 3
  Joseph 56
  Samuel 21
  William 15, 25, 97
BOYCE
  Richard 15, 17
BOYD
  Elisha 44
  James 15, 17, 83
  John 55, 97
  William 16
BOYER
  Charles 123
  Henry 84
  John 33, 56, 64
  Philip 14
BOYIER
  John 56
BOYLE
  Fran. 53
BOZELL
  Mathew 22
BRADLEY
  () 85
  C.C. 83, 96, 98, 118
  Daniel 24
  H. 87, 98, 118
  Harrison 84
  P.B. 78
  William 114
BRADY
  John 40
BRANDON
  James 56, 63, 64
BRAY
  William 56
BREEN
  James 90
BREITHAUPT
  John G. 85
BRENER
  John 85
BRENGLE
  Henry 89, 95, 98
BRENNEN
  John 123
BRENT
  George W. 125
  Henry 16
  John 15, 25, 34, 43
  John H. . . . 85, 88, 96, 99, 113, 117,
                                          118, 123
  William 43, 46
BREWER
  J.H. 128
BREWIS
  Thomas A. 118
Bridges:
  Abutments 89
  Washington 78
BRIGHT
  John 119
  William 119
  Windel 8
BRITTON
  Benjamin 23
BROADWATER
  Charles 22, 33
  Charles L. 15, 23, 33, 35

BROCCHUS
  Thomas 56, 100
BROCK
  Thomas 43
BROCKET
  Robert 35, 47, 55, 64, 66
BROCKETT
  F.L. 87, 90
  F.S. 83
  R.L. 109
  Robert 83, 86, 90
BRODER
  T.A. 43
BRODERS
  Joseph 18, 22
BROKET
  Robert 23, 28
BROMLEY
  William 8, 15, 17, 18, 25, 35
BRONAUGH
  Benjamin 53
  John 25
  William 42
BROOK
  William W. 53
BROOKE
  Barnabas 70
  Fran. 17
  Francis 14
  John 84
  Richard 55, 70
  Walter 15, 17, 25, 40
BROOKS
  John 56
  John T. 64
BROWN
  Addison 129
  C.F. 83
  Coleman 24
  Edward 22
  George 54
  H.M. 126
  James 56
  John 40, 52, 90, 97, 128
  John B. 129
  John D. 86, 95, 102
  John L. 83
  John R. 126
  Jonathan 53
  Joseph 16
  O.M. 88
  Samuel M. 8, 14, 17, 28, 33
  Septemous 128
  Thomas 22
  Thomas P. 83
  W. 9, 14, 18, 23, 27, 34
  William 12, 33, 34
  William H. 127
  William N. 83, 87, 109, 118, 128
  Windsor 2

BROWNE
  A. 34
  John 98
BRUMBACK
  John 30
BRYAN
  Bernard 48, 55, 66, 69, 70
  Charles 3, 6, 18, 22, 34, 43
  George 83, 85, 95, 118
  James D. 83, 95, 98, 118
  John 19, 48, 55, 62, 63, 66, 70
  Joseph 14
  M. 6
BRYANT
  George 86
  William 33
BRYCE
  Nicols. 18
BRYMAN
  Alexander 56
BRYSON
  And. 66
BUCHAN
  Alexander 14, 20, 28
  John 55
BUCHANAN
  James 84
  James H. 90, 97
  R.E. 84, 87, 98
  Robert E. 89
BUCHER
  William 24
BUCKINGHAM
  I. 119
  Isaac 85, 87, 89, 105, 117
  J. 123, 127
  Thomas 123
BUCKLEY
  John 22, 30
  Joshua 22
  William 30
BUCKNER
  Richard 55
  Thornton 46
BUDD
  Henry 14, 18, 25, 35
BUDDICOM
  William 35
BURCH
  John 85
  Oliver 22
BURCHELL
  E. 83, 92, 95, 102, 109, 122
  Edward 86
  G. 118
  M. 123
  Norval W. 116
BURFORD
  Henry 70
  R. 69

BURGER
  Thomas 31
BURGESS
  William 84
BURKE
  Edward 56
  George 112
  James 22
  John 43
BURN
  Terrence 24
BURNES
  John 24
  Thomas 24
BURNETT
  Robert 109
BURNS
  John 15, 17, 33
  Thomas 84, 98, 118
BURRAGE
  Thomas 83, 84
BURRESS
  Thomas 86
BURRLY
  Peter R. 84
BURRS
  John 25
BURTON
  John 47
BURWELL
  Lewis 36
  Nathaniel 42
BUSH
  Dennis 19
BUSHBY
  James 25
  Jos. 16
  Joseph 15, 27, 48
  William . . 3, 8, 14, 25, 27, 35, 39, 43,
    48

Businesses:
  () & Triplett 47
  A. & Jacob Swoope 25
  A. Jamieson & Co. 130
  A.C. Cazenove & Co. 87, 92
  Abraham D. Powell & Son 121
  Addison, Wallace & Co. 130
  Albert W. Gray & Co. 129
  Allison & Ramsay 4
  Allison & Young 47
  Andrew & William Ramsay . 39, 45, 63
  Andrew Jamieson & Son 87
  Ashby & Herbert 118
  Bakers & Brown 88
  Barley & Triplett 129
  Bartleman & White 65
  Bayne & Co. 129
  Benjamin A. Hamp & Co. 39
  Benjamin Hamp & Co. 24
  Benjamin W__ & Son 42

Bennett & Watts 45, 48
Berkley & Harper 118
Blacklock, Marshall & Co. 130
Bolte & Foeke 64
Bryan & Adam 130
Burke & Herbert 123
C.A. Baldwin & Co. 129
C.C. Smoot & Son 130
C.F. Suttle & Co. 127, 129, 130
C.G. Wildman & Co. 86
C.M. & F. Taylor 85, 86, 109
Campbell Wilson & Co. 71
Carne & Slade 48
Casenove & Walker 39
Catlett & Meeks 63-65, 69
Cazenove & Co. 118, 128
Cazenove & Walker 43
Cazenove Co. 100, 105
Clark & Brother 87
Clemson & Cookson 130
Cook & Peck 118
Creighton & Bodkin 118
Creighton & McNair . . . 118, 121, 123
D. & J. Blacklock 110
D. & S. Blacklock 118
D.R. Wilson & Co. 123
D.S. Gwin & Son 127, 129
Darling & Earp 28, 39
Davis & Smoot 111
Delius & Weidemeyer 63
Dixon & Littlepage 22
Dow & McIver 4
Dunlap & Craig 39
Edward K. Thompson & Co. . . . 15, 25
F. & A. Schneider 126
F. & M. Taylor 118, 123
Fendall & Hipkins 40
Fishburk & Brother 121
Fitzgerald & Peers 4
Fleming & Douglass 109, 118
Fletcher & Otway 43, 45, 47
Fletcher, Otway & Co. 39
Ford & Wickliffe 127
Ford, Patton & Co. 45
Forrest & Seton 39
Foster & May 48
Fowle & Co. . 99, 105, 106, 110, 123,
    126, 129
Fowle Co. 118
G.K. Witmer & Bros. 130
Geo. Dixion & Co. 92
Geo. H. Payne & Co. 118
Geo. H. Smoot & Uhler 92
Geo. Sweeney & Co. 43
George ? & Co. 87
George H. Smoot & Uhler . . . 105, 121
George Moore & Co. 42
George O. Dixion & Co. 100, 118
George W. Johnston & Co. 86
Gleese & Co. 62, 70

Gray, Miller & Co. 129	Lancaster & Gardiner 118
Green & Tuttle 128	Leml. Bent & Co. 43
Grimes & Kincheloe 118	Leven Powell, Jr. & Co. 45
H. Bradley & Son 87	Lewis & Quigley 118
H. Eldridge & Co. 129	Lewis & Stover 43
H. Grimes & Co. 92	M. Trenman & Co. 130
H. Peel & Co. 87	MacIver & MacKenzie 43
Harper & Baruch 128	Markell & Co. 129
Harper & Bro. 123, 130	Masters & Co. 87
Harper & Davis 64	Matthew Robinson & Co. . . 43, 46, 47
Hartshorne & Donaldson 39	McCrea & Mease 4
Henry Cook & Co. 130	McVeigh & Bro. 88
Hepburn & Dundas 39, 101	McVeigh & Bro. & Co. . . 92, 99, 110, 118
Hewes & Miller 63, 71	McVeigh & Chamberlain 127
Hezekiah Smoot & Co. 64	McVeigh, Harper & Chamberlain . . 121
Hill, Brown & Patton 127	Meade & Marye 130
Hodgson, Nicholson & Co. 39	Monroe & Funsten 125
Hooe & Harrison 4, 5	Moore & Young 39
Hooe & Powell 87	Murray & Wheaton 39, 43
Hugh O'Neal & Co. 48	Nalls & Co. 121
Isaac Kell & Bro. 123	Nevett & Snowden 127, 128
J. English & Bro. 130	Norwood & Warfield 39
J. Levyson, Jr. & Co. 39	P. Wise & Co. 64
J. McVeigh & Chamberlain 128	Partlow Hill & Co. 129
J.H. Harper & Co. 130	Paterson, Taylor & Co. 33
J.H. McVeigh & Son 130	Paton & Butcher 25, 39
J.H. Wheat & Bro. 110	Peel & Stevens 129
J.J. Wheat & Bro. 92	Pennybacker & Perry Bros. 129
J.J. Wheat & Bros. 86, 105, 118	Perrin & Brothers 14, 18, 20
J.N. Harper & Co. 129	Perrin Brothers 48
J.W. McVeigh & Chamberlain 127	Perrin Brothers & Co. 35
James & John Camock 39, 43	Perrin Frères 39
James Green & Son 121	Peterson & Taylor 47
James Russell & Co. 71	Pethen & Davis 87
Janney & Irish 45	Pettit & Power 15
Jas. Entwisle & Son 130	Pomery & Isabell 48
Jas. Patton & Davd. Finlay 42	Powell & Co. 127
Jenckes Winsor & Co. 28	R.H. Miller & Son & Co. 130
Jesse Taylor, Jr. & Co. 43	Richard Latham & Co. 66
Jesse Wherry & Co. 42	Ricketts & Newton 40, 42, 45, 47
John & Thomas Vowell 45, 71	Ridgely Hampton & Co. 129
John Corse & Son 86	Robert & James Hamilton 50
John Dundas & Co. 101	Robert B. Jamiesson & Co. 42
John Gill & Co. 48	Robert Hamilton & Co. 40, 43
John Hickman & Co. . 15, 18, 25, 39, 47	Robert Young & Co. 43
John Murray & Co. 15	Roberts & Griffith 64
Joseph & Samuel Harper 45, 50	Robinson & Payne 127, 128
Joseph Kirkbride & Co. 40	Robinson, Sanderson & Co. 40
Joseph Riddle & Co. 39, 71	Robinson, Sanderson & Rumney . . . 14, 16, 25
Josiah Faxon & Co. 63, 64	Rogerson & Dabney 39, 42
Josiah Watson & Co. 25, 29, 39	Rolle & Foeke 62
Kephart & Barker 121	S. Hartley & Son 130
Kinch & Washington 123	S. Schoolherr & Bro. 123
Kincheloe & [Swain?] 130	S.S. Masters & Son 106, 118
Knox & Brother 129	Smith & Bartleman 70, 71
Koones & Dean 87, 92, 95, 116	Smith & Clark 84
Korn & Wisemiller 40, 45	Smith & McClean 71
Lambert & McKenzie 87, 91, 92, 100, 106, 110	Smoot, Uhler & Co. 130

Sparhawk & Jarvis 42
Stephen Shinn & Son 118, 128
Strayer & Heidey 28
Stump & Ricketts 40, 41
T.M. McCormick & Co. 87
T.N. Bemis & Co. 127
T.W. & R.C. Smith 87, 92
Thomas & Dyer 87, 92
Thomas & James Irvin 39
Thomas & Lloyd 105
Thompson & Veitch 64
Thos. Patten & Co. 43
Thos. Vowell & Sons 42
Washington & Co. 127
Waters & Zimmerman . . . 87, 92, 110, 118, 121
Waters & Zimmerman & Co. 130
Wheat & Bro. 127-130
William Armistead & Co. 45, 47
William H. Powell & Co. 25
William Hartshorne & Son 50
William Hartshorne & Sons 45
William L. Powell & Son 105
William Lowry & Co. . 13, 15, 17, 25, 27, 28
William Newton & Co. 25
Williams & Cary 39, 42, 45, 47
Williams, Cary & Co. 14, 16
Wise & Co. 130
Wm. H. Fowle & Son 130
Wm. L. Powell & Son 118
Wm. Miller & Co. 88
Wm. Stabler & Bro. 118
BUTCHER
   J. 70
   John . 2, 3, 6, 13, 27, 34, 43, 47, 50, 63, 64, 66, 90
   Jonathan 55, 63
BUTLER
   Isaac 55
   Thomas 127
   W.B. 78
BUTT
   Adam 15, 17, 33
   John 16
BUTTS
   Jacob 8, 17, 25, 28, 33, 35
BYRNE
   Patr. 33
   Patrick . . . 18, 28, 43, 55, 64, 66, 70

C

C__THE
   D. 55
CABELL
   W.M. 126
CALVERT
   C.C. 123

CAMOCK
   James 43
   John 43
CAMP
   Lieut. 80
CAMPBELL
   Collin 19
   D. 70
   Daniel 56
   George 62
   J.J. 124
   James . . 25, 55, 63, 65, 71, 87, 121
   John W. 83, 89, 123
   Samuel L. 98
   W.R. 121
   William R. 84, 90, 109
Canals: 78, 89, 96, 99, 102
CANTWELL
   Thomas 40
CARAN
   James 71
CARD
   James 55
CAREY
   James G. 83
CARICO
   Abel 30
   William 30, 32
CARLEY
   Michael 56
CARLIN
   James F. . . . 83, 84, 86, 102, 118, 121
   W.H. 128
   Wesley 85, 128
   William 35
CARLYLE
   George W. 5
   John 1, 5
CARNE
   Richard 87
   Richard L. 119
   William 48, 63, 66, 70, 71
CARNES
   Arthur 23
CARNICLE
   John 16
CAROLIN
   Hugh 55, 64
   James 64
CARPENTER
   Benjamin 42
   Burbon N. 121
   George 19
   Matthew 19
CARR
   Joseph G. 86, 92, 96, 98
CARREL
   James 24
CARRELL
   Denise 24, 42

Edward 42
John 42
CARRIL
   Daniel 16
CARRINGTON
   Timothy 16, 31
   William 66
CARROLL
   James 84, 98
CARSON
   Andrew 121
   George 97
   J.M. 33
   James 97, 106
   John M. 28
   Joseph 85, 98, 118
CARTER
   James 42
   Jesse 63
CARTWRIGHT
   Jonathan 14, 16
   Seth 43, 46, 50
CARY
   Joseph 18, 24, 28, 39, 46, 56, 62, 64
   Virginia 90, 91
CASE
   James 52
CASEY
   D. 40
   Dan 43, 53
   John 15, 97
   Thomas 66
   William 43
CASH
   Joseph 97
   Robert 92
   William 24, 55, 62, 63, 65, 70
CASSETT
   Solomon 24, 31
CASSIDY
   Solomon 70
CASTEEN
   S.M. 56
CASTLEMAN
   C.M. 123
   David 19
CATHER
   Samuel 56
CATLETT
   David 19
   Henry 19
   John 19
   Peter 70
CAVAN
   Frances 50
   James 45, 47, 55
CAVERLY
   Jos. 3
   Joseph 6, 25, 34, 36
   Peter 49

Phebe 36
CAWOOD
   Daniel 84, 87, 92, 106, 110, 118,
                              127, 130
   Joseph 110
   Mary 91
   Mrs. 90
   Sally 82
CAYOL
   Antoine 16
CAZENOVE
   Anty. Chs. . . . 56, 62, 64, 71, 85, 87
            91, 92, 110, 116, 118, 121
   L.A. 89
   Louis 91
   Louis A. 83, 86, 99, 102, 116
   Louis C. 87
   W.G. . 85, 86, 89, 90, 102, 110, 117,
                                     123
CHAMBERLAIN
   James L. 83, 123
CHANDLER
   Walter S. 15
CHAPIN
   Gurden . . . 14, 16, 25, 28, 33, 34, 39,
                  43, 47, 55, 62, 66, 70
   Hiram 9, 16, 22
CHAPMAN
   Allan M. 56, 66, 70
   G. 15
   George M. 56
   James 3
   Nathaniel 1, 6
   William 65
CHAPPLE
   Jesse 32
   John 32
CHARLES
   Duncan 56
CHARTERS
   Charles 24
CHASE
   John 17
   Judah 127
   Sylvester 127
   Theophilus 127
CHATHAM
   Henry 85, 95
   James 23, 85, 98
CHATTAM
   James 43
CHATTER
   Thomas 23
CHATTOM
   Stephen 90
CHENAULT
   Elijah 77
CHERUS
   Paul A. 43

Chesapeake and Ohio Canal . . 78, 96, 99, 123
CHEVIS?
   Elizabeth 104
CHEW
   John 15, 33
   Roger 3, 8, 18, 21, 27, 33, 35
   William 27
CHICHESTER
   Daniel M. 32
   Doddridge P. 32
   Richard 32
CHILTON
   Sam 125
CHINN
   Thomas 41
CHIPLEY
   Samuel N. 95
CHURCH
   Jesse 33
   Robert 32
   Thomas 32
Churches:
   Christ Episcopal 37
   Evangelical Lutheran 69
   First Presbyterian 11, 36, 111
   Protestant Episcopal 113
CLAGETT
   Anne 90, 91
   H.B. 129
   Nathaniel 15
   P.A. 123
   R.H. 95
   W.E. 129
CLAMPITT
   W.H. 128
CLAPDORE
   Jacob L. 97
   John M. 98
CLARK
   () 88
   James C. 84, 95
   James T. 128
   John 23, 31, 34, 83, 128
   John M. 31
   Josiah 31
   Josias 23, 31
   Peyton 85
   Richard 23, 56, 63
   Thomas 56, 63
CLARKE
   John 32
   Joshua 55
   Michael 25, 28
   Peyton 98
   Richard 23
   Robert 55, 57
   Thomas 42, 63
CLARRIDGE
   James H. 85, 95

CLARVINS
   John F. 97
CLAUGHTON
   H.C. 125
   P.C. 84, 92, 109, 118
CLAXTON
   E. 85
CLAY
   Odin G. 126
CLEARY
   Michael 56
CLEGG
   John 63, 64, 66, 70
CLEMENTS
   Edward 126, 128
   George 22, 28
   John 3
CLEMENTSON
   George 43, 56
CLEVELAND
   James 24
   William 24
CLIFFORD
   Jeremiah 18, 21
   Nehemiah 18, 21, 70
   Obadiah 56
CLINGMAN
   Jacob 46, 50
CLOWE
   Thomas 95
COBBS
   J.G. 86, 92
COCHBURN
   Martin 47
COCHRAN
   James 19, 21
COCKBURN
   Martin 30
COCKERILL
   Jeremiah 25
   Joseph 24
   Sampson 30
COCKERILLE
   R.H. 78
   Sampson 18
   William 24
COCKRELL
   Benjamin 24
COFFER
   Francis 23, 32
   Joshua 22, 31, 32
COFFEY
   C.H. 56
COHAGAN
   John 79
COHAGEN
   John 109
COHEN
   William 55

COLE
  James 98, 111
COLEMAN
  James 18, 23, 40, 43, 117
  James P. 87, 95, 102, 118
  Joseph 46, 63
COLES
  Daniel M. 55
COLLARD
  John R. 110
COLLINS
  James 3, 15, 23
  John 14, 16
COLLINSWORTH
  A.D. 87, 118
COLTAR
  Thomas 27
COLTART
  Roger 20, 29
COLVILLE
  Ann () 37
COLWELL
  Cor. 56
COM__
  Frederick 40
COMBS
  Robert 41
COMMARGILL
  T. 55
COMPTON
  E.G. 95, 98
  John R. 126
  William 22
  Zebedea 31
CONDON
  Joseph 31
CONKLING
  A. 15
CONN
  Gerrard S. 28
  Gerrard T. 3, 8
  Hugh 24
  Philip 15, 17, 22, 27, 48
  Robert 9, 18, 28, 35
  Thomas . 9, 12-14, 17, 20, 27, 35, 43
CONNER
  Edward 15
  James 16, 32
  Terrence 30, 32
CONRAD
  John 40
CONWAY
  Andrew 113
  Andrew J. 110, 113
  Mary (Vansant) 113
  Mary A. 110
  Richard 1, 3, 5-7, 14, 18, 24, 27,
         33-35, 39, 42, 47, 57, 63, 71, 100,
                                113, 114
  Robert 5, 100

COOK
  Bryan 70
  Henry 84, 87, 109, 123, 130
  John 44
  Leonard 65, 70
  Lewis 17, 22
  Thomas 65, 71
COOKBURN
  Robert 44
COOKE
  Giles 18, 23, 71
  Lewis 56
  Stephen 39, 46, 50, 65
  T. 47
  William 77
COOLEY
  David 85
COOPER
  Joel 3, 8, 35
  Samuel 55, 63, 66, 70
COPPER
  Cyrus 3, 8
  Thomas 28
CORBETT
  S.B. 126
CORBIN
  Thomas 73
CORN
  M.P. 88
CORNBARGER
  John 97
CORNFIELD
  Owing 22
CORRYELL
  Junius 35
CORSE
  J.D. 109, 119
  John 86
  M.D. 83, 95
  M.P. 89, 92
  W. 83
  W.D. 92, 109
CORYELL
  George ... 15, 17, 27, 33, 39, 43, 47,
                    51, 55, 57, 64, 66
CORYTON
  Josiah 47, 48, 62, 63, 66, 70
COTTOM
  Peter 55, 62, 64, 65
COTTON
  E. 22
Counties:
  Albemarle 126
  Alexandria . 77, 80, 83-86, 88, 89, 97,
         98, 100-104, 106-109, 114, 119,
                         121-123, 125-128
  Alleghany 102
  Amherst 126
  Augusta 53
  Buckingham 53

144

Campbell 126
Charlotte 53
Culpeper 114-116, 119, 126
Cumberland 78
Fairfax . 2, 4, 5, 9, 15, 25, 26, 29, 35,
    37, 38, 45, 47, 49, 52, 53, 57, 67,
    75, 77, 78, 81, 83, 88, 89, 104,
    105, 110, 114-117, 119, 122, 125,
    128
Fauquier . 46, 111, 114-116, 119, 125
Fayette 38
Frederick 12, 18
Greene 114-116, 119
Hampshire 124
Jefferson 123
King & Queen 79
Loudoun . 52, 53, 73, 76, 78, 81, 114-
    116, 119, 123
Louisa 53, 95
Madison 114-116, 119, 126
Nelson 126
Orange 53, 114-116, 119, 126
Prince Edward 53
Prince William ... 105, 106, 110, 111,
    114, 115, 119, 125
Rappahannock 126
Rockingham 111
Shenandoah 111
Warren 111
Washington 78
COUPAR
    Robert 14, 18, 25, 29, 33
COUPER
    Alexander 8, 9, 18, 21, 35
Court: 3, 77, 105
    Alexandria 45, 96
    Circuit 103, 107
    Circuit, Chancery .. 103, 104, 107, 108
    Clerk of 3, 102, 127
    Corporation 30
    County . 26, 29, 30, 35, 36, 101, 105,
        111, 112, 114
    District 36, 45, 49
    District of Columbia 82
    Hustings .. 19, 36, 37, 48, 95-99, 102
    Orange 119
    Prince William 105
    Records of vi
    St. James 7
    Supreme 49, 85, 101
COURTENAY
    John 70
Courthouse: 29, 35, 53, 120, 124
COURTS
    John 15
COWMAN
    Charles H. 83, 84
COX
    Ambros 23
    Charles F. 98

Jacob ... 3, 6, 14, 17, 25, 27, 35, 39,
    43, 45, 46, 65
R.A. 123
William 14, 16, 35
COXEN
    Daniel T. 22
COYER
    Philip 16
COZZENS
    John 22
CRABBS
    Joshua 128
CRAFERD
    John 55
CRAGHILL
    William 44
CRAIG
    Charles 24
    Samuel ... 28, 40, 42, 45, 47, 50, 51,
        56, 62, 64, 66, 71
CRAIK
    George W. 66
    James 8, 29, 40, 63, 64
CRANDELL
    Samuel 62
    Thomas 48, 62, 66
CRANE
    John 42
CRANFORD
    John 30
CRANSTON
    John 55, 70
CRAVEN
    John 89
CRAVIN
    Thomas 84
CRAWFORD
    Hartly 86
    John 56
CRECH
    William 48
Creeks:
    Four Mile 2
    Four Mile Run 76
    Great Hunting 2, 5, 48, 122
    Hunting 1, 5
    Oxen 66
    Smith's 4
CREIGHTON
    John 87, 109
    John L. 87
    John T. 102, 109, 130
    Thomas B. 84, 98
    Thomas R. 95
CROFT
    George 14
CROMWELL
    J. 128
CROOK
    Bernard 55, 64, 121

145

Joseph 84
CROSBY
   George 41
CROSS
   Newman 84
   R.Y. 109, 118, 130
   Reid 86
   Richard Y. 83, 86, 112
CROUCH
   Peyton 90
CROUGHON
   Mathew 23
CROUSE
   Paton 84
CROWCH
   John 14, 18
CROWE
   Lanty 33, 43, 48, 62, 70
CRUIT
   Robert 126
CRUMP
   George 30
   Stephen 30
   William 16, 23, 30
CRUPPER
   John 41
   R. 86, 88, 92, 96, 129
   Robert 84, 91, 99, 112
CRUSE
   Thomas 66, 70
CRYSS
   Henry 84, 90, 95, 98
CUITER
   Edward H. 55
CULPEPER
   Thomas 7
CUMMINGS
   William 55, 70
CUMMINS
   Daniel 41
   Joseph 42
   William 42
CUNNINGHAM
   William 48
CURTIS
   John 24
   Joseph 43
CURTTS
   John S. 97
CURY
   Joseph 39

D

D'ESSEX
   Arthur W. 113
DABNEY
   John B. 28, 34, 43
DADE
   B. 43
   Baldwin . 5, 8, 13, 14, 16, 22, 27, 29,
                           35, 37-40, 67
   Charles S. 111
   James 81
   Jane 81, 82
   Jane (Adam) 111
   Townsend 15
   Townshend 15
DAINGERFIELD
   Edward 84, 87, 99, 103, 118
   H. 42
   Henry . . . 85, 88, 89, 92, 96, 99, 102
   John B. . . . 86, 89-92, 100, 105, 110,
                    117, 118, 121, 128
   Margaret B. 91
   Mrs. 90
DALBY
   Philip 14, 16, 18, 25, 34
DALEY
   Thomas 24
DALGARN
   John 24
DALRYMPLE
   John 39
DALTON
   John 34, 48
   Mr. 1
   William 22, 35
   Wm. 9
DANA
   Charles B. 92
DANBURY
   George 66
DANENMARKER
   John 27
DANFORTH
   Jane J. 91
   Mrs. 90
DANHAM
   Lewis 42
DANIEL
   John 23
   Stephen 23, 32
   William 126
DANIELS
   Henry 89
DARLING
   George . . . 18, 21, 27, 34, 43, 47, 55,
                             63, 64
DARNALL
   James M. 84
DARNE
   Thomas 66
   William 23
DARRELL
   Sampson 15
   Samson 25
   William 15, 18, 23
DAUGHERTY
   F. 42

DAVENPORT
  James 65
  Joseph 31
DAVEY
  Thomas 87
DAVIDSON
  Francis J. 129
  Francis R. 84
DAVIES
  Benjamin 54
  David 24
  Edward 55
  H.G. 97
  J. 57
  John 23
  John G. 54
  R.J. 97
DAVIS
  Allen 24, 31, 55, 70
  Aquilla 31
  Benj 70
  Benjamin 16, 22
  Benjamin B. 22
  Charles 16
  Edward 17, 23, 30, 32
  George 83, 97, 109, 124
  H. 109
  Henry 15, 31, 70
  Henry W. 92, 99, 102-104
  Isaac 16
  James 84
  John 17, 32
  Joseph 32
  Joseph H. 123
  Joseph W. 129
  Joshua H. 110
  Josiah 117
  Josiah H. . 83, 92, 95, 117, 127, 130
  Nehemiah 23
  Peter 95, 98
  Robert W. 109
  Samuel 50, 51
  Simon 22
  Theophilus 48
  Thomas 43, 48, 57, 64
  W.F. 97
  William 24, 84, 109
DAVISS
  James 32
DAVY
  David 62, 66
  Thomas 109
DAWE
  Philip 14, 16
DAWES
  William 31
DAWS
  Frederick 84
DAWSON
  John 23, 30

  William 30
DEALE
  A.M. 56
DEAN
  J. 63
  Joseph 55, 64, 69-71
  William A. 83
DEARBORNE
  George W. 123
DEARING
  Elias 57
DEAVERS
  Gilbert 30
  Richard 30
  William 30
DEBILL
  William 41
DECKER
  John 66
DEETON
  George L. 83, 89, 95, 98, 119
DELAROUCHE
  Michael 16
DELARUE
  Augustus 8, 14, 18, 23, 35
  J. 14
DELAWAR
  J.J. 27
DEMAIN
  John 84, 89
DEMAINE
  John 95
DEMAN
  Hen. B. 8
DEMPSEY
  James 87, 95, 109, 119, 121
  Thomas 62, 66
DEMPSTER
  Hugh 33
DEMUTH
  Reuben 55
DENEALE
  G. 57
  George . . . 18, 34, 39, 42, 47, 51, 62,
                                            65, 75, 77
  James 22
  William 30
DENNIS
  John 42
DENNISON
  Benjamin 128
DENT
  George W. 43
  S.M. 129
DENTY
  Jonathan 31
DERRY
  Michael 55
DEVAUGHAN
  John 24, 31

147

DEVAUGHN
  J.H. 130
  James H. 84, 87
  John 18
  Jonathan 30
  S.H. 87
  Samuel H. 83, 90, 92, 118
  W.H. 98
  William 84
DEWERY
  Davey 63
DICK
  Archibald 40
  David 70
  Elisha C. . . 15, 27, 39, 43, 47, 51, 62, 64
DICKIN
  J.W. 97
DICKINS
  Edward A. 128
  Francis A. 128
DICKSON
  Richard 16
DILLON
  Josiah 41
DILLS
  Nicholas 33
DINES
  John B. 69
DINWIDDIE
  Robert 36
DISNEY
  John 128
  John C. 128
  Robert 128
District of Columbia . . 72, 75-77, 80, 83, 92, 107
Districts:
  Constable in 122
  Court 36, 45
  Federal 52
  Kentucky 37
  Overseer of the Poor 25, 26
Divorces:
  Arell, David 36
  Baare, Eliza J. 113
  Conway, Mary A. 110, 113
  Horwell, Susan 106
  Jacobs, Alfred 107
DIX
  John 97
  Thomas 98
DIXION
  George 92
  George O. 83, 90, 99, 118, 123
  John 97
  John A. 110, 123
DIXON
  Benjamin 24
  James 55

  John 112
  John A. 130
  Page 19
  Sarah 112
  Turner   85, 89, 96, 98, 118, 123, 127
DOBBIN
  A. 47
  Archibald 25
  Robert 47
DODSON
  John 31
  Thomas 31
  Walter 48
DONALDSON
  Alfred 88
  B.S. 97
  Elizabeth 111
  Elizabeth (Muir) 117
  James 126
  John 40, 97
  Mitchell 28
  Robert . . 14, 16, 25, 29, 35, 97, 117, 128
  Spencer 23
  William 30
DONNELL
  John 39
DOOREN
  Mickel 55
DORSEY
  H. Carlin 98
DOUGHERTY
  Mrs. 100
  P. 40
DOUGLAS
  Ch. 52, 56, 62, 64, 66, 71
  Eliza 91
  G. 39
  R. Stuart 118
  R.S. 89
DOUGLASS
  Adam 40
  D. 43, 46
  Daniel 55, 63, 65, 71
  Gray 15, 18
  James 27, 39, 42, 85, 90
  James S. 89
  John 119
  Malcolm 128
  Mrs. 90
  W. 97
DOVE
  James 22, 30
  James H. 98
  Thomas 16, 23, 30
  Zechariah 32
DOW
  Peter 3, 12, 15
DOWDALL
  John 17, 40

Samuel 40
DOWDLE
   John 22
DOWLING
   Daniel 66
DOWNS
   James 42
DOWNY
   Henry 42
DOYLE
   Conrad 18
   Garret 55
DRINKER
   George 47, 51, 56, 62, 64, 70
   Jon. 40
DROWN
   Thomas 70
DROWNS
   Thomas 97
DRULL
   J. 128
DRUM
   Charles 21
DRUMMOND
   William 23
DRUMMONDS
   Noah 128
DUCKET
   John 97
DUCKETT
   Thomas 23
DUDLEY
   J. Saunders 97
   James S. 90
   Joseph 55, 101
DUFFEL
   Felix 23
DUFFEY
   George 87, 118, 120
   George H. 95
   John 48, 63, 64
DUFFIL
   Felix 30
DUFFY
   Bartholomew 22
   John 56
DULANY
   Benjamin . . 12, 15, 25, 35, 47, 50, 57, 100
   William H. 105
DULIN
   Atwell 31
   Atwill 32
   Charles 42
   Edward 23
   George 42
   John 23, 31, 42
   Thaddeus 24
DUMAX
   Andrew 55, 63

DUN
   William 23
DUNBAR
   William 24
DUNCAN
   Charles 46
   Coleman 15, 24
   George 3, 6
   Henry 78
   J.A. 123
   W.A. 127
DUNDAS
   Agness (Hepburn) 101
   Eliza 101
   John . . 8, 14, 18, 20, 33, 35, 37, 43, 44, 46, 48, 52, 55, 57, 62, 63, 65, 70, 71, 100, 101
   Thomas 101
   William H. 100
DUNLAP
   John . 12, 14, 16, 25, 27, 39, 43, 46, 47, 56, 57, 62, 66, 70, 71, 101
   Samuel 65
   William 33
DUNTON
   Steven 127
DURESS
   George 22
DURHILL
   Thomas 70
DUVALL
   John 70
   Richard 9
   William . . . 3, 6, 8, 13, 14, 18, 20, 27, 28, 33, 35, 40, 43
DWYER
   Robert D. 92
DYE
   Amos 128
   Thomas 31
DYER
   Archibald 128
   James 32
   John F. 83, 90, 91, 109, 117
   Robert 128
   Thomas 32, 118
DYKES
   James 50, 55, 57
   Mungo 21, 27, 43, 47
DYSON
   James L. 123
   Joseph 63
   Josh. 64, 70
   Phily 42

E

EACHES
   Joseph 83, 99, 102
   William 96

EAKIN
   Frederica A. 74
   James 8
   Mathew 63
   Matthew 74, 75
EALES
   () 31
Earl of Albemarle 36
EARLE
   Benjamin 5
   C. 19
   Elias 19
   Henry S. 63, 65
   Samuel 19
EARLY
   William 116
EARNSHAW
   John 14, 17
EARP
   Caleb 16, 18, 23-25, 34, 43, 47
   Matthew 22
EASTBURN
   A.W. 124
EASTER
   John D. 118
EASTON
   David 40, 43
   Tildon 84
EATON
   Francis 31
   William 30, 32, 42
EBERT
   Adam 18, 22, 28
ECKRIDGE
   Charles 22
   William 22
EDD
   J.T. 98
EDDONS
   Samuel 79
EDELEN
   Thomas J. 97
EDELIN
   Robert J. 95, 98
EDGAR
   Mark 43
EDIE
   Robert 66
EDMONDS
   Edmund 18, 22, 28, 43, 47, 51
EDMONS
   John 22
EDMONSTON
   Thomas 40
EDWARDS
   Ephraim 8
   John 16
   W.L. 105
EGAN
   Daniel J. 118

EGGBORN
   Perry J. 116
EICHBERG
   Isaac 130
ELDRIDGE
   H. 129
Elections: 2, 12, 25, 26, 69, 88
ELLICOTT
   Nathaniel 63
ELLIOTT
   John 84
   William 41, 128
ELLIS
   C.B. 86
   Clement B. 85
   William 8, 97
ELLZEY
   T. 23
   Thomazin 31
ELZEY
   William 19
EMERSON
   Aquila 84, 110
   Harrison 119
   John P. 119
   William R. 84
EMERY
   James 97
EMMET
   Josiah 16, 63, 66
EMMONS
   William 65
ENGLISH
   J. 130
   James 83, 92, 98, 119
   James A. . . 106, 109, 112, 117, 118,
                                          123
ENNIS
   W. 85
ENTWISLE
   Isaac 124
   James . . 83, 86, 109, 116, 118, 123,
                                       129, 130
   W.J. 83, 92, 129
EPP
   Peter 19
ERSKINE
   John 23
ERWIN
   William 63
ESKRIDGE
   George 42
ESSEX
   William 30-32
ESTAVE
   Andrew 46, 48
EUSTACE
   Edwin 53
   Hancock 53
   William 53

EVANS
  Ephraim 15, 16, 25, 43, 56, 66
  Gunter 83
  Guy 3, 18, 21, 28
  J.T. 83
  James 97
  Jery. 53
  John 18, 22, 28, 66, 70
  John J. 130
  John T. 109
  Robert 18, 21, 43, 62, 63, 66
  Samuel 41, 56, 83
  Thomas 56
EVELETH
  John 95
EVERARD
  William 56
EWING
  M.C. 85

F

FADELEY
  James 90, 121
FADELY
  John 56
FAIRBANK
  Samuel 16, 22
FAIRBANKS
  Henry 116
FAIRFAX
  Albert 123
  Henry .. 78, 104, 107, 111, 112, 121, 124
  Hezekiah 16
  O. 84, 95, 119
  Orlando 91
  Robert 6
  T. 47
FAIRFIELD
  Eugene V. 129
FALVEY
  Cornelius 43
FARIS
  George 41
Farmers' Bank of Alexandria 86
FARNSWORTH
  R.C. 128
FARRELL
  W. 33
  William 33
FASSON
  N. 19
FAUNTLEROY
  D. 92
Fauquier and Alexandria Turnpike
  Company 82, 129
FAW
  A. 55, 57, 62, 65, 70, 71
  Abraham 77

  J. 57
  Jonathan 55, 62, 65
FAXON
  Josiah ... 43, 46, 47, 56, 63, 64, 66
FAZAN
  Samuel B. 22
FEAGAN
  Edward 42
FEBREY
  H.W. 127
  John 127
  M.A. 128
  Nicholas 86, 97, 127
FEBRY
  Moses A. 97
FEGURRAN
  Robert 50
FELSER
  Adam 22
Female Free School 90, 103
Female Free School Society 91
FEMISTER
  John 23
FENDALL
  Benjamin T. 87, 92, 95, 102, 105
  Philip R. ... 17, 39, 42, 45, 47, 55, 63
  Townshend C. 129
  Townshend D. 86, 95, 102, 123
FENLEY
  James 24
FENTHAM
  John G. 55
FERGESON
  Zachariah 16
FERGURRON
  Robert 55
FERGUSON
  C. 14
  Cumberland 16, 56
  Josiah 23
  William 8, 23, 31, 32
FERNEAU
  Philip 56
FERNO
  Philip 16, 56
Ferries: 6, 64, 66
  Coles' 53
  Dix's 53
  Georgetown 103
FERVALL
  Jeremiah 33
FICKLEN
  George 116
FIELD
  Henry C. 130
  John 42
  John A. 109, 124
  R.H. 125
  Richard H. 116
  Stephen 95

151

FIELDER
   George 18, 24, 31
FIELDS
   John A. 85
FINALL
   Joseph 40
FINDLEY
   William 15, 17
FINKENS
   Theron 22
FINLAY
   David 25, 33, 42
FINLEY
   Charles 43
   Charles B. 27
   David 28
   John 2, 6
   John B. 22, 35
   William 8
FINLY
   Henry 55
Fires: 5, 29, 79
   Department 120
FISHER
   Charles 113
   Eliza J. 113
   H.F. 98
   Robins. 97
   William 27, 97
FITZGERALD
   John   2, 9, 12, 17, 19, 27, 28, 33-35,
                              39, 42, 47
FITZHUGH
   A.M. 112
   Battaile 47
   Cook 104
   Frances () 104
   Francis 104
   Fugus R. 104
   George 74, 104
   Giles 47
   John 104
   John J. 74
   Lucy 104
   Lycurgus 104
   Mary F. 104
   N. . 15, 40, 47, 50, 55, 62, 70-72, 75
   Richard 15
   W. 50
   William C. 74
   William G. 104
   William H. 112, 123
FITZSIMMONS
   James 42
FLANAGEN
   Edward 90
FLANNERY
   M. 43
   Michael 39, 55, 66, 70
   Richard 47

FLEMING
   A. 83, 98
   A.J. 90
   Andrew 22, 27
   Andrew J. 87, 95, 109, 117, 118,
                                124, 127
   Hugh 16
   Thomas 1, 3
FLETCHER
   E.C. 92
   Edward C. 85, 123, 129
   George . 17, 84, 86, 89, 96, 100, 105
   James 8, 16
   John W. 46
   Joshua 42
   Thomas 3
   William 63
FLETZER
   Henry 33
Flour: 52, 106, 111
   Inspection . . . 28, 40, 41, 45, 97, 106
FOEKE
   Charles 56
FOLEY
   D. 57
   Dennis 56
FOLLAN
   William 23
FOLLIN
   William 56
FOLMAR
   Christian 84
FOOTE
   Mary M. 103, 104
   W. Haywood 104
   William 104
   William H. 103, 104
FORD
   Cornelius 24
   Edward 23, 31
   James 31, 62
   John E. 9, 20, 28, 39
Foreign:
   Persons 4, 14, 71
   Ports 115
   Trade 8, 62
FORREST
   Joseph 42
FORST
   Abrm. 43
FORTENY
   George 66
FORTNEY
   Jacob . 18, 22, 28, 34, 48, 55, 64, 70,
                                       84
   James 84
FOSSETT
   James 85, 98, 119
FOSTER
   Francis 56

John . 34, 39, 43, 46, 47, 50, 56, 57,
62, 64, 66, 70, 71
  Thomas 56
FOUCH
  Isaac 22
FOUCHE
  John B. 27
FOUCHEE
  Dr. 82
FOUDRAY
  Samuel 62
FOUNTAIN
  William 83
FOUSHEE
  John 21
FOWLE
  B. Rollins 123
  George D. 96, 102, 117
  W. 86, 92, 96, 105, 123
  William 78, 79, 116
  William H. . . 87, 91, 96, 99, 102, 111,
116, 127, 128, 130
FOX
  Gabriel 78
  James 24
  Morris 24
  Uriah 42
FOY
  James 56, 57
FR___
  Thomas 30
FRANCE
  Philip 16, 25, 28, 34
FRANCIS
  Emanuel 83, 109
  John 42
FRANCK
  Reuben 42
FRANKLAND
  Thomas 55, 64
FRANSESS
  Thomas 24
FRASER
  Anthony R. . . . 85, 98, 126, 127, 129
  John 31
  Joseph 97
  William 17, 56
FRAZIER
  Joseph 111
FREEMAN
  Garr. A. 116
  Richard 23
  William 14, 17
FREMON
  Richard 32
FRENCH
  G.C. 130
  George E. 123
FREND
  James 22

FRESHER
  William 23
FREWEL
  John 55
FRIEND
  William 66, 70
FRISBY
  John 3
FRIZELL
  Luke 24
FRYER
  Tapley 30
FUGATE
  Jeremiah 32
FUGITT
  Benjamin 87, 89
  Gustavus 95
  W. 85
FULLER
  Joseph 42
FULLMER
  Joseph 8, 22, 25
FULTON
  Robert 27, 33, 35, 41
FUNSTEN
  D. 127
FUNSTON
  David 124
Furniture: 2, 12, 107
  Billiard Tables 12

G

GADSBY
  John 55, 57, 64, 70
GAHEN
  Walter 98
GALE
  James 55
GALLAT
  James 55
GALLENTINE
  Jacob 43
GAMBLE
  James C. 89
GAMELL
  James C. 95
GANT
  Henry 22
  Joseph 23
GARCIA
  Francis 83, 86, 95
GARDEN
  Nobert 56
GARDINER
  A.G. 126, 129
GARDNER
  Anthony 80
  Charles 24
  Eliza F. 91

Henry 18
L. 62
Mrs. 90
Z. 64, 65
Zachariah 70, 71
GARLAND
   S.M. 126
GARLEN
   John 23
GARNER
   William 42
GARNETT
   () 24
   James C. 119
GARRETT
   John 42
   Nicholas 30
   Robert 41
GARY
   William J. 128
GATES
   William 15
GAY
   Benjamin F. 92
GEASLIN
   W.L. 90
GEIGER
   Jac. 56, 66
GEISELING
   William 85
GEISENDAFFER
   William H. 89
GEMEN
   R.H. 129
GEMENY
   R.H. 119
GEOGHEGAN
   Michael 22
GEORGE
   Joseph 53
GERMAIN
   E.S. 97
GERMAN
   M. 97
GERRARD
   Richard M. 3
GESS
   John 24
GHEQUIERE
   Ber. 47
   Bernard 50, 51, 55, 62, 63
   Bernd. 43
GIBE
   Jean 14, 18
GIBSON
   Albion 55
   George 42
   Isaac 66
   John 63

GILBRETH
   Henry 97
GILDEA
   John 55
GILES
   John 24
GILKERSON
   John 40
GILL
   James 24, 31, 32
   John 40, 45, 48, 50
GILLIES
   James 39, 47, 50, 55, 57, 63
GILLIS
   Rev. 113
GILLISON
   James 53
GILPIN
   George . . 3, 7, 14, 15, 33, 34, 39, 43,
          47, 50, 55, 62, 64, 65, 71
   J. 43
   Joseph 28, 33
   William 31
GINNACOM
   George W. 128
GIRD
   Christopher 55, 57, 64
   Henry 48, 51, 62, 66
   William 55, 56
GIST
   Joshua 30
GLADDING
   John 24, 30
GLADMON
   Asa 127
GLASCOCK
   John 42
   William 19
GLASS
   William 35
GLASSCOCK
   Archabald 42
   Gregory 42
   Hezekiah 42
   Peter 42
GLASSGOW
   Milton 83, 90
GLINGAN
   George 55
GLINN
   Jesse 42
GLISH
   George 97
GLOSTER
   James 31
GLOUDELET
   Petit en 18, 34
GLOVER
   Thomas 21

GLOYD
  George H. 48
GO___
  John 24
GOING
  John 85
GOLATT
  Charles 97
  William 97
GOODEN
  William 31
GOODES
  George 33
GOODHAN
  Nathaniel 103
GOODING
  John 30
  Peter 78
  W.H. 78
GOODRICH
  W.W. 98
GOODRICK
  Richard 15
GOODS
  James C. 83
GOODWIN
  Nathaniel 84
GORDEN
  Joshua 30
  Robert 64
GORDON
  () 47
  Alexander 23, 39
  Allen 43
  John 56, 65
  Lewis 66
  Robert 57, 63
GORETZ
  Peter 43
GOSSOM
  Thomas 31
GOSTLING
  Isaac 3
GOUGH
  James 84
GOULD
  John 63, 64, 71
GOVER
  A.P. 86, 109
GRA__BURY
  James 25
GRADY
  Frank T. 129
  Joshua 85
  Joshua Y. 90
GRAFFORT
  Thomas 44-46, 55
GRAHAM
  Charles 86
  David 65

George 56, 63, 64, 66
James 44, 48
John 16, 18, 22, 27, 35
GRATER?
  Charles 64
GRAY
  () 39
  Albert W. 129
  Ann 63
  Edward 56
  Fra. 16
  George 42
  John 70
  John H. 98
  Robert 40, 70, 100
  Vincent 42, 47, 50
  William 16
  William F. 70
GRAYSON
  Benjamin 47
GREEN
  Barsilla P. 90
  Beel 24
  C.W. 130
  Clement 62
  Edmund 85
  Edward 89, 97
  Frederick 100
  James 87, 91, 92, 99, 118, 121, 123,
                                 130
  James E. 129
  James W. 118
  Jesse 70
  Jesse C. 83, 87
  Job 28
  John 55, 62, 66
  John W. 87, 119
  Joseph 42
  Samuel 30
  Stephen A. 119
  William 32
GREENE
  Barriella N. 97
  D. 123
  D.C. 92
  L. Edward 90
GREENLEES
  James 16
GREENUP
  Christopher 37
GREENWAY
  Joseph ... 12, 14, 16, 25, 28, 34, 39
GREENWOOD
  John 121
GREER
  Alexander 43
GREEVES
  Robert 18, 25
GREGHAGAN
  Michael 8, 14, 17

155

GREGORY
- Douglas L. 92
- Douglas S. 95, 109, 118, 130
- H.J. 130
- Mary D. 91
- Mr. 90
- Mrs. 90
- William 85-87, 91, 109, 123, 129

GREIR
- Clement 56

GRESSLER
- M'h. 56

GRETTER
- John 3, 8, 18, 21, 27, 33, 55
- Michael 3, 18, 21, 27, 33, 35

GREY
- John 98

GRIFFIN
- () 70
- Henry 32

GRIFFITH
- D. 17
- Daniel 98
- David 9, 13, 37, 38, 43
- Hannah () 37
- John H. 84
- K. 98
- Kinzey 87
- Sally W. 91
- Samuel G. 62
- Sarah 90

GRIGG
- Joseph 87, 95, 109, 118

GRIGSBY
- James 42

GRIMES
- () 87
- Enoch 87, 89, 121
- George 18, 22
- H. 92
- James 17, 27, 56
- John 15, 23
- Joseph 89, 92
- Joseph P. 103
- Nicholas 24
- Stephen 24
- William 24, 54

GRIMLER
- Michael 33

GRIMSLEY
- James 30, 31

GROVE
- John 19

GROVERMAN
- William ... 40, 56, 57, 62, 64, 66, 71

GROVES
- Robert 21

GRUBB
- J.H. 87
- James H. 123

John 87
John S. 83, 87

GRUSH
- Michael 30

GUEST
- Robert 55

GUIN
- D.S. 129

GUINN
- D.H. 118

GULLATT
- Charles 63
- Peter 22

GUNNELL
- H. 70
- Henry 31
- John 31, 32
- Presley 32
- Robert 22, 32
- Thomas 32, 40, 43, 47, 70
- William 18, 32, 43, 47
- William 3d 40

GUNYON
- William 53

GUY
- Benjamin 83

GWIN
- D.S. 127

GWINN
- B. 47
- Benjamin 15, 23

H

HAGEN
- Frank 31

HAGERMAN
- Adam 42

HAGERTY
- Patrick 18, 21, 27, 34

HAGUE
- John 23

HAINES
- Robert 40
- Simeon 42

HALBERT
- Isaac 16
- William 56

HALL
- Jacob 23
- James B. 87
- John 128
- Michael 24
- Richard 32
- Robert 92
- Sylvester 22
- W. 46
- W.J. 63
- William 24, 31
- William J. 64, 66

William V. 56
HALLEY
  George 30, 43
  James 30, 31, 40
  John H. 78
  Richard 24, 32
  Sylvester 30
  Thomas 30
  W. 70
  William 18, 23, 29, 42, 55
HALLIDAY
  James 8, 18, 35
HALLOWELL
  Benjamin 124
  Caleb S. 95, 109
  James S. 123
HALLSLAUGH
  John 97
HAMERSLEY
  William 90
HAMILTON
  James 43, 50, 56, 57, 64
  James H. 56
  John 28
  Robert 43, 45, 50, 56, 57, 64
HAMMADINGER
  C. 95
HAMMER
  Charles 98
HAMMOND
  Gervus 23
  James 127
  Jarvis 18
HAMP
  Benjamin A. 14, 16, 24, 27, 28, 34, 39
HAMPSON
  Bryan . . 42, 47, 56, 57, 63-65, 70, 71
  J.H. 89
  Joseph H. 85, 87, 92, 106, 118
HAMPTON
  Jeremiah 42
  John 32
  Ridgely 129
  Samuel 31
  William 32
HANCOCK
  John B. 92, 119
HANDY
  S. 85
HANKINS
  John 25
HANNA
  James 56
HANNAH
  Alexander 18, 22
  John 25
  Nicholas 24, 43
  Richard 39
HANSBROUGH
  John 62

HANSON
  S. 13, 18, 23, 28, 35, 43
  Samuel 12, 13, 15, 18, 23, 28, 35, 43
  T. 14
  T.H. 105
  William 15
HANY
  William 24
HARDING
  Edward 15
HARDWICK
  Younger 22
HARDY
  Henry 85
HARLEY
  George 31
  John 31
HARMAN
  Jacob 35
HARMON
  A.D. 87, 96
  Daniel 109
  N.D. 84
HARPER
  Charles 56
  Edward . 8, 14, 16, 25, 29, 34, 56, 64
  G. 85
  George G. 86, 98, 111
  J.H. 130
  J.M. 95
  J.N. 86, 129
  John . . 3, 5, 6, 9, 11, 14, 16, 23, 25,
    27, 28, 33, 39, 43, 46, 47, 56, 62,
                                        64, 66
  John N. 109, 118
  Joseph . . . 45, 46, 48, 50, 51, 55, 62,
                                    63, 66, 70
  Lemuel D. 83
  Mary A. 91
  Mrs. 90
  Robert . . 6, 86, 102, 109, 118, 123
  Samuel . . . 15, 17, 25, 33, 39, 43, 46,
           47, 50-52, 56, 62, 64, 65, 70
  Samuel D. 109, 118
  W. 113
  W. Walton 118, 123
  W.A. 89
  W.T. 92, 98, 106, 118, 127
  W.W. 118, 122
  Washington T. 86, 113
  Wells A. 83, 88, 92, 109, 123
  William . . . 14, 25, 27, 43, 46, 47, 50,
        51, 65, 69, 71, 95, 109, 118
  William T. 96
  William W. 92
  Wm. 16
HARRIS
  Edward 123
  George W. 87, 92, 95
  James 41

Monroe 97
Theophilus 55
Thomas 22, 62
W. 85
Walter 87, 92, 109
HARRISON
() 85
B.E. 125
Col. 79
Elias 90
George 31
J.D. 95, 118
John 24, 30, 31, 34, 55, 66
John D. 88
John T. 41
Jos. W. 16
L.D. 88, 109, 118
P. 41
R. 33, 34
Robert 70, 97
Thomas 31, 48, 74
W. 41
William 22, 30, 32, 33
HARRISS
James 24
HARROW
Gilbert 22, 27, 33
HARROWAY
Merryman 24
HARROWER
John 30
Merryman 30
William 30
HART
John 83
John T. 129
W.A. 130
W.D. 126
HARTLEY
George 55
Mark 128
S. 130
HARTSHORNE
John 97
William . 2, 3, 6, 8, 12-14, 16, 25, 27,
28, 34, 40, 41, 42, 45, 47, 50, 51,
56, 62, 64, 65, 70, 72
HARUE
Richard 92
HARVEY
George C. 83
HARYWAY
Merryman 30
HASTINGS
Robert 44
HATCHELL
John 85
HATCHER
Henry 16
HATTON
Samuel 56
HAUCK
Peter 43, 56
HAWDERFER
John 16
HAWKINS
Charles 83, 87, 89
John 14-16, 35
HAY
Robert 3
HAYCOCK
William 18, 23
HAYES
Alonzo 126, 128
George 27
John 55
Maria 128
HAYS
Andrew 8
HAZELL
Ignatius 42
HEAD
John T. 90
HEAL
George 55
HEALE
George 15, 17
HEATH
Andrew 55, 66
James E. 99
HEDRICK
Thomas 16, 23, 27
HEIDE
Philip 33
HEINEMANN
Jacob 18, 21, 27, 43, 48, 62
HEISKELL
P. 64, 65
HEITES
George 25
HELPHINSTINE
Philip 19
HEMSLEY
W. 85
HENDERSON
Alexander 40
Andrew 41
Charles A. 85, 86
David 55, 64, 65
G. 95
Hugh 42
J.E. 95, 97, 118
James 30, 124
James L. 84, 89, 97
John E. 83, 86
Peter G. 83, 89, 92
Peter J. 117
Robert 47
Samuel 42

William 22
Willis 87, 98
HENDRICKS
  James . 3, 6, 8, 11-14, 17, 20, 29, 35
  John . 6, 8, 12-14, 18, 20, 27-29, 35
HENDY
  Patrick K. 56
HENING
  James 19
HENLEY
  David 34
HENNEY
  James 16, 22
HENNINGER
  Francisca W. 68
  Frederick 45, 69
  John F. 67, 69
  John M. 69
  Mary M. 67, 69
HENRETTY
  James 41
HEPBURN
  Agness 101
  John 23
  Juliana E. 113, 114
  Letty 113
  Moses 100, 102
  William .. 6, 8, 14, 18, 20, 33, 35, 43,
    44, 46, 55, 62, 64, 71, 101, 114
Herald, The 49
HERBERT
  Daniel D. 83, 90
  George 15, 17, 35
  Thomas 17, 22, 42, 57, 66
  W. 114
  W.U. 97
  William .. 2, 3, 13, 14, 18, 20, 27, 29,
    33, 39, 42, 47, 50, 55, 57, 63,
    69-71, 100, 101
HEREFORD
  John 32
HERLIHY
  Maurice 21, 56
HERMAN
  Henry 31
HERMON
  Henry 32
  Peter 31
HERNE
  William 84
HERREFORD
  Thomas A. 41
HESS
  Jacob 8, 14, 18
HESSE
  David 56
HEWES
  Aaron ... 6, 8, 14, 16, 25, 27, 35, 43,
    47, 51, 56, 63, 64, 65, 69
  Abram 45-47, 50, 51, 57, 63, 65

O.C. 83
HEWITT
  John 30
  Peter 89, 98, 110, 116, 118
  Richard 48
HICKEY
  John 30
HICKMAN
  John 15, 18, 25, 35, 47
  Thomas 25
  William 28, 34, 47
HICKS
  N. 84
  William 31
HIERONYMUS
  Henry 42
HIGDON
  J.H. 83
  W.J. 121
HIGGINBOTHAM
  John 55
HIGGINS
  William 66, 70
HIGGS
  Benjamin F. 78
HILL
  Bennett 16, 24, 32
  George 29, 56, 85
  John 56, 123
  John T. 121
  Thomas S. 125
  William 116
HILLS
  Josiah B. 83, 86
HILTON
  Samuel 56, 65, 97
HIPKINS
  Lewis 23, 39
HITE
  Isaac 38
HOAKES
  Jacob 32
HODES
  W.B. 55
HODGKIN
  Daniel 22
  John 55, 70, 98
  Raphel 16, 32
  Robert 97
  Walter 55
  William F. 97
HODGKINS
  John 87
  Robert 119
HODGSON
  W. 33, 39, 42
  William 34, 45, 47, 50, 63, 64, 66, 67
HODSKIN
  Daniel 32

HOFFMAN
   Jacob 56, 57, 63, 64, 71-74
   P.E. 84, 92
HOGAN
   Edmund 57
Hogs: 128
HOKE
   Michael 22, 28
HOLDEN
   Charles G. 31
HOLEMON
   William 32
HOLLENSBURY
   John 90
HOLLIDAY
   William 40
HOLLINGSWORTH
   D. 88
   George 34
HOLMES
   H. 40
   Joseph 40
   Stephen 28
HOOD
   R. 43
HOOE
   B. 78, 79, 92, 96, 98
   Bernard 106
   Daniel F. . 85, 90, 105, 106, 109, 118,
                                         130
   Henry D. 15
   J.H. 65
   James H. 39, 62, 64, 72
   John 15, 23, 40, 98
   R.   3, 6, 8, 14-16, 24, 28, 35, 40, 45,
              47, 50, 51, 56, 62, 64, 71
   R.T. 28
   Robert T. 33
HOOFF (Hoof)
   Charles 24
   Charles R. 129
   J.H. 86
   J.W. 129
   James 22
   John 88
   L.W. 86
   Lawrence . . 3, 6, 8, 9, 18, 24, 27, 35,
              40, 43, 47, 48, 55, 57, 65
   Lewis 88, 92, 129
   P.H. 88, 119, 127, 130
HOOFMAN
   Christopher 42
HOOKES
   Jacob 56
HOOMES
   George 43
   John 19
HOOPER
   John 57

HOOVER
   H. 128
   John 127
HORD
   Thomas 81, 82
HORNBUCKLE
   Richard 31
   Solomon 25
   Thomas 24
HORNER
   John 43, 56, 63
   William 15
HORSBAUGH
   John 66
HORSEMAN
   E. 95
   Elijah 98
   John 16, 23
HORWELL
   Charles 70
   E.C. 83
   John 55, 70
   Richard 62, 64, 106, 107
   Susan () 106, 107
HOSKINE
   T.H. 110
HOSKINS
   James O.C. 84
HOUGH
   Edward S. 85, 90, 116
HOUGLAND
   Aaron 27
HOUSE
   David 97, 98
   Richard 95
Houses: 5, 45, 46, 48, 54, 67, 100,
                              101, 108, 124
   Brick 100
   Brick, Stone or Wooden 1
   Counting 45
   Court 29, 125
   Custom 125
   Ferry 67
   Hospital 80
   Mansion 76, 77
   Market 36
   Poor 26, 27
   Post Office 125
   Public 29
   Rolling 20
   Store 44
   Worship 11, 12, 37
HOWARD
   Beal 27, 55
   George T. 90
   John 89, 97
   Samuel 18, 23
HOWE
   P. 17

HOWELL
  John 85, 95, 98, 109, 123
HOXTON
  William W. 84
HOYE
  William 43, 63
HUBBALL
  John 56, 66
HUBBARD
  Eppa. 19
HUCK
  Richard S. 118
HUFF
  John 42
HUFMAN
  John 16
HUGHES
  Constantine 24
  Thomas 126
HUGUETY
  George F. 84
HULL
  George I. 12, 20
  Samuel 16
HULLS
  Samuel 22
HULSPRINGER
  Christian 89
HUME
  Charles 53
  James 53
  Theo. 66, 69
  Thomas 70
HUMFREYS
  Thomas T. 17
HUMMER
  Benjamin A. 128
HUMPHREY
  Jesse 42
HUMPHREYS
  A.J. 129
HUNT
  Benjamin 14
  Henry 30
  James 32
  John 30
  Thomas 30
HUNTER
  Alexander 15, 17, 78
  B.W. 128
  Benjamin 18
  Bushrod W. 127
  George . . . 14, 16, 25, 27, 39, 43, 46
  Ichabod 14, 16, 25
  J.R. 129
  John . 15, 24, 25, 28, 33, 51, 55, 66,
                                            67, 71
  John C. 15, 25, 49
  Moses 44
  Nathaniel C. 15

  Robert 25, 95, 98, 109, 118
  William . 3, 6, 8, 9, 11-14, 18, 23, 25,
                  28, 33-35, 37, 39, 56, 67
HUNTON
  Eppa 125
HUNTT
  N.L. 129
HURDLE
  Levi 89, 98, 110, 121
HURFORD
  James 31
HURLEY
  Daniel 23
HURST
  H. 22
  Henry 32
  James 23, 31, 40
  John 22, 24, 31
  K. 51
HURTT
  John 97
HUSEY
  Henry 23
HUTCHENSON
  Cockrell 24
  George 24
HUTCHINS
  William 97
HUTCHINSON
  Isaac 24
  John 24, 84
HUTCHISON
  Elijah 78
  Ely 78
  Joshua 78
HUTT
  William H. 129
HYLOR
  Edward 31

I

INATZCOUF
  Anthony 66
INGLE
  Henry 62, 63, 66
  Joseph 55
INGRAHAM
  Nathaniel 33
IRATZCALF
  Peter 14
IRISH
  George 50, 63, 64, 66, 71
IRVIN
  James 29, 39, 48, 64, 98
  Thomas 39
IRVINE
  James 12, 10
IRWIN
  James 23, 83, 105, 110, 118

Thomas .. 29, 34, 43, 46, 56, 57, 64, 65, 70	JAMIESSON
William H. 83, 95, 96, 116, 118	Andrew 27, 28, 34, 40
ISABEL	Andrew W. 62
William 52, 56, 70	R.B. 63, 66, 70
ISABELL	Robert 33
Jonah ... 55, 62, 63, 65, 70, 71, 101	Robert B. 39, 42, 47
William 63, 66	JANNEY
ISERLOAN?	A. 52, 71
Jesper 33	Abel 56, 63, 66, 69, 70
	Aquila 70, 71
	E. 72

J

	Elisha .. 39, 43, 46-48, 50, 62, 66, 71
	John . 39, 43, 47, 50, 51, 55, 57, 63, 64, 66, 71, 125
JACKINAN	John A. 110
G. 127	John H. 87, 109, 118
JACKSON	Joseph 34, 55, 63, 66
Daniel...................... 42	Phineas 73, 74, 78, 79, 86
George C. 126	Thomas 62, 71
Hannah 100	JAVAIN
Harry 31	P. 55
James W. 126	JAVINS
John 18, 22, 23, 31, 32, 40	Charles 89
Joseph 32, 34	Daniel 31
Philip 3	Harrison 89, 97
Robert 84	J.D. 90
Samuel 22	J.L. 109
Solomon 31	James A. 84, 98
Spencer 32	John 24
JACOB	John D. 97, 129
Michael 67	Richard 97
JACOBS	Thomas 97
Alfred 107, 108	Thompson 98
Ann V. 108	William 98
Con. 105	JEFFERSON
Cornelius 87, 89, 98	Clo. 84
Edward 23, 90	James 90
H. 95	John 47
John 56	Robert 90
Joseph 32	Thomas 55
Joshua 15, 17, 31	William 84
Margaret A. 107, 108	JEFFREY
Mordecai 32	F. 47
Presley 105	Jerem. 23
Presly 87	JEFFRIES
Sarah E. 108	Joseph 42
Thomas 43, 56, 95	JENKIN
William 32	W.M. 56
JAMES	JENKINS
Benjamin 53	B.H. 118, 121
JAMESSON	Benjamin H. 84
R.B. 62, 71	Daniel 32
Robert B. 55	Henson 32
JAMIESON	James 31
A. 130	James T. 83, 84
Andrew .. 18, 23, 37, 43, 46, 47, 57, 63, 87	Richard 15, 23, 25
Charles 47, 56, 63	Thomas 24
John 55, 119	William 98, 121
Robert 83, 86-91	JENKS
	William 129

162

JENNINGS
  A. 19
JEST
  George 56
  John 24
JETT
  Charles W. 129
  Je. 8
JEWELL
  Henry C. 126
  Thomas 33
JEWETT
  Joseph 95
JINKINS
  Daniel 23
JOHN
  Andrew 15, 16
  Benjamin 42
  Daniel 42
JOHNSON
  () 35
  A.H. 123
  Bennett 16
  Bennit 22
  David 22
  Dennis M. 65
  George 83
  Isaac M. 47, 50
  J.E. 97
  James 42, 101
  John 32, 56, 64, 98
  John F. 89
  John J. 109
  John T. 90, 103, 121, 124, 127
  Lancelot 32
  Mason 24
  Robison 84
  Samuel 32, 70
  Strother 22, 31
  Thomas 15, 16, 23, 31, 32
  Walter 15, 30, 31
  William 22, 30, 32, 85, 87, 95
  William S. 97
JOHNSTON
  Arran 18
  Dennis 86, 88
  French 84
  George W. 86
  J.R. 126, 128
  John .35, 48, 56, 63, 65, 66, 70, 97, 101
  John T. 83
  Lancelot 16, 24
  M. 92
  R. 83, 89, 90, 95, 99, 102, 103, 105, 119, 122, 127
  Reuben 88, 117
  Robert 41
  Samuel 17
  W.C. 83

  Wilfrid 24, 42
  William 23, 40
  William C. 87
JOLLY
  John 8, 14, 18, 22, 25, 27, 35
JONES
  Charles 3, 15, 16, 34, 47, 57, 70
  David 18, 22
  E. 97
  Henry 23
  J.W. 97
  John 19, 23, 31, 98
  P.B. 126
  Roger 114
  Samuel 15, 83
  Stephen 89
  T.F. 70
  T.H. 97
  Thomas 17
  Thomas ap C. 114, 116
  Walter 65, 70
  William 16, 23
JORDAN
  James 44
JORDEN
  Hugh 33
  Joshua 16
JOURDAN
  Francis 116
JULIAN
  Dr. 82
JUNIGEL 43
  Ignatius 48, 56, 64
  Ignatius J. 63
JURDEN
  Willm. 16

K

KAY
  J.W. 126, 128
KEAN
  John 22, 27
KEARNS
  William 53
KEARSHALL
  Samuel 41
KEATING
  William 23
KEEFER
  E.R. 92
KEEN
  Francis 24
  Kent 32
  William 32
KEENAN
  Michael W. 44
KEENE
  Nancy () 101
  Newton 101

KEITH
    Alexander 18, 22, 56
    Isaac S. 11, 12, 37
    James . 9, 11, 15, 17, 23, 25, 33, 39,
        42, 46, 47, 50, 51, 62, 64, 66, 71,
        72
    John 15, 42
    John C. 25
    Smith 34, 56
    W. 35
    William 18, 23
KELL
    Isaac 62, 65, 83, 89, 98, 123
    John 89, 123
    Nathan 84, 89
    Robert 129
    Thomas 98, 119
KELLY
    John 42
    Samuel 3
    Vincent 33
    William 56, 64
KELLYHAM
    James 34
KEMPFF
    Jo. 14, 16, 27, 43, 47, 64, 66
KENNEDY
    Dr. 101
    James 20, 27, 28, 39, 43, 47, 50, 55-
        57, 62-65
    Matthew 42
KENNER
    James 56
KENT
    Daniel 32
    John 31, 32, 70
    Sampson 24
    Stephen 83, 97
KEPPEL
    William A. 36
KEPPELL
    Henry 66
KERCHEVAL
    James 19
    John 40
    Samuel 19
KERCHNER
    Fredrick 56
KERN
    Alexander 63
    James 31
    William 31
KERNS
    Robert 53
KERR
    Alexander 62
    C.D. 123
    James 39
    James D. 83, 85

KEY
    Martin 53
KEYS
    Francis 121
KEYTH
    John 23
KIDWELL
    Hezekiah 24, 31
    J.W. 97
    Joshua 31
    Samuel S. 98
    Thomas 22
KIEFER
    E.R. 83
KILST__
    Andrew 95
KILTON
    George 63
KINCAID
    John 55, 57, 62, 63, 66, 70
KINCHELOE
    Cornelious 32
    Daniel 23
    E.W. 87, 89, 92
KING
    Daniel 24
    Edgar C. 123
    G.W. 97
    Hargess 24, 32
    Henry 77
    John 32
    Laurence 32
    Samuel D. 97
    Stephen 32
    William 30
KINGS
    Cornelius 42
KINGSTON
    F. 118
    Nicholas 56, 63
KINSEY
    James 23
    John F. 95
    Zenas 95, 118, 122
KINZER
    J. Louis . 96, 98, 105, 111, 117, 124,
        125
KIPP
    A. 126
    C. 126
KIRBY
    Charles 85
    Thomas 31, 32, 47
KIRK
    James 8, 34
    Rubin 31
    Samuel 55, 62, 63
KIRKBRIDE
    Joseph 40

KIRKE
  Grafton 18, 22, 31, 35
KIRKNEY
  Richard 127
KIRKPATRICK
  Thomas 3, 8
KISENDAFFER
  John 89, 98
KITSON
  John 64
KITTEN
  John 43
KNIGHT
  John T. 21
  William 35
KOONES
  Charles 87, 89, 95, 98, 118
  T.A. 83
KORN
  John 3, 14, 22, 25, 33, 56, 57, 63-65
KREIST
  George 98
KROUSE
  Peter 34
KUHN
  E.F. 83

L

LABILTZ
  L. 62
LACY
  W.B. 126, 128, 129
LADD
  John G. 50, 56, 62, 64, 65, 72
LAKE
  John 41
LAKENAN
  J.D. 84
LAKEWAN
  J.D. 90
LAMBERT
  Benjamin H. 83, 89, 90, 116, 117,
                                       119, 126, 128
  William H. 123
LAMMOND
  A. 83, 87, 102, 109, 118, 120
  Alexander 96
LANCASTER
  George B. 98
  Thomas 19, 43
LANE
  James 24
  James H. 17
  Richard 17
LANG
  John 16
LANGDEN
  John 43

LANGMARCH
  Christian 3
LANHAM
  Edward 32
  G.H. 55
LANPHIER
  Going 55, 101
  Robert G. 55, 101
  William 57, 63, 65, 70, 84
LANSTON
  Benjamin 17, 33, 43
LAPHEN
  John 92, 98, 119
LARKIN
  L.A. 130
  William W. 129
LARMOUR
  J.H. 88
  Joseph H. 95
  Robert M. 85, 88
LARRENCE
  John 84
  William R. 84
LATHAM
  Hugh 87, 89, 98, 119
  Richard 62, 66
LATHRAM
  Thomas H. 86
LATIMER
  Alexander 55
LATOUCHE
  John 130
LATRUITE
  () 43
LAURANCE
  William R. 98
LAURENCE
  James 65
LAW
  A.W. 126
LAWRASON
  J. 64, 71
  James 3, 6, 8, 12, 14, 16, 25, 27, 34,
                35, 39, 50, 51, 57, 63, 69
  Thomas 66, 71
LAWRENCE
  John 24
LAWSON
  Charles 90
  James 41
  John 84, 86, 92, 118
  Robert 15
LAY
  Abraham 24
LEACH
  John G. 98
LEADBEATER
  John 87, 92, 99, 109
LEAHY
  Dennis 23

LEAP
  Jacob 25, 46, 48, 63, 66, 71
LEE
  () 87
  Alfred 110
  Cassius F. . . 86-90, 95, 109, 119, 123
  Chapin 84
  Charles 12, 17, 33, 39, 45
  Edmund J. 47, 56, 64, 65, 69
  Jacob 27
  Ludwell 43, 57
  R.E. 127
  Theodorick 25
  Thomas 36
  William A. 23
  William L. 118
LEECH
  Thomas 42
  William T. 9
LEIGH
  H. 9
LEMOINE
  John 56, 64, 66, 70
LEWIS
  Britain 53
  Daniel 18
  Edward 56
  Henry 55, 69
  James 41
  John 16, 32
  John C. 25
  Joseph 25
  Richard 55, 66, 69
  Samuel 55
  Thomas 23, 37, 38, 42
  William 24, 32
LIBBY
  Richard 63, 66, 70
Licenses: 112
  Pilot 121, 126
  Selling Wood 130
  Tavern 12, 102
LIGHTFOOT
  Samuel 16
  William 23, 32
LIMERICK
  John 55
LIMRICK
  John 43, 48
LINCH
  Daniel 31
LINDSAY
  Samuel 86, 109, 118
  Thomas 18, 24
LINE
  George R. 121
LINN
  Francis 41
LIPSCOMB
  W.C. 128

Liquor: 13, 14, 107
LITTLE
  Charles 12, 17, 27, 39, 40, 48
  Robert 16
  Webster 23
Little River Turnpike Company . 72-74, 77, 78
LITTLETON
  Lawson 114
LIVINGSTON
  Cornelius 19
  John 55
LLOYD
  Francis L. 98
  Henry 98
  John 51, 63
  John F. 89
  John J. 127
  Richard B. 87, 98
LOCKE
  Benjamin 56
  Thomas 56
  Thomas M. 62
LOCKWOOD
  A. 83, 86, 99, 102, 118
  J.W. 86, 118, 129
  John 43, 99, 123
  William F. 83
LOEFBOURNES
  David 23, 30
LOMAX
  John 3, 6-9, 18, 35
  Stephen 31
LOMBARD
  Thomas 32
LONG
  Samuel 54
LONGDEN/LONGDON
  John . . . 3, 8, 18, 28, 33, 51, 57, 64
  Ralph 3, 24, 33
LONGLEY
  Joseph 24
LONGRON
  James 128
Lord Arlington 7
Lord Cornwallis 79, 80
Lord Culpeper 7
Lord Fairfax 6, 7
LORE
  Thomas 62
Lots: 1
  Sales and Leases of 2
LOTT
  John 3
Lotteries: 33, 34, 36-38, 73, 82
LOUDAN
  John 9
LOURY
  William 9

LOVE
    Charles 43, 47, 56, 62, 64, 65
    F.R. 105
    J. 29
    James 22
    John 32, 43
    John C. 64
    Robert 22
    Samuel 57
    Thomas 24
    Thomas R. 114
LOW
    Charles 31
    Robert 25
    Thomas 14, 16, 25, 56, 71
LOWE
    Charles 22
    David A. 127
    Henry 16
    Henry F. 48
    I.F. 91
    J.R. 55
    James 63
    John F. 122
    Walter 22
LOWNES
    James 28, 34
LOWRY
    James D. 70
    Robert K. 70
    William   13, 15, 18, 27, 28, 37, 56, 57
LOYD
    Henry 31
    James 84
    William D. 97
LUCAS
    Lindores 24
LUCKETT
    Ignatious 30
LUGENBEEL
    John W. 92
LUKE
    John 42
LUMSDON
    John 48, 55, 63
LUNT
    Arthur 87
    Samuel 86, 88, 92, 99, 109, 118
LUPTON
    David 40
    Joseph 84, 98
LUTZ
    M. 15
    Mi. 17
LYLE
    Robert . 6, 12, 14, 17, 20, 21, 27, 35, 70
    William 21
LYLES
    Enoch M. 56

Henry 6, 35
James 23
Robert 3, 14, 17
William   6, 13, 17, 25, 27, 28, 34, 84
Zacharias 47, 56
LYND
    John 66
LYNN
    Adam . . 2, 3, 6, 8, 35, 43, 55, 57, 62, 66
LYON
    Walter 48

M

M'GINNIS
    John 19
M'GWIN
    Edward 33
MACHEN
    Thomas 8, 17
MACHIN
    Thomas 15
MacINTOSH
    John 31
MacIVER
    Charles 8, 18, 21
    Colin 8, 14, 16, 25, 35
MACKAY
    Michael 55
MacKENZIE
    Alexander . 33, 47, 50, 56, 62, 64, 66
    James 66
    William 43
MACKINTOSH
    John 64
MacLEOD
    Daniel 48, 55, 63
    John 48, 64, 65, 69
MacMASTERS
    Andrew 18
MacREA
    W. 39
MACY
    T.E. 97
MADDEN
    Alfred 118
    John 43
    M. 18, 20
MADOX
    Martin 123
MAGRUDER
    Nathaniel J. 43
    Philip 50, 57, 64, 70
    Thomas 55
MAHONY
    Jeremiah 8
MALONE
    Alexander 70

MANDEVILLE
  John 18, 22, 46, 47, 70
  Jonathan . 22, 33, 39, 43, 47, 55, 62,
                      63, 65, 70, 71
  Joseph 47, 55, 57, 65, 100
MANERY
  John 95
MANKIN
  James E. 83, 98
  Mark 87, 121
  William 84, 85, 98
MANKINS
  Charles 84
  David 55
MANLEY
  George 32
  John 23
  William 97
MANLY
  J.H. 32
  John H. 31
MANSELL
  John 31
MANSFIELD
  Henry 83, 92, 107, 109, 118
  William H. 88
MANUM
  William 55
Manumissions: 112
MARBURY
  F.A. 116, 126
  Fendall 125
  Francis A. 83
  Jo. 15
  M. 123
  Thomas 83, 86
  W.H. 83, 119, 123, 129
MARCEY
  Alexander 32
MARCKLEY
  William H. 121
Marine Insurance Company of Alexandria .
                             50
MARKELL
  George H. 84, 86, 124, 130
MARKES
  Robert 127
MARKS
  Elisha 42
  William G. 48, 63
MARLENDE
  John 42
MARMONTELL
  Frederick 24
MARSHALL
  Edward C. 111, 116
  James E. 56
MARSHEL
  John 32

MARSTELLER
  F. 65
  N. 28
  P. 13, 14, 16, 25, 28, 33, 34, 40, 43,
                      47, 55, 62, 65, 71
  Philip 33, 57
  Philip G. 47, 62, 64, 66, 70
MARTEN
  James 24
MARTENI
  John C. 18
MARTIN
  () 30
  Bartin 16, 24
  Bastin 30
  C. 69
  Cyrus 129
  Denny 6
  Edward 42
  Franklin W. 87
  J.M. 85
  James 30, 43, 70
  John 43, 70
  Joseph 56, 62
  Lewis 129
  Peter 23
  William 8, 70
MASON
  Francis 30
  French 32
  G. 39
  George 18, 21, 30-33, 35, 47
  J. 40, 42
  John 22, 48, 55
  Richard R. 92
  Thomas 32
  Thomson 75, 78
  Thomson F. 79
  William 31
Mason's Hall 38
MASSEY
  John 128
  Lee 30
  Linus 42
  Rud. 92
  Rudolph 95
  W.D. 83, 90, 122, 125, 130
  William B. 84
  William D. 87, 102, 109, 113
MASSIE
  William 126
MASTER
  J.S. 123
MASTERS
  John R. 127
  Joseph 119, 121
  Richard 56
  S.S. 118
  Samuel A. 92, 119, 123, 127
  Solomon S. 110

Wallace 123
William K. 123
MASTERSON
  Mark E. 83
MATHEWS
  John 22
MATING
  John 55
MATTHEWS
  Griffin 22
MAUZEY
  Peter 24, 30
MAXWELL
  A. 14
  A.W. 8
  Anthony 27
  Arthur 18, 34
  Cl. 56
  Clo. 64
  Close 62
  Fa. 44
  G.W. 121
  George W. 83
  Hugh 70
MAY
  Edward 62
  Joshua 16
MAYRE
  William S. 73

Mc__
  William 86
McALISTER
  James G. 56
  John 40
McATIE
  William 32
McCAFFREY
  James 42
McCAGILL
  Archibald 40
McCANNE
  Patrick 55
McCARDALL
  James 16
McCARTHY
  Patt. 22
McCARTY
  Daniel 15, 30-32
McCAUGHEN
  Hugh 14, 17, 22, 27, 33, 35, 64
McCLAGHEN
  Charles 56
McCLEAN
  Archibald 51, 57, 70
  Daniel 55, 62, 64, 70
  Honoria 81
  Honoria (Barry) 81

McCLEISH
  G. 109
  George W. 129
  James 56
McCLELAND
  Thomas 112
McCLENACHAN
  James 41
  John 12, 14, 27, 71
McCLIESH
  Archibald 22, 27, 63
  G. 87
  George 119
  James 18, 22, 27, 64, 70
McCLINACHAN
  John 25, 33
McCLOUD
  Hugh 66
  Samuel 48, 55, 62, 65
McCLURG
  Walter 82
McCONCHIE
  William 15
McCONNEKEY
  John 41
McCONNELL
  Alexander 43
McCORMICK
  J. 118, 129
  James 25, 41, 118
  John 95, 102
  Samuel J. 85
  T. 84
  T.M. 87, 106
  Thomas 40, 90-92
  Thomas M. 88
McCRACKEN
  () 87
  J.C. 118, 127
  John 98
  John C. 111
McCREA
  Richard 14
  Robert 3, 5, 6, 11, 12, 18, 27, 29, 33,
                               37, 48
McCREADY
  James 43
McCUE
  Henry 33, 70
McDANIELS
  W. 90
McDAWNEY
  James 41
McDONALD
  Alexander 24, 31
  Archibald 19
  James 3, 34, 40
  M. 23
McDOUGALL
  Daniel 56, 64

McDOWELL
  William 24
McFADON
  James 70
McFAGIN
  J.J. 87
McFARLAND
  John 43
McFARLING
  Ignatius 23
McGAHAN
  James 55
McGAW
  James 46
McGEE
  John 21
McGILL
  James 43
McGINNIS
  Laurence 16
McGLUE
  John B. 84
McGOUGH
  Henry 56
McGRAW
  J.E. 95, 118
  James E. 84, 87
McGUIRE
  Edward 42
  J. 64
  James 55, 70, 91
  William 40, 42
McGWIN
  Edward 28
McHENRY
  James 23
McINTOSH
  James 23
  John 16, 22, 43
  Th. 16
McIVER
  Charles 28
  Colin 3, 12
  John 12, 25, 28, 46, 47, 56
McKEA
  James M. . . 12, 18, 20, 27, 35, 43, 47,
                                              50
  William 20
McKENNA
  James 14, 18, 20, 34, 43, 47, 55, 66
  Peter 24
McKENNY
  Francis 19
McKENZIE
  Alexander 71
  James 89, 123
  Lambert 105
  Lambert S. 92
  Lewis 83, 86-91, 95, 99, 102,
                116-118, 121, 122, 123

McKIM
  Alexander 24
McKNIGHT
  Charles . . 43, 65, 70, 71, 86, 95, 118
  John 28, 66
  R. 8, 34
  W. . 6, 12, 18, 22, 25, 28, 29, 34, 47,
                          48, 55, 63, 64, 70, 71
  W.H. 83, 87, 92, 121
  William 2, 3, 8, 13, 39, 43, 57
McLAUGHLIN
  Jesse 16
McLEAN
  A. 85
  Archibald 101
  Bernard 22
  E. 25
  Evan 14, 16
  Isabella ( ) 48
  James 89
  James H. 98
  Jane 48
  Joseph 90, 98
  Margaret 48
  Samuel 22, 27, 35, 48
  Thomas 48
  William 128
McLEOD
  William 19
McLOR?
  John L. 8
McLOWE
  John F. 95
McMASTERS
  Andrew 23
McMECHEN
  James 56
  William 56, 64
McMOORY
  John 25
McMUNN
  G. 47, 56, 64, 71
  George 40
  Robert 40
McMURRAN
  E.M. 129
McNAIR
  J.B. 118
  James B. 95, 109
McPHERSON
  Daniel 9, 14, 16, 24, 28, 34
  Isaac . . 9, 14, 16, 27, 28, 34, 39, 40,
                                43, 46, 57, 64
  John 100
  Samuel 15
  William 31
McRAE
  James M. 57
McREA
  James 57

James M. 34, 40, 51, 64, 66, 70
John 66
William 27, 34
McREADY/McREDY
   James 21, 34
McSAVAGE
   Thomas 35
McTAGUE
   J.J. 95
McTRUE
   John 35
McVALE
   Thomas 25
McVEIGH
   J. 128
   J. Humphrey 99
   J.H. 90, 109, 118, 130
   J.W. 127
   James H. 83, 91, 99, 123
   Jesse 41
   Jesse H. 83
   Jonathan 42
   William 123
   William N. 83, 87, 91, 99, 117
McWHIR
   William 12, 17

MEARA
   John 32
MEASE
   Robert .. 1, 3, 12-14, 18, 20, 27, 29,
      34, 40, 43, 47, 51, 55, 57, 63, 70
MELLIUS
   C. 84
MENDINHALL
   William 40, 43, 47
MERCER
   Charles F. 74
MERCHANT
   William 16
Merchants Bank of Alexandria 77
MEREDY
   James 18
MERRYMAN
   Joshua 15, 17
MERSHAM
   William 83
METCALFE
   Charles 41
MEYERSBERG
   S.W. 130
MEYLER
   J. 3
   James 18
MEZARVEY
   Thomas 47, 55, 64, 71
MICHAEL
   Daniel 24
   Henry 69

   Jacob 45, 69
MICKY
   Michael 97
MIDDLETON
   F. 113
   James P. 95, 102
   James T. 87
   Thomas 42
MIFFLETON
   Henry 98
MIKELLS
   L.B. 64
MILBOURNE
   Joseph 57
MILBURN
   B.C. 84
   Joseph 64
   Timothy 129
Military:
   175th Regiment 120
   60th Regiment 62
   Certificates 29
   Mexican War 104, 111, 112, 116,
                     121, 124
   Patent 38
   Revolutionary War ... 79, 81, 82, 111
   Service 79, 81, 111, 113
   Supplies Furnished to . 107, 111, 112,
                  116, 120, 124
   Warrant 38
MILLER
   Conrad 28
   E.J. 109, 118, 123
   Ephraim 55
   Godfrey 35
   J.W. 126
   James 44, 52, 57
   Joseph 55
   Mordecai 29, 42, 47, 51, 55, 64
   P. War. 27
   R.H. 118, 130
   Robert H. ... 78, 79, 86, 91, 99, 117
   Samuel 118
   W. Baker 88
   W.A. 84, 85
   William 21, 34, 88
MILLON
   Flavius 56
MILLS
   George 31
   J.W. 97
   John 3, 16, 23, 63
   John T. 85
   Robert Adam 2
   Thomas M. 84
   William 31
   William N. 83, 87, 95
MILNOR
   William 51, 56, 57

MILTON
  Elijah 16, 40
  J. 40
  Moses 16
MINCHIN
  John 14, 16, 25
MINOR
  D. 86, 87
  George 23
  John 63
  Robert M. 86
  William 87, 97
MITCHEL
  Adam 24
MITCHELL
  Benjamin 63
  Hugh 34
  John 31, 90
  Judson 84, 87, 95, 109
  Randle 34
  William 16, 22, 63, 65, 70, 71
MOLCHEN
  Robert 32
MONCURE
  Charles P. 116
MONDAY
  Charles 41
  John 41
MONES
  William 53
MONROE
  Andrew 23, 31
  Edwin 98
  Harrison L. 122
  James T. 89, 98
  John H. 109
  John M. 84, 95, 97
  Sarah 22
  Slighter S. 98
  Spenc 22
  Thomas M. 124
  William 31
  William H. 22
MOODY
  Benjamin 62, 64, 66
  James 84
MOON
  William 32
MOONEY
  Neal/Neil/Neill ... 3, 7, 18, 27, 34, 64
MOORE
  Alexander 101
  C.H. 89
  Charles S. 124
  Cleon . 13, 18, 20, 29, 34, 35, 47, 50,
                                55, 57
  George 42
  Henry 55, 57, 63, 65
  Jacob 25, 41
  Jeremiah 47
  Jesse 17, 43, 57
  John 15, 17, 24, 63, 66, 87, 89
  Joseph C. 125, 127
  Phoebe (Caverly) 36
  Stephen 36, 64
  Thomas 64, 116
MORE
  Eliza 22
  Manery 16
MORELAND
  Archibald 31
  Enos 24, 31
  Jacob 30
  John 24, 31
MOREY
  John 24
MORGAN
  Abraham 44
  Daniel 42, 129
  David 56
  Enoch 8, 18
  Jesse 23
  William 33, 85, 87, 89, 90
MORRIL
  Mrs. 90
MORRILL
  Mary 91
MORRIS
  John 55, 63
  Nehemiah 31
  Nicholas 30
  Zechariah 31, 32
MORRISON
  Hugh 43
  James 17, 28
MORTIMORE
  Ch. 34
  Chs. 9
MORTON
  Jer. 126
  Noah 31
MOSS
  Alfred 105, 125
  John 17, 23
  William 65
MOTHERSHEAD
  Lewis 90
MOUNSHER
  William 25, 27, 34
MOXLEY
  George 22, 31
  Hector 22
  James 16, 24
  John 32
  Spencer 32
  Thomas 1, 3, 17, 35
  William 22
MOZEA
  John 53

MUIR
  Elizabeth 117
  Elizabeth (Wellman) 37
  George 27, 37
  J. 85, 118
  James 3, 37, 48, 51, 56, 57
  John . . . 1, 9, 24, 28, 34, 42, 56, 90,
                                    113, 117
  Robert 3, 6
  Tibbie (Wardlaw) 37
  W.H. 130
  William H. 87, 118, 120, 121
MULLAN
  Thomas 55
MULLIKIN
  N. 97
MULLIN
  Daniel 55
MUNCASTER
  J.L. 98
  John . 42, 46, 47, 50, 56, 64, 65, 70
  Zachariah 64
MUNDAY
  William 2, 3
MUNY
  Park 34
MURCHANT
  Thomas 95
MURPHY
  F.G. 118
  Francis 63, 66, 70, 99
  Francis G. 86
  Stephen 78
MURRAY
  George 19
  James 33, 47, 64
  James E. 128
  John . . 8, 12, 15, 17, 25, 27, 28, 33,
                                       34, 37
  Patrick 2, 8, 15, 17, 27
  Peter 47
  Ralph 42
  Reuben 42
  Robert L. 90
  Samuel 14, 16
  Thomas 47
  Thomas J. 105
MURRY
  John 32
  Robert 84
MUSE
  Laurence 43
MUSGROVE
  Cuthbert 42
MYERS
  E. 71
  William 55, 62, 63, 65, 69, 70
MYTINGER
  Daniel 19

N

N___
  Joseph 48
NALL
  Robert 87
NALLEY
  Aaron 31
  O. 22
NALLS
  James W. 90, 98, 109
  R.W. 129
NASH
  George 3
  Robert J. 83, 95
Natural Resources: 111
  Timber 128
  Timber and Wood 126
  Wood 130
Navigation: 8, 79, 92, 96, 110
NEALE
  Charles 83
  Charles C. 87, 95
  Charles L. 95
  Christopher . . . 24, 87, 96, 105, 125
  Francis 66, 70
  Joseph 66, 70
  Thomas 22
NEBLON
  John J. 43
NEILL
  Abraham 40
  Doras 23
  John 43, 46, 47
NEILSON
  William 114
NELSON
  George W. 84
  William 85
NESWANGER
  Jacob 19
NEVETT
  James C. 123, 129
  Joseph 95
NEVITT
  Nehemiah 16
NEWBY
  Prichd. 39
NEWMAN
  Th. 22
  Ths. 116
Newspapers:
  Alexandria Gazette 36, 82
  Columbia Mirror and Alexandria
      Gazette 48, 52
  Pennsylvania Gazette 12
  The Herald 49
  Virginia Gazette 36
  Virginia Gazette and Alexandria
      Advertiser 36, 38, 40, 44
  Virginia Journal and Alexandria

    Advertiser 34
    Virginia Journal and Alexandria
      Gazette 7, 9, 12, 36
NEWTON
    A.G. 85, 86, 92, 118
    Chs. 97
    James 55
    Robert C. 34
    William . . . 25, 39, 47, 50, 51, 55, 57,
                            62, 66, 71
    William C. 63
NICHOLASSON
    Thomas 98
NICHOLS
    Amos 44
    Frederick 24
    Henry 66
NICHOLSON
    Henry 69
NICKELSON
    Joseph 23
NICKLIN
    J.R. 123
NICKOLLS
    George 32
    J. 47
    J.B. 47, 50, 57, 66
    James B. 43
    Scudamore 43, 64, 70
NIGHTGILL
    James 89
NIGHTINGALE
    John 85
    Toby 85
NILES
    Amos 42
NIVEN
    Duncan 22, 56, 70
NIXON
    W.B. 98
NOBLE
    William F. 56
NOLAND
    Charles 16, 24
    F.A. 97
NOLLAND
    William 98
NOLTE
    Luis 84
NORFLET
    S. 83
NORRIS
    John 85
    William 34
NORSBROUGH
    John 55
NORSBURGH
    John 63
NORTON
    John I. 83

NORWOOD
    John 45-47, 66
NOWLAND
    Nimrod H. 89
    Theophilus 89
NOWLES
    Charles W. 84
    Gilmore 84
NUTT
    William D. 84, 95, 126, 129

O

O'BRIAN
    W. 66
O'CONNOR
    John 55
O'DANIEL
    John 22
O'DONALD
    Hugh 55
O'KELLY
    John B. 39
O'LANDRY
    William 14
O'NEAL
    Hugh 48, 55
    Thomas N. 95
    William 95
O'RYAN
    T. 34
    Thomas 16
O'SULLIVAN
    Daniel 16
Occupations:
    Adventurer to Sea 4
    Artist 112
    Assessor 96
    Attorney 82, 103
    Auditor 81
    Baker 68, 69
    Banker 69, 71, 72, 86
    Cabinet Maker 2
    Capt. 98
    Chaplain 82
    Churchwarden 26
    Clergyman 12
    Clerk 3, 9, 102, 105, 127, 129
    Commissioner of the Revenue 98, 109,
                                  112, 113
    Constable 3
    Director 51
    Doctor 111
    Escheator 117
    Farmer 118, 128
    Ferry Man 67
    Fisherman 110
    Flour Inspector 28, 46, 97
    Flour Merchant 40
    Governor 36, 81, 102

Joiner 2
Justice of the Peace . 3, 4, 46, 53, 69, 77
Lawyer 96, 99
Librarian 51
Magistrate 2, 89
Manufacturer of Flour 40
Manufacturer of Wheat 40
Mariner 110
Mayor 19, 45, 48, 51, 52, 106
Mechanic 69, 121
Merchant .. 2, 4, 8, 9, 13, 20, 28, 39, 45, 50, 62, 63, 69, 71, 91, 105, 110, 112, 117, 118, 121, 126-128, 130
Miller 41, 45
Minister 11, 12, 37, 90, 113
Overseer of the Poor 25, 26
Pilot 121, 126
Planter 110
Printer 72, 125
Registrar of Wills 101
Senator 99
Sheriff 9
Shoemaker 112
Stage Coach 19
Surgeon 80-82
Surveyor 9, 13
Tobacco Inspector 22, 44, 45, 71
Trader .. 8, 28, 40, 45, 69, 117, 118
Tradesman 63, 127, 128
Treasurer 51

ODANIEL
  John 16
OF___
  John 44
OFFICER
  James 16
OFFUTT
  Rezin 23
OGDEN
  A.J. 87, 89
  John 130
  Thomas 23
  William 30
OGDON
  Henry 23
  William 23
OGLE
  Benjamin 23
  John 23
OISENS
  Thomas 32
OLDDEN
  James 51
OLIPHANT
  John 3, 8, 18
OLIVER
  John 22
OPLETELER
  George 14

Orange and Alexandria Railroad   111, 114-116
Orange and Alexandria Railroad Company   106, 119, 120, 124, 125
ORISON
  Andrew 24
ORM
  Reason 128
Orphans: 49
  Asylum 90, 91
ORR
  James L. 55, 70
  John D. 48
OSBOURN
  Luke 88
OSWALD
  John 56, 70
OTWAY
  Thomas 66
OVERALL
  John 62
OWEN
  Edward 87
OWENS
  Edward 3
  John 32
  John E. 98
  Joshua 41
  Mason 42
  Thomas 32
  William 85
OWNBREAD
  William 8
OWSLEY
  Anthony 42
  Henry 42

P

PACKARD
  Samuel 28
PADGETT
  J.G. 98
  James 84
  John W. 95
  Joseph 84
  William 84
  William F. 87
PAGE
  Charles 43, 56, 66
  J. Dixon 123
  Susan S. 127
  Washington C. 84, 92, 123
  William ... 33, 83, 95, 106, 110, 119
  William B. 50, 66
PAIN
  Thomas 30
PALMER
  Thomas 22

PANCOAST
   David 8
PANE
   William 17
PARK
   John 24
PARKER
   Lawson 31
   Nathaniel 23
PARKINS
   John 83
PARMER
   Thomas 30
PARRITT
   Samuel 127
PARRY
   John 42
PARSONS
   James 2, 3, 6, 8
   John 22
   Thomas 95
PASCOE
   Charles 55
   John L. 84, 87, 92, 124
PATON
   T.M. 16
   William .. 3, 6, 12-14, 27, 28, 35, 42,
       47, 50, 51, 55, 63, 64, 70, 71
PATTEN
   Hezekiah 90
   James 57
   Thomas 43, 46, 55, 64, 66
PATTERSON
   Robert 41
PATTON
   F. 47
   James 14, 20, 34, 42, 47, 50, 56, 63,
                66, 71, 72
   John 22
   R.H. 129
   Robert 42
PAUL
   Isaac 129
   Joseph 55, 62, 66
PAYELS
   Peter 63
PAYNE
   () 15
   And. 23
   Benjamin C. 25
   Charles 97
   George H. 109, 110, 118
   P. 123
   Sandford 24
   Sanford 30
   T. 97
   W. 23, 39
   William 110
PAYTON
   Andrew 43

PEACH
   J. Gibson 96
PEACOCK
   John 16, 31
PEAKE
   G.R. 116
   Henry 18, 23
   John 24
   William 18, 23
PEARCE
   Allan 126
   Allen 128
PEARL
   Elijah C. 126
PEARLE
   Samuel 41
   William 42
PEARSON
   John 30
PEEL
   Cook S. 109
   Henry 84, 109, 123
PEERS
   Valentine 2, 3, 16, 35, 43
PELL
   Henry 30
PELTEN
   Enoch 56
PENDLETON
   Philip 44
PENKSTONE
   Henry 42
PENN
   Walter L. 95, 98, 118
PEPPER
   Michael 25
PERRIN
   Jh. M. 55, 57, 64, 65
   Joseph M. 28
   Mathzarin 55
   Math<u>z</u>urin 64, 65
   Mr. 14
PERRY
   Alexander 18, 23, 55
   Edmund 129
   J.T. 105
   John 109, 123
   John S. 91
   John T. .. 87, 92, 109, 110, 118, 123
   John T.B. 85
   William 129
PERRYMAN
   John 22
PERTH
   Christian 27
PETERKIN
   Thomas 65, 70
PETERSON
   Peter 25, 47

PETTIGREW
   John 28
PETTIT
   B. 25, 43
   J. 28
   John 84
   Mr. 15
PETTYJOHN
   Jos. 126
PEYTON
   Andrew 39
   Cha. 42
   Francis ... 14, 18, 24, 28, 39, 42, 45,
             47, 50, 51, 55, 57, 62, 122
   Henry 41
   J. 40
   L. 96
   Lauren 97
   Lucien 84, 95, 98
   R. 20
   Sophia () 101
   T.W. 56, 62
   Thomas W. 101
   Valentine 33
PHILLIPS
   James 95
   John 32
   Thomas 42
   William 32, 83
PICKELL
   Thomas B. 89
PICKETT
   Thomas B. 97
PICKIN
   James H. 89
PICKRELL
   Richard 15, 17
PIERCE
   Jacob G. 41
PIERCY
   Henry 39, 43, 47
PIERPOINT
   John R. 86, 118
PILES
   Jacob 84
   Peter 18, 22, 28, 57
PITMAN
   Andrew 19
PITTMAN
   John 56, 63
Places:
   Addison's 6
   Alexandria Harbour 5
   Ball's Cross Road 88
   Baltimore . 34, 39, 41, 63, 65, 73, 82,
                88, 92, 110, 111, 126
   Bel Air 37
   Bellemont 9
   Blue Ridge 73
   Blueridge 74

Boswell's 53
Brooklyn, N.Y. 82
Cape Francois 4
Carolina 5
Chester Co., Pa. 100, 101
Colross 37
Cotton Factory 87
Craney Island 52
Criswell's 53
Culpeper Courthouse 119
Delaware 130
District of Columbia 72, 73, 75-77, 80,
                          83, 92, 107
Dowdel's 100
Dumfries 7
England 113, 117
Europe 50, 52
Fairfax Co. 2, 4, 5
Fairfax Courthouse 82
Fairfax Parish 49
Falmouth 1
Fort Cumberland 8
Fort Washington 110
Frederick Co. 2
Frederick, Md. 82
Fredericksburg 20, 117
Georgetown 46, 65, 78
Georgia 52
Germany 45, 67, 74
Gloucester Point 79
Gloucesterton 79, 80
Gordonsville 95, 119, 120
Great Britain 1, 117
Great Falls 8, 114, 116, 119
Great Hunting Creek 5
Guilford 53
Gum Spring 74
Hampton 19
Harper's Ferry 88, 123
Harrisonburg 111
Hawkin's 6
Hayfield 103
Haymarket 49
Hayti 114
Hettenhousen, Ger. 69
High Point 110
Hooff's Run 122
Hunting Creek Warehouse 1, 5
Indian Head 110
Kentucky 37, 38
Keys' Gap 74
Leesburg 73, 74
Lexington, Ky. 38
Liverpool Point 110
Lynchburg 119, 120, 124
Martin Key's Ford 53
Maryland . 4, 5, 65, 75, 91, 105, 110,
                          128, 130
Mexico 111
Mill Dam 2

177

Mississippi	119
Missouri	104
Mrs. Waller's Landing	110
Mushpot Run	122
Naval Office	4
Ninety-Six	53
Norfolk	71, 117
Norman's Ford	52, 70
Northern Neck	6
Notley Hall	9
Ohio	81
Paddytown	124
Pennsylvania	5, 128
Philadelphia	39, 41, 50, 100
Pohick	30, 32
Point Lookout	126
Point West	1
Port au Prince	113
Portsmouth	36
Preston	76
Price's Ordinary	35
Prussia	113
Quantico	7
Raccoon Ford	53
Ravensworth	112
Richmond	19, 54, 112, 116, 120
Rozier's	6
Ruckey Cock	100
Salisbury	53
Scotland	117
Sheridan's Point	110
South Lowell	114, 115, 119
Spier, Ger.	69
St. Domingo	113, 114, 120
St. Louis, Mo.	113
Staunton	73
Thornton Gap	73
Warrenton	82, 88
Washington, D.C.	82, 95, 106, 108, 110, 111, 113, 119
Williamsburg	79
Winchester	18, 97, 111
Winchester, Va.	2
Windmill Point	79
Wormley's Gap	74
York	79, 80
Yorktown	79

PLAIN
George	87, 88, 95, 109, 117

PLANT
Joseph	84
Joseph K.	98

PLEASANTS
John	25

PLOWMAN
James	33

PLUM
George	84

PLUMMER
B.T.	83, 95, 102, 109, 123

E.	85

POESSEY
Charles	24

POLK
Charles	15

POLKINHORN
Henry	48

POLLARD
Henry	84
Thomas	23, 31
William	84

POLLOCK
James T.	44

POMERY
George	56, 63, 64, 66, 70, 71
Walter	55, 62, 63, 66, 70
Walter L.	87
William	48, 56, 63, 66, 84

POOL
Edward	31
Thomas	16
William	24

POOLL
Thomas	23

POPE
William	15

PORTER
Betsey	82
Daniel	82
James	46, 47, 50, 63, 66
Sarah R.	82
Thomas	14, 16, 33-35, 39, 56, 64

POSTON
Frances	23

POTTEN
H.J.	22

POTTER
Edward	31, 32
John	97
Joseph	30, 32
Reuben	32
Sanford	18, 31
Stanford	23
William	32

POTTS
John	8, 14, 17, 20, 25, 29, 34, 35, 39, 43, 47, 50, 55, 62, 64, 101

POWELL
Abraham D.	121
Burr	41
Col.	38
Cuthbert	64, 70, 72, 76, 121
Edw. B.	86, 102, 119, 123, 128
Edward B.	85
John	15, 30, 31, 97
Joseph	15, 16, 23, 32, 35
Leven	9, 11, 41, 45, 47, 73, 74
W.	41
William	24, 84
William H.	14, 16, 28, 41

William L. . 85, 88, 99, 102, 105, 106, 118, 120
William T. 123
POWER
  Mr. 15
POWERS
  John 52
PRATHER
  James 25
  John S. 24
  Thomas 21
PRATT
  Shubael 3, 7
  William 86
PRESCOTT
  R. 34
PRESGRAVES
  Richard 31
  William 16, 22, 31
PRESTON
  Henry 25
  John S. 98
  T. Gardner 83
  Thomas 46, 56, 66
PRICE
  Benoni 16, 23, 31
  Charles 87
  Charles S. 83, 123
  Ellis 51, 56, 62, 66
  Ellis L. 83
  George 98, 105
  Hezekiah 31
  Jacob 33
  John T. 98
  Oliver . 3, 6, 9, 18, 19, 25, 27, 33, 34, 43, 48
  Will. 16
  William 31, 87, 95
  William B. 87, 92, 102, 109
  William D. 83
PRICHARD
  James 31
PRIEST
  Thomas 42
PRITCHARD
  Lewis 30
PROCTER
  Richard 31
PROCTOR
  John J. 87, 102, 109, 124
Prostitution: 36, 108
PUGH
  Jesse 63
PUPPO
  Daniel C. 56, 70, 71
PURDY
  James 14, 16, 22
PYLES
  Peter 43

Q

QUAID
  James 85, 97, 98, 108
QUIRK
  Richard 55

R

RADCLIFF
  John S. 89
Railroads: . . 88, 95, 103, 105, 111, 114, 119, 123, 124, 125, 127, 128
  Freights 129
RAMSAY
  A. 50, 71
  Andrew 39, 45, 47, 56, 63
  Dennis . 3, 5, 7-9, 18, 20, 27, 28, 33, 35, 39, 46, 51, 56, 62, 65, 71, 82
  Edward . . . 3, 6, 9, 14, 18, 25, 33, 43
  Edward M. 2
  Family 5
  G.W. . 83, 86, 92, 102, 105, 110, 129
  G.W.D. 118
  George W. 82
  J.T. 89, 96
  J.W. 123
  Jane A. 82
  John . 22, 50, 56, 63, 66, 70, 71, 101
  R.T. 83, 92, 102, 105, 110, 118
  Robert T. 82
  Thomas 18, 22, 27
  William . . . 1, 6, 8, 13, 18, 24, 27, 28, 35, 39, 45, 50, 56-57, 62, 63, 82
  Yeaton 63
RAMY
  Michael 31
RAND
  John 31
RANDOLPH
  R.B. 118
RATCLIFF
  E.D. 32
  Ignatius 55
  John 16
  Richard 14, 18, 35
RATCLIFFE
  Richard 32, 43
RATLIFFE
  John 23
RATLLIFF
  Edward 23
RATTLE
  James 18, 22, 28, 32
RAWLINGS
  B. 43
READ
  John S. 30
  William 22

REARDON
  George 30
  Henry 16
  John 56
  William 16, 30, 31
REAS
  Hensley 16
RECTOR
  Henry 42
  William 42
REDMAN
  Thomas 18, 56
REDMON
  Thomas 43
REDMOND
  Edward 55
REED
  Andrew 34
  Charles 30
  James 42
  John 98
  Samuel 44
  Thomas 3, 18, 22
REEDER
  Ben 15
REEDOR
  Thomas 9
REESE
  Hiram 89, 98
  Samuel 95, 98
  William L. 98
REEVES
  Leonard 21, 64
REID
  J.H. 118
  Joab 32
  Thomas 28, 32
REIGHLEY
  Joseph 32
REILLY
  John 63
REINTZEL
  Andrew 43
  Jacob 43
  Nicholas 56
REINTZELL
  Andrew 34, 56
REIS
  John 83
RENO
  Hanson 55, 63, 70
  Rents: 1, 27, 49, 99, 100
RESLER
  Jacob 34, 56, 63
Retrocession: 83, 84, 86
  Suspension of 85
REVES
  James 24
REYNOLDS
  Cornelia 42

  John . . 8, 14, 16, 25, 28, 33, 35, 43, 46
  Michael 15, 25, 34
  William 43
  William C. 84, 95, 97
RHODES
  John 70
  W. 83
  William 33
RICE
  B. 19
  David 84
  Hopkin 31
RICHARDS
  C.L. 95
  Caleb 23
  Caleb L. 87
  David 55
  E.L. 118
  George 9, 14, 27, 35
  Henry 31
  James 16, 24, 31
  John 62, 66, 70, 85
  Richard 50
  Thomas 18, 22, 28, 43
  W.B. 130
  W.C. 98
  William 17, 22, 31, 48
  William B. 87, 119
  William C. 87, 118
RICHARDSON
  James 64, 66, 71
RICHTER
  Charles 43, 55
  John 55, 62, 63, 66, 70
RICKETTS
  J.T. 47
  John T. 50, 56, 57, 62, 64, 71
RIDDLE
  J. 72
  J.R. 92, 95
  James R. 64
  Joseph . . . 42, 45, 47, 50, 56, 63, 64, 66, 71, 76
  Joshua 44, 50, 56, 63, 64, 66, 70, 71
RIDGWAY
  Coats 55, 65
RILEY
  Benjamin 31
  James 31
RIPTLER
  Peter 126
RISDON
  John 84
RITSON
  Russell 63
Rivers:
  Appomattox 53
  James 19, 39
  Lands on 102

Little 72, 73, 77
  Ohio 96
  Potomac . 2, 8-10, 13, 15, 20, 27, 39,
     40, 48, 51, 64, 71, 78, 83, 102,
     103, 110, 114, 115, 119, 121, 122,
     126
  Rappahannock 52
  Rivanna 53
  Saluda 53
  Shenandoah 92
  Slate 53
  South Potomac 13
  South Potowmack 4
  York 79, 80
RIVES
  W.C. 126
ROACH
  Frances 127
  J. 85, 90, 97, 106, 126
  James 127, 128
  John 109
Roads: 5, 34, 52, 70
  Alexandria Turnpike 127
  Colchester 2
  Fauquier & Alexandria Turnpike . . . 82,
     129
  Leesburg and Georgetown Turnpike . 52
  Little River Turnpike . . . 72-74, 77, 78,
     82, 122
  Repairs 73
  Thornton Gap 73
ROBERDEAU
  Daniel 12, 14, 16, 25, 29, 35, 43
  Isaac 14, 16, 29
ROBERTS
  John 62, 70
ROBERTSON
  John 16, 22, 25
ROBEY
  Elisha 22
  Josiah 63, 64
  Michelhines 22
ROBINSON
  George H. 129
  James H. 84
  John 31, 42
  John C. 23
  Joseph 6, 8, 35
  Matthew 43, 46, 47, 55, 63, 65
  Mr. 14
  Richard 83
  William 84
ROBISON
  William 23
ROBY
  Elias 31
  J.T. 95
  Levi 31
  Lish T. 31
  Michael 31
  Michael H. 31
ROCK
  George W. 95, 109
  Micajah 40
  William 83, 87, 95, 102
  William W. 121
ROGERS
  Asa 99
  Benjamin 31
  Isaac 30
  John 31
  William 16, 23, 24, 32
  William H. 96, 99, 118, 123, 130
ROGERSON
  Thomas . . 25, 28, 33, 34, 46, 47, 51,
     65
ROOKLEY
  Reuben 32
ROOKSLEY
  Jacob 32
ROONEY
  Michael 30
ROSE
  Alexander M. 84
  Henry 47
  Jesse 84
  Thomas 3
ROSENTHAL
  J. 130
ROSS
  J. 87, 90, 96
  John 53
ROTCHFORD
  Barth. 98
  Bartholomew 98
  Philip 98, 118
  Richard 98
ROW
  George 3
ROWE
  William N. 85, 87
ROWLAND
  Gilbert 30
  Henry 32
  James 24, 30, 32
  Thomas 32
ROXBURY
  J. 109
  Jacob 86, 87, 90, 102
ROY
  Thomas 46
ROZIER
  Henry 3
  John 43
RUDD
  Charles D. 89
  James S. 98
  James T. 95
  John A. 89
  John W. 89

R.A. 89, 121
Richard 96
RUDER
   Jacob 41
RUFFNER
   Joshua 73
RUMNEY
   John 27
   Mr. 14
   William 3, 81, 111
RUNDEL
   John 85
RUSH
   Daniel 24
RUSSAN
   Henry 32
RUSSELL
   James 55, 63, 66, 71
   R. 85
   Thomas 42
RUST
   Matthew 43
RUTTER
   George 15, 17, 33, 64, 65, 70
   Mike 55
RYAN
   Frances (l) 49
   John 24
   Michael 49
   Thomas O. 14
   Timothy 55
RYE
   Jesse 98

S

SALLMON
   James 30
SAMPLE
   William 48
SANDERS
   Benjamin 22
   Daniel 24
   John 23
   Lewis 16, 22, 32
   Robinson 28
   S.S. 119
SANDERSON
   Mr. 14
   Robert 34
   Samuel 84
SANDFORD
   John 4
   Lawrence 5
   Mrs. 90
SANFORD
   Daniel 24
   Edward . 3, 7-9, 14, 17, 21, 27, 33, 43
   Esther 91
   John 6, 8

Richard .. 3, 7, 18, 24, 25, 34, 35, 47
Robert 18, 24, 35
Th. 95
Thomas 56, 86, 109
William 56
SANGSTER
   Samuel 70
   Thomas 22, 31, 32
SARAT
   George 127
SAUNDERS
   John 2, 6-8, 14, 16, 25, 27
SAXTON
   John 30
SCEARCE
   William B. 89, 98, 118
SCHAFER
   Christian 98
   Christopher 87
SCHEWE
   C.F. 70
SCHIESE
   Sebastien 15, 17
SCHMIDT
   John 55
SCHUTER
   Henry 97
SCHWARZ
   Henry 130
SCOOPE
   Jacob 25
SCOT
   James 18
SCOTT
   C.R. 57
   Charles R. 20, 43, 64
   D. 126
   David W. 62, 64, 66, 70, 71
   Gus. H. 78
   Hugh 42
   James 22
   James L. 55
   John 23, 31, 55
   R.E. 125
   Richard M. 63, 64, 83
   Samuel 128
   Zacrahia 23
SCRIVENER
   Richard 31, 32
SEARS
   James W. 83, 84, 95
SEATON
   James 53
   William 53
SEBASTIEN
   Nicholas 16
SELDEN
   L. Cary 97
SELDNER
   S. 123

SELMON
  George 23
SEMMES
  D.R. 129
  William H. 96
SENGEL
  William R. 37
SETON
  John C. 39
SEWELL
  J.W. 85
SEXSMITH
  Matthew 43, 48, 55, 63, 66, 70
SHACKELFORD
  B.H. 125
  John 92
SHACKLETT
  George W. 123
  Henry 78
  Hezekiah 42
SHAKESPEAR/SHAKSPEAR
  William 15, 17, 28
SHAW
  C.P. 117, 125
  Charles P. 92, 118
  John 3, 18, 87
SHAY
  S. King 83, 89, 95, 119, 120
SHECKLE
  Diedrick 56
SHED
  John 24
SHEEHY
  Edward 98
  Edward L. 92
  Edward S. 98
  James 85, 88, 98
  R.J. 88
  Robert J. 98, 118
SHEHEE
  Stephen 22
SHEKLE
  Diedrick 22, 47, 66
SHELLER
  John 97
SHEMES
  Martin 22
SHEOBALDS
  Samuel 34
SHEPPARD
  William 48
SHERD
  Francis 56
SHERER
  John 97
SHERMAN
  S.H. 123
SHERRER
  John 84
SHERRON
  Daniel W. 27
  Peter 62, 65
SHERTELL
  Luke 48
SHERWOOD
  George L. 118
  J.W. 128
  John B. 97
  Thomas 23
  William 98
SHEVERLANE
  Catharine 101
SHIELDS
  Thomas 42
SHILTS
  William 98
SHIMAKER
  Junius 127
SHINN
  J.A. 123
  John A. 92
  Stephen 87, 90-92, 96, 99, 100, 102,
           103, 105, 118, 124, 128, 130
  William 44
Shipping: 96, 126
Ships: 1, 6, 51, 79, 99, 121
  Custis 38
  Repairing 103
  Schooner Sidney 4
  Swan 121
SHIRLEY
  Chs. B. 83
  Davey 55
SHIVELEY
  Jebob 24
SHORE
  Michael 17
SHORT
  C. 87
  E. 92, 98
  Edward 83
  John 8, 17, 25, 27, 30
  Truman 84
SHORTILL
  Luke 42
SHORTRIDGE
  John 24, 32
SHREVE
  B.F. 88
  Benjamin . . . 6, 12, 14, 16, 25, 27, 28,
           35, 40, 46, 47, 50, 56, 62-65,
           69-71
  Benjamin F. 97
  Reuben 55
  Richard L. 128
  Samuel 128
  Thomas 55
  William 23, 25, 128

SHRINER
  John 97
SHROPESHIRE/SHROPSHIRE
  William 42, 56, 63
SHRYER
  Daniel 102
SHUCK
  Jacob 34, 55, 57
SHUGART
  Zachariah 15, 17, 25
SHULTHEIS
  Henry 69
SHUMAKER
  Shedrick 33
SHUMAN
  J.H. 95
SHUMATE
  B. 125
  Bailey 53
  Barley 53
  Benjamin 53
  Daniel 53
  George 53
  John 53
  Joseph 53
  Lewis 53
  Thomas 53
  Toliafer 53
SHURTON
  C.M. 40
SHUTT
  W.H. 127
SIDEBOTTOM
  Winfred 84
SIM
  Robert 14, 18, 33
SIMMENS
  Thomas 23
SIMMONDS
  Samuel 8, 27, 33
SIMMONS
  Samuel 3, 43
  Thomas 16, 24
  William 24
SIMMS
  Alexander 31
  Ch. 6, 24, 27, 33, 39, 47, 51, 56, 65,
                            71, 73, 74
  Charles 9, 11, 12, 33
  Chs. 57
  J. 18
  Jesse . 16, 28, 40, 42, 43, 47, 50, 57,
                            63, 65
  John 84
  Samuel 18
  Thomas 63
  William 24, 31, 32
SIMPSON
  A.M. 98
  Aaron 30
  French 16, 30
  George 23, 30, 32
  Gilbert 23, 30, 92
  Henry 83, 87
  Henry L. 92, 118
  J. 32, 97
  James 30
  James M. 95
  James W. 84
  John 23, 30-32
  Joseph 32
  Peter 98
  Richard 32, 40
  S. French 98
  Spencer 30
  Thomas 30
  William 15, 30, 32
SIMS
  Robert 22
SIMSALL
  James 40
SIMSON
  Levi 24
SINCLAIR
  Charles G. 39
  John W. 95
  Thomas 24
SINGLETON
  Joshua 42
  Samuel 42
  William 42
SINKLER
  James 42
SIPPLE
  Waitmon 43
SISSON
  J. 89
  J.L. 128
  William 16, 30
SKIDMORE
  J.W. 97
  Jesse 98
  L.E. 84
  T.W. 97
SKIDWELL
  Joshua 24
SKINKER
  William 15
SKINNER
  A. 35
  John 30
  John T. 83, 90
  Samuel 41
  William 30
SLACK
  Samuel R. 89
SLACOM/SLACUM
  Gabriel 15, 17, 56
  George 39, 46, 47, 56, 63, 70
  John 56, 102

SLADE
  Charles 63, 71
SLATER
  John 127
SLATFORD
  George 23
  George W. 48, 55
  Thomas 84
SLAUGHTER
  D.F. 125
SLAUGHTON
  Smith 40
Slaves: 75-77, 100
  () Esther 100, 101, 114
  () Frank 76, 77
  () Hanson 77
  () Harry 76, 77
  () Henny 76, 77
  () Henson 76
  () Jack 76, 77
  () James 76, 77
  () Jenny 76
  () Jerry 100
  () Joe 77
  () John 77
  () Letty 100, 113
  () Lucy 77
  () Mary 77
  () Moses 100, 101
  () Nace 76, 77
  () Ned 76, 77
  () Old Harry 76
  () Oswald 76
  () Ozzy 77
  () Sall 76
  (), Juliana E. 100, 113, 114
  Dixon, John 112
SLAYMAKER
  John B. 129
SLIMMER
  J. 123
  Peter 43
SLOAN
  John 63, 70
SLOWEN
  Andrew 33
SLY
  Thomas 34
SMALLWOOD
  Charles 56
SMARR
  Robert 41
SMITH
  Alexander .. 8, 14, 16, 18, 25, 27, 29,
     33, 34, 39, 43, 45, 46, 47, 55, 63,
     65, 70
  Augustine J. 73
  Benjamin 14, 16
  C.F. 125
  Ch. 23

Charles 16, 31
D. Boyd 103
D.B. 117, 118, 127, 130
D.C. 84
E. 90
Edmund 40
Elizabeth H. 90
Elizabeth J. 91
Enoch 23
Flenoy 25
Francis L. 84, 86-88, 90, 96, 99, 103,
                         104, 111, 125
George 24, 32
Gideon 24
H.C. 87, 90, 99, 109, 118
Hesselius 129
Hugh .. 55, 74, 78, 79, 86, 120, 129
Hugh C. . 84, 87, 90-92, 99, 102, 123
Isabella K. 91
J. 89
James 22, 28, 30, 32, 56, 98
James P. 123, 129
John . 18, 19, 23, 24, 27, 28, 40, 42,
                         47, 66, 97, 100
John L. 98, 119
John W. 95
Joseph 17
Leonard 30
Nathan 15
R.C. 87, 92, 95
Richard C. 83, 103
Robert 15, 19, 22, 55, 66
Robert I. 85
Robert J. 105, 117, 119
Samuel 15, 17, 23, 27, 30, 70
T.W. 87, 92
Tempel 15
Tempile 47
Thomas .. 38, 62, 64, 66, 70, 82, 83,
                                   88
Thomas W. 116, 129
W.M. 92, 123, 127
Weathers/Wethers 24, 32
William .. 15, 16, 22, 25, 32, 43, 48
William H. 97
SMITHER
  Gabriel 52
SMITHERMAN
  Hugh 31
  Samuel 24, 31
SMITHSON
  William 69
SMOCK
  Robert 66
SMOOT
  C.C. 84, 90, 117, 130
  Charles C. 85, 91, 92, 109
  George H. 83, 86, 88, 92, 95, 99,
        100, 103, 105, 117, 119-121, 123
  Hezekiah 56, 63-65

James E. 86
James R. 119
W.H. 110
SMUDERMAN
　Samuel 24
SMULL
　William 25
SMYTH
　Edward 98
SNICKERS
　William 40
SNIDER
　John 34
SNOW
　Gideon 16
SNOWDEN
　E. 90
　Edgar . . . 83, 91, 112, 113, 123, 129
　Edward 109, 123
　Mr. 103
　Samuel 72
SNYDER
　George 97, 118
　John 110, 119
　R.R. 123, 129
　Robert B. 109
　Robert R. 84, 119
SOLOMON
　Michael 63, 70
　Samuel 86
SOMERVILL
　James 18
SOMMERS (also see Summers)
　A. 97
　J.W. 128
　John 43
　John W. 97
　S.L. 97
　Simon 71
SOTHORON
　Richard 85
SOUTHERN
　Richard 97, 126, 129
SOUTHWARD
　Laurence 24
SPEAKE
　Robert 30
SPENCER
　Francis 16
　John 16
SPIERS
　Joshua 8
SPILMAN
　Edwd. M. 125
　William C. 87, 89
SPINKS
　James 83, 95
　Joseph 18
SPOONER
　Nath. 17

Nathaniel 43
SPRAGUE
　John 85
SPRINGS
　Gerard 16
SPRINKS
　Chandler 17
SPURR
　John 27
SQUIRES
　Caleb 42
　Thomas 42
STABLER
　Edward . . . 40, 43, 46, 56, 57, 63, 64
　Francis 83
　R.H. 119
　Richard H. 95
　William 109, 118
STANSBURY
　Joseph S. 124
　Samuel 51
STARK
　Thompson 71
STARKEY
　James 44
STARR
　Seth 25
STAUNTON
　E.H. 95
STEAL
　Thomas 56
STEEL
　John 18, 22, 34
　Thomas 66
　William 24
STEELE
　H.N. 89, 97
　William 16
STEPHEN
　Robert 44
STEPHENS
　John 22
　Stephen 55, 70
STEPHENSON
　James 44
　John 85, 95
STEUART
　H. 23
　J.M. 86, 109
　James 3
　James M. 70, 87
STEVENS
　Joseph 19
　William 22
STEVENSON
　Clotworthy 70
STEWART
　Andrew 2
　Charles 78
　David 12

J.M. 109, 123, 130
  John . . . 8, 15, 17, 22, 54, 62-64, 70
  John A. 55, 65, 101
  John W. 129
  Mrs. 90
  Robert 63
  Thomas 22, 27, 33, 43, 54
STIER
  C.J. 50
  Charles J. 57, 64
STIMER
  Joseph 55
STITH
  Buckner 16
STODDARD
  Thomas 27
STOHR
  Adam 16
STOKES
  Harry 97
STONE
  Benjamin 16, 24
  Caleb 31
  Daniel 31, 32
  Eli 31
  Elie 18
  Francis 32
  Frank 22
  John 31, 32
  John S. 40
  Samuel 30, 31
  William 16, 31
STONSTREET
  Basil 23
STOOP
  James 85
STOOPS
  James 87, 89
  William 70
STORM
  Jacob 16
STORY
  Daniel 32
STOTS
  Henry 24
STOVIN
  Charles 42
  George 39
STRAITH
  Alexander 44
  Streets: 2, 9, 33, 34, 49
    Cameron 39, 122
    Columbus 120
    Duke 2, 72, 73, 117
    Fairfax 122
    Franklin 10
    Hooff's Alley 100
    King 9, 52, 100, 122, 125
    Lee 6
    Montgomery 48

  Oronoka/Oronoko . . . 1, 13, 20, 45, 52
  Pitt 100, 117, 123, 125
  Prince 99, 123, 125
  Princess 100, 101
  Queen 13, 51, 100, 120
  Royal 2, 123
  St. Asaph 2, 99, 100
  Union 6, 10, 101, 125
  Washington 9, 10, 13, 51
  Water 6, 10, 11, 20, 44, 101
  West 48
  Wolfe 2, 12
STRIBLING
  Thomas 40
  William 40
STRIDER
  J.L. 90
STROMAN
  Henry 3, 8, 18, 22, 27, 55
STROTHER
  Benjamin S. 42
  J.F. 126
  James 53
STUART
  Albert 99, 102, 108, 125
  Alexander 78
  Ann L. 91
  Charles 102
  Charles T. 83, 95, 109, 118
  Charles W. 99
  D. 40, 71
  David 40, 41
  Henry L. 83
  Philip 15
  W. 15, 71
  William 71
SUDDETH
  Benjamin 30
  James 31
  Lewis 32
SULLIVAN
  Enoch 56
  J.B. 62
  John 22, 42
  Owen 42
  Timothy 48
SUMMERS (also see Sommers)
  Daniel 24
  Francis 23, 24, 32
  Geo 16
  George 18, 22, 35
  J. 65
  John   17, 32, 98, 109, 117, 123, 124
  Lewis 70, 71
  Wesley 84, 87, 102, 118
  William . . . 17, 23, 29, 32, 33, 43, 47
SURRATT
  Alphonsus 18
  G.D. 97

SUTTER
  George 56
SUTTLE
  C.F. 127, 129, 130
SUTTON
  D. 43
  J.A. 55, 66, 70
  John 14, 18, 20, 21, 35, 66
SWAIN
  Archibald 34
  George 95
  Stephen 124
SWAINE
  J.G. 84, 87
SWAN
  Charles A. 121
  George 3
SWANN
  Eli D. 98
  J.C. 85
  T.C. 89
  Thomas 25, 64, 70, 75
  William T. 75-77
SWEARINGEN
  James 44
  Joseph 44
SWEENEY
  George 43
SWIFT
  Jonathan . 13, 14, 16, 25, 27, 34, 37,
    39, 47, 50, 51, 55, 62, 64, 66, 70
SWINGSFIRE
  Francisca W. 68
SWOOPE
  A. 25
  James 17
  Michael 17
SWOPE
  A. 17
  Adam S. . . 25, 28, 40, 43, 56, 63, 66
SYDNOR
  William F. 19
SYFORT
  Mathis 28
SYNIER
  G.C. 129

T

T_
  Joseph 56
TALBOT
  Elisha 117
  Levi 16, 18, 21, 27, 35, 64
  McKinzey 16, 23
TALBOTT
  Benjamin 22, 33
  Sampson 22, 31
  William 51

TALIAFERRO
  H.B. 129
  John A. 123
TALTON
  John 56
TANDY
  Moses 3, 18, 20, 27, 38
TASCOE
  James 30
TATERSON
  Francis 89
TATSAPAUGH/TATSPAUGH
  Charles C. 109
  E.H. 92
  George 84, 98
  Henry 95
  John 104, 117, 118
  Peter 34
TATUM
  Nath. 126
Taverns: 29, 102
  Licenses 12, 102
  Price's Ordinary 35
Taxes: 5, 97, 112, 125, 127-129
  Clerk Fees 109
  Distilled spirits 14
  Foreign Articles 62
  Landed Property 49
  On brown sugar 14
  On coffee 14
  On salt 14
  Tithables 53
  Wharfage 6
TAYLER
  Edward 24
TAYLOR
  Alexander 18
  Andrew 48, 55
  Archibald 47
  Archibald J. 43, 69
  Archibald L. 45
  C.M. 85, 86, 109
  Charles M. 91, 102
  F. 85, 95, 109, 118
  Francis 22
  G.W. 127
  George 25, 29, 34, 39, 43, 45-47, 50,
    57, 62, 64, 65, 70, 129, 130
  J.A. 56, 66
  James . . . 22, 30, 39, 43, 46, 48, 50
  Jesse . . 6, 11, 12, 14, 18, 20, 28, 29,
    33-35, 37, 39, 43, 45, 47, 55, 62,
    64, 65
  John 84, 97
  Joseph 90, 97
  Joshua 84, 119
  L.B. 125
  Lawrence B. . 83, 84, 86, 95, 99, 102-
    105, 123-125
  M. 118

R.J. 55, 66
Reazon P. 97
Richard 56
Robert 98, 118, 127
Thomas 24
W. 19
W. Arthur 89, 99, 102
W.A. 86, 109, 125
William 16, 18, 34, 127
William F. 97
William T. 42
TEATUM
  Warren 92
TELLIER
  Adrien 28
TENESSON
  Charles 83
TENNENT
  A.F. 128
TENNISON
  Samuel 95
TERRALL
  John 48
TERRETT
  Alexander N. 97
  John 128
  W.H. 15, 35
TERTZBACH
  Peter 27
THEDRICK
  Thomas 18
THOM
  Mary () 12
  William 12
THOMAS
  Alexander 35
  Benjamin 30, 83, 86, 92, 95
  G.J. 95, 100
  George 24
  George A. 118
  George J. 91
  J. 70
  J.I. 83, 121
  John 42
  John V. . . 47, 55, 57, 62, 63, 66, 69
  Joseph 34, 66, 67
  P. 39
  Robert 24, 42
  T. 95
  Thomas 8
  William 42
  William H. 98
THOMPSON
  Cornelious 32
  Daniel 31
  Edward K. 15, 17, 25, 29, 34
  George 97
  George W. 88, 128
  H. 15
  H.C. 128

  Henry 84
  James 18, 22, 31
  John 31, 32, 84
  Jonah . . 9, 12, 14, 25, 27, 28, 34, 35,
    39, 42, 45, 47, 48-50, 56, 57, 65,
    71, 78
  Josiah 16
  Samuel 22, 31
  Thomas 129
  William 31, 43
THOMSON
  Daniel 23
THORN
  John 16
  Michael . . . 3, 6, 8, 14, 16, 25, 27, 33,
    35, 43
THORNTON
  Anthony 116
  James B. 104
  John 55
  Joseph . . 47, 52, 55, 62, 64, 65, 70
  Sally () 104
  Thomas 53
THRIFT
  Charles 18, 24
  George 8, 24, 42
  Hambleton 18, 32
  James 117
THROCKMORTON
  Robert 15
  Thomas 40
  William 40
THROOP
  John 64
THRUSTON
  C.M. 42
  Charles 8, 42
TIBBETT
  Jonathan 89
TILLET
  Samuel 22
TILLETT
  James 32
  John 23, 32
TINBALL
  J. 42
TIPPETT
  Thomas 42
TITUS
  Samuel 126
Tobacco: 91
  Inspection 5-7, 15, 17, 18, 20, 22, 44,
    45, 52, 71, 91, 92, 105
  Rolling House 20
  Warehouse 1, 5
  Warehouses 15, 17, 22, 44, 46
TOBIN
  John 14, 16
  Thomas 34

TODD
   D.M. 126
   Robert 38
TOF__
   Jonathan 42
TOFFLER
   Peter 56
Tolls: ...... 72-74, 78, 99, 129, Cover
TOMLIN
   Robert 98, 119
TOMPSON
   John 22
   Samuell 22
TONSDALL
   John 27, 34
TOWERS
   John 31, 65
TRAISELER (see Tressler)
   Lewis 22
TRAMEL (Trammell)
   Thomas 23, 31
TRAMELL (Trammell)
   Gerrard 17, 23, 47
TRAVERS
   John W. 126
   Thomas 83, 123, 127
   Thomas B. 127
TRAVIS
   J. 89
   John 84
TREAKLE
   William H. 127
TREDEL
   John 53
TREIDLE
   Friederick 55
TRENMAN
   M. 130
TRESSLER (see Traiseler)
   Lewis 22, 30
TRIPLETT
   Catherine () 104
   George 14, 16
   Reuben 42
   Simon 41, 42
   Thomas 23, 56
   William 5, 18, 21, 22, 35, 71
   William H. 92, 98, 104
TRIPLITT
   Greenberry 42
   Thomas 42
TRIPP
   Othniell 14, 16
TRIRVEY
   William 24
TRISLER
   George 56
TRUNNELL
   George 22

TUCKER
   Meshack 70
   Samuel 84
   William 82
TULEMAN
   James 98
TURLEY
   Charles 22
   James 23
   Joseph 40
   Sampson 24, 31
TURNBAUGH
   Henry 18, 23
TURNBULL
   William 89
TURNER
   Charles 21, 27, 39, 47, 65
   Chs. 39
   Joseph 18, 21
   Thomas 31
   William 24, 31, 32, 55, 65
   Z. 126
TWINING
   Natt. 15
TWYMAN
   T.J. 126
TYCEN
   Louis 98
TYLER
   James 18, 23
   John W. 125
   Joseph T. 39
   Thomas 23
   Thompson 95
   William 8, 55, 57, 70
TYSON
   John 97

U

UHLER
   P.G. 83, 89, 109, 118, 127
   Valentine/Valentin .. 9, 18, 22, 27, 34
UMBEREIT
   John 33
UNRUH
   C.B. 87
UPTON
   Edward P. 126, 129
USHER
   G.T. 114

V

VALE
   Joseph 54
VALENDEHAM
   James 23

VALENTINE
  Edward 90
VALLENTINE
  Jacob 18
VALLETTE
  Elie 25
VALLINDIGHAM
  John 32
VANCE
  James A. 40
VANDERWERKEN
  G. 126
VANHAVRE
  J.M. 57, 64
  T.M. 50
VANHORN
  Gerrard 42
  William 42
VANSANT
  James 87, 91, 92, 113, 118
  Mary 113
VARDEN
  Jos. 70
  Joseph 55
VASSOY
  Peter 56
VAUGHAN
  Thomas 19
VEITCH
  Chs. W. 83
  M.P. 83
  Richard 47, 50, 57
  William . . . 83, 84, 95, 102, 109, 118
  William C. 126
VERNON
  Henry T. 55
  James 85
  John 31
  P.B. 83
  R. 84
VILKE
  Peter 28
VIOLET
  Whaley 15, 32
VIOLETT
  Alexander 98
  C.W. 85
  E.R. 87
  H.F. 86
  J.W. 87
  John 31
  John W. 84
  R.G. 86, 95, 109, 117, 127
  Robert G. 83, 102, 118, 129
  William 23
Virginia and Tennessee Railroad 125
Virginia Gazette and Alexandria
    Advertiser 38
Virginia Journal and Alexandria Gazette . 36

VIVENT
  F. 48
VORCE
  Nelson 126, 128
VOSS
  Alexander 32
  Nicholas 55, 66, 70
VOWELL
  Ebenezer 43
  John 45, 50, 71
  John C. . . 51, 62, 64, 65, 71, 87, 92,
                                   109, 118
  Thomas . . 42, 45-47, 50, 51, 62, 64,
                              65, 71, 72
VOYLET
  Hugh 16

W

W__
  Benjamin 42
WADDEY
  John 87, 109
WAGENER
  Beverly R. 53
  J. 23
  Robert 39
WAGGENER
  A. 44
WAILES
  Levin C. 25
WAITE
  Obed. 40
WALDEN
  John 116
WALDER
  Christifer 22
WALES
  Andrew . 6-8, 12, 14, 16, 25, 27, 29,
                       35, 39, 43, 47, 48, 56
WALEY
  Andrew 43
WALKER
  Henry 42, 47
  James 84, 98
  John 42
  John S. 97
  Joseph 24
  Marion 84, 98
  Robert 89
  Spencer 42
  W.D. 87, 95
  William 89
WALKOM
  John 56, 70
WALL
  W. 47
WALLACE
  Aron 127
  Hugh 55

James 64
John 56
John R. 127
WALLACH
  W.D., Mrs. 129
WALLER
  Mrs. 110
WALSH
  Richard 64, 65
WALTON
  M. 55
WANENMACKER
  John 22
WANTON
  P. 16
  Philip 39, 47, 56, 57, 62-64
WARD
  Enoch 24, 31, 32, 97
  F. 86
  John 31, 85, 95
  Jonathan 24
  Josias 31
  T. 85
  William . . . 3, 8, 9, 12, 14, 18, 21, 24,
                           27, 31, 84
  Zachariah 16, 32, 62
WARDEN
  Richard 24
  William 8, 14, 22
WARDLAW
  Tibbie 37
WARE
  James 19
WARFIELD
  A.D. 95, 109
  Abel D. 84
WARING/WARRING
  Arthur 114, 120
  Juliana E. 114
  Thomas 87, 95
WARNER
  Henry 22
  John C. 87
  Joseph 32
WARREN
  Erasmus 95
WARRICK
  William 18
WARRINER
  Edmund 18, 21
WASHINGTON
  Bushrod 34
  Edward 15
  George 12, 112
  George F. 98
  Henry 15
  John A. 17, 92
  Lawrence 1
  N. 98
Washington and Alexandria Railroad . . 127

Washington and Alexandria Railroad
  Company 127, 128
WATERMAN
  Simon 130
WATERS
  Thomas A. 83, 92, 98
WATKIN
  Edward 23
WATKINS
  Joseph 28
  W.T. 121
WATSON
  James 43
  John 66
  Josiah   3, 5, 6, 11-14, 16, 29, 34, 42,
                                    46, 47
  Robert 64, 66
  Robert T. 63
  William 23
WATTLES
  C.W. 118, 125, 129
  N.S. 116
  Nathaniel 66
WATTS
  J. 47
  John 50, 55, 62, 63, 65, 70, 71
  Samuel 70
WAUGH
  James 24
  Tylor 30
WAYMOTH
  John 84
WEADON
  F.M. 89, 121
  Francis M. 87
WEAVER
  Frederick 16, 22, 33
WEBBER
  Michael 31
WEBSTER
  George 84
  Hiram 97
  John 84
  Nailor 84
  Nathaniel 56
  Philip 6, 8, 20, 25, 29, 34, 43
  Richard 7
  Thomas 84
  William 84
WEDDERBURN
  William 79, 80
WEEDON
  Richard 41
  Samuel 16, 30
WEEKS
  J.T. 87
  Thomas 41
WEELBRIGHT
  Barneby 22

WEEMS
  Nathaniel C. 15
WEIGHTMAN
  Richard 18, 21, 27, 33, 70
WEIR
  Benjamin 43
WEISMULLER
  Jacob 27, 33
WELCH
  Erasmus 34
WELLER
  Michael 22
WELLMAN
  Elizabeth 37
WELLS
  Alfred 128
  Daniel 97, 129
  J.W. 97
  James 16
  John 97
WELSH
  John 84
WESLEY
  Richard 24
WEST
  Anne () 67
  George 30
  Hugh 5, 32, 67
  Jeremiah 86
  John 15, 25, 84, 95, 100
  R. 47
  Roger 15, 25
  Sibyl 5
  Sybil 5, 18, 67
  Thomas   3, 18, 21, 23, 25, 30, 33, 43,
                                     56, 67, 97
  William 17, 32
WESTBROOK
  William 53
WESTCOTT
  James 69
  James D. 51, 55, 63, 66
WESTON
  C.C. 126, 128
  Lewis 3, 6, 9, 15, 27, 33, 35
  William 32
WEY
  Henry 41
WEYLIE
  Ephraim 34, 48, 55
  John 70
WHALEY
  George 78
  Gibson 32
  Gilson 15
  James M. 124
  John 24
  R.H. 125
  William 23

WHARTON
  W.A. 84
  William A. 98
WHEALEN
  John 98
  Wheat 52
  Inspection 41
WHEAT
  () 97
  B. 86
  Benoni 83, 88, 96, 102
  J.H. 110
  J.I. 86
  J.J. 86, 92, 105, 118
  John J. 117
  Robert W. 83, 97, 100
WHEATLEY
  J.W. 127
WHEATON
  John 25
  John B. 47
  John R. 43
WHEELER
  Drummond 24, 31
  Jabez 87
  Nathan 16
  Richard 23, 30
  Samuel 63, 64
WHELER
  Nathen 23
WHERRY
  Jesse 42, 46, 47
WHIPPLE
  E.A. 126
WHITACRE
  Caleb 15, 17
WHITAIN
  Robert 8
WHITE
  Abednego 30
  Ambrose 63
  Bar. 48
  Bart. 70
  Bartemus 51
  George 86, 92, 98, 118
  J. 48
  James 41
  John 41, 43, 64, 85
  John T. 109, 119
  Jonathan 42
  Thomas . . 43, 48, 51, 55, 56, 64, 66,
                                          69-71
  Thomas M. 83, 87, 92, 102, 109,
                                     121, 123
  W. 22
WHITEFORD
  Samuel 18
WHITESIDE
  Edward 21

WHITESIDES
   John 24
WHITING
   Thomas 35
WHITMAN
   Frederick 16
WHITMORE
   John P. 83
WHITNEY
   John 23
WHITTAKER
   Thomas 43
WHITTINGTON
   ( ) 87
   H.B. 84, 118
   Thomas 84
WICKES
   N.K. 116
WICKS
   S.S. 127
WIGGANTON
   Benjamin 22
WIGGINS
   William 55
WIGGS
   John 24, 30
WIGINTON
   Henry 22
WILBAR
   John J. 119
WILCOXON
   Rezon 30
   Thomas 22
WILDMAN
   C.G. 86, 95, 118
WILEY
   George W. 95, 109
   James 22, 43
WILKE
   Peter 14, 16, 18, 22
WILKES
   Alderson 41
WILKINS
   S.M. 84
WILKINSON
   Thomas 3, 6, 8, 25, 35
WILLAMS
   John 97
WILLIAMS
   Alexander 63
   Bazel 24, 128
   Bazil 97
   Bazzel 32
   David 84
   George 15, 17, 23, 24, 30, 32
   Hezekiah 16, 24
   James 78, 97
   Jeremiah 22
   John 90, 98
   John A. 84
   John F. 84
   John S. 19
   Josias 34
   Peter 18, 23, 27, 33
   Richard 127
   Robert 97
   Thomas . . 23, 24, 29, 34, 40, 50, 57,
                                63-65, 84
   Thomas S. 19
   William 23, 27
WILLINGTON
   William 52
WILLIS
   A.S. 85
   Abel 16, 25, 63
   B.F. 83
WILSON
   C.F. 89, 95
   C.W. 106
   Charles 110
   Charles F. 97
   Chs. 92
   D.R. 123
   David 19
   George 14, 16, 25, 34
   H. 116
   J.H. 92
   James . . 12, 29, 33, 39, 43-47, 50, 57,
                                63, 66, 71
   John 16, 42
   Joseph 8, 15, 17
   Moses 16
   R.J. 106, 118, 127
   R.T. 110
   William . 8, 12, 14, 18, 20, 28, 34, 39,
         42, 43, 45, 46, 47, 50, 54, 62, 64,
                                        71
WILY
   George 66
Winchester and Potomac Railroad 89
WINDSOR
   Richard 88
   Richard W. 87, 98
   Thomas 30
   William 98
WINGATE
   Henry 23, 31
WINN
   A. 32
   Lewis T. 16
WINSER
   Thomas 23
WINSHIP
   Winn 44
WINSOR
   O. 14, 33, 34
   Olney 34
WINSTON
   J. 102

WINTERBERY/WINTERBURY
  John .. 3, 25, 28, 43, 47, 56, 64, 66
WINTERHOUSE
  Reuben 22
WISE
  Charles J. 130
  Frank 129
  G. 123
  George 62, 66, 87, 96, 98
  George P. 110, 119
  John   8, 9, 18, 20, 27, 28, 34, 35, 38,
                       40, 43, 47, 55
  Mrs. 90
  P. 57, 62
  Peter 2, 3, 6-8, 12-14, 18, 23, 28, 34,
      35, 40, 43, 52, 62, 64, 66, 70, 129
WISEMILLER
  Jacob 56, 63, 64, 66
  James 57
WISENDAHL
  Lewis 14, 16
WITHERS
  John 91, 110, 117, 118
  Lyttleton 129, 130
  Mr. 90
WITMER
  G.K. 118, 130
  George K. 85
WOLF
  William 97
WOOD
  Andrew 55
  Elijah 16
  George 16
  John 42, 85, 109, 118
  Joseph 32
  Robert 40
  Thomas W. 83
  William 56, 66
WOOD__
  John 56
WOODARD
  J. 14
  Ja. 16, 25, 27
  James 34
WOODEN
  Joseph 64
WOODROW
  H. 56
  Henry 51, 66
  John 64
WOODWARD
  Thomas 23
WOODYARD
  Jeremiah 30
WOOLBRIGHT
  Jacob 32
WOOLLS
  Stephen 96, 109
  William 18, 23, 34, 55, 87

WORDEN
  William 18, 33
WORNALD
  James 41
WORRELL
  Benjamin 23
  Morris 18, 23, 63
WORTHIN
  Edward 30
  Henry 31
WREN
  David 56
  James 16, 31, 47
  John 16, 18, 22, 23, 31
  Thomas 42
  William 23
WRENN
  J.W. 130
WRIGHT
  Anthony 23
  Charles 30
  D. 83
  George H. 98
  Israel 23
  Israel S. 25
  John 55, 66
  Matthew 40
  Richard 92, 119
  Robert 24
  Samuel 8
  William . 15, 17, 25, 27, 46, 109, 123
  Zachariah 95
WROE
  Absalem 33
  Absolem 56, 70
WUNDER
  George O. 128
  H.S. 128
WYLD
  John 64, 66
WYLEY
  George 30
WYLIE
  John 62

Y

YEATMAN
  Henry L. 63
YEATON
  Richard S. 56
  Sprague 65
  W. 65, 97
  W.C. 105, 125
  Warren 123
  William 63, 96, 123
YOHE
  C.M. 128
  E. 126

195

YOUNG
- () 46, 47
- Charles 43
- David 22
- James 16, 56, 64, 70, 83, 92
- John 32
- John T. 130
- Motley 15
- Nimrod 53
- R. 45, 88
- Robert 43, 65, 70-72, 89, 95
- William 22, 33, 42

YULER
- E. 128

Z

ZIMMERMAN
- () 55
- H.F. 84
- R. 83, 90, 109
- Reuben 124
- Timothy 3
- Tobias 3, 8, 21, 34

Other Books by Wesley E. Pippenger:

Alexandria (Arlington) County, Virginia Death Records, 1853-1896

Alexandria City and Arlington County, Virginia Records Index: Vol. 1

Alexandria City and Arlington County, Virginia Records Index: Vol. 2

Alexandria County, Virginia Marriage Records, 1853-1895

Alexandria Virginia Marriage Index, January 10, 1893 to August 31, 1905

Alexandria, Virginia Marriages, 1870-1892

Alexandria, Virginia Town Lots, 1749-1801 Together with the Proceedings of the Board of Trustees, 1749-1780

Alexandria, Virginia Wills, Administrations and Guardianships, 1786-1800

Alexandria, Virginia 1808 Census (Wards 1, 2, 3, and 4)

Alexandria, Virginia Death Records, 1863-1896

Alexandria, Virginia Hustings Court Orders, Volume 1, 1780-1787

Connections and Separations: Divorce, Name Change and Other Genealogical Tidbits from the Acts of the Virginia General Assembly

Daily National Intelligencer *Index to Deaths, 1855-1870*

Daily National Intelligencer, *Washington, District of Columbia Marriages and Deaths Notices (January 1, 1851 to December 30, 1854)*

Dead People on the Move: Reconstruction of the Georgetown Presbyterian Burying Ground, Holmead's (Western) Burying Ground, and other Removals in the District of Columbia

Death Notices from Richmond, Virginia Newspapers, 1841-1853

District of Columbia Ancestors, A Guide to Records of the District of Columbia

District of Columbia Death Records: August 1, 1874-July 31, 1879

District of Columbia Foreign Deaths, 1888-1923

District of Columbia Guardianship Index, 1802-1928

District of Columbia Interments (Index to Deaths) January 1, 1855 to July 31, 1874

District of Columbia Marriage Licenses, Register 1: 1811-1858

District of Columbia Marriage Licenses, Register 2: 1858-1870

District of Columbia Marriage Records Index, 1877-1885

District of Columbia Marriage Records Index October 20, 1885 to January 20, 1892: Marriage Record Books 21 to 30

District of Columbia Probate Records, 1801-1852

District of Columbia: Original Land Owners, 1791-1800

Early Church Records of Alexandria City and Fairfax County, Virginia

Georgetown, District of Columbia 1850 Federal Population Census (Schedule I) and 1853 Directory of Residents of Georgetown

Georgetown, District of Columbia Marriage and Death Notices, 1801-1838

Husbands and Wives Associated with Early Alexandria, Virginia (and the Surrounding Area), 3rd Edition, Revised

Index to District of Columbia Estates, 1801-1929

Index to Virginia Estates, 1800-1865 Volumes 4, 5 and 6

John Alexander, a Northern Neck Proprietor, His Family, Friends and Kin

Legislative Petitions of Alexandria, 1778-1861

Pippenger and Pittenger Families

Proceedings of the Orphan's Court, Washington County, District of Columbia, 1801-1808

The Georgetown Courier *Marriage and Death Notices: Georgetown, District of Columbia, November 18, 1865 to May 6, 1876*

The Georgetown Directory for the Year 1830: to which is appended, a Short Description of the Churches, Public Institutions, and the Original Charter of Georgetown, and Extracts of the Laws Pertaining to the Chesapeake and Ohio Canal Company

The Virginia Gazette and Alexandria Advertiser:
Volume 1, September 3, 1789 to November 11, 1790

The Virginia Journal and Alexandria Advertiser:
Volume I (February 5, 1784 to January 27, 1785)

Volume II (February 3, 1785 to January 26, 1786)

Volume III (March 2, 1786 to January 25, 1787)

Volume IV (February 8, 1787 to May 21, 1789)

The Washington and Georgetown Directory of 1853

Tombstone Inscriptions of Alexandria, Volumes 1-4

www.ingramcontent.com/pod-product-compliance
Lightning Source LLC
Chambersburg PA
CBHW051053160426
43193CB00010B/1172